Entrepreneurial Innovation and Economic Development in Dubai and Comparisons to Its Sister Cities

Heather C. Webb
Dubai Men's College, UAE

Hussain A. Al Numairy
Dubai Men's College, UAE

A volume in the Advances in Business Strategy and Competitive Advantage (ABSCA) Book Series

IGI Global
DISSEMINATOR OF KNOWLEDGE

Published in the United States of America by
IGI Global
Business Science Reference (an imprint of IGI Global)
701 E. Chocolate Avenue
Hershey PA, USA 17033
Tel: 717-533-8845
Fax: 717-533-8661
E-mail: cust@igi-global.com
Web site: http://www.igi-global.com

Library of Congress Cataloging-in-Publication Data

Names: Webb, Heather C., 1979- editor. | Al Numairy, Hussain A., 1986-
Title: Entrepreneurial innovation and economic development in Dubai and comparisons to its sister cities / Heather C. Webb and Hussain A. Al Numairy, editors.
Description: Hershey PA : Business Science Reference (an imprint of IGI Global), 2020.
Identifiers: LCCN 2019002057| ISBN 9781522593775 (hardcover) | ISBN 9781522594284 (softcover) | ISBN 9781522593782 (ebook)
Subjects: LCSH: Entrepreneurship--United Arab Emirates--Dubai. | Economic development--United Arab Emirates--Dubai. | Small business--United Arab Emirates--Dubai.
Classification: LCC HB615 .E57785 2020 | DDC 338/.04095357--dc23 LC record available at https://lccn.loc.gov/2019002057

This book is published in the IGI Global book series Advances in Business Strategy and Competitive Advantage (ABSCA) (ISSN: 2327-3429; eISSN: 2327-3437)

British Cataloguing in Publication Data
A Cataloguing in Publication record for this book is available from the British Library.

Advances in Business Strategy and Competitive Advantage (ABSCA) Book Series

ISSN:2327-3429
EISSN:2327-3437

Editor-in-Chief: Patricia Ordóñez de Pablos, Universidad de Oviedo, Spain

MISSION

Business entities are constantly seeking new ways through which to gain advantage over their competitors and strengthen their position within the business environment. With competition at an all-time high due to technological advancements allowing for competition on a global scale, firms continue to seek new ways through which to improve and strengthen their business processes, procedures, and profitability.

The **Advances in Business Strategy and Competitive Advantage (ABSCA) Book Series** is a timely series responding to the high demand for state-of-the-art research on how business strategies are created, implemented and re-designed to meet the demands of globalized competitive markets. With a focus on local and global challenges, business opportunities and the needs of society, the **ABSCA** encourages scientific discourse on doing business and managing information technologies for the creation of sustainable competitive advantage.

COVERAGE

- Economies of Scale
- Globalization
- Foreign Investment Decision Process
- Innovation Strategy
- Competitive Strategy
- Value Creation
- Strategy Performance Management
- Co-operative Strategies
- Core Competencies
- Value Chain

IGI Global is currently accepting manuscripts for publication within this series. To submit a proposal for a volume in this series, please contact our Acquisition Editors at Acquisitions@igi-global.com or visit: http://www.igi-global.com/publish/.

The Advances in Business Strategy and Competitive Advantage (ABSCA) Book Series (ISSN 2327-3429) is published by IGI Global, 701 E. Chocolate Avenue, Hershey, PA 17033-1240, USA, www.igi-global.com. This series is composed of titles available for purchase individually; each title is edited to be contextually exclusive from any other title within the series. For pricing and ordering information please visit http://www.igi-global.com/book-series/advances-business-strategy-competitive-advantage/73672. Postmaster: Send all address changes to above address.

Titles in this Series

For a list of additional titles in this series, please visit:
https://www.igi-global.com/book-series/advances-business-strategy-competitive-advantage/73672

Handbook of Research on Corporate Restructuring and Globalization
Antonio Carrizo Moreira (University of Aveiro, Portugal) and Pedro Silva (University of Aveiro, Portugal)
Business Science Reference • ©2019 • 408pp • H/C (ISBN: 9781522589068) • US $295.00

Responsible, Sustainable, and Globally Aware Management in the Fourth Industrial Revolution
Ziska Fields (University of KwaZulu-Natal, South Africa) and Stefan Huesig (Chemnitz University of Technology, Germany)
Business Science Reference • ©2019 • 396pp • H/C (ISBN: 9781522576389) • US $225.00

Handbook of Research on Entrepreneurial Leadership and Competitive Strategy in Family Business
José Manuel Saiz-Álvarez (Tecnológico de Monterrey, Mexico) and Jesús Manuel Palma-Ruiz (Universidad Autónoma de Chihuahua, Mexico)
Business Science Reference • ©2019 • 559pp • H/C (ISBN: 9781522580126) • US $345.00

The Belt and Road Strategy in International Business and Administration
Wei Liu (University of Sydney, Australia) Zhe Zhang (University of Sydney, Australia) Jin-Xiong Chen (Wuyi University, China) and Sang-Bing Tsai (University of Electronic Science and Technology of China Zhongshan Institute, China & Capital University of Economics and Business, China & Wuyi University, China)
Business Science Reference • ©2019 • 273pp • H/C (ISBN: 9781522584407) • US $225.00

Global Considerations in Entrepreneurship Education and Training
Luísa Cagica Carvalho (Instituto Politécnico de Setúbal, Portugal & CEFAGE - Universidade de Évora, Portugal) and Ana Dias Daniel (Universidade de Aveiro, Portugal)
Business Science Reference • ©2019 • 322pp • H/C (ISBN: 9781522576754) • US $215.00

For an entire list of titles in this series, please visit:
https://www.igi-global.com/book-series/advances-business-strategy-competitive-advantage/73672

IGI Global
DISSEMINATOR OF KNOWLEDGE

701 East Chocolate Avenue, Hershey, PA 17033, USA
Tel: 717-533-8845 x100 • Fax: 717-533-8661
E-Mail: cust@igi-global.com • www.igi-global.com

Table of Contents

Detailed Table of Contents

It has become vital to understand the economic, environmental, and social impact "going green" has on the region as well as on the interlinked relationship between sustainable consumption and production. This chapter focuses on Dubai's green growth strategy and the process for anticipating success while comparing its policy and initiatives to other major cities. In addition, the chapter reviews current regulations along with low carbon initiatives as part of Dubai's green, sustainable development. As Dubai prepares for Expo 2020, the city is focusing on generating sustainable, green innovations. Indeed, climate change has shaped the need for cities and countries to be more aware of their surroundings, and Dubai is no exception in developing a fully, sustainable city to become a green, economic leader.

Innovation economies are a departure from traditional modes of development. Where the latter privileges activities like resource extraction and infrastructure construction, the former emphasizes less material approaches such as knowledge-building and talent creation. In its drive to become a knowledge-based economy, Dubai may face challenges of perceptual legitimacy in its newly formed innovation clusters. At the same time, however, a strength of image bulwarks its established clusters like finance and logistics. This chapter summarizes best practices and existing theory on cluster branding, briefly examines several innovation clusters in Europe and the United States, and finally ruminates on the opportunities and challenges faced by Dubai in creating strong brands that communicate innovation.

Rapid national infrastructure growth, as witnessed today in many countries such as the United Arab Emirates, commonly makes fast-tracking demands of what are already highly complex multi-stakeholder projects. Considering the long history of airport project failures in a number of fast-growing cities, the chapter explores risk management enhancements for addressing the challenges associated with transitions from project completion to commencement of operations. The proposed solution in the pages that follow is to have in place dedicated risk management teams spanning the transitions. These teams should provide a locus for stakeholder collaboration based on a shared concern to build excellence into the customer experience from commencement of operations onwards.

The Gulf states, attempting to diversify their economies, have focused largely on transforming their economies. Part of their transformation focus areas is the technology sector. FinTech is a generic term used for all financial technology developments, and has gained a lot of traction in the recent years. As Financial services is one of the main sources of GDP for the GCC states, the GCC governments have focused in promoting the FinTech entrepreneurship spirit, through different initiatives. In the chapter, the authors analyze the FinTech ecosystem development mode for all the GCC countries, focusing on understanding the reason that have made it one of the most successful FinTech ecosystems globally.

The importance of the SME is well established in the literature. These account for the majority of economic contribution in many economies. In the case of emerging markets, SMEs make significant contributions to the local income generation, employment support, and innovation development. The aim of this chapter is to provide an overview of how the world's largest emerging economy—China—helps promote its SMEs. This chapter provides a brief history of Chinese SMEs throughout the Great Economic Reform that started in 1978. Next, the SMEs' achievements and current constraints are outlined. Last, this chapter discusses how the SMEs in China upgrade through innovation and branding to embark on future pathways. Through this timeline approach, the experience of Chinese SMEs development will provide some insights for other emerging regions.

Innovation has an essential impact on SME creation, and governments are concerned with stimulating adoption of innovation by SMEs to strengthen growth and development and adapt to the ever-changing business environment. Innovation by SMEs requires operating within a generally embracing economic and financial environment. The availability of various formal and informal financing options and a growing economy encouraging consumer spending, innovation-driven investment spending and export, and a policy favoring enhancing private equity, economic diversification, and market competition are incipient factors contributing to a culture of private initiatives by entrepreneurs and SMEs.

This chapter explores the extent and characteristics of small and medium enterprises (SMEs) in Dubai and their innovative practices. Within this context, considerable emphasis is placed on evaluating the propensity of these SMEs to adopt new

Being an entrepreneur encompasses a number of traits. Used as an "umbrella term," it constitutes self-motivation, leadership, resilience, proactivity, creativity, and a sense of light-hearted preparation to deal with potential failure in different aspects of the startup. These individual traits are prevalent in most people; however, it is the combination of them, alongside sound physical health and access to social resources that allows an entrepreneur to enjoy success in due time. Psychological theory and practice may inform techniques in developing and facilitating what it takes to succeed as an entrepreneur. Specifically, health psychology explains how individuals' unique biological, psychological, and social factors, as informed by biopsychosocial theory, together produce adaptive or maladaptive behaviors. To translate this for the context of entrepreneurship, only an individual, who is physiologically healthy or otherwise manages their physical condition well, might enjoy entrepreneurial success.

Entrepreneurship is a driving force to modern economies if organizational excellence is achieved. High-quality outputs are important at the local, regional, and international level due to e-commerce evolution in business industries. Therefore, factual approach to solve managerial challenges toward quality at the micro and macro level is on demand to outreach global markets. Even local companies selling locally will have to compete globally with high quality and cost-cutting strategies to gain customer loyalty. The quality challenge is to have consistency in all products and services sold anywhere in the world; this can only be achieved if standardized processes, systems, and training are adopted in a quality culture. As an entrepreneur, acquiring "Quality Strategic Management" approach helps prevention of poor outcomes by keeping failure and appraisal costs to the minimum through quality planning and quality training, quality testing, and quality auditing to avoid factors preventing competitive advantage strategies promptly.

Preface

Dubai is one of the seven Emirates that forms the United Arab Emirates (UAE). The city has transformed from being a meager, sandy village to becoming a model of the future packed with architectural landmarks and luxury resorts. Thus, the term 'Dubai' is being fashioned as a global brand. The future of Dubai is resilient in regards to economic development as well as economic diversification. Therefore, we hope this book can offer organizational and governmental decision makers an informed policy perspective. Additionally, we hope this book can be of benefit to academics and researchers for educational and learning opportunities as well as to a wide range of individuals wanting to innovate and start their own business in the region.

Historically, the leaders of Dubai have taken risks where others were critical and skeptical of success. Nonetheless, these risks were the best use of Dubai's oil reserves, and instead of ensuing what the other emirates and geographical neighbors were doing, it chose to diversify its economy (e.g. tourism and logistics industry) in non-oil sectors. Nonetheless, Dubai is focusing on building an entrepreneurial and small-medium enterprise industry. Undeniably, being an entrepreneur is risky, but when leaders can see beyond the risks and how entrepreneurs and small businesses can help the community and country, then upon reflection, the country becomes economically stronger.

Currently, these are exciting times for Dubai and the UAE because of their pace of development. The UAE is in a transformation process. Specifically, Dubai offers talent and the groundwork for innovation and SMEs startups. The progressive government policies are attracting overseas investments and elevating the status of UAE, and Dubai is being seen as a hub of business and innovation creation. There has also been tremendous structural changes which are continuing to create modern infrastructures. The country has always been attractive for foreign multinational corporations, and accordingly, the book highlights the economic and social policy changes that are of fundamental importance for the continued process.

The original idea of the book was to showcase to outsiders what is happening in regards of innovation and small businesses in Dubai. We wanted to present the challenges and barriers that others may have encounter in order to learn for future innovation development and businesses. For books, topics can be general or specific and for this book, it becomes a challenge to provide an exhaustive review of the history and development landscape of the UAE. We wanted to present the opportunities and the challenges that others may encounter in terms of business start-up and policy implications. The endeavor was to overcome the disillusionment of economic development for the region. The world is becoming much more collaborated in a distributed global network, which is impacting everyday life. We want to showcase that on an observation level, the process of development is properly underway for success. A successful business requires infrastructure. Infrastructure comes from government enablement and market acceleration. Considering that there are not many books specifically on the innovation development of Dubai, this book sheds light on the exciting prospects for potential entrepreneurs to consider Dubai as a place to headquarter their businesses.

Parallel with the growth of Dubai, there has been an increase of research on the emirate from within the UAE and abroad. Thus, there continues to be a process of scholarly research in producing valuable new data on a wide range of topics. This book brings together a collection of these research topics such as: economic development, entrepreneurial activities, entrepreneurial education, and financial innovation focus. In the present, readers should find important policy analysis as well as what the region offers and the different barriers or challenges that could affect business development decisions. The book leads readers to a positive understanding of the region while offering some comparisons to other major cities in order to discover if there is a specific Dubai model being formulated. Consequently, the benchmarking of other major cities is minimal, but it gives the book a practical angle that differentiates from other economic development books. Additionally, this book was edited as a resource for students and practitioners.

The chapters presented in the book include such topics as sustainability, digital marketing, risk management of the logistics industry, financial innovation, Islamic financing, small-medium-enterprises (SMEs) development, quality management, the role of public governance and the mental reflection on the difficulty of being an entrepreneur and starting a new business. Some chapters are organized as case studies and other chapters offer smaller case study discussions that can be used in academic settings. Overall, the chapters give the book a practical approach that can, hopefully, lead to future research. Thus, this book is an important topic of discussion on the future of the region and the knowledge being developed. We hope that others will view this region positively and this can be an informal guide for future strategic decision makers and managers.

APPROACH TO THE CHAPTERS

The first chapter of the book, titled "The Sustainable Falcon: Dubai's Path to Becoming a Green Economic Leader," offers an interesting analysis of the definition of sustainability, green economy and green development. The literature review gives an understanding of the economic, environmental and social impact of 'going green' has on the region. Specifically, the chapter focuses on Dubai's green growth strategy while offering some policy benchmarks to other major cities. Also, the chapter reviews Dubai's current regulations and sustainable innovation developments in what Dubai is doing to counteract and tackle climate change. This chapter was chosen as the opening of the book because sustainability is at the forefront of innovation and economic development solutions being implemented.

The second chapter, "Cluster Branding: The Art of Communicating Innovation," looks at how innovative economies are a departure from traditional economic development moods. Dubai is driven to become a knowledge-based economy and faces challenges of perceptual legitimacy. Thus, the strength of the image becomes very important in established industries such as finance and logistics. The chapter offers a definitional perspective of cluster branding and examines several innovation clusters in Europe and the United States while finally reflecting on the challenges faced by Dubai in creating strong brands that communicate innovation. Image is very important to economic development.

The third chapter, "Risk Management as Knowledge Production: Application to Fast-Tracked Complex Multi-Stakeholder Airport Projects," focuses on Dubai's fast development of their logistic industry. The UAE is witnessing a rapid national infrastructure growth and is making fast-track demands of highly complex multi-stakeholder projects. Specifically, this chapter explores the risk management for addressing the challenges associated with transition from project complementation to actual commencement of the operations. The chapter offers a proposed solution in enlisting a dedicated risk management team to be involved in such transitions. Fundamentally, the teams should provide support with other stakeholders based on a shared concern to build excellence into the customer experience from commencement to operations.

The fourth chapter, "FinTech Strategies in the GCC: Developing a Growing FinTech Ecosystem – A GCC Perspective," presents a discussion how most of the Gulf States are attempting to diversity and transform their economies to rely less on oil. Part of this transformation of economic diversification is developing the FinTech industry. FinTech being a generic term for all financial technology developments, there has been an increase in FinTech entrepreneurship through different initiatives. The chapter analyses the FinTech ecosystem development while focusing on understanding the reasons that makes it, globally, one of the most successful.

The fifth chapter, "Historical Development of Chinese SMEs," takes a step back from the Middle East region and Dubai to present the importance of SMEs on economic growth. It uses China as an analytical framework for benchmarking against other countries who are focused on creating an SME stronghold. Dubai can learn about China's approach to local income generation, employment support and innovation development. The chapter aims to provide an overview of how the world's largest economy, China, helps promote its SMEs. It outlines China's SMEs' achievements and current constraints while, lastly, discussing how the Chinese SMEs promote through innovation and branding. The Chinese experience provides some helpful insights for other emerging regions such as Dubai.

The sixth chapter, "Survey of Financing Options and Key Challenges Faced by SMEs in the UAE: Economic, Environment, Finance, and Regulatory Landscape," showcases the involvement of entrepreneurs and SMEs towards achieving the economic and social objective of the UAE. A flourishing SME ecosystem is essential for a thriving economic and social structure characterized by better allocation of resources driven by inherent innovation, efficiency, and competitiveness. The chapter presents a discussion on how innovation has an essential impact on SMEs as well as how the UAE is concerned with stimulating adoption of innovation to strengthen growth and development. Additionally, the chapter surveys the various formal and informal financing options for SMEs and entrepreneurs in the UAE.

The seventh chapter, "The Characteristics of SMEs in Dubai and Their Impact on Innovation," explores the extent and characteristics of SMEs in Dubai. The chapter evaluates the propensity of these SMEs to adopt new technology. The industries that are being developed from these SMEs play a crucial role in not only economic growth, but more importantly, job creation. Thus, the connection between economic successes in SMEs is fundamental since these firms are able to incorporate innovation in their operations and organizational practices. The chapter presents various aspects to Dubai's SME development.

The eighth chapter, "Entrepreneurship in the United Arab Emirates," continues the discussion on how entrepreneurship innovates an economy. This chapter carries on the conversation from Chapter 6 and Chapter 7 in describing the UAE's economy and contributions of SMEs. However, this chapter also presents how the role of women play in SME development and offers mini-case studies on successful SMEs in the UAE. Finally, it conjectures the future of entrepreneurship in the UAE.

The ninth chapter, "The Impact of Entrepreneurship Education on Entrepreneurs' Skills," presents a study designed to measure the impact of entrepreneurship education on entrepreneurs' skills. Entrepreneurial skill set includes, but not limited to, technical, business management and personal abilities. The chapter presents the results of the survey where respondents were required to rank their perceptions on the impact of their education to become successful entrepreneurs. The survey was based on a five-point Likert scale techniques.

The tenth chapter, "Using Health Psychology to Inspire Entrepreneurial Innovation in Dubai," continues the discussion on the skills and traits an entrepreneur encompasses for success. Traits, in this chapter, comprises of self-motivation, leadership, resilience, proactivity, creativity and a sense of light-hearted preparation in order to deal with potential failure in different aspects of starting a business. Most people have these traits, but it is the combination of them, along with sound physical health and access to social resources that allows an entrepreneur to enjoy success in due time. The chapter presents psychological theory and practice that may inform techniques in developing and facilitating what it takes to succeed as an entrepreneur.

The eleventh chapter, "Quality Management Obsession: Drive Out Fear, Create Innovative Climate in a Quality Culture," focuses on the managerial challenges towards entrepreneurship. The chapter presents the challenges towards quality at the micro and macro level in competing globally. It looks at standardized processes, systems and training currently being adopted in quality culture and, being an entrepreneur, how can that help prevent poor outcomes. Several factors are offered as analysis such as quality planning, quality training, quality testing and quality auditing in order to create strategic competitive advantages.

Finally, the twelfth chapter, "The Moderating Role of Public Governance on the Relationship Between the Entrepreneurship and Economic Growth: Evidence From United Arab Emirates," investigates the role played by public governance in relation between entrepreneurship and economic growth in the UAE. The chapter presents a study that uses a twenty year time series of 1996 to 2015. The results show a positive impact of entrepreneurship activities within the framework of public governance. The chapter offers recommendations that focuses on continued support for entrepreneurship activities.

Heather Webb
Dubai Men's College, UAE

Hussain Al Numairy
Dubai Men's College, UAE

Chapter 1
The Sustainable Falcon:
Dubai's Path to Becoming a Green Economic Leader

Heather Webb
Higher Colleges of Technology, UAE

Shubo Liu
Central University of Finance and Economics, China

ABSTRACT

It has become vital to understand the economic, environmental, and social impact "going green" has on the region as well as on the interlinked relationship between sustainable consumption and production. This chapter focuses on Dubai's green growth strategy and the process for anticipating success while comparing its policy and initiatives to other major cities. In addition, the chapter reviews current regulations along with low carbon initiatives as part of Dubai's green, sustainable development. As Dubai prepares for Expo 2020, the city is focusing on generating sustainable, green innovations. Indeed, climate change has shaped the need for cities and countries to be more aware of their surroundings, and Dubai is no exception in developing a fully, sustainable city to become a green, economic leader.

DOI: 10.4018/978-1-5225-9377-5.ch001

INTRODUCTION

In the United Arab Emirates (UAE), the Emirate of Dubai has transformed from a 40-mile long coast of fishing and trading ports to a city of skyscrapers, tourism and global, logistics. The weather in Dubai ranges from a low of 65-degrees Fahrenheit in the winter months to a high of 105-degrees Fahrenheit in the summer. In order to keep residents cool, Dubai burns fossil fuel to air-condition buildings, and boils hundreds of gallons of seawater daily. The emirate has asserted itself as becoming a global hub for innovation and start-ups. However, when one thinks of innovative cities, Dubai is not front-of-mind as a nucleus for business start-ups and innovation.

Innovation is a core element of growth, and Dubai is a young, energetic and ambitious city. To catapult itself to a position of global preeminence with respect to innovation, it has employed a strategy focused on economic development. In the past few years, the emirate has seen a new phase in her socio-economic transformation towards becoming one of the first "smart" cities, embracing the vision of a green economy balanced between economic, social and environmental considerations. However, it is not without its struggles. Indeed, Dubai did not get her first paved road until 1961 (Kunzig, 2017). Since then, however, the city has grown exponentially to where it can be a global example.

In the last decade, the idea of global environmental change has taken more notice and there is more comprehensive coverage of policy development. Compared to Dubai's sister cities, Dubai is in a unique geographical location. For that reason, the emirate deals with more heat related issues and development has to take the hot temperature and sand storms into consideration. However, weather is not a new problem, rather, it is how one reacts to it via policy development that can change the path of sustainability and development.

This chapter focuses on Dubai's narrative role of becoming a green economy leader. On a global scale, economic development policies in every city should have a sustainability strategy. Much of the discussion in this chapter is conceptual and does not address the uncertainties or possible failures of sustainable initiatives. Instead, this chapter concentrates on how the concepts of sustainability and the drive for a green economy have been applied. In addition, by benchmarking policies with other major cities, there are limitations. Limitations to the comparisons include that cities are not all the same economically, politically and socially. Some have more policy flexibility while others are more constrained by larger governmental authorities. Therefore promoting sustainability and green growth are translated in different ways. The next section focuses on the definition of green economy and sustainability followed by Dubai's goal of obtaining a green economy.

DEFINING SUSTAINABILE DEVELOPMENT

The Brundtland Report was one of the first reports to give context to sustainability with the definition "sustainable development is development that meets the needs of the present without compromising the ability of future generations to meet their own needs" (World Commission on Environment and Development, 1987). This report introduced, on a global level, the term *sustainable development.* The term sustainable development combines technological advances while considering the costs aspects while seeking to improve the quality of life. Whereas, the United Nations Environment Program (UNEP) defines green economy as "one that results in improved human well-being and social equity, while significantly reducing environmental risks and ecological scarcities" (UN, 2018). Technology slowly mediates between society and the environment in a green economy. A green economy is sustainable infrastructure that takes all human needs into consideration regardless of profitability aims. Indeed, sustainability is a strategic verb in getting companies to take action where governments support with policy creations.

There are slightly modified definitions of sustainability, however, one common aspect is that these working definitions provide an initial framework for more extravagant definitions that are suitable for each city developing sustainability initiatives. One city, San Francisco (Zeemering, 2009), has defined sustainability in terms of urban design combined with traditional economic development terms, and the definitional ideal of community engagement. Termed another way, San Francisco looks at the architecture of buildings, however, what was not mentioned in their definition was waste management and environmental equity despite conceptualizing the foundations of sustainability.

The idea of sustainability is not a completely new concept, but the focus has been, more-or-less, on individual consumers' behaviors and private sector companies' activities under the heading of corporate social responsibility (CSR) initiatives. Thus,, governments are becoming more efficient with sustainable focused policies. Government activities on a worldwide level are visible in the way roads are designed, in how public transportation is provided, in the manner in which recycling is implemented, and in how architectural designs are constructed. More importantly, however, government policy influences behavior change among residents.

Green Economy

Another phrase in line with green sustainability is the 'green economy.' Defined as the "triple bottom line" that adds additional performance measurements to organizations besides profitability (Elkington, 1998). This term originated in accounting nomenclature in the late 1990s. The paradigm focuses on three aspects: the traditional financial bottom line, the social/ethical performance, and the environmental performance (Norman & MacDonald, 2004). The paradigm is complex to apply as an organizational performance system, but it at least gives weight to bringing attention to CSR concerns on an economic level.

Business start-ups with a primary green product or service are either classified as being ecopreneurs (Schaper, 2002), environmental entrepreneurship (de Bruin & Lewis, 2005), green entrepreneurship (Berle, 1991), or enviropreneurship (Menon & Menon, 1997). Notwithstanding the various classifications, these categories describe how new products or services are *socially* committed in meeting environmental market opportunities (Lober, 1998; Isaak, 1997). Being green in business model development and strategy is not a new concept because these terms have historically been acknowledged for the last three decades or so. Nonetheless, there should be research that showcases measured success of companies gaining a competitive advantage who focus on improving their environmental performance. Success being the optimal word for measuring not just multi-national corporations increasing their reliance on environmentally certified raw materials in their supply chain, or packaging being environmentally friendly, or even having energy-efficient light bulbs. There needs to be stronger evidence, and that is harder to prove without a change in standardized processes, and a change in measuring outcomes; not outputs.

INSTITUTIONAL CONTEXT OF POLICIES

Environmental policies and regulations are central to the development of a green economy. They provide investment direction, determine the system of development, and define the governmental role. Policy instruments are developed by governmental authorities to wield their power so as to either ensure support for, or prevent the occurrence of, social change (Vedung, 1998). There are more-or-less three types of policy instruments: regulatory, economic, and informational (De Bruijn & Hufen, 1998). Regulatory policies are regulations that are traditional government policies and are often referred to as the obligatory rules, orders, directives, norms, standards and statutory provisions (Vedung, 1998). Economic policies are fiscal incentives that incorporate environmental costs and benefits into budgets. These policies include taxes and fees or charges on permits or waste collection (United Nations Statistical Division, 1997). Whereas informational instruments are government involvement that formally influences social and economic acts through information (Krott, 2005) such as knowledge transfer, communicating an argument, advice, and/or moral appeal.

By enacting policy, governments can place restrictions on the use of scarce resources and spur technological change. But, more importantly, governments can provide the best direction that is beneficial to society; unlike the private sector who reacts to the changes. Governments regulate business behavior through institutional pressures, and, in a way, enforce "green" innovation to be conducted by businesses. Thus, this can produce positive results not only for the economy and businesses, but for society overall with a focused strategic response (Sorli & Stokic, 2009).

Sustainability and green economics is not without debate and controversy. In fact, it is difficult to monetize environmental contamination and intangibilities such as fresh air. An economic principle is simple how to report, measure and account the outcomes. There is no international accounting framework to measure CSR as well as financial reporting (Lewis & Russell, 2011). By developing a more green economic system, it is not necessarily about balancing, in economic terms, supply and demand in order to avoid recessions. Instead, it is basically about how to overcome resource constraints, or lack of supply, where natural resources are being depleted, and hence, production cannot maintain status quo (Cabezas & Diwekar, 2012).

LEARNING FROM OTHERS' SUSTAINABILITY OUTCOMES

The obligation of any government to be environmentally responsible and sustainable is not a minor focus nor is it trivial for cities and countries to ignore how much the climate is changing. Without a doubt, there is no formal international organization that is an authority of forcing sustainability policies, but the United Nations (UN) has had an invisible hand in guiding and promoting government policy developments. The UN focuses on facilitating voluntary agreements by countries and developing frameworks (e.g. UN Framework Convention on Climate Change). However, the UN addresses that everyone has to consider climate change, but they cannot force the responsibility to address climate change. There will always be difficulty in achieving broader international agreement on sustainability issues because countries simply have different economic strengths where developed countries, who are the most pollutant countries, intimidate developing countries, the least polluters, to engage in more green economic development.

There is no global rubric or matrix to assess how sustainable outcomes are successful. With economic development plans, it takes years to see if the outcomes have had a positive effect. Efforts by cities to be include sustainability initiatives involve working incrementally toward changing established policies and behaviors that align with the goals complementary of sustainability results. Undeniably, creating a green economy is challenging and is not without limitations and constraints of certain approaches, which is why cities are focusing on creating sustainability communities built from scratch. These sustainability communities are small in scale and purposely built experimental projects to study what works and what does not work in order to guide future policy changes or creations.

Two largest economic powerhouses, the US and China, overall on federal level, have done very little to systematically push for greater sustainability policies. The US has only taken modest steps to promote sustainability. Indeed, it has been up to each individual states to design policies. Whereas, China has focused on economic growth by expanding manufacturing and increased exporting of goods. This has resulted in increase of air pollution in urban cities. However, China does recognize there is a health issue of workers because of air pollution and is developing large-scale sustainable cities and communities to counteract carbon emissions. China, in light of their focus on expanding manufacturing, has, in essence, been one of the leading countries in constructing numerous experimental sustainable-built communities, or what can be termed as cluster green economic communities.

In the 1970s, Japan shifted to a more aggressive policy encouraging energy-efficient innovation. As a result of this shift, Japan became one of the leading economies in the world for innovation (Portney, 2015). Switzerland has developed policies that recognize the need that their different government levels are involved in creating a green economy. Nevertheless, Denmark is another example of a government designing policies and referencing the need to incorporate a reaction of climate change. Denmark's policies are very explicit compared to other major economic countries. They have 23 objectives within the three pillars of sustainability (Portney, 2015). Their main focus is on climate change policies mitigated within agriculture, energy, and transportation aspects.

DUBAI'S GREEN DEVELOPMENT

Creating a sustainable, green economy is not easy, and focusing on a more sustainable society costs time and money. Communication, dedication and data sharing has to happen amongst government ministries because government policy- and decision-makers have to consider the societal and economic impact. In addition, there has to be a positive impact in addressing climate change where sustainability is affordable. This can happen through exploring how data analytics, digitalization and technology can drive the green economy. Below discusses just some of the aspects of what Dubai has been doing on her path to becoming a global, green economic leader.

In 2014, Dubai's National Innovation Strategy was developed to put the country on the path towards becoming the world's most innovative nation within seven years (Step Feed, 2018). The National Innovation Strategy is part of Dubai's "Vision 2021" where the aim is to create an environment that cultivates, encourages, and more importantly, supports the development of innovations through institutions and policy legislations. Thus, the month of February has turned into an annual event termed "UAE Innovation Month" which is one of the largest innovation festivals globally. For the month of

February, the UAE hosts events, workshops and innovation competitions across not only Dubai, but the seven other emirates as well. The vision includes His Highness Sheikh Mohammed bin Rashid Al Maktoum's innovation fund to support UAE-based companies as well as apply over $81.7 billion to developing a Science, Technology and Innovation policy (Step Feed, 2018). The government of Dubai has been heavily involved in the promotion of innovation with 'The Mohammed bin Rashid Centre for Government Innovation.'

Consequently, 'sustainable' becomes a strategic term. Indeed, it can be the complete model and strategy that businesses should strive for, but it is not easy. The central story of Dubai's green economic climb has been powerfully assembled by a network of five government ministries. This process is owed to His Highness Sheikh Mohammed bin Rashid Al Maktoum. He has declared that Dubai will get 75% of her energy from clean sources by 2050 in order to have the smallest carbon footprint globally. In January 2012, Sheikh Mohammed launched the Green Economy initiative where he posits Dubai in becoming not only a global hub, but a successful model of the being a purely a green economic powerhouse. These initiatives have six aspects (Government of Dubai, 2018):

1. The first field of green energy aims to promote the production and use of renewable energy.
2. The second field includes government policies aimed to encourage investments in green economy and to facilitate the production, import, export and re-export of green products and technologies.
3. The third field relates to developing urban planning policies that preserve the environment and to raise the efficiency of housing and buildings environmentally.
4. The fourth field consists of means for dealing with the effects of climate change, promote organic agriculture, maintain biodiversity and protect the ecological balance.
5. The fifth field aims at rationalizing the use of water resources, electricity and natural resources and recycle waste.
6. The sixth field includes development and promotion of green technology.

Dubai's Green Fund

Dubai has also created the Dubai Green Fund in November 2015 as part of the "Dubai Clean Energy Strategy 2050" (Government of Dubai, 2018). This fund is the investment focus side of Dubai Electric and Water Authority (DEWA) in offering loans to companies in the clean energy sector for investing directly on green projects. The intention of the fund is not necessarily focused on shareholders or mainly profitability, but to focus on multiple projects of renewable energy, energy efficiency, and innovative ways of balancing electricity demand and supply. For instance, DEWA produces most of Dubai's electricity and drinking water. Natural gas is burned to generate electricity where the leftover heat is used to distill seawater and remove the salt (Kunzig, 2017).

The Sustainable City

Specifically, Dubai is creating a new housing development called "Sustainable City" on the outskirts of city. The plan is to have 500 townhouses and villas that have the lowest environmental footprint while maintaining a high quality of life. Not without challenges, this city is focused on the triple bottom line in addressing the three pillars of sustainability (social, environmental, economic) and happiness. The Sustainable City produces more electricity than it consumes because of solar power panels as well as all waste is recycled in greenhouses. The houses will all have UV reflective pain to reduce thermal heat and charging stations for electric cars.

Solar Decathlon Middle East

Additionally, Dubai skillfully hosted an international competition to increase environmental knowledge exchange. The Solar Decathlon Middle East (SDME) was an international competition for universities to design, build and operate solar powered houses. These houses need to use renewable energy as the only main energy source and are equipped with innovative technologies that maximize energy efficiencies (Power Technology, 2018). Currently, Dubai has the land and space to host initiatives such as these.

Dubai Green Hotel Innovation

Another initiative to develop green innovation is through the "Dubai Green Hotel Innovation" that presents ideas on lasting impact on energy efficiency solutions in hotels (Dubai Green Hotel Innovation, 2018). Dubai is a city that is relying less on oil and more on tourism, and because of this, hotels want to reduce operating costs and improve sustainable performance. By being focused on the hotel industry, this creates benchmarks for other tourist cities. Dubai is now constructing 300 hotels to add to their current 700 hotels. This increase in hotels will escalate the environmental impact from natural resource usage

Solar Park

Dubai is also creating a solar park officially known as the "Mohammed Bin Rashid Al Maktoum Solar Park." This park hopes to be the largest single-site in the world by installing 2.36 million First Solar FS Series 3 Black photovoltaic (PV) modules over a 4.5 million square meter area (Power Technology, 2018). In addition, the park will create hydrogen mobility by powering a number of fuel-cell vehicles with hydrogen generated at the Mohammed bin Rashid Al Maktoum Solar Park (The National, 2019). The flagship, pioneering project is in partnership with German based Siemens.

Hydrogen Innovation

Hydrogen is a renewable energy source that has been in existence for more than 100 years within the chemical industry. Currently, the automobile industry is developing hydrogen fuel cell vehicles because it reduces the carbon footprint as compared to petroleum vehicles. Once this innovation becomes more focused in the automobile industry, then production costs should decline since hydrogen is very expensive to develop. Al-Futtaim Motors launched the first hydrogen station in the Middle East in October, 2017 (Air Liquide, 2017). The technology is become more customized for higher temperature regions since hydrogen compression process has to be cooled to compensate for an increase of heat.

CONCLUSION

This chapter discussed definitional aspects of sustainability and green economy. It also benchmarked some of Dubai's sister cities in regards of policy development. Some cities and countries do more than others in developing a green economy and creating sustainability advantages. Certainly, more cities need to be engaged in the pursuit of sustainability because climate change cannot be ignored. It is subjective whether these policies have made the cities more sustainable and the economy more "green." Policy development is important because it can change industries and the capabilities of innovation and technology. However, what is not a clear is if regulation can change the willingness of businesses to integrate sustainability into their strategy besides imposing taxes (Holt, 2011). Taxes get passed onto the consumer. Therefore, regulation and policy needs to be "smart" (Janicke, 2008). However, it comes down to commitment level of not only individuals, but companies and governments too in creating more effective ways of sustainability. There is no shortage in seeing the consequences of global warming, increased carbon emissions, manufacturing, fishing and other economic workings. In addition, by understanding the cause-and-effect of the environment needs as dire effects from not just the individual perspective, but the effects on the country as a whole, regulations and policies can be specifically shaped. Technologies and green communities offer the promise of time and long-term solutions, however, multilateral action will always be necessary.

Dubai cleverly adapts to changing fads without departing from their overall "smart" imitative objective to create measures of environmental responsibility and green economic growth reforms. They are creating pioneering initiatives to invoke green innovation. There is no suggestion, though, that cities, such as Dubai, can, somehow miraculously make the world sustainable. However, the government competitions and initiatives are creating a knowledge roadmap for Dubai in becoming a global, sustainable city. Nevertheless, the world can become more sustainable if more cities are involved in being "glocally" in thinking globally and acting locally. Additionally, Dubai will find success because it has the drive, the support and the space to focus on being one of the global leaders in developing a green economy.

FUTURE RESEARCH

Indeed, the Dubai example is not a mirage that conceals itself from economic development. Certainly, when a policy is created to conserve household water usage (e.g. DEWA), then it is with the thought that this can extend water supplies. Or when there is an increase in the usage of renewable energy, it is with the hope that carbon emissions will decline. Therefore, a future study should be conducted in 5-10 years' time looking at the effect of currently policies to see if there are positive outcomes of sustainability. Although program success centers on how they are implemented and, more importantly, how they are managed. It is with hope that in a decade, the benefits of such development of the Sustainable City will be seen.Future research can focus on how businesses in Dubai and the region react to Dubai's institutional policies in regards of green innovation and green economic development. There are few studies that actually relate to the green innovation process. Some cities are focused on designing a green economy, whereas others have enacted policies that undercut the definition of sustainability. The focus of this chapter is on presenting what current policies are and is not trying to offer a critical reflection of a wide array of policies. Instead, one can hope that knowledge can be gained for practitioners and designers of government policies.

Businesses strategic responses to environmental policies in the Middle East region is under-researched. Therefore, research can focus on how businesses adapt their innovation processes under new institutional policies for the green economy. In addition, other research can focus on how businesses behave in a strategically proactive manner within their innovation practices based on environmental criteria (Gupta & Kumar, 2013) as well as green technology push and green demand pull on innovation systems.

Since the effects of sustainability and green economic development policies are very long-term focused, future research is time consuming and expensive. However, it will be essential in order to understand if the policies are working and, if necessary, any environmental risk is being taken. Historically, research has focused on current environmental problems and the consequences of those problems, and has created an increase of public misperceptions. The discrepancies between perceived risk and actual risks influences governmental policy makers. Repeatedly saying climate change is going to happen or an individual has to live more sustainably do not create innovations or personal changes. There is very little evidence on how successful a particular, sustainable program become more sustainable which can hamper future policy making. However, sustainability is complex and requires adaptation from everyone. People, businesses and governments cannot prevent climate change, but they can slow down the progress. The reality is, though, that it comes down to effective leadership of governments as well as business executives to increase their genuine behavior towards social responsibility (Ayson, 2011). It cannot simply be a marketing ploy or public relations stunt to avoid being responsible. Conversely, it is neither about economics nor technology, but human behavior to deal with the paradigm shift. Economics and technology are just the consequences of the reaction. Ultimately, it is about organizational change process of management and leaders to learn to take action.

REFERENCES

AirLiquide Magazine. (2017). *Hydrogen mobility gains momentum in Middle East.* Retrieved from https://www.airliquide.com/magazine/hydrogen-mobility-gains-momentum-middle-east

Ayson, S. (2011). Sustainable Management Education: A Graduate Skills Approach. In Business and Sustainability: Concepts, Strategies and Changes (pp. 293-308). Bingley, UK: Emerald Group Publishing Limited.

Berle, G. (1991). *The green entrepreneur: Business opportunities that can save the earth and make you money.* Blue Ridge Summit, PA: Liberty Hall Press.

Cabezas, H., & Diwekar, U. (2012). *Sustainability: Multi-disciplinary perspectives.* Bentham Science Publishers Ltd. doi:10.2174/97816080510381120101

De Bruijn, H. A., & Hufen, H. A. M. (1998). The traditional approach to policy instruments. In P. B. Guy & F. K. M. van Nispen (Eds.), *Public Policy Instruments: Evaluating the Tools of Public Administration.* Cheltenham, UK: Edward Elgar.

De Bruin, A., & Lewis, K. (2005). Green entrepreneurship in New Zealand: a micro-enterprise focus. In M. Schaper (Ed.), *Green Entrepreneurship in New Zealand: A Micro- Enterprise Focus.* Aldershot, UK: Ashgate Publishing.

Dubai Green Hotel Innovation. (2018). Retrieved from http://www.dubaigreenhotelinnovation.com/

Elkington, J. (1998). *Cannibals With Forks: The Triple Bottom Line of 21st Century Business.* Stony Creek, CT: New Society Publishers.

Government of Dubai. (n.d.). *Solar Decathlon Middle East Dubai, 2018.* Retrieved from https://www.dubaisolarshow.com/views/sdme.aspx

Gupta, S., & Kumar, V. (2013). Sustainability as corporate culture of a brand for superior performance. *Journal of World Business, 48*(3), 311–320. doi:10.1016/j.jwb.2012.07.015

Holt, D. (2011). The Longitudinal Evolution of Environmental "Ecopreneurs" from the 1990s: Mergers and Acquisitions and the Waste Management Industry. In G. Eweje & M. Perry (Eds.), *Business and Sustainability: Concepts, Strategies and Changes* (Vol. 3). Bingley, UK: Emerald Group Publishing Limited. doi:10.1108/S2043-9059(2011)0000003013

Isaak, R. (1997). Globalisation and green entrepreneurship. *Greener Management International.*, *18*, 80–90.

Janicke, M. (2008). Ecological modernisation: New perspectives. *Journal of Cleaner Production, 16*(5), 557–565. doi:10.1016/j.jclepro.2007.02.011

Kunzig, R. (2017, April 4). *The World's Most Improbable Green City.* Retrieved from https://www.nationalgeographic.com/environment/urban-expeditions/green- buildings/dubai-ecological-footprint-sustainable-urban-city/

Larcom, S., & Swanson, T. (2013). Economics of Green Economies: Investment in Green Growth and How it Works. In P.-M. Dupuy & J. Vinuales (Eds.), *Harnessing Foreign Investment to Promote Environmental Protection.* Cambridge, UK: Cambridge University Press. doi:10.1017/CBO9781139344289.007

Lewis, L., & Russell, S. (2011). Premating boundaries: Accountability at the nexus of water and climate change. *Social and Environmental Accountability Journal.*, *31*(2), 37–41. doi:10.1080/0969160X.2011.593812

Lober, D. J. (1998). Pollution prevention as corporate entrepreneurship. *Journal of Organizational Change Management, 11*(1), 26–37. doi:10.1108/09534819810369554

Menon, A., & Menon, A. (1997). Enviropreneurial marketing strategy: The emergence of corporate environmentalism as marketing strategy. *Journal of Marketing, 61*(1), 51–67. doi:10.1177/002224299706100105

Mowery, D. (1995). The Boundaries of the US Firm in R&D. In N. R. Lamoreaux & D. M. G. Raff (Eds.), *Coordination and Information: Historical Perspectives on the Organization of Enterprise* (pp. 147–172). Chicago: Chicago University Press.

Norman, W., & MacDonald, C. (2004). Getting to the bottom of "Triple Bottom Line.". *Business Ethics Quarterly, 14*(2), 243–262. doi:10.5840/beq200414211

Portney, K. (2015). *Sustainability.* Cambridge, MA: MIT Press.

Power Technology. (n.d.). *Mohammed bin Rashid Al Maktoum Solar Park Phase II, Dubai.* Retrieved from https://www.power-technology.com/projects/mohammed-bin-rashid-al- maktoum-solar-park-phase-ii-dubai/

Schaper, M. (2002). The Essence of Ecopreneurship. *Greener Management International., 38*(38), 26–30. doi:10.9774/GLEAF.3062.2002.su.00004

Sorli, M., & Stokic, D. (2009). *Innovating in Product/Process Development: Gaining Pace in New Product Development.* Springer Science & Business Media. doi:10.1007/978-1-84882-545-1

Step Feed. (2018). Retrieved from https://stepfeed.com/here-s-how-the-uae-is-creating-the-next-wave-of-innovators-0348

The National. (2019). *Dubai home to first solar-powered hydrogen facility in Mena.* Retrieved from https://www.thenational.ae/business/energy/dubai-home-to-first-solar-powered-hydrogen-facility-in-mena-1.821303

The Official Portal of the UAE Government. (n.d.). *Green Economy for Sustainable Development.* Retrieved from https://government.ae/about-the-uae/economy/green-economy-for-sustainable-development

United Arab Emirates Ministry of Climate Change & Environment. (n.d.). *UAE State of Green Economy Report 2017.* Retrieved from http://un- page.org/files/public/uae_state_of_green_economy_report_2017_0.pdf

United Nations Environment Program. (2011). *Towards a Green Economy: Pathways to Sustainable Development and Poverty Eradication.* Retrieved from http://www.unep.org/greeneconomy

United Nations Statistical Division. (1997). *Glossary of Environment Statistics, Studies in Methods (Series F, No. 67).* New York, NY: United Nations.

Vedung, E. (1998). Policy instruments: Typologies and theories. In M. L. Bemelmans-Videc, R. C. Rist, & E. O. Vedung (Eds.), *Carrots, Sticks and Sermons: Policy Instruments and Their Evaluation.* London, UK: Transaction Publishers.

World Commission on Environment and Development. (1987). *Our Common Future (Brundtland Commission).* Oxford, UK: Oxford University Press.

Zeemering, E. (2009). What Does Sustainability Mean to City Officials? *Urban Affairs Review, 45*(2), 247–273. doi:10.1177/1078087409337297

Chapter 2
Cluster Branding:
The Art of Communicating Innovation

Toby Nelson
https://orcid.org/0000-0001-6695-1376
Independent Researcher, USA

ABSTRACT

Innovation economies are a departure from traditional modes of development. Where the latter privileges activities like resource extraction and infrastructure construction, the former emphasizes less material approaches such as knowledge-building and talent creation. In its drive to become a knowledge-based economy, Dubai may face challenges of perceptual legitimacy in its newly formed innovation clusters. At the same time, however, a strength of image bulwarks its established clusters like finance and logistics. This chapter summarizes best practices and existing theory on cluster branding, briefly examines several innovation clusters in Europe and the United States, and finally ruminates on the opportunities and challenges faced by Dubai in creating strong brands that communicate innovation.

DOI: 10.4018/978-1-5225-9377-5.ch002

INTRODUCTION

Michael Porter (1990) defined the early contours of what would become known as "innovation clusters" — networks of geographically co-positioned and thematically related companies and institutions that, through collaboration and competition, could produce greater results as a group than they could individually. The drivers for cluster development have been well-documented. Autio, Chaminade, et al. (2016) include among them "skills, accommodating policy framework, infrastructure, low cost structures (in early stages), a good lifestyle offering and serendipity." To that hexad of innovation drivers, however, perhaps we can add a seventh —effective branding.

A brand represents a "shared reality" (Ballantyne and Aitken 2007, 365), or how we collectively perceive a product, person, or place. It is a method of distilling a complex set of ideas into a simple and easily understood image. Cluster branding, therefore, is about the creation of a recognizable and enduring image for an innovation cluster.

Dubai, the subject of this volume, is not a single, self-contained cluster. Rather, it is a panoply of clusters. It does not project one image of itself. Rather, it is a city of images. Each of its clusters magnifies a different and unique brand to its residents, customers, and investors, all of which ultimately feed into the larger place brand of Dubai.

In this chapter, we examine the function and theory of cluster branding and its importance to both the individual companies and institutions that form the cluster brand, as well as the place brand in which the cluster sits. We then briefly explore Dubai's innovation clusters, juxtapose them against clusters in other regions, and finally ruminate on how or if the brands projected by Dubai's clusters contribute towards innovation and entrepreneurship in this "city of images."

CLUSTER BRANDING

Of Places, Brands, and Clusters

Cluster branding can logically be described as a subset of place branding. Where the place brand is a specific image of a city or region generated in the mind of a receiver, the cluster brand represents a more nuanced sense of an area as the place point for an innovation cluster; it is our shared perception of why and how that area is innovative. Cluster branding is ultimately "the process of identifying the identity of a particular cluster brand and reflecting this core value ... to build brand awareness, visibility, credibility, and loyalty." (Mauroner and Zorn 2017, 291)

Figure 1 relates the cluster brand, the brands of its constituent companies and institutions, and the brand of the place in which it's located to an avocado. The brands of individual companies and institutions form the seed of the avocado; they are ensconced by the cluster brand, represented by the meat. Holding it all together is the skin of the fruit, representing the place brand.

For a company or institution, the image and identity it shares by virtue of being part of a cluster may be as important as some of the more obviously tangible business benefits of cluster membership, such as infrastructure development and regulatory improvement. Sölvell, Lindqvist, and Ketels

Figure 1.

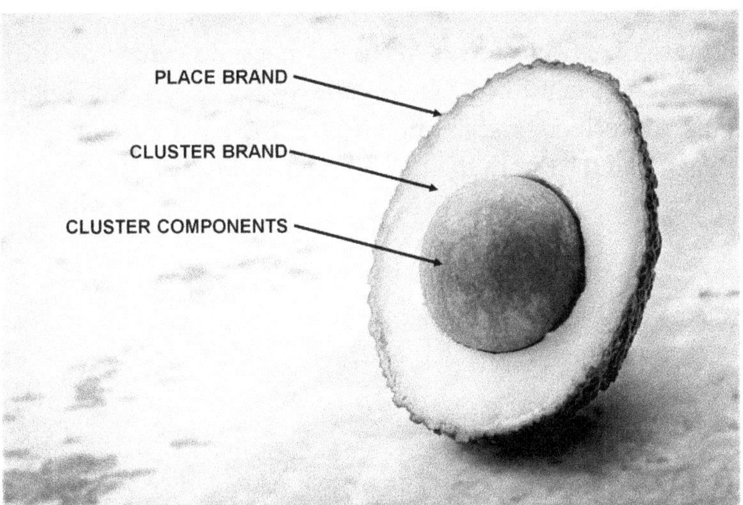

(2003) surveyed more than 200 individuals involved in cluster-related work across a number of regions. They found that survey participants considered brand building one of the most important contributions of a cluster. In fact, more than 80 percent of respondents agreed that "creating a brand" was a key objective of a cluster initiative (ibid.).

When thinking about the importance that comes from association with a powerful cluster brand consider, for instance, the built-in challenges an upstart vehicle manufacturer located in Santa Fe, New Mexico might face. Not only is it removed from the resources, infrastructure, and creative foundation of more established automotive clusters like Michigan, but it also faces a question of perceptual legitimacy. Who, after all, associates auto manufacturing with Santa Fe? For the vehicle manufacturer located in a recognized cluster like Michigan or Germany, however, the strength of the cluster's brand can elevate and support the member company's individual brand.

The elevation of the individual brands of a cluster's constituent companies by the umbrella brand of the cluster itself was observed by Yao Lu (2012) in her study of Chinese textile clusters. And, Mauroner and Zorn's (2017, 301) interviews with stakeholders in two German technology clusters discovered that the cluster brand operated as a "paperclip whose function is to signal the coherence of the actors and make them visible outside of the cluster as a unit with specific characteristics and standards." It could probably be posited that a continuous transfer of energy between the cluster brand and its constituent brands exists; the constituent brands help establish the cluster brand while the cluster brand helps mold the constituents into a more coherently branded whole.

Figure 2 visualizes a cluster and its brand in less abstract terms by focusing on that most iconic cluster, Silicon Valley, and its vertical relationships. As previously described, and as shown here, the cluster brand is formed of influences generated by both the place brand and the cluster components.

Figure 2.

At this point, however, it's important to distinguish the cluster initiative from the cluster brand. The organization supporting and advancing the brand is not the same as the brand itself. Indeed, the world's most enduring cluster brands are not the product of a planned or intentional branding initiative at all. While the name Silicon Valley has become inseparably entangled with the image of high-tech innovation, it is despite the absence of a single, central organization claiming the right to curate, defend, and advance a Silicon Valley brand.

In fact, past research into established clusters — places like Hollywood (as a film and television cluster) and Silicon Valley (as a high technology cluster) — strongly suggests a blend of organic factors were the principal drivers in establishing their success. Speaking at a symposium hosted by the United States' National Research Council in 2011, Maryann Feldman of the University of North Carolina observed that many of these iconic clusters appear to be the result of historical happenstance and chance events. Echoing this observation, Muro and Katz (2010) frankly declare that:

Clusters can't be created out of nothing and cluster initiatives should only be attempted where clusters already exist. The preexistence of a cluster means that an industry hotspot has passed the market test. By contrast, efforts at wholesale invention will likely be fraught with selection issues, inefficiency, and probable failure and waste.

In that sense, the process of cluster formation may be more a process of cluster discovery — the identification of existing institutions which can be bound together through, among other things, an effective and unifying brand.

The Transnational Alliance of Clusters Towards Improved Cooperation Support (TACTICS), an *ad hoc* European Union policy group, outlined four key elements in the construction of a cluster brand. First, is the identification of the cluster's core values and attributes. (What does the brand stand for and in what does it believe?) Next, is the definition of the cluster's value proposition. (What benefit does it provide that its competitors don't?) Third, is the description of its personality. (Is it wholesome, refined, youthful, reliable, innovative, adventurous?) And, finally, comes the creation of the brand's visual identity. (What color palette will the brand select for its external communications; what is the logo and wordmark; what font face will the brand use?)

These elements, of course, are no different than those used in a brand building exercise for any product, service, or place. To be effective, they must be an actual projection of the values, attributes, proposition, and personality as they exist in the cluster, or towards which the cluster realistically aspires. Purely arbitrary selection of branding elements results in an image that doesn't square with the brand's reality.

Perhaps more importantly, it bears remembering that the major elements used in the construction of the brand are only support structures for its underlying value, or brand equity. The equity of the brand are the thoughts and feelings that come to mind when the public thinks about it. If the public associates the brand with bad experiences they've had in terms of quality and competence, no number of new logos and color palettes can rescue it. The cluster brand, like all brands, must deliver on its promise.

A Lifecycle of Brands

A lifecycle of brands was identified in the 1990s by advertising agency Young & Rubicam. Their Brand Asset Valuator model defined four pillars of brand equity. They are:

- Differentiation, or the uniqueness of the brand in relation to its competitors.
- Relevance, or the perceived import of the brand.
- Esteem, or the perception of the brand's quality and popularity.
- Knowledge, or the level of awareness the brand enjoys.

These four pillars, in turn, combine to establish two cornerstone brand characteristics. Differentiation and relevance represent a brand's vitality, while esteem and knowledge describe its stature. These characteristics can be plotted on a matrix to help visualize a brand's place in the lifecycle (Figure 3).

Figure 3.

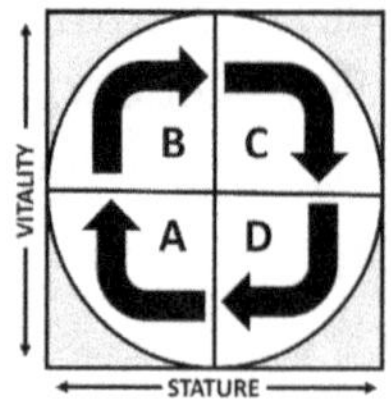

A brand begins its life as a new and unfocused entity with low stature and low vitality. This is quadrant "A" of Figure 1. Increasing vitality, created by growing relevance and differentiation, moves the brand into quadrant "B" where it has a building, but unrealized, potential. With more awareness and greater esteem comes a move into quadrant "C" where the brand enjoys both high stature and high vitality; it is a leader and innovator in its category. Brands that stagnate and lose momentum begin to fade. While they continue to enjoy high stature, their vitality suffers and they fall into quadrant "D." They may ultimately fade away entirely, effectively placing themselves back into quadrant "A."

The Young & Rubicam model was created to assess the status of consumer brands, but its flexibility and universality make it a useful building block in examining any brand type, including cluster brands.

In the next part of this chapter, we briefly explore several major clusters before narrowing our focus to Dubai, specifically.

CLUSTER BRANDING: CASES AND COMPARISONS

Boston's Biotech Cluster

The Boston area has an organically developed biotech cluster that dates to the mid-1970s when the city council of Cambridge, Massachusetts first licensed Biogen to conduct DNA experimentation (Bernsau 2018). The biotech and pharma companies that later followed Biogen into eastern Massachusetts were supported by a rich educational network bulwarked by institutions such as Harvard University, Boston College, and the Massachusetts Institute of Technology, and coupled with an excellent transportation network and conducive regulatory environment.

However, the first intentional efforts to brand the Boston area as a biotech cluster didn't come until a generation later. Recognizing that Boston risked being supplanted as America's life sciences leader by up-and-coming areas like North Carolina and California, in the early 2000s Massachusetts retained branding consultancy KHJ to fortify the region's established reputation as a biotechnology innovation cluster. To emphasize the centrality of resources Boston offered in the way of business networks, an educated workforce, and regulatory support, KHJ renewed the Boston area's biotech brand under the tagline "Massachusetts: It's All Here." (ibid.)

During the roll-out of the new initiative, Mitt Romney — then Governor of Massachusetts — described the importance of effective cluster branding: "We're not going to keep the best jobs here if we adopt the 'Field of Dreams' strategy — if you build it they will come. We need to do a better job of getting the word out." (Collins 2003)

In 2018 *Genetic Engineering & Biotechnology News (GEN)* placed Boston on the top of its list of "Top U.S. Biopharma Clusters." In describing the reasons for this rank, the publication cited the fact that the region had received more National Institutes of Health funding than any other, that 18 of the 20 leading biopharmaceutical companies had a corporate presence in Boston, and that an impressive 7,565 patents had come out of the Boston biotech cluster in the preceding year. (Philippidis 2018)

The *GEN* ranking is a manifestation of the Boston brand. But it is not one borne out of taglines and magazine ads. It is a projection of the region's reality. Successful branding requires that the brand's storyteller has something tangible to communicate and, likewise, that the cluster's tangible qualities are effectively communicated.

Photonics Network Thuringia

The German state of Thuringia, and particularly its second-largest city of Jena, has long been a center of innovation in the optics industry with world-leading companies like Carl Zeiss AG based there, as well as important research entities such as the Fraunhofer Institute for Applied Optics and Precision Engineering.

Like Boston, intentional efforts to elevate and enforce the organic Jena optical innovation brand did come about until well after many of the cluster's characteristic elements were already in place. In 1999 OptoNet was established as an organized initiative to support the cluster. The creation of OptoNet might be considered a defensive response to similar efforts already underway in competitive clusters. Seven years prior to OptoNet's creation, for instance, the Arizona Optics Industry Association was created to help grow the image of Tucson, Arizona as "Optics Valley."

According to OptoNet (2018), which is funded partly by the German Ministry of Education and Research, it "represents the leading players of Photonics in Jena region, creates a communication and cooperation platform, strengthens the international visibility of the cluster, initiates activities for talent promotion and is committed to marketing of the Photonics region."

In his 2015 study of the Jena optical innovation cluster, Mauroner interviewed executives of the region's companies and discovered there were widespread feelings of satisfaction with the work OptoNet had done in communicating the brand to the outside world, such as its advertising and media relations initiatives. He drew particular attention to OptoNet's organization of a cooperative trade show presence at major industrial fairs which company executives described as a "door opener that makes it easier ... to penetrate markets that would not be accessible when going it alone." In total, these efforts helped develop and solidify a common brand and image for the existing Jena optics innovation cluster.

However, as Mauroner also noted, the common aspects of the Jena brand were an identity "built up over the course of time." In other words, the work which OptoNet had done was more a process of refining and communicating the brand than making it, a situation and observation not dissimilar to that seen in the case of the Boston biotechnology cluster.

Medicon Valley

Medicon Valley is a geographically interesting innovation cluster, straddling Denmark and Sweden and made possible, in part, by the 1999 completion of the Øresund Bridge which linked the two countries. In the late 1990s when its formal cluster initiative, the Medicon Valley Alliance, was created the region was home to more than 50 percent of Scandinavia's pharmaceutical and biotechnology firms, headlined by companies such as AstraZeneca, Novo Nordisk, and Leo Pharma. It's also the site of major life sciences education and research programs at Lund University, the Copenhagen Business School of Pharmacy[1], the Technical University of Denmark, and the Research Center of the Danish Cancer Society. (Horton 1998)

Originating as the Medicon Valley Academy, the Alliance has been aggressive in branding Medicon Valley as northern Europe's leading life sciences innovation cluster. Its branding strategy has embraced the cluster's binational character by elevating common Scandinavian qualities and highlighting the region's modern infrastructure and educated workforce. Meanwhile, "the cultural and geographical differences between the two countries" is continuously minimized (Boesso, D'Orazio, and Torresan 2012, 54).

While the Medicon Valley Alliance employs traditional marketing techniques to project its brand — its collateral, interestingly, emphasizes the dichotomous values of uniqueness and uniformity (ibid.) — it has also made a heavy investment in the "soft" technique of relationship marketing. In a case report, Anderson, Solitander, and Ekman (2012) described the Medicon Valley Alliance's Life Science Ambassador Programme:

It is not a network of volunteers per se, but rather a systematic effort to build international partnerships and linkages with companies, academia and organisations in other life science clusters, which is done by posting ambassadors to leading life science cluster regions in the world.

The program's exchange with British Columbia, Canada, for instance, saw a representative from the British Columbia Innovation Council posted for three years to Copenhagen and, in return, a representative from the Medicon Valley Alliance stationed in Vancouver. While the representatives were principally tasked with developing business linkages between the two regions, according to the Tendensor report (ibid.), the exchange also helped heighten "awareness and recognition among key target groups in business and academia in the host regions."

Medicon Valley, born of the type of serendipity previously discussed as a hallmark of the successful cluster, embraces an organic view of its own self. Like the previous two clusters examined, the branding approach taken by Medicon Valley has been more about communicating an existing brand than about making a new one. The Medicon Valley Alliance's 2018 marketing strategy handbook drives this point home:

The idea of developing a communications and marketing strategy for Medicon Valley arose because the cluster's "power of particularity" has been unknown – or at least unclear – to stakeholders both in and outside Medicon Valley ... For years, terms such as "worldclass" and "world-leading" have been utilized to describe Medicon Valley. While these buzzwords may be accurate by some parameters, they say very little about Medicon Valley and its "power of particularity" and they certainly do not make the cluster stand out from the many other life science clusters around the world that also claim to be "world-leading" or "worldclass".

The Alliance seems to recognize a truth in Muro and Katz's caution about "efforts at wholesale invention" of a cluster and that such a caution, by extension, extends to a cluster's brand as well.

The Clusters of Dubai

The Dubai Creative Clusters Authority is a government entity that provides regulatory oversight to nine "free zones" forming seven diverse clusters: media and entertainment, information and communications technology, higher education, outsourcing, human capital development, design, and life sciences Established in 2014 as the successor to a similar organization, its self-described mandate is "to foster the economic development of Dubai's creative clusters and related knowledge industries." Charged with the actual development and operation of each cluster's physical infrastructure is the TECOM Group, a company owned by the state-run Dubai Holding investment firm.

For Dubai, the zones are instrumental to its continuing development. Martin Hvidt (2009) notes that the emirate and city long ago planned to bypass industrialization and advance directly to a knowledge economy; an economy, in other words, centered on "a greater reliance on intellectual capabilities than on physical inputs or natural resources." (Powell and Snellman 2004, 199) Part of this strategy involves creating and capturing opportunities to make Dubai home to companies with a global reach.

The benefits offered to businesses choosing to locate in one of Dubai's cluster zones are impressive. They include a 50-year exemption from taxes and customs duties, the ability to fully repatriate profits to the company's home country, and "one-stop services" like permitting and work authorizations. Unlike other areas of the emirate, in which most companies must have 51-percent local ownership, businesses operating out of one of the cluster zones are allowed full foreign ownership.[2] These benefits are in addition, of course, to each cluster's well-developed residential and commercial properties, and the built-in convenience of being located within a four-hour plane flight from one-third of the world's population.

However, Dubai's new creative clusters face the perceptual challenge of artificiality. That is, unlike well-established clusters such as Hollywood and Silicon Valley, they were not born out of serendipity but, rather, were the conscious constructs of the emirate's government. The need to establish legitimacy and to redefine Dubai from oil sands to knowledge center must undoubtedly be a point of central concern to the city's brand makers.

However, innovation clusters in Dubai are not limited to those of the Creative Clusters Authority. An older echelon of clusters has more-or-less organically developed within Dubai, principally encompassing the logistics and financial sectors. These are directly tied to the emirate's history as a centrally positioned trading state and the longstanding policies of the country's leaders; as far back as 1894 then ruler Sheikh Maktoum bin Hasher Al Maktoum exempted foreign traders from taxes. These traditional clusters are bulwarked by their own special economic zones, such as the Jebel Ali Free Zone and Dubai International Financial Centre. The established image and identity of the traditional clusters may have a "spillover effect" on the branding of those rooted in newer sectors (Hafeez, Foroudi, et al. 2016).

As has been observed, the cluster brand is inseparably entangled with both the brands of its members and the larger place brand in which it is situated. Dubai's place brand is rooted in its history as a cosmopolitan trading state, sitting at the nexus of Africa and Asia. Previously described was the challenge of artificiality perhaps faced by some of the innovation clusters that have been conjured into existence in Dubai. Writing in *The Independent* in 2015, Willis dismissed the Dubai Design District, the city's arts and design cluster, as "an attempt to manufacture cool by erecting some flatpack graffitied warehouses in the middle of the desert." In their research on Dubai's clusters, Hafeez, Foroudi, et al. (2016) noted that they each tended to offer similar or identical value propositions:

... lower cost, reduction in administrative bureaucracy, excellent infrastructure, provision of support services, ability to have complete foreign ownership and exemption from corporation taxation and import duty.

The challenge, therefore, for Dubai's newest innovation clusters is that what differentiates their brands from those of other clusters is easily replicable by competitors. Nothing in it cannot be recreated in other markets or by other clusters; regulations can be legislated and infrastructure can be built. The country's traditional clusters of finance and logistics, however, may offer value propositions better insulated from competition. Each are built upon a critical mass of important companies and institutions as well as deep, established pools of talent. These are recognizable elements of their respective clusters and form part of our shared reality of them.

SUMMARY

This short chapter has briefly explored the idea of the innovation cluster and established how its creation is often a result of the confluence of organic forces and serendipity. We've also seen how several powerful clusters recognize some level of truth in this belief and approach cluster branding as a method of communicating an existing reality rather than a method of making a new one.

Ultimately, however, the question of whether clusters can form through accident or artifice may be less relevant than the undeniable realization that the cluster brand exists in a state of symbiosis between its place brand and its component elements. It is nurtured and developed by each of them and draws on their strengths for its vitality. A cluster brand cannot be used to create a place brand, nor can it somehow generate its own constituents. Cluster branding, therefore, is very much a matter of sequence; it occurs after cluster formation and not as a precursor to its genesis.

How could Boston or Medicon Valley as biotech and life sciences clusters, or Jena as an optics innovation cluster, be compared to any of Dubai's traditional or emerging clusters using the Brand Asset Valuator model? By placing each of these clusters on the valuation matrix, companies seeking to position in one or the other might help identify how they could contribute to, and benefit from, that continuous transfer of energy which exists between the cluster brand and its component elements. Of course, this is not a matchmaking process; fading brands do not want to associate with other fading brands. It is, instead, about finding a place of mutuality and positional symmetry.

Innovation-based development represents a break from traditional models of development. Where the latter privileges activities like resource extraction and infrastructure construction, the former emphasizes less material approaches such as knowledge-building and talent creation.

But innovation is unbounded by geographic concerns. Oil can only be drilled in places where there's oil to be drilled and gold can only be mined in places there's gold to be mined. Knowledge, however, has no such spatial restriction. When all is said and done, the only advantage one innovation cluster has over any other innovation cluster is the power of its brand. And, unlike oil wells or gold mines, access to the trophy of brand preeminence can be captured or taken unless constantly protected, curated, developed, and improved.

REFERENCES

Anderson, M., Solitander, A., & Ekman, P. (2012). *Cluster branding and marketing*. Kalmar: Tendensor.

Autio, E., Chaminade, D., & Corbett, A. (2017). *Innovation clusters: Understanding life cycles*. New York: Economist Intelligence Unit.

Ballantyne, D., & Aitken, R. (2007). Branding in B2B markets: Insights from the service-dominant logic of marketing. *Journal of Business and Industrial Marketing, 22*(6), 363–371. doi:10.1108/08858620710780127

Bernsau, M. (2018) Fifteen years later: A reflection on the Mass. biotech sector. *Boston Business Journal*. Available from: https://www.bizjournals.com/boston/news/2018/05/31/fifteen-years-later-a-reflection-on-the-mass.html

Boesso, I., D'Orazio, M., & Torresan, A. (Eds.). (2012). *Supporting cluster marketing and branding*. Venezia: TACTICS.

Collins, J. (2003, June 18). New campaign markets bay state to businesses. *Boston Globe*, p. D4.

Hafeez, K., Foroudi, P., Dinnie, K., Nguyen, B., & Parahoo, S. (2016). The role of place branding and image in the development of sectoral clusters: The case of Dubai. *Journal of Brand Management, 23*(4), 383–402. doi:10.1057/bm.2016.18

Horton, B. (1998). Medicon valley: A bridge to collaboration. *Nature, 395*(6700), 412–413. doi:10.1038/26542 PMID:9759734

Hvidt, M. (2009). The Dubai model: An outline of key development-process elements in Dubai. *International Journal of Middle East Studies, 41*(3), 397–418. doi:10.1017/S0020743809091120

Lu, Y. (2012). *An investigation of the relationship between cluster brands and individual brands: A place branding perspective*. Ames, IA: Iowa State University; doi:10.31274/etd-180810-2983

Mauroner, O. (2015). Innovation clusters and public policy—The case of a research-driven cluster in Germany. *American Journal of Industrial and Business Management, 5*(12), 736-747.

Mauroner, O., & Zorn, J. (2017). Cluster branding – a case study on regional cluster initiatives, cluster management, and cluster brands. *International Journal of Innovative Research and Development, 7*(4), 289–312. doi:10.1504/IJIRD.2017.086234

Muro, M., & Katz, B. (2010). The new "cluster moment": How regional innovation clusters can foster the next economy. *Brookings Institution.* Available from: https://www.brookings.edu/research/the-new-cluster-moment-how-regional-innovation-clusters-can-foster-the-next-economy/

National Research Council. (2011). *Growing Innovation Clusters for American Prosperity: Summary of a Symposium.* Washington, DC: The National Academies Press.

OptoNet. (2018). A powerful network. *OptoNet.* Available from: http://www.optonet-jena.de/english-pages

Philippidis, A. (2018). Top 10 U.S. biopharma clusters. *Genetic Engineering and Biotechnology News.* Available from: http://www.genengnews.com/lists/top-10-u-s-biopharma-clusters-5

Porter, M. (1990). *The competitive advantage of nations.* New York: Free Press. doi:10.1007/978-1-349-11336-1

Powell, W., & Snellman, K. (2004). The knowledge economy. *Annual Review of Sociology, 30*(1), 199–220. doi:10.1146/annurev.soc.29.010202.100037

Sölvell, Ö., Lindqvist, G., & Ketels, C. (2003). *The cluster initiative greenbook.* Stockholm: Ivory Tower.

Willis, K. (2015). Can Dubai's design district 'hipster village' attract the right type of goatee-wearing individualist? *The Independent.* Available from: https://www.independent.co.uk/arts-entertainment/architecture/can-dubais-design-district-hipster-village-attract-the-right-type-of-goatee-wearing-individualist-10277373.html

ENDNOTES

1 The Cophenhagen Business School of Pharmacy has since been merged into the University of Copenhagen to become that institution's School of Pharmaceutical Sciences.

2 Businesses operating in cluster zones are, however, generally prohibited from selling goods or services to the UAE market itself unless they operate with a domestic partner company.

Chapter 3
Risk Management as Knowledge Production:
Application to Fast-Tracked Complex Multi-Stakeholder Airport Projects

Alasdair James Marshall
University of Southhampton, UK

Udechukwu Ojiako
University of Sharjah, UAE

Terry Williams
University of Hull, UK

Jumah Rashid Al-Mazrooie
Dubai Aviation Engineering Projects, UAE

Fenfang Lin
University of Southampton, UK

Maxwell Chipulu
University of Southampton, UK

ABSTRACT

Rapid national infrastructure growth, as witnessed today in many countries such as the United Arab Emirates, commonly makes fast-tracking demands of what are already highly complex multi-stakeholder projects. Considering the long history of airport project failures in a number of fast-growing cities, the chapter explores risk management enhancements for addressing the challenges associated with transitions from project completion to commencement of operations. The proposed solution in the pages that follow is to have in place dedicated risk management teams spanning the transitions. These teams should provide a locus for stakeholder collaboration based on a shared concern to build excellence into the customer experience from commencement of operations onwards.

DOI: 10.4018/978-1-5225-9377-5.ch003

INTRODUCTION

Being comprised of stakeholders in such a way as to ensure a thorough environmental scanning mix, the risk management teams advocated for in the present chapter should approach risk management not just as a process matching identified risks to controls, but - much more ambitiously - as an active intelligence gathering and knowledge production activity which continually informs and yet also transcends that process. Accordingly it can be argued that risk management, considered in both interconnected aspects, should take operational readiness and commissioning factors as their focus for developing abstract-categorical risk knowledge.

In other words these categories should be considered important for sensitising the minds of all who manage risks on projects, to specifc risks likely to arise which might otherwise be invisible owing to the overwhelming complexity of the projects. Such practice can be explained as harnessing abstract-general risk categories for purposes of top-down risk identification to capture logically aligned subsets of concrete-specific risk. To complement this view, it can be further explained in terms of the risk management metaphor which calls for project risk radars to be pointed towards where risks are most likely to materialise.

Pointing the Risk Radar

In cases of fast-tracked complex multi-stakeholder airport projects, such sensitivity, cutting through complexity to focus on what is most important, is clearly vital. The risk management of such projects needs to be able to cope with accelerated countdowns to project completion by time-compressing all its management effort. That includes all its effort to anticipate and protect against the heightened risks that threaten often delayed and very heavily time-compressed transitions from project completion to commencement of operations. Under these challenging circumstances, an important question for project management practitioners is how project risk management might best focus its attention towards the risks that are most likely to matter during the transitions and early days of operations in particular. However that leaves the even more challenging question of how the exercise of foresight by project management during these critical periods might also result in actions which help create more resilient and risk aware airports over the longer term.

To address these questions some brief theoretical preliminaries are necessary. First, it is necessary to need to set out the view of risk management as a time-pressured knowledge production activity applicable to fast-tracked complex multi-stakeholder airport projects. Following Marshall et al. (2018), the risk management function will be theorised as aiming to critically juxtapose and co-produce two necessary and complementary types of risk knowledge:

1. **Abstract Risk Knowledge:** Learned isomorphically from previous similar projects. *That is,* where A gains recognition within the project management profession as a type of risk tending to associate to risk exposure type B through vulnerability type C[1]). *For example,* it is well known that project schedule risks (A) often escalate for planned deadlines required for coordinated transitions (B) when Principal Contractors are financially and managerially unprepared (C) for deviations from their anticipated schedules).
2. **Concrete Risk Knowledge**: Formed from risk information generated wholly from the conditions of some particular project, creating localised project concern for a specified future possibility affecting specified parties for specified reasons. *That is* where project-specific risk A associates to project-specific risk exposure B through project-specific vulnerability C). *For example* (taking the case of an ongoing and highly problematic airport project in Germany), where project schedule risk (A) to the Brandenburg airport terminal completion schedule of the company Flughafen Berlin Brandenburg GmbH (B) intensified in the period 2014-2016 due to failure to incorporate adequately compliant fire protection and alarm provision (C) into the project.

In order to appreciate why both *abstract* and *concrete* types of risk knowledge are necessary and complementary, the risk imagination can usefully be theorised as striving for balance as it is both *pushed* by more general abstract risk knowledge deriving from professional experience, and *pulled* by more project-specific risk knowledge that is either passively encountered or actively gathered in what can be called *risk intelligence gathering*. Arguments can be constructed for erring too far towards either extreme. As Marshall et al. (2018) explain, overreliance on abstract risk knowledge in combination with a paucity of concrete risk knowledge can be theorised as allowing risks triangulated in this manner to be labelled as *'known-unknowns'*. Excessive focus on these within fast-tracked complex multi-stakeholder airport projects can be highly problematic, for example because doing so may invite false assumptions and neglect of novelty and the exotic within the risk environment of the project. The converse circumstances can then be described as ones of *'unknown-known'* risk. Focus on these can also be highly problematic, for example because views of such risks are likely to be far more tacit, subjective and therefore relatively unamenable to structured and coordinated planning and control. Accordingly, the risk knowledge production challenge for risk management in fast-tracked complex multi-stakeholder airport projects can be theorised as one of raising *'unknown-unknowns'* into *'known-knowns'* by pushing through either intermediate phase of partial risk knowledge.

Hence the question: how to push through? This is where the *critical* juxtaposition of abstract and concrete risk knowledge becomes important. For example, sometimes a project may begin to show signs of failure in subtle ways that cause managerial anxiety yet are hard to assign to the risk categories that are in use. Having abstract categorical risk knowledge to hand may be very useful in such cases because it allows the risks on the project to be explored through the lenses of various alternative risk categories. Risk categories so applied may play a number of risk-sensitising roles, for example by focusing mindfulness of project management practitioners towards certain kinds of exposure and/or vulnerability, or (in more formal, planned ways) by directing both passive environmental scanning and more active risk intelligence gathering activities to seek concrete risk knowledge that fits the theoretical template provided by the abstract risk category. In this way the robustness of the category can be tested in terms of its level of perceived relevance to the project and either incorporated more fully or rejected in accordance with findings.

A simplifying metaphor for expressing such use of risk categories can be expressed in terms of situating and pointing the 'risk radar' to be sensitive to particular risk exposures and vulnerabilities within projects. In what is now regarded as the traditional approach to organisational risk management, 'risk identification' take place at - or close to - the front end of the risk management process (ISO, 2009). By contrast, in the more recently evolved resilience-based approach to risk management the 'risk radar' constantly scans the environment at the front end of the resilience process (Franken et al., 2014). Whereas in projects, 'risk identification' commonly informs planning activities, the 'risk radar' is typically viewed, within resilience literatures at least, as scanning the environment in *real time,* to enable early detection and strong/rapid *ex-ante/ex-post* project management responses to unexpected/fast-onset risks. Most notably, this is a metaphor fit for fast-paced project environments such as fast-tracked complex multi-stakeholder airport projects where both time-compressed risk anticipation and planning, as well as urgent management handling of risks which have not been anticipated, are vital ingredients of project risk management practice.

To conclude this section, then, the metaphorical question of where to 'point' the risk radar, within project risk management, can be viewed essentially as one of which complexity-reducing risk ontology – and more specifically which risk 'categories' - to use, in order to render more of project risk visible under very time-pressured, resource-limited circumstances where there is a high premium on responding urgently to weak signals that things many be going wrong. Clearly this relies on learning isomorphically from the past, and more specifically in terms of the method adopted here, of distilling from literature the risk categories that offer most relevance, so that this knowledge can be available when required urgently on projects. Moreover, given that this chapter will argue for stakeholder representation and participation within project risk management teams, the high level risk categories proposed therein are intended to serve as a common professional language for stakeholders from very different backgrounds.

Project Risk Management Context: Avoiding 'Disastrous Airport Openings'

The political and economic consequences of the 'disastrous openings' of major complex multi-stakeholder airport infrastructure projects are well documented (House of Commons, 2008; Brady and Davies, 2010). Mention has already been made above of risk relating to insufficient fire safety provision within terminal building construction, which was just one of many problems to have marred the Brandenburg Airport Construction project in Berlin since its inception in 2004 (Fiedler and Wendler, 2016). The cumulative effect of this project risk experience appears to be, at the present time of writing, that the airport opening will now not occur until 2020 or later.

This experience is obviously a valuable learning example for project managers of the present Al Maktoum International Airport Expansion in Dubai. Approved in 2014 with a planned 6 or 8 years to completion, this aims to make the airport the world's biggest (both physically and by passenger capacity) by 2050. The managers of this and similar projects in the Gulf region understand well that all schedule delays bring with them time-compressed remedial and catch-up management effort which can further increase project risk and therefore lead to overall project failure.

Media criticism and reputational damage can be particularly serious considerations when such failures are of significance for national infrastructure development. In a scathing report following the 'disastrous opening' of London's Heathrow Airport Terminal 5 on 27 March 2008, the United Kingdom House of Commons highlighted that "What should have been an occasion of national pride was in fact an occasion of national embarrassment" (House of Commons, 2008; p. 3). The report's various lessons and recommendations illustrate how national governments can play important roles in facilitating isomorphic learning from project failure. Such learning will be invaluable not only to individual project management practitioners, but also to the much wider project management profession. It will be especially pertinent for project management teams such as the Dubai Aviation Engineering Projects which are currently embarking on airport projects of national significance in the United Arab Emirates.

Notably, the likely durations of these complex multi-stakeholder airport projects are sufficient as to necessitate managing and maintaining collaborative relationships with both the national government and the regulator (Dubai Civil Aviation Authority). It can be argued that if such teams wish to cultivate their regulatory environments well, both by recognising ways in which regulatory support offered may reflect lessons of past failure, and by dealing more proactively with risk, then they should engage in ongoing project risk stakeholder dialogue dedicated to advancing the risk knowledge production activity outlined at the start of this chapter. In particular, governments and regulators might be expected to contribute more abstract views, with the far more closely involved project management teams contributing more concrete (and therefore complementary) views.

These various observations and suggestions are intended to illustrate that the view of project risk management for fast-tracked airport projects advanced in the present paper is intended to be sensitive to how the principal contractors and their various stakeholders might often differently see risk and yet contribute to productive risk dialogue based on two closely interrelated shared understandings: *firstly,* the risk management of such projects can usefully be regarded as risk knowledge production which synthesises different forms of risk knowledge from multiple stakeholder knowledge bases; *secondly,* what brings these parties together in this common enterprise is often a very conspicuous need to avoid 'disastrous airport openings' which may lead the general public to blame all of them. Given this shared reputational risk exposure, disastrous airport openings stands out very clearly as a sensible focus for collaborative project risk management by mutually concerned stakeholders who might otherwise vary considerably in their risk exposures on the project.

Our risk-knowledge-production-based view of project risk management is also intended to offer practitioner support at a time when many large and complex multi-stakeholder infrastructure projects in general, and for airports specifically, are moving into their construction development stages in both the United Arab Emirates (Faridi and El-Sayegh, 2006; O'Connell, 2011; Ponzini, 2011; Kardes et al., 2013). Other countries in the Gulf region have also either recently commenced or completed large complex multi-stakeholder airport projects. For example, in March 2018, the US$1.8 billion Muscat International Airport in the Sultanate of Oman was completed. On the other hand, The Kingdom of Saudi Arabia is planning a US$67 million airport to be built in the City of Jazan.. Given the significance of such projects for ongoing national infrastructure development, the need for a study that sets out to explore the factors that need to be taken into consideration to preclude *disastrous openings* cannot be overemphasised. Although this chapter is concerned most with the UAE and other countries where airport expansion is regarded as key to national infrastructure development, it is in the nature of isomorphic learning that much of the literature considered below derives from a far broader range of project, organisational and theoretical contexts. Accordingly, it is hoped that the recommendations proposed will pertain strongly to fast-tracked complex multi-stakeholder airport projects in particular, as well as to fast-tracked complex multi-stakeholder *infrastructure* projects in general.

As a final comment on stakeholder management to conclude this section, it is worth adding that the theorisation of improved risk management of fast-tracked complex multi-stakeholder airport projects does not seek an even more complex managerial division of labour on the project teams concerned. This division of labour is itself an important source of risk, which is further *complexified* by the need for the project management team to bridge the gap between project completion and commencement of operations. Herein, what is proposed is the consolidation of environmental scanning and other intelligence gathering effort within a risk-knowledge-production-focused risk management process where all stakeholders and represented and work in tightly coupled collaborative project teams. This risk management process should, arguably, take pre-existing operations readiness and commissioning factors as the basic risk categories through which abstract risk knowledge is applied to sensitise the project risk management mind to actual risk on the project. Optimal selection of risk categories (taking airport openings as the focus) hinges on isomorphic learning from the long history of failure on previous similar projects which offer at least some isomorphic learning value owing to the existence of some shared project characteristics. Well-established interest with *readiness* and *commissioning* issues within the project management profession, it can be argued in this vein, holds the key to integrating better risk management within numerous management practices which project risk managers are already very familiar with. It can be concluded that the present day experiences of cities such as Dubai, that are unusually reliant on rapid infrastructure expansion, provide perhaps the best learning sources for developing risk categories suitable for time-pressured as well as managerially complex and disjointed projects which are at serious risk of failure in their transitions to commencement of operations.

OPERATIONAL READINESS FACTORS

Accordingly there is a need to focus most on the risk management value of project management practices which have grown substantially concerned with readiness issues at points of transition from project completion to commencement of operations. Fortunately, a substantial literature (e.g. Lee, 2000; Davies et al., 2009; Brady and Davies, 2010) has already reviewed operations readiness factors for airport projects in particular. Furthermore, many post-mortem reports have commented on why complex and high profile airport projects have experienced *disastrous openings* (House of Commons, 2008; Hong Kong Government - Legislative Council, 1999; Hong Kong Government - Office of the Ombudsman, 1999).

One important learning point arising from these literatures is that operations readiness failures often need to be understood as arising from interactions between contributory causes. For example it can be inferred from various sources (see Brady and Davies, 2010; Kierzkowski and Kisiel, 2015; Zerjav et al., 2018) that in the case of London's Heathrow Airport Terminal 5, operations failure at commencement resulted from both the overtly technical nature of the systems *and* also from managerial complacency. Clearly, therefore, there are important issues of granularity, related to capture of multiple synergising risks, to be considered when selecting operational readiness categories for risk management use.

Drawing from the earlier work of Stevens (2013), it can be argued that conceptualising operations *readiness* instrumentally, as a way to manage the tight-coupling of what have traditionally been conceptualised as two distinct phases in large complex multi-stakeholder infrastructure project delivery, is necessary to appreciate their criticality in ensuring successful airport openings. This idea derives support from the academic literature which has largely opined that readiness remains not only a critical and key antecedent to successful implementation (Armenakis et al., 1993; Armenakis and Harris, 2002; Cassidy, 1994; Hardison, 1998; O'Connor and Fiol, 2006; Weiner et al., 2008) but also of any transition from the project to operations stage of any implementation or delivery.

COMMISSIONING FACTORS

The term 'commissioning' implies some systematic process of ensuring that project systems are designed, installed and operating as planned (Kats et al., 2008). Accordingly, it is observable from related literature that definitions of commissioning tend to relate to systems in particular, regardless of who runs the operations. This literature also generally recognises that commissioning activity is critical for the success of any project (Lawry and Pons, 2013). This has led to some scholars such as Archibald et al. (2012) viewing it as a major project phase in its own right. Tribe and Johnson (2008) recognise the importance of commissioning as a task directed at ensuring systems serve the functions they are designed for. Taking stock of the above, one way to try to differentiate commissioning from operations readiness (in order to appreciate their overlaps and complementarities) is in terms of differing specificities. However the point made here may seem counter-intuitive, by inviting a view of 'commissioning' as a relatively narrow subset of 'readiness' considerations. Operations readiness can be viewed as spanning much broader integrative concerns relating to systems interaction by juxtaposing systems readiness (which can be conceived narrowly as 'commissioning') alongside people readiness, facility readiness, and indeed more process and organisation focused forms of readiness. All of these forms of readiness might then usefully be theorised in terms of their mutual reliance so as to set narrow 'commissioning' within far broader context as one of several readiness considerations, albeit a vital one.

However, whereas the reasonableness of such theory is one thing, agreement about it within the project management profession and academia is quite another. Perhaps due to its breadth of scope, the reality is that within project management and operations management literatures, readiness often remains poorly defined; hence it is common to find it interpreted quite ambiguously in terms of its relatedness to similar concepts (Lawry and Pons, 2013). This entails a need to be wary of possible differences in meaning and also eclectic in drawing from readiness and commissioning literatures to select appropriate abstract risk categories to suit the present purpose. In particular this chapter refers to literatures which bridge these concepts through expanded views of projects that extend into operational phases, and which adopt service-focused views of project risk management which, by their nature, think ahead to the operational experiences of clients who will own/run facilities and their customers who will use them.

READINESS-RELATED LITERATURE

Academic and professional interest in operations readiness has been growing over time and has increased rapidly from the year 2000. For example, a search for "operations readiness" on SCOPUS and the Web of Science from 1958 to 2016 resulted in 577 matches in SCOPUS and 649 within the Web of Science. However, a cursory examination of the literatures suggests that, overall, the notion of operations readiness does not appear to be a part of traditional project management academic literature. A developing interest in operations readiness is however very discernible (see Morris, 1983, 1997; Rodrigues and Williams 1998; Brady et al. 2005; Weiss and Maher 2009; Brady and Davies 2010; Archibald et al. 2012; Artto et al. 2015; Winch and Leiringer 2015).

Similarly, advocacy of various operations readiness practices is available in practitioner manuals and guides such as the Integrated Readiness Assurance Process and (IRAP) (Nossair et al., 2012), the BSI BS6079 Standard for Project Management produced by the British Standards Institution (2010), the Project Management Body of Knowledge (PMBOK 5th edition) (Project Management Institute 2013) and the Code of Practice for Project Management produced by the Chartered Institute of Building (CIOB, 2014). The PMBOK, for example, presents an important discussion on the relationship between project management and operations management with an emphasis on intersection points between the two. So too does CIOB (2014), which also addresses the need for testing and commissioning as well as operations in its Code of Practice for Project Management. While the CIOB Code of Practice does not mention operations readiness as a standard process or a stage in its lifecycle, it does (in comparison to other guides) lay particular emphasis on hand-overs before operations.

More detailed examination of project management literatures, in particular, is as follows. Early studies by Morris (1983, 1997) focused on project interfaces and called attention to opportunities for project value creation through dynamic transitional interfacing between project and operations phases. In Rodrigues and Williams (1998), this idea was carried forward with an acknowledgement that traditional project management planning models were unlikely to provide an effective base for operations after the completion of the project phase. Rodrigues and Williams (1998) again emphasised the need for transition between project and operations phases by proposing an integrated system dynamic model that goes further than traditional project planning. The main justification for this proposal was that traditional planning and control tools are ineffective at modelling desired transitions between project and operational phases.

Brady et al. (2005) drew from the emergence of 'newer' forms of infrastructure project procurement such as Build-Operate-Transfer which involves granting delivery consortiums concessions to finance, design, construct (deliver) and operate specific infrastructures over specified timeframes. They also explored how projects might usefully focus more on integrated solutions rather than one-off deliveries. Most importantly, Brady et al. (*ibid*) highlighted that delivering such integrated solutions requires not only systems integration capabilities, but also operational (downstream) service capabilities. More specific reference to operations readiness in project management context comes from a discussion by Doherty (2008) of this as a practice in use by project managers and operations. However Doherty did not refer to any operations readiness theoretical base or background, or discuss related practical effectiveness issues.

The work of Weiss and Maher (2009) can also be construed as of relevance to the development of operations readiness literature. Their study explored how operational hedging can mitigate against severe operational disruptions. Arguably, their study serves as one foundation to the main thesis of this chapter that operations readiness-based risk categories hold the key to mitigating exposure of complex multi-stakeholder infrastructure projects to 'disastrous openings'. This point requires explanation as follows. Heeding their claim that operational hedging instruments (e.g. for fleet standardization, ownership policy and in-sourcing) can protect organisations from severe operational disruptions, it can be posited that operations readiness instruments (e.g. for process standardization, process ownership policy, project data accuracy and completeness, operational flexibility, efficient commissioning, avoiding unresolved constructions (defects) and contractual issues, early involvement of operations team and asset owners etc.) can serve as mitigating factors against 'disastrous openings' of large complex multi-stakeholder infrastructure projects on the first day of operations. Hence an important question is how to group such risk control instruments together within a number of high level risk categories which best span the full range of relevant issues and therefore permit project risk management identification effort and control resource to be structured to enable exhaustive drilling-down into risk contexts of transition into commencement of operations.

Other notable works of interest to the development of operations readiness literature include that of Brady and Davies (2010). They found that in large complex multi-stakeholder infrastructure projects such as London's Heathrow Airport Terminal 5, the likelihood for 'disastrous openings' (p. 152) increased with centralisation of decision-making which reduced management capacity to respond urgently and flexibly to unanticipated events. Extending this resilience-against-the unexpected focus to operations readiness in particular, it can be contended that inability of delivery teams to engage complexity is a near inevitable consequence of tight-coupling between project and operations phases. Done et al.'s (2011) work exploring the relationship between best practice interventions (defined as discretionary activities which organisations develop towards routinisation as new best practice procedures) and sustained operational improvements, is also of interest. Although their study identifies a number of contextual, implementation and change factors likely to deliver desired operational improvements, they tend to conceptualise such interventions as being big/quick win-oriented, i.e. oriented towards delivering "dramatic improvements within a focused operational area" (p. 500). They also point out that best practice interventions are likely to be implemented more effectively if the organisation is well prepared and committed to change. They define such state of preparedness and commitment as "organizational readiness" (p. 501), which of course reminds us of the importance of considering the concept in its softer psychological and cultural aspects at the theoretical intersect between risk culture, change culture and mindfulness.

Another study of interest is Archibald et al. (2012), who emphasised the need for comprehensive and holistic management of the entire project life cycle, spanning project feasibility phases all the way through to post-project close-out phases. While not addressing operations readiness explicitly, they advocate for expanding the scope of projects beyond the traditional start-plan-execute-closeout phase (p. 1) to a point well after the project has been completed. They emphasize that expanding the scope of projects to encompass a post- project phase, will stem the trend of 'moving along' unresolved problems to the next phase, whose consequence is often that problems with projects often get pushed towards their most overt manifestations at the operational phase. Their corresponding advocacy of broader and more forward-looking project risk management conceptualisation is well recognised in project management literature (Pinto and Winch, 2015; Svejvig and Andersen, 2015; Winch and Leiringer, 2015; Geraldi and Söderlund, 2018). However, Winch and Leiringer (2015) note that the need for such broader conceptualisations of projects nonetheless remain under-recognised. Of particular interest in that regard is their observation that "literature on project and commercial capabilities does not distinguish between dynamic and operational capabilities" (p. 222). Underlying this point is their construal of operational capabilities as related to making provisions for the effective and efficient delivery of goods and services to customers and users.

Notably this perspective is in line with the earlier view of Rust (1998) which held that "…most goods businesses now view themselves primarily as services, with the offered good being an important part of the service" (p. 107). Recognising the value offered by this service perspective, Pinto and Winch (2015) have called for project managers to be equipped with more knowledge and greater competency, not only to manage and control the execution phase of the project, but also to manage "… critical actions and interfaces" (p. 4) relating to the service user experience. These interfaces, which had earlier attracted the attention of Morris (1983, 1997) and Rodrigues and Williams (1998), have also been considered by Artto et al. (2015). They proposed mechanisms for integrating project and post-project operations phases, thus ensuring value creation for a wide range of project stakeholders. While again not explicitly discussing 'operations readiness', their study identified two key service-focused success criteria for projects; one focused on business success and the other focused on preparing for the future – which might be taken to represent a form of 'operations readiness'. Most importantly, both criteria were only measureable "a long period of time after completion of the project" (p. 260). In effect, this broadened conceptualisation allows for a view of project risk management focused on producing knowledge that will at least retain and perhaps increase its use value, both throughout successful delivery of a project, and thereafter during early operations.

From the above discussions there arises an expanded view of operations readiness as flexible in both its positive orientation towards change and in its dedication towards service. Some longstanding theoretical literature can help explore and structure this view further. Readiness as a method for reducing resistance to change was used in a classic research study by Coch and French (1948), which demonstrated the value of allowing an organisation's members to participate in planned changes. Lewin's (1951) notion of 'unfreezing' is also relevant for conceptualising readiness, as it can be utilised as a readiness creation strategy. According to Lewin (1951), the fundamental idea was to use a concept of change as unfreezing to develop new behaviours, values and attitudes among an organisation's members. Other scholars such as Bartlem and Locke (1981) and Gardner (1977) identified other factors that have contributed to the readiness-creating literature. In principle, the readiness's preparation for the change in the organisation will act to prevent the likelihood of resistance to change from employees, which in turn will increase the possibility for change efforts to be more efficient and ultimately, successful (Armenakis et al., 1993; Armenakis and Harris, 2002). This implies that operations readiness does on occasion focus on preparing the operations team for new operational procedures and operating new systems.

An early example of some strategies for dealing with readiness and resistance to change was provided by Kotter and Schlesinger (1979). It includes education and communication and the desired changes and reasons for them. Participation and involvement in the organisation may provide opportunities for employees to participate in the decision-making. This offers employees incentives to support change (Armenakis et al., 1993; Armenakis and Harris, 2002), which might often prove crucial for achieving forward-looking, service-focused operational readiness within project risk management practice.

While acknowledging the role of operations readiness as a mechanism for employee participation in change within projects, it is also important that attention is drawn to closely related theory and research on "organisational readiness" (Weiner et al., 2008; Weiner, 2009), which focuses on organisational change initiated by management to provide organisations with competitive advantages. Such change is usually conceived to involve moving the organisation from its present state to some desired future state in order to increase organisational effectiveness and productivity. This literature especially Stevens, 2013) has advanced a number of underlying theoretical perspectives. These have included, for example, (i) the 'trans-theoretical model of change', espoused by Prochaska and DiClemente (1983) and drawn into change management scholarship by Harris and Cole (2007), (ii) the 'commitment to change' theory (Herold et al., 2007), which was drawn into readiness literature by Weiner et al. (2008), (iii) the 'openness to change' theory (Wanberg and Banas, 2000), and (iv) the 'readiness as capacity' theory (Nelson et al., 1999; Weiner et al., 2008).

Drawing from Stevens (2013), there are two dimensions to the 'readiness as capacity' theory which are of particularly strong relevance to any understanding of operations readiness. The first of these dimensions focuses on key organisational capabilities and characteristics supportive of transitions to new operations. Focusing on key organisational capabilities and characteristics implies ensuring that the right 'organizational climate' (Stevens, 2013; p. 341) exists for managerial accessing and harnessing the resources which organisations require for routinely managing transitions to new operations. On the other hand, the second dimension to the 'readiness as capacity' theory espouses the existence of specific readiness factors that serve to measure key drivers for successful transitions. Literature on these dimensions is supplied by Molla and Licker (2005), Burnett et al. (2010), Antony (2014) and Al-Balushi et al. (2014).

Important Readiness Categories for Preventing Disastrous Airport Openings

Taking stock of the above theories pertaining to operational and organisational readiness, this literature review will now focus back towards more airport-project-related (and other highly relevant) literature, and identify four broad readiness categories capable of playing the sensitising roles in the risk knowledge production process, as outlined at the start of the chapter. This chapter's purpose in highlighting these readiness categories is, to reiterate, to better structure and direct the project risk imagination to prevent disastrous airport openings. The key is arguably for routine risk management processes, which span project and early operations, to employ abstract risk categories based on operational readiness categories which are most salient in the relevant literature, and whose subject matter also intersects with and spans the broad areas of theoretical concern traversing the readiness and commissioning issues explored in the last section. Hence the chapter now looks in turn at: (1) *facility readiness*, (2) *people readiness*, (3) *technology readiness* and (4) *organisation readiness*.

Facility Readiness

Looking specifically at '*facility readiness*', the availability of the physical asset becomes highly significant as an operations readiness enabling factor. Non-flight-based commercial revenues are vital for airport operations and highly dependent on facility considerations (Graham, 2009). Hence replacing, upgrading or creating new airport facilities can be crucial from the business risk standpoint (Zaneldin, 2006; Arif *et al.*, 2013). One particularly important linked consideration is customer service (Wilson et al., 2004; Gupta et al.,

2014). However, although as earlier argued, readiness may actually commence prior to the delivery of the physical asset (the facility), its completion and availability for customers is nonetheless widely recognised as an indispensable factor in successful openings (Gardner, 2001; Wilson et al., 2004; Hickey, 2008; Lyons and Powell, 2010; Nossair et al., 2012; Brereton and Papp, 2013; Krauss, 2014; Kidd and Howe, 2014).

Various literatures suggest that one of the main problems facing airport operations is that increasingly, due to the popularity of air transport (driven by a number of factors including the growth of the low cost 'no frills' airlines - see Takebayashi, 2012; Jimenez et al., 2017), most airports facilities are unable to consistently provide facilities appropriate for positive customer experiences in busy public spaces (Evans and Schäfer, 2011). The result is that airport facility development is often undertaken in a reactive and ad-hoc manner in response to adverse circumstances where poor customer experiences have generated complaints and reputational challenges (Mumayiz, 1989).

Various studies (see for example, Lee, 2000; Brereton and Papp, 2013) have looked at contributions of facilities readiness to operations readiness more generally. In Lee's (2000) examination of the fiasco experienced during the opening of the new Chek Lap Kok (Hong Kong International) Airport, a lack of readiness leading to the eventual malfunctioning of key systems supporting the various facilities interfaces was identified as a major reason for operational failure at opening. Masrom et al. (2015) correlated facilities readiness and project success, finding that facilities readiness strongly influences project stakeholder satisfaction which in turn increases project success. The key point arising is that to assure facilities readiness, the various stakeholders who contribute towards and participate within risk management can usefully conceive of themselves as sharing a common concern alongside other stakeholders to build a positive customer experience from day one of operations.

People Readiness

On the issue of '*people readiness*', relevant literature emphasises the need for individual skills, commitment and adaptability (Armenakis et al., 1993). Accordingly, the risk management of people readiness can be regarded as a knowledge management challenge, where aspects of human capability that are sometimes very hard to codify, must nonetheless be captured in some rigorous yet simplifying way, for example by using lists of desired and undesired human attributes. Accordingly Del Giudice et al. (2015) refer to the need for multidisciplinary effort to compile such information.

Of course, readiness for change can nonetheless be recognised as an individually nuanced notion (Jansen, 2000), such that there will inevitably be some socially distributed tacit knowledge, pertaining to relevant human attributes, that must be sourced when establishing a management overview of people readiness. Much literature has emphasised human resistance factors when explaining high project failure rates among change initiatives (Burke and Biggart, 1997; Beer and Nohria, 2000a, 2000b; Burnes, 2004). Choi (2011) and Choi and Ruona (2011) argued that a major driver for such failure resided in *people readiness factors* in particular. To the forefront of their concern lay problems of limited organisational capability to recognise and influence workforce attitudes about particular changes. According to Del Giudice et al. (2015), failure to address human factors (and by implication, *people readiness factors)* can only lead to sub-optimal systems design and, as a consequence, to poor service user experiences.

Similarly Weiner (2009) counted human factors and staffing as important determinants of organisations readiness more generally. Likewise, Kidd and Howe (2014) found the training of both new and existing staff to add significant readiness value for a new hospital facility. Similar findings were also reached by Ventre et al. (2014). Earlier, Jones et al. (2005) had found that reshaping employee capabilities exerted a significant positive effect on readiness for change. Results of their analysis (which covered airlines and airport operators) show change readiness correlating more strongly with people readiness than with facility readiness. This strong link between people readiness and change readiness should, arguably, be very strongly borne in mind, particularly on airport projects where there are problems and delays requiring non-routine problem-solving and management agility under conditions of severe time constraint.

Next *technology readiness* is considered. The literature (Kalakou et al., 2015) suggests that technology can play a major role in improving the effectiveness of airport operations. Its influence upon the customer experience appears quite often to be the most critical factor in determining such effectiveness. This is simply because technology offers airline operators new ways of interacting with their customers while at the same time reducing the high costs associated with managing the customer interface (for example, through the use of contact self-service systems – see Gures et al., 2018). This means customers can benefit both from reduced costs and from shorter and less anxious queueing experiences. In particular, technology in the form of biometric security systems can quicken boarding and verification of passenger information in ways that minimise informational demands on customers in busy queues (Kirschenbaum et al., 2012; Morosan, 2016). Similarly, when such technology fails all its value-added for the customer experience can quickly transform into customer refund costs and (significantly more worrying) reputational costs amplified through social media. These possibilities matter greatly for ongoing operational risk management because they strongly underscore the need for non-technological (or less technologically vulnerable) back-up systems to be planned for swift availability in the event of relatively new or untested technology failing or becoming subject to unanticipated cyberattack, electrical supply failure etc.

In other words it would be inappropriate to conceive of *technology readiness* at the project stage without planning forward extensively for possible operational circumstances where the technology may need to be very urgently repaired or circumvented altogether through the use of substitute low-tech practices where appropriate human skills will need to be in place. Although this problem very clearly underscores the importance of considering human-technology interaction within planning, it further implies a need for a holistic view of operational readiness where an appreciation of high level readiness categories and their interdependencies is utilised to build a complete picture of problems and solutions associated with technological failure. Focusing within that broad territory, it seems likely that the interface between technology readiness and human/change readiness may often matter most when planning ahead for technological failure within busy airport environments. According to Parasuraman (2000), fundamental to technology readiness is "people's propensity to embrace and use new technologies for accomplishing goals" (p.308). This is not just a question of skills and training, but also of differing dispositions individuals have towards technology and change, where factors such as age and experience might matter greatly.

Corresponding to the above discussion, some literature (see for example, Davies et al., 2009; Davies and Mackenzie, 2014) views *technology readiness* as heavily impacted by the organisation's ability to integrate its various systems and manage the risk factors associated with technology infusion within the broader context of organisational integration. A commonly recognised adverse circumstance is where technology is infused into airport operations in a largely reactive and ad-hoc manner (Mumayiz, 1989) rather than with appropriate planning based on a holistic view of readiness. Similarly, Ojiako et al. (2013) have cautioned against the over- infusions of technology at the expense of enhanced human interaction. Their notion that technology infusion can be de-humanising and detrimental to sometimes latent human networks that can matter during crises, leads us to recommend bearing in mind that holistic thinking about readiness might require contemplation of a multitude of possible trade-offs where gains within one readiness category may be accompanied by losses in others.

Having technological systems available and backed-up, along with other supporting systems, is of course essential in ensuring the consistent and ongoing operability of any new airport facility (Gardner 2001; Cosenzo et al. 2007; Kingston et al. 2007; Deloitte 2011; Brereton and Papp 2013; Del Giudice. 2015). This requirement underscores the need for a project risk management approach which is focused not just on commencement but also ongoing future-proofing of operations, which is also reflective upon why different forms of readiness are mutually reliant. Several studies help us further understand this mutual reliance. One study undertaken in the Oil and Gas industry (see Nossair et al., 2012) found a significant correlation between technology readiness and operations readiness in particular. Similarly Hastings (2015) drew attention to the importance of operations readiness encompassing systems and asset integration. In terms of the practical impacts of technology readiness on project success, Lee (2000) found that collaboration between the project management delivery team and operations team were crucial elements required to ensure systems and technology readiness and, ultimately, project success.

Organisation Readiness

The last of the four high level abstract risk categories is *organisation readiness*. Care is needed when differentiating this from the previous three. As explained, each of the four high level risk categories can only add value to project risk management if they can contribute to a holistic understanding of readiness by standing clearly apart from the other three contributory categories. Weiner (2009) has earlier defined '*organizational readiness*' as '…organizational members' change commitment and change efficacy to implement organizational change'. This definition would, for present purposes, be inappropriate because it would overlap with *people readiness*, particularly as this chapter has previously represented it in terms of 'change' being a key theme. And yet Weiner's definition does capture an important aspect of organisation readiness: the organisational (and not human-individual) property of capacity for effectively managed change without which an organisation cannot be innovative and agile.

Partly at issue here is organisational culture. Carver (2012) examined the relationship between organisational culture and readiness to change among U.S. Army officers and concluded that by addressing organisational-cultural readiness, military leaders were able to increase force readiness to change with positive organisational effects. Both Motwani et al. (2005) and Ahmadi et al. (2015) found organisation readiness, similarly conceived, as having major positive effects on implementation success. Studies by Zerjav et al. (2015) suggested a progressive confidence in organisational readiness as enhancing the smooth transition from implementation to operations of newly constructed airport facilities. Lyons and Powell (2010) focused on 14 international airports' activation and readiness plans. They concluded that the divergent processes and organisational cultures among different operational stakeholders required careful consideration for successful airport terminal facility activations.

The concept of organisation readiness therefore draws to light one of the most problematic challenges facing project management teams drawn from multiple contributing stakeholder entities, and whose focus on ensuring 'readiness' should commit them to anticipate complexities not just of airport openings but also ongoing operations. Without the commitment to future-proof ongoing operations advocate for here, organisational culture would lack significance. However, in taking a more far-sighted view of readiness, the cultural 'engineering challenge' within readiness building stands out as potentially making an enormous contribution to readiness overall. And it is also one that requires us to take a holistic view of readiness spanning architectural, technological and potentially many other factors already covered in this chapter, all of which are likely to set the cultural tone for the service environment, and in so doing strongly influence the service user experience. Arguably, even simple architectural considerations such as creating public spaces which facilitate stakeholder networking in daily airport life (e.g. where technicians from one service provider might socialise with customer-facing staff from another) might create what could be called a positive 'readiness culture' from the first day of operations onwards. This early *'readiness culture'* could then provide the behavioural foundation for ongoing continuity and improvement within what would later more appropriately be named the *'risk culture'* or the *'resilience culture'* of the airport.

CONCLUSION

Here the chapter concludes with some further brief observations on the importance of using readiness/commissioning factors as risk categories for project risk management within complex and often fast-tracked multi-stakeholder airport projects. In advocating use of *facilities readiness*, *people readiness*, *technology readiness* and *organisation readiness* as generic risk categories, the key concluding point is that these 'high level' abstract categories, as sketched in the four dedicated subsections above, will inevitably matter for all such projects because they supply a universal starting point for building more complete risk taxonomies whose further details will vary between projects. More fully, the four readiness categories can be regarded as contributing towards the most abstract-general 'top layer' in risk categorisation matrices used for all complex airport projects. Risk subcategories can then be designed to fit under these, in order to represent more concrete-specific readiness issues which are (increasingly as one moves down through successive sub-levels) more likely to be mutable between projects. This argument should not insinuate that the resilience categories and any logically linked subcategories must dominate project risk management for complex airports. Instead it is advocated here that the four categories should be *designed into* existing risk matrices as enhancements, and that the logic in support of their use be considered in matrix redesign. Any airport project concerned to avoid disastrous openings should ensure they are incorporated strongly.

At the start of this chapter the importance of project risk management as co-production of abstract and concrete risk knowledge (which a longer chapter might have linked to the knowledge-based view of the firm) was discussed. Here it is appropriate to recapitulate and expand slightly on that theory's relevance. It can be concluded that risk categorisations cascading downwards from the proposed top layer can juxtapose and invite critical reflection upon, the combinations of abstract and concrete risk knowledge that are likely to matter on complex airport projects. For purposes of risk anticipation in stressed and fast-paced project environments, the distinction between abstract and concrete risk knowledge might at first appear to offer no practical value. However, the top layer categories can play important sensitising roles – for the most part very straightforwardly by mapping out the highly complex risk environment as a theoretical space where more of concrete risk can become visible in theoretical terms of its affinities with one or more of the four top level categories.

The above conclusion further serves to permit us to clarify the value of the risk radar metaphor within project management practice. The co-production of abstract and concrete risk knowledge advocated for here is intended to be useful within contexts of not just project planning but also of non-routine trouble-shooting and quickly halting problems in the making before they escalate. The four high-level risk categories essentially tell the project risk radars where to point towards, in order to detect the problems that are most likely to result in disastrous opening. The specifications are intended to be appropriately simple and straightforward, for purposes of sharpening the mental habits of risk professionals to think more *critically*, *causally* and *thoroughly* about risk, under very difficult, time-pressured and information poor circumstances. And yet at the same time they equip project risk management with the theory that is necessary for projecting the risk imagination quite far into the future to consider aspects of the staff and service user experience which they might otherwise fail to consider.

REFERENCES

Ahmadi, S., Papageorgiou, E., Yen, C., & Marin, R. (2015). Managing readiness-relevant activities for the organizational dimension of ERP implementation. *Computers in Industry*, *68*, 89–104. doi:10.1016/j.compind.2014.12.009

Al-Balushi, S., Sohal, A., Singh, P., Al Hajri, A., Al Farsi, Y., & Al Abri, R. (2014). Readiness factors for lean implementation in healthcare settings–a literature review. *Journal of Health Organization and Management*, *28*(2), 135–153. doi:10.1108/JHOM-04-2013-0083 PMID:25065107

Antony, J. (2014). Readiness factors for the Lean Six Sigma journey in the higher education sector. *International Journal of Productivity and Performance Management*, *63*(2), 257–264. doi:10.1108/IJPPM-04-2013-0077

Archibald, R. D., Di Filippo, I., & Di Filippo, D. (2012). The six-phase comprehensive project life cycle model including the project incubation/feasibility phase and the post-project evaluation phase. *PM World Journal*, *1*(5), 1–40.

Arif, M., Gupta, A., & Williams, A. (2013). Customer service in the aviation industry - An exploratory analysis of UAE airports. *Journal of Air Transport Management*, *32*, 1–7. doi:10.1016/j.jairtraman.2013.05.001

Armenakis, A., Bernerth, J., Pitts, J., & Walker, H. (2007). Organizational change recipients' beliefs scale: Development of an assessment instrument. *The Journal of Applied Behavioral Science*, *43*(4), 481–505. doi:10.1177/0021886307303654

Armenakis, A., & Harris, S. (2002). Crafting a change message to create transformational readiness. *Journal of Organizational Change Management*, *15*(2), 169–183. doi:10.1108/09534810210423080

Armenakis, A., Harris, S., & Mossholder, K. W. (1993). Creating readiness for organizational change. *Human Relations*, *46*(6), 681–703. doi:10.1177/001872679304600601

Artto, K., Ahola, T., & Vartiainen, V. (2015). From the front end of projects to the back end of operations: Managing projects for value creation throughout the system lifecycle. *International Journal of Project Management, 34*(2), 258–270. doi:10.1016/j.ijproman.2015.05.003

Artto, K., Ahola, T., & Vartiainen, V. (2016). From the front end of projects to the back end of operations: Managing projects for value creation throughout the system lifecycle. *International Journal of Project Management, 34*(2), 258–270. doi:10.1016/j.ijproman.2015.05.003

Bartlem, C., & Locke, E. A. (1981). The Coch and French study: A critique and reinterpretation. *Human Relations, 34*(7), 555–566. doi:10.1177/001872678103400703

Beer, M., & Nohria, N. (2000a). Cracking the code of change. *Harvard Business Review, 78*, 133–141. PMID:11183975

Beer, M., & Nohria, N. (2000b). Introduction: Resolving the tension between theories E and O. In M. Beer & N. Nohria (Eds.), *Breaking the code of change* (pp. 1–33). Boston: Harvard Business School Press.

Brady, T., & Davies, A. (2010). From hero to hubris – reconsidering the project management of Heathrow's Terminal 5. *International Journal of Project Management, 28*(2), 151–157. doi:10.1016/j.ijproman.2009.11.011

Brady, T., Davies, A., & Gann, D. (2005). Creating value by delivering integrated solutions. *International Journal of Project Management, 23*(5), 360–365. doi:10.1016/j.ijproman.2005.01.001

Brereton, S. J., & Papp, F. (2013). Assuring operational readiness of the National Ignition Facility. *Health Physics, 104*(6), 597–605. doi:10.1097/HP.0b013e31828d2e4c PMID:23629065

British Standards Institute (BSI). (2010). *BS6079-1: Project Management — Part 1: Principles and Guidelines for the Management of Projects*. BSI.

Burke, W. W., & Biggart, N. (1997). Interorganizational relations. In D. Druckman, J. E. Singer, & H. Van Cott (Eds.), *Enhancing organizational performance* (pp. 120–149). Washington, DC: National Academy Press.

Burnes, B. (2004). *Managing change: A strategic approach to organisational dynamics*. London: Prentice Hall.

Burnett, S., Benn, J., Pinto, A., Parand, A., Iskander, S., & Vincent, C. (2010). Organisational readiness: Exploring the preconditions for success in organisation-wide patient safety improvement programmes. *BMJ Quality & Safety*, *19*(4), 313–317. doi:10.1136/qshc.2008.030759 PMID:20211961

Carver, T. (2012). *The Relationship between organizational culture and readiness to change in a U. S. Army organization within japan* (PhD thesis). Northcentral University.

Cassidy, J. (1994). System analyzes readiness for integrated delivery. *Health Progress (Saint Louis, Mo.)*, *75*(3), 18–20, 22. PMID:10132874

Chartered Institute of Building. (2014). *Code of practice for project management for construction and development* (5th ed.). Wiley-Blackwell.

Choi, M. (2011). Employees' attitudes toward organizational change: A literature review. *Human Resource Management*, *50*(4), 479–500. doi:10.1002/hrm.20434

Choi, M., & Ruona, W. (2011). Individual readiness for organizational change and its implications for human resource and organizational development. *Human Resource Development Review*, *10*(1), 46–73. doi:10.1177/1534484310384957

Coch, L., & French, J. R. P. Jr. (1948). Overcoming resistance to change. *Human Relations*, *21*(10), 512–532. doi:10.1177/001872674800100408

Cosenzo, K. a., Fatkin, L.T., & Patton, D. (2007). Ready or not: enhancing operational effectiveness through use of readiness measures. *Aviation Space and Environmental Medicine, 78*(5).

Davies, A., Gann, D., & Douglas, T. (2009). Innovation in megaprojects: Systems integration at London Heathrow terminal 5. *California Management Review*, *51*(2), 101–125. doi:10.2307/41166482

Davies, A., & Mackenzie, I. (2014). Project complexity and systems integration: Constructing the London 2012 Olympics and Paralympics Games. *International Journal of Project Management*, *32*(5), 773–790. doi:10.1016/j.ijproman.2013.10.004

Del Giudice, K., Hale, K., & Johnston, M. (2015). Development of a scale for quantifying a system's human factors readiness. *Procedia Manufacturing*, *3*, 671–677. doi:10.1016/j.promfg.2015.07.580

Deloitte. (2011). *Operational excellence operational readiness assurance.* Available at: https://www2.deloitte.com/con- tent/dam/Deloitte/ca/Documents/energy-resources/ca-en-energy-resources-operations-excellence-asset-management-brochure.pdf

Doherty, S. (2008). *Heathrow's T5 history in the making.* West Sussex, UK: John Wiley & Sons.

Done, A., Voss, C., & Rytter, N. (2011). Best practice interventions: Short-term impact and long-term outcomes. *Journal of Operations Management*, *29*(5), 500–513. doi:10.1016/j.jom.2010.11.007

Evans, A., & Schäfer, A. (2011). The impact of airport capacity constraints on future growth in the US air transportation system. *Journal of Air Transport Management*, *17*(5), 288–295. doi:10.1016/j.jairtraman.2011.03.004

Faridi, A. S., & El-Sayegh, S. (2006). Significant factors causing delay in the UAE construction industry. *Construction Management and Economics*, *24*(11), 1167–1176. doi:10.1080/01446190600827033

Fiedler, J., & Wendler, A. (2016). Berlin Brandenburg Airport. In G. Kostka & J. Fiedler (Eds.), Large Infrastructure Projects in Germany: between ambitions and realities (pp. 87–145). Academic Press. doi:10.1007/978-3-319-29233-5_4

Franken, A., Goffin, K., Szwejczewski, M., & Kutsch, E. (2014). *Roads to resilience: Building dynamic approaches to risk.* Cranfield Management School.

Gardner, D. (2001). *Operational readiness—is your system more "ready" than your environment.* Project Management Institute annual seminars and symposium, Nashville, TN.

Graham, A. (2009). How important are commercial revenues to today's airports? *Journal of Air Transport Management*, *15*(3), 106–111. doi:10.1016/j.jairtraman.2008.11.004

Gures, N., Inan, H., & Arslan, S. (2018). Assessing the self-service technology usage of Y-Generation in airline services. *Journal of Air Transport Management*, *71*, 215–219. doi:10.1016/j.jairtraman.2018.04.008

Hardison, C. (1998). Readiness, action, and resolve for change: Do health care leaders have what it takes? *Quality Management in Health Care*, *6*(2), 44–51. doi:10.1097/00019514-199806020-00006 PMID:10178159

Harris, S. G., & Cole, M. (2007). A stages of change perspective on managers' motivation to learn in a leadership development context. *Journal of Organizational Change Management*, *20*(6), 774–793. doi:10.1108/09534810710831019

Hastings, N. (2015). *Physical asset management: with an introduction to ISO55000* (2nd ed.). Springer.

Herold, D., Fedor, D., & Caldwell, S. D. (2007). Beyond change management: A multilevel investigation of contextual and personal influences on employees' commitment to change. *The Journal of Applied Psychology*, *92*(4), 942–951. doi:10.1037/0021-9010.92.4.942 PMID:17638456

Hickey, M. (2008). *Operational readiness - making it happen. CORE 2008: rail; the core of integrated transport*. Railway Technical Society of Australasia: Engineers Australia.

Hong Kong Government - Legislative Council of the Hong Kong Special Administrative Region. (1999). *Report of the Select Committee to Inquire into the Circumstances Leading to the Problems Surrounding the Commencement of the Operation of the New Hong Kong International Airport at Chek Lap Kok since 6 July 1998 and Related Issues* (Vol. 1). Hong Kong: Government Printer.

Hong Kong Government - Office of the Ombudsman. (1999). *Executive Summary of the Report of the Investigation into the Commissioning and Operation of the New Airport at Chek Lap Kok*. Hong Kong: Government Printer.

House of Commons: Transport Committee. (2008). *The opening of Heathrow Terminal 5*. London: House of Commons.

ISO. (2009). *ISO 31000: Risk management – principles and guidelines.* Geneva: International Standards Organisation.

Jansen, K. (2000). The emerging dynamics of change: Resistance, readiness, and momentum. *People and Strategy*, *23*(2), 53–55.

Jimenez, E., Claro, J., de Sousa, J., & de Neufville, R. (2017). Dynamic evolution of European airport systems in the context of Low-Cost Carriers growth. *Journal of Air Transport Management*, *64*, 68–76. doi:10.1016/j.jairtraman.2017.06.027

Jones, R., Jimmieson, N., & Griffiths, A. (2005). The impact of organizational culture and reshaping capabilities on change implementation success: The mediating role of readiness for change. *Journal of Management Studies*, *42*(2), 361–386. doi:10.1111/j.1467-6486.2005.00500.x

Kalakou, S., Psaraki-Kalouptsidi, V., & Moura, F. (2015). Future airport terminals: New technologies promise capacity gains. *Journal of Air Transport Management*, *42*, 203–212. doi:10.1016/j.jairtraman.2014.10.005

Kardes, I., Ozturk, A., Cavusgil, S. T., & Cavusgil, E. (2013). Managing global megapro- jects: Complexity and risk management. *International Business Review*, *22*(6), 905–917. doi:10.1016/j.ibusrev.2013.01.003

Kats, G., Alevantis, L., Berman, A., Mills, E., & Perlman, J. (2003). *The costs and financial benefits of green buildings: a report to California's sustainable building task force*. Sustainable Building Task Force. Available at https://noharm-uscanada.org/sites/default/files/documents-files/34/Building_Green_Costs_Benefits.pdf

Kidd, L., & Howe, R. (2014). Operational readiness: An integral part of the facility planning process. *Healthcare Quarterly*, *17*(4), 63–67. doi:10.12927/hcq.2015.24120 PMID:25906468

Kierzkowski, A., & Kisiel, T. (2015). Functional Readiness of the Check-In Desk System at an Airport. In W. Zamojski, J. Mazurkiewicz, J. Sugier, T. Walkowiak, & J. Kacprzyk (Eds.), *Theory and Engineering of Complex Systems and Dependability* (Vol. 365). Springer. doi:10.1007/978-3-319-19216-1_21

Kingston, J., Frei, R., Koornneef, F., & Schallier, P. (2007). *Defining operational readiness to investigate, DORI* (White Paper). The Noordwijk Risk Initiative Foundation (NRI) and the Royal Society for the Prevention of Accidents (RoSPA). Available at: http://www.nri.eu.com/WP1.pdf

Kirschenbaum, A., Mariani, M., Van Gulijk, C., Rapaport, C., & Lubasz, S. (2012). Trusting technology: Security decision making at airports. *Journal of Air Transport Management*, *25*, 57–60. doi:10.1016/j.jairtraman.2012.08.005

Kotter, J., & Schlesinger, L. (1979, March). Choosing strategies for change. *Harvard Business Review*, 106–114. PMID:10240501

Krauss, E. (2014). How does operational readiness assist in asset management : It surely is an operations function? *Australian Journal of Multi-Disciplinary Engineering*, *11*(1), 1–11. doi:10.7158/14488388.2014.11464878

Lawry, K., & Pons, D. (2013). Integrative approach to the plant commissioning process. *Journal of Industrial Engineering*, *2013*, 1–12. doi:10.1155/2013/572072

Lee, E. (2000). The new Hong Kong international airport fiasco: Accountability failure and the limits of the new managerialism. *International Review of Administrative Sciences*, *66*(1), 57–72. doi:10.1177/0020852300661006

Lewin, K. (1951). Field theory in social science: selected theoretical papers. In D. Cartwright (Ed.), Field theory in social science: Selected theoretical papers. New York: Harper.

Lyons, A., & Powell, D. (2010). *Airport terminal facility activation techniques*. Available at: http://www.nap.edu/catalog/14394

Marshall, A., Ojiako, U., Wang, V., Lin, F., & Chipulu, M. (2018). Forecasting Unknown-Unknowns by Boosting the Risk Radar within the Risk Intelligent Organisation. *International Journal of Forecasting*.

Masrom, M., Rahim, M., Mohamed, S., Chen, G. K., & Yunus, R. (2015). Successful criteria for large infrastructure projects in Malaysia. *Procedia Engineering*, *125*, 143–149. doi:10.1016/j.proeng.2015.11.021

Molla, A., & Licker, P. (2005). Perceived e-readiness factors in e-commerce adoption: An empirical investigation in a developing country. *International Journal of Electronic Commerce, 10*(1), 83–110. doi:10.1080/10864415.2005.11043963

Morosan, C. (2016). An empirical examination of US travellers' intentions to use biometric e-gates in airports. *Journal of Air Transport Management, 55*, 120–128. doi:10.1016/j.jairtraman.2016.05.005

Morris, P. (1983). Managing project interfaces — key points for project success. In D. I. Cleland & W. R. King (Eds.), *Project Management Handbook*. Van Nostrand.

Morris, P. (1997). Managing project interfaces—key points for project success. In D. I. Cleland & W. R. King (Eds.), *Project management handbook* (2nd ed.). Hoboken, NJ: John Wiley & Sons, Inc. doi:10.1002/9780470172353.ch2

Motwani, J., Subramanian, R., & Gopala Krishna, P. (2005). Critical factors for successful ERP implementation: Exploratory findings from four case studies. *Computers in Industry, 56*(6), 529–544. doi:10.1016/j.compind.2005.02.005

Mumayiz, S. (1989). Development of airport terminal design concepts—A new perspective. *Transportation Planning and Technology, 13*(4), 303–320. doi:10.1080/03081068908717408

Nelson, J., Raskind-Hood, C., Galvin, V. G., Essien, J., & Levine, L. (1999). Positioning for partnerships - Assessing public health agency readiness. *American Journal of Preventive Medicine, 16*(1), 103–117. doi:10.1016/S0749-3797(99)00003-3 PMID:10198687

Nossair, A., Al-Tamimi, A., Al Amri, A., Al-Katheeri, K., Hann, T., & Finigan, T. (2012). Mega projects integrated readiness assurance process. In Abu Dhabi international petroleum conference and exhibition. Abu Dhabi, UAE: Society of Petroleum Engineers. doi:10.2118/159116-MS

O'Connell, J. (2011). The rise of the Arabian Gulf carriers: An insight into the business model of Emirates Airline. *Journal of Air Transport Management, 17*(6), 339–346. doi:10.1016/j.jairtraman.2011.02.003

O'Connor, E., & Fiol, C. (2006). Creating readiness and involvement. *Physician Executive*, *32*(1), 72–74. PMID:16509406

Ojiako, U., Maguire, S., & Chipulu, M. (2013). Thematic elements underlying the delivery of services in high-contact public service encounters. *Production Planning and Control*, *24*(6), 532–545. doi:10.1080/09537287.2011.642485

Parasuraman, A. (2000). Technology Readiness Index (TRI) a multiple-item scale to measure readiness to embrace new technologies. *Journal of Service Research*, *2*(4), 307–320. doi:10.1177/109467050024001

Pinto, J., & Winch, G. (2015). The unsettling of 'settled science:' The past and future of the management of projects. *International Journal of Project Management*, *34*(2), 237–245. doi:10.1016/j.ijproman.2015.07.011

Ponzini, D. (2011). Large scale development projects and star architecture in the absence of democratic politics: The case of Abu Dhabi, UAE. *Cities (London, England)*, *28*(3), 251–259. doi:10.1016/j.cities.2011.02.002

Prochaska, J., & DiClemente, C. C. (1983). Stages and processes of self-change of smoking: Toward an integrative model of change. *Journal of Consulting and Clinical Psychology*, *51*(3), 390–395. doi:10.1037/0022-006X.51.3.390 PMID:6863699

Project Management Institute. (2013). *A guide to the project management body of knowledge (PMBOK Guide)* (5th ed.). Project Management Institute.

Rodrigues, A., & Williams, T. (1998). System dynamics in project management: Assessing the impacts of client behaviour on project performance. *The Journal of the Operational Research Society*, *49*(1), 1–24. doi:10.1057/palgrave.jors.2600490

Rust, R. (1998). Editorial: What Is the Domain of Service Research? *Journal of Service Research*, *1*(November), 107. doi:10.1177/109467059800100201

Stevens, G. (2013). Toward a process-based approach of conceptualizing change readiness. *The Journal of Applied Behavioral Science*, *49*(3), 333–360. doi:10.1177/0021886313475479

Svejvig, P., & Andersen, P. (2015). Rethinking project management: A structured literature review with a critical look at the brave new world. *International Journal of Project Management, 33*(2), 278–290. doi:10.1016/j.ijproman.2014.06.004

Takebayashi, M. (2012). Managing the multiple airport system by coordinating short/long-haul flights. *Journal of Air Transport Management, 22*, 16–20. doi:10.1016/j.jairtraman.2012.01.004

Tribe, M., & Johnson, R. (2008). Effective capital project commissioning. In *Pulp and Paper Industry Technical Conference, 2008. PPIC 2008. Conference Record of 2008 54th Annual* (pp. 106-119). IEEE. 10.1109/PAPCON.2008.4585812

Ventre, K., Barry, J., Davis, D., Baiamonte, V., Wentworth, A. C., Pietras, M., ... Barley, G. (2014). Using in situ simulation to evaluate operational readiness of a children's hospital-based obstetrics unit. Simulation in Healthcare. *Journal of the Society for Simulation in Healthcare, 9*(2), 102–111. doi:10.1097/SIH.0000000000000005 PMID:24401917

Wanberg, C. R., & Banas, J. (2000). Predictors and outcomes of openness to changes in a reorganizing workplace. *The Journal of Applied Psychology, 85*(1), 132–142. doi:10.1037/0021-9010.85.1.132 PMID:10740964

Weiner, B. (2009). A theory of organizational readiness for change. *Implementation Science; IS, 4*(67). doi:10.1186/1748-5908-4-67 PMID:19840381

Weiner, B., Amick, H., & Lee, S. (2008). Conceptualization and measurement of organizational readiness for change: A review of the literature in health services research and other fields. *Medical Care Research and Review : MCRR, 65*, 379–436. doi:10.1177/1077558708317802 PMID:18511812

Weiss, D., & Maher, M. W. (2009). Operational hedging against adverse circumstances. *Journal of Operations Management, 27*(5), 362–373. doi:10.1016/j.jom.2008.10.003

Wilson, M., Hejna, W., & Hosking, J. (2004). Activation and operational planning: ensuring a successful transition. *Journal of Healthcare Management / American College of Healthcare Executives, 49*(6), 358–362.

Winch, G., & Leiringer, R. (2015). Owner project capabilities for infrastructure development: A review and development of the 'strong owner' concept. *International Journal of Project Management, 34*(2), 271–281. doi:10.1016/j.ijproman.2015.02.002

Zaneldin, E. (2006). Construction claims in United Arab Emirates: Types, causes, and frequency. *International Journal of Project Management, 24*(5), 453–459. doi:10.1016/j.ijproman.2006.02.006

Zerjav, V., Edkins, A., & Davies, A. (2018). Project capabilities for operational outcomes in inter-organisational settings: The case of London Heathrow Terminal 2. *International Journal of Project Management, 36*(3), 444–459. doi:10.1016/j.ijproman.2018.01.004

ENDNOTE

1 Exposure/vulnerability nomenclature sometimes causes confusion but can be understood simply. Above the term *exposure* is used to label some combination of *who* and *what* can be at risk within a project. In other words the term covers some entity engaged in some purposeful activity which can be considered at risk. The complementary term *vulnerability* is then used to describe what makes the exposed entity practice susceptible to harm and thus the exposed entity susceptible to loss. The key to avoiding confusion here is to recognise the difference between saying that some entity and related practice *can be* at risk and saying that the same *are* at risk. It is possible to be exposed to risk and yet not vulnerable. People working on numerous tasks on building sites are exposed to many risks, yet their use of personal protective equipment reduces their vulnerability. It may be dangerous to regard such reduction in vulnerability as also reducing risk exposure, because vigilance focused on risk exposure should remain necessary no matter what vulnerability reduction effort there has been. A concern with risk exposure and not just vulnerability may discipline the risk imagination to contemplate where risk might impact while avoiding false confidence in risk controls.

Chapter 4
FinTech Strategies in the GCC:
Developing a Growing FinTech Ecosystem - A GCC Perspective

Konstantinos Tsanis
Hult International Business School, UAE

ABSTRACT

The Gulf states, attempting to diversify their economies, have focused largely on transforming their economies. Part of their transformation focus areas is the technology sector. FinTech is a generic term used for all financial technology developments, and has gained a lot of traction in the recent years. As Financial services is one of the main sources of GDP for the GCC states, the GCC governments have focused in promoting the FinTech entrepreneurship spirit, through different initiatives. In the chapter, the authors analyze the FinTech ecosystem development mode for all the GCC countries, focusing on understanding the reason that have made it one of the most successful FinTech ecosystems globally.

DOI: 10.4018/978-1-5225-9377-5.ch004

INTRODUCTION

The Gulf has long been famous for two things: its oil and the lavish spending on extravagant initiatives made possible by oil windfalls. Yet, in this age when humanity is aligning its efforts to achieve a more balanced (Sustainable Development, n.d.) and sustainable (The Paris Agreement, n.d.) path to growth and systems of production face rapid technology-driven transformation, perhaps unexpectedly, Gulf countries are leading the way.

In the recent years, all the Gulf countries have launched long term plans to transform their economic models to embrace the opportunities created by the 4th Industrial Revolution (Lanteri, 2017), by leveraging, experimenting, and exploiting different emerging technologies. This is a result of the changing economic environment globally, and the associated risks and opportunities. As a result, the gulf countries have been performing quite well on Innovation indices, making them very attractive places to test and implement these technologies. Such examples include the Hyperloop, which is supposed to cut the time needed between Dubai and Abu Dhabi in 10 minutes, the use of robots in different companies and departments, and self-driving cars, among others.

While these technologies are successfully deployed across multiple domains, what presently seems their most promising application in the Gulf is in finance (AMP, n.d.). This seems to be aligned with the fact that the GCC countries, apart from oil exporters, are also popular financial hubs. Such success holds precious lessons for the region, highlighting the importance of both a clever strategy and an effective execution.

In order to understand in depth, this chapter is structured in the following sequence: In the following section, we describe the traditional economic structure of the Gulf countries. We then explore further the meaning of fintech, and how it is affecting company operations.

THE TRADITIONAL ECONOMIC STRUCTURE OF THE GULF COUNTRIES

The Gulf Cooperation Council (GCC) is a group of six oil exporting countries – namely Bahrain, Kuwait, Oman, Qatar, Saudi Arabia and the United Arab Emirates. It was formed a regional intergovernmental political and economic union in 1981, with its ultimate aim to expand the economic ties between its members. In 2008 a common market was launched and discussions about the introduction of a single currency were started.

The six countries show similarities in terms of their economy and how they are governed. Specifically, their economies have largely been based in the Oil revenues. This was associated with large government expenditure, with particular focus in the construction and real estate industries. Following the Arab spring, these amounts of money were used to benefit the countries' population, so again there was an increase in the public expenditure.

At the same time however, some of the economies, specifically the UAE and Qatar, have attempted to diversify their economies in more areas. They have done by adopting dedicated policies in specific areas. First of all they have attempted multinationals, in order for them to build their regional headquarters. Furthermore, they have tried to develop specific ''niches'', in the aviation, tourism and education industries. As a result, Emirates contributes 10% of the UAE's GDP, while at the same time tourism numbers have been growing with a steady pace the recent years. Concerning education, both the UAE and Qatar have formed partnerships with leading universities, attracting them to relocate to these emirates, while at the same time attracting very large numbers of international students.

In the recent years however, all of the GCC countries have tried to focus on their SME development. In order to do that they have developed long term plans and national policies with specific industry focus. As a result, there have been some SMEs that have been growing very rapidly in the recent years. A particular focus has been on technology and start ups. Specifically, there have been multiple attempts to engage in policies to promote education technology, aviation, oil and gas, and the finance industry, also known as fintech, as all of these industries have been the pillars of these economies. We analyze more in the fintech industry in the following part.

FINTECH: WHY, WHAT, HOW?

As discussed in the previous paragraphs, the regional economies in the GCC countries have attempted to diversify their economies in the recent years. This is mainly by embracing innovation in every industry. However, as the

Figure 1. The areas of FinTech

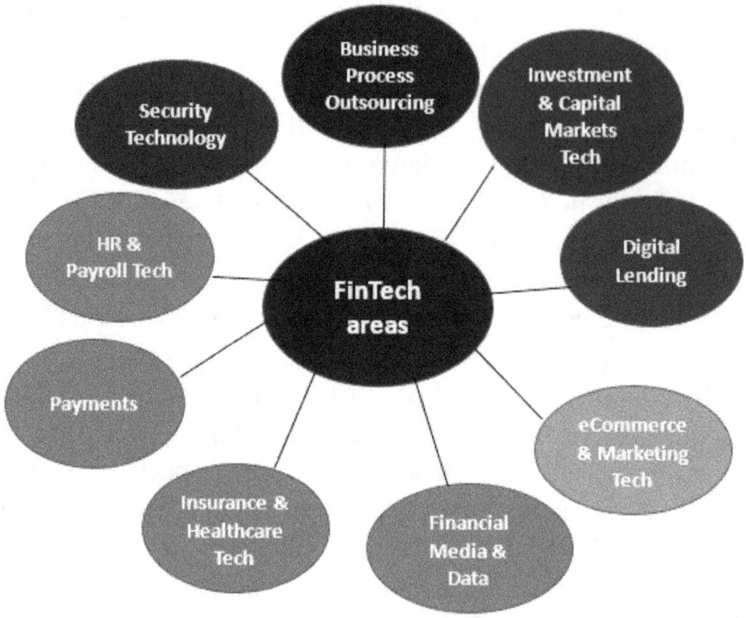

financial services are an important area in terms of GDP contribution of the GCC,there are different approaches that each country has engaged, to develop a FinTech ecosystem. Before describing them in detail, the next paragraphs discuss in depth the FinTech environment.

What Is Fintech, and its Impact?

The word "fintech" is simply a combination of the words "financial" and "technology". It describes the use of technology to deliver financial services and products to consumers. FinTech covers a few different areas. These can be seen on diagram 1 below.

This could be in the areas of banking, insurance, investing – anything that relates to finance.

Fintech is changing the world of finance for consumers in a myriad of ways. For example, you can now open a bank account over the internet, without physically visiting a bank.

Figure 2. Caption

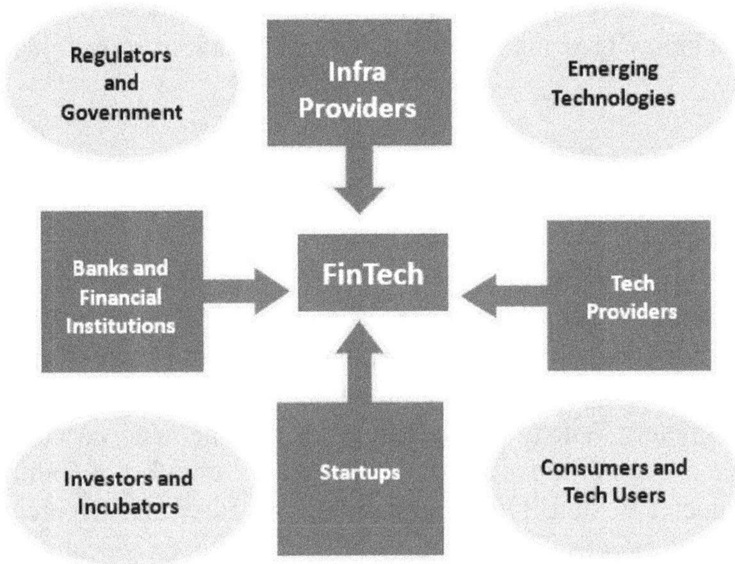

You can link the account to your smartphone and use it to monitor your transactions. You can even turn your smartphone into a "digital wallet" and use it to pay for things using money in your account.

Advances in technology means consumers can also invest over the internet on an "execution only" basis without any face-to-face interaction. In time, you may be able to get automated financial advice or "robo advice" with little or no human interaction.

The FinTech Ecosystem

Together, governments, financial services companies, and FinTech startups form an ecosystem. From an innovation perspective, one's efforts help further another's. Companies see what the other is doing and make similar adjustments to their product offerings. There is also increased acceptance of new technologies, as one's addition of a certain technology helps fuel adoption. Ultimately, FinTech ends up being a very small world. The people with the financial expertise needed to inform FinTech projects and those with the technological abilities to make those suggestions come to life often move between companies, either through mergers, a consulting basis, or employment. Diagram 2 below presents in more details the different stakeholders of the ecosystem.

Broad FinTech Categories

Mobile Banking

Mobile banking refers to the service that banks and other financial institutions provide to their customers by allowing them to conduct a range of transactions using an app. The app allows the customers to access and transact with their accounts remotely. With mobile banking, you can open a new account; check your balance, transfer funds and pay bills from the comfort of your house. A study conducted in the US in November 2016 revealed that 72 percent of the financial services consumers use digital channels to open checking accounts.

Internet Banking

Also referred to as e-banking or online banking, internet banking is closely related to mobile banking. The difference is that instead of using an app, customers use the web. You may access the web by use of your smartphone, tablet or a PC. All the transactions are conducted through the website of the financial institution. Statista notes that the share of individuals using internet banking in the UK increased from 30 percent in 2007 to 60 percent in 2016, pointing to the increasing popularity of internet banking.

Blockchain

Blockchain refers to a decentralized digital ledger that can record transactions across multiple computers such that the recorded transactions cannot be altered retrospectively. Participants can, therefore, audit and verify the transactions in a simple and cost-effective way. Blockchain is an online platform for digital assets. Bitcoin is the digital currency commonly used in blockchain transactions and it is gaining popularity as more and more people embrace fintech.

Insurtech

Insurtech is the use of financial technology in the insurance industry. Many insurance companies are adopting the use of technology and it is now possible to take an insurance cover without having to physically present yourself to the company. An individual can also file claims online.

Predictive Analytics

Predictive analytics is the use of big data to forecast future occurrences. The fintech sector involves the use of Big Data by finance institutions to determine market trends and future profitability. Established financial institutions such as the Bank of America, Goldman Sachsand Morgan Stanley are currently seeking to make use of the data that they have accumulated over time.

Crowdfunding

Crowdfunding is a rapidly growing fintech sector. Every year, up to $3 billion is raised on US-based crowdfunding platforms. Entry of early startups in the sector has significantly contributed to its overall growth with 24 percent campaign success rate.

Peer-to-Peer Lending

Peer-to-peer lending is one of the sectors that take the big financial institutions head-on by targeting their most profitable products, i.e. loans. It's no surprise that it attracts the most investors. It's an alternative form of financing that puts individuals and young startups in contact with potential investors. The chances of getting approved for credit is much higher than through banks and provided at a much lower cost. In doing so, it further fuels growth and innovation by giving small businesses much-needed funding to get projects off the ground. It's also one of the sectors that produces the most unicorns ($1 billion startups), including Lufax, LendingClub, ComonBond, Prosper, Funding Circle and Jimubox, to name a few.

Smart Finance Management

The advancement in fintech makes personal finance management easier to all irrespective of their academic background. Apps are capable of managing accounts, automatic budgeting, asset management and finance planning. Mint.com provides one app that performs all these functions.

Innovative Payments

Innovative payments are an important fintech sector especially in the light of increasing globalization and e-Commerce. It is predicted that by 2019, over 5 billion people will be making digital payments.

Robo-Advisors

Robo-advisors are software that uses algorithms to help people make informed investment decisions. Robo-advisors are gaining prominence in the financial industry particularly in portfolio management and stock markets where they make trading intuitive, cheap and mobile. Prominent examples include Wealth front and Betterment.

Remitances

The global remittance market is worth $530 billion annually.

With today's ever-increasing globalization, more and more people process gross border transfers on a regular basis. This is more prominent in developing countries where global remittance increased by 51% between 2007 and 2016.

The problem is that traditionally, it's incredibly expensive to make an international transfer. In Southern Africa, it costs on average close to 15% of the total transfer amount.

This means that disruption in the remittance sector is especially important, making it viable for people to send large or small amounts of money around the world at a fraction of the cost.

One of the biggest FinTech remittance companies is TransferWise. $500 million is moved through the platform every month and the company recently raised a further $280 million in funding, pushing the company value to $1.6 billion.

Mobile Wallet

Mobile wallets could be seen as a sub-section of the payments sector as it not only provides a safe place to store your money but also offer seamless payment solutions.

Between 50% and 70% of people in developing countries do not have access to traditional financial services, like a bank, while around 80% of individuals do own a mobile phone.

Due to the huge opportunities for FinTech startups to make a real difference in the lives of the unbanked individuals around the globe, the sector attracts around 10% of total FinTech investments. Some of the most successful startups include Mozido and Dwolla. The sector is so lucrative that big tech companies have developed their own wallets, such as Apple (Apple Pay), Google (Google Wallet) and Samsung (Samsung Pay). It is also seen as the birthplace of FinTech, with PayPal one of the first ever platforms to leverage technology in order to disrupt traditional financial services.

IMPACT OF FINTECH IN BANKING IN THE GCC

As mentioned, innovation and financial technology have impact in different areas of organizations.

The rise of the smartphone has massively changed the behavior of consumers. Whether it's checking to pay for goods online or making bank transfer via a mobile app, customers are now getting used to handling financial affairs as easily and conveniently as they do their email or Facebook page.

Banking

FinTech is the major cause of all the recent disruptions we are experiencing in the banking sector today, with the UAE having the highest number of digital banks in the world. Emirates can access top-notch financial services without stepping into a bank.

Fintech uses technology in a better way to make people feel convenient living in the modern age. FinTech helps people who are 'unbanked' but a desire to buy or sell online have access to quick and affordable banking operations just by using a mobile phone.

Lending

FinTech has fueled the growth of alternative lenders which offer both higher yields to investors and faster, cheaper, more convenient loans for borrowers compared to traditional banks.

Private lenders like Beehive, Sarwa,, PayLater, QuickCheck, and Lidya are continuing to plow hundreds of millions of dirhams into alternative-lending space in the GCC states making it easy for anyone to access quick loans (business or personal) when needed.

Financial Management

FinTech is changing the way we manage our money for the better. FinTech startups are introducing simple ways to manage and track your finances.

Instead of relying on a pen and paper or spreadsheet, you can now use digital financial solutions to manage your finances in real time. Good examples of Nigerian startups playing in this space are Payit for saving, Bayzat for invoicing and Souqalmal for expense management.

Payments

As per the PwC FinTech Global Report, 60 percent of all survey responders highlighted payments as the most likely sector to be disrupted by FinTech due to the introduction of cash-less payments such as Apple Pay and Bitcoin.

The GCC payments landscape has significantly evolved over the past decade. The cost of integrating online payments to a website 5 years ago was over 150k now thanks to FinTech, the cost of accepting online payments is Zero.

With the rapid adaptation of card payments in Nigeria, platforms like Paytabs are playing the lead role in making it easy for businesses to start accepting online payments with the click of a button.

KYC and Security

There is an increasing demand for Know Your Customer (KYC) solutions to support the prevention of money laundering and fraud. Presently, KYC operations need to adopt new technology to cut costs, reduce labor time, and efficiently adapt to regulatory changes. The cost of non-compliance is apparent as the Governor of the Bank of England Mark Carney highlighted that the cost of global banks' misconduct reached more than $320 billion.6 Therefore, financial institutions are starting to adapt FinTech verticals, such as AI, to support KYC guidelines.

DIFFERENT APPROACHES ON DEVELOPING A FINTECH ECOSYSTEM WITHIN THE GCC

As mentioned, all GCC countries have recognized the need for transformation, with one of their priorities being the development of the FinTech industry. In the following paragraphs we discuss in more depth how each country is competing in this space.

UAE

Country Approach

The UAE have been pioneer in being the first country that has diversified successfully its economic model with only 1% of its revenue coming from oil, which isn't the case for other countries. This has been achieved through a series of activities. First of all, both Abu Dhabi and Dubai have pushed for the creation of multiple accelerators. The operation of these accelerators along with invitations to large regional corporates permits for real time innovation. This is then excarbated with the availability of funding from start ups from different networks. The successful alignment of different stakeholders has resulted to multiple success stories.

Success Story One: Blockchain

A good example of UAE's execution muscle is the articulation of its 2021 Blockchain Strategy (Government, n.d.) aimed at becoming the first blockchain-powered government in the world. It was directly implemented in targeted government areas, with specific KPI's. Specific initiatives include:

urban planning, digital currency, digitalisation of government records through blockchain, and transaction processing. To drive the strategy, a blockchain council was established with regional and global subject matter experts, with a range of different specialisations. This approach has already resulted in several viable plans with realistic expectations, enabling a constantly improvement in blockchain implementation in different government areas.

One of the earliest success stories is DubaiPay (Das, 2018). The app processed $35 million of payments in 2017, which was its first year of operations. The government now aims to have more than 50% of its transactions on blockchain software. Other similar examples are now flourishing across different government departments and partner private institutions [*is this true?*]. The Dubai Electricity and Water Authority and the Human Development Authority also embraced DubaiPay and are now moving to the decentralised ledger to process their transactions, and have already processed more than five million transactions in the first six months of application. The Roads and Transport Authority is testing a vehicle management system. The bank Emirates NBD is piloting a fraud detection software and many other use cases are being developed across the country.

These examples also illustrate the power of creativity under the discipline imposed by a clear vision and a rigorous execution framework.

Success Story Two: Fintech Acceleration

Another illustration of UAE's approach is the development of its fintech acceleration ecosystem. The government established two acceleration programs focused on fintech, each under the supervision of one of the two main financial authorities of the country: Abu Dhabi Global Market (ADGM, n.d.) and Dubai International Financial Center (Webdesign, n.d.). These authorities took a pragmatic approach to deciding the fintech themes for their accelerators. They had to be aligned with the government's targets to support growth in other sectors. So, each summoned the financial institutions under their authority and asked them to identify the main issues they encountered. They then invited fintech startups that addressed exactly those problems. Specifically, they focused on attracting FinTech start ups that are their very early phases (pre series A), based in the world's FinTech hubs, as these were indicated from the WEF. Ultimately this would help the accelerator bring intellectual capital and knowledge, from company that are ready to offer their product, and they only needed local market access.

This pragmatic approach fast-tracked the acceleration programs. Having direct access to the main financial institutions of the country, and under the auspices of the main financial authorities, fintech startups can immediately test their prototyped solutions. Furthermore, since the accelerator focuses on existing issues, as soon as they graduate from the program, startups can offer their services to address the existing demand of a clearly defined market. This is highlighted from the success that some of the start up companies of the accelerator have had. Sarwa, for example, that focused on offering Robo-advisory services, was among the companies that successfully graduated, and were able to secure funding up to 2 million, to further expand in the region. Another interesting case is Norblock, which is a start up focusing on implementing KYC through Blockchain. Following the accelerator, the start up got access to multiple large regional banks, and other major European banks, having a very accelerated product testing, helping them be ahead of any competitor within this space.

As the UAE decided to differentiate its sources of income beyond oil, it established a clear vision (Vision, 2021) and a corresponding country strategy that pursues multiple growth drivers and with a strong focus on building and enabling a digital infrastructure. This vision also offers a broad umbrella policy framework with two distinguishing features that make it stand out with respect to similar visions in neighbouring countries. Vision 2021 was designed with an emphasis on implementation, through a framework of coherent and aligned strategies, ensuring that each decision follows a clear plan and is clearly aligned with the final outcomes of the vision. While fintech is a broad concept that spans from insurance to financial literacy and from wealth management to payments, the UAE took a selective approach to support only the initiatives aligned with the goals of Vision 2021. The combination of execution muscle and disciplined creativity resulted in a coherent overall strategy with specific and yearly measurable milestones to ensure constant progress towards the ultimate goal. At least two compelling success stories illustrate this well.

Bahrain

Country Approach

Bahrain was a regional success story before the UAE take the lead. As a result, they have a more mature financial ecosystem. Its relatively smaller size, also allows for an ease of adaptation to changes. Despite its early entry in the market however and its size, the protests of 2011 resulted on Bahrain losing a few of the companies located there. Despite these changes, the country has been able to successfully adopt a strong FinTech approach.

Success Story One: Credit Scoring

Bahrain, assisted perhaps from its smaller size, is the only country in the GCC that has available a full credit scoring for all the Kingdoms entities available online for free. This is a distinctive advantage, given ie the very large number of credit frauds that happen in the region. The vision of the countrys' leader enabled them to start very early the work on building a strong data infrastructure. This was followed by a very strong execution muscle, where all the companies of the country were forced to behave according to the required reporting standards. As a result, the country has build a very strong and transparent credit database, resulting in market transparency and a more attractive investment environment

Success Story Two: FinTech Bay

In a similar with the UAE, FinTech Bay is a government run accelerator from Bahrain's main financial authority. The impact of this accelerator program has been profound, as it has engaged all the ecosystem to work with international startups. As a result, there has been much adoption of innovation, compared to other regional economies. Furthermore, FinTech Bay has successfully established multiple global partnerships for knowledge, while having also enhanced innovative banking partnerships, such as the KFH, Al Baraka and Bahrain Development Bank partnership to have a common desk for FinTech research and adoption.

Saudi Arabia

Saudi Arabia is the regional giant, dominating the regional economy for more than 50 years. The main source of income traditionally has been Oil revenues. This has resulted in an economy that has largely ignored technology, who was the slowest mover in the FinTech space from its neighbors. Its size however (30 million, making it equal to the population of all the other GCC countries) makes it a very attractive investment environment. Because of its potential, it has had some quick wins with a large impact.

Success Story One: Ripple Blockchain Partnership

Ripple is one of the most successful digital currencies. Saudi Arabia Monetary Authority (SAMA), one of the oldest financial institutions in the region is responsible for the monetary policy within Saudi. Recognizing the potential of digital currencies, the authority decided to partner with Ethernet, in order to ensure efficient currency adoption in the future. This has received world wide recognition, and the work towards 2020 plan has already started. Following the success of the pilot, the oldest and largest bank of the country (National Commercial Bank) was then able to test and fully implement this technology, in order to capture the very large remittance market that exists in Saudi.

Success Story Two: Paytabs

Paytabs is a payments start up from Saudi. Despite its relatively delayed launch, compared to other payment providers, it has captured a big market share within Saudi, and keep growing. In addition, it has started expanding internationally. At the same time, the company acts as a regional fintech success story, working on further enhancing the regional ecosystem.

Qatar

Qatar's economy is one of the richest economies in the world based on GDP per capita, ranking between fifth and seventh on world rankings for 2015 and 2016. Petroleum and natural gas are the cornerstones of Qatar's economy and account for more than 70% of total government revenue, more than 60% of gross domestic product, and roughly 85% of export earnings. Qatar has the world's third largest proven natural gas reserve and is the second-largest exporter of natural gas.

The country has followed a somehow similar policy to the rest GCC countries, on that it is using a lot its public companies and authorities to implement its policies. Once of its main differences however is the way it has leveraged partnerships. Following their successful implementation of the education industry partnerships, which has resulted in some of the largest universities to be based in Qatar, they are now trying to implement this paradigm in the FinTech industry. This has resulted in multiple large scale strategic partnerships, which are discussed in the following paragraphs.

Success Story One: Knowledge Exchange

The country, despite its small size, has performed best in leveraging their 'partnerships' capability. Among others they have partnered with B-Hive, which is an EU knowledge exchange platform. This has enabled them to leverage large scale innovation to build a major fintech hub. Keeping on mind that Qatar is home to the biggest regional bank in terms of assets (Qatar National Bank), the scalable benefiting that partnerships can have is clear.

Success Story Two: International Partnerships

Qatar is the only country that has established strategic fintech partnerships with other countries within the region. Specifically, they have signed strategic alliance agreement with France, on Paris EUROPLACE and Finance Innovation, to support the growth of Qatar's booming digital industry. Paris EUROPLACE is responsible for promoting and developing the Paris financial marketplace. Finance Innovation was launched by the French Ministry for the Economy and Finance in 2007 to stimulate the Paris financial centre, and encompasses 480 member organisations and companies. By establishing these unique partnerships, Qatar has been able to form some of the largest knowledge networks, where people and organization from the private and the public sector collaborate through an online international platform. This has resulted in an alternative way of Innovation Engagement and has benefits at scale for the country.

RECOMMENDATIONS

Young Is Better

As a young region, the GGC has relatively little established legal and financial infrastructures. While this can be a limiting factor for fintech startups, forward-looking and supportive government policies have proved capable of overcoming these limits. Besides, having few established infrastructures allows the government to introduce and implement change more easily. So, our expectation is that the UAE will not only emerge as a leader in the development and deployment of the new technologies that drive the 4th Industrial Revolution. It will also emerge as an innovator in the policy frameworks that make such technologies possible and their applications successful.

Execution Matters Mostly

As mentioned during the text, all of the GCC countries have actually followed a similar path, on their growth choices. Specifically, all of them have more or less developed based in oil money, which has then be channeled to other areas. However, by observing the overall 30 years of growth, it can be safely said that what matters mostly is execution. Specifically, all of the countries have adopted different SME policies and national plans. What we can see however is that only a couple of them have really followed them. So the conclusion we can safely draw is that Execution Muscle is one of the most critical success factors.

Importance of Being ''Open''

Another critical factor that can explain the difference performance of economies is their ''openeness'' to partnership, knowledge exchange, and for the international attraction of multination companies. Being ''open'' is particularly important, as it attracts international companies to be headquartered in the country. Furthermore, this is also beneficial for knowledge exchange, as it can be seen in the case of Qatar.

CONCLUSION

The world is in constant change. And so do the GCC economies. Given the traditional structure of their economies, and the relatively 'safe' oil income that dominated their economies over the years, the predictions from economists over the future economies wasn't clear.

All of the countries however have engaged successfully in their digital transformation trips. As mentioned in this chapter, all of the GCC countries have exhibited a particularly successful execution muscle. This is combined from the available resources to create an enabling infrastructure. The regulators have been pivotal in driving FinTech engagement in the region, while they have been pushing for 'disciplined creativity'. As a result, the fintech industry in the GCC is expected to attract more than 2 billion investment in the next few years, while at the same time making their digital transformation journey a paradigm within emerging economies.

REFERENCES

ADGM Home. (n.d.). Retrieved from https://www.adgm.com/

Das, D. (2018, September 24). *Dubai Govt Upgrades Payment Portal DubaiPay with Blockchain technology.* Retrieved from https://www.ccn.com/dubai-govt-upgrades-payment-portal-dubaipay-with-blockchain-technology

Emirates Blockchain Strategy 2021. (n.d.). Retrieved from https://government.ae/en/about-the-uae/strategies-initiatives-and-awards/federal-governments-strategies-and-plans/emirates-blockchain-strategy-2021

Lanteri, A. (2017, November 26). *How CLEVER companies dominate the 4th Industrial Revolution.* Retrieved from https://medium.com/@alelanteri/how-clever-companies-dominate-the-4th-industrial-revolution-f250472ba93c

Middle East Makes a Play for Fintech Glory. (n.d.). Retrieved from https://amp.ft.com/content/201a0580-e72d-11e8-8a85-04b8afea6ea3

Sustainable Development Knowledge Platform. (n.d.). Retrieved from http://sustainabledevelopment.un.org/

TenTwenty. (n.d.). *DIFC: The Leading International Financial Hub & Destination for Lifestyle, Arts & Culture.* Retrieved from https://www.difc.ae/

The Paris Agreement. (n.d.). Retrieved from https://unfccc.int/process-and-meetings/the-paris-agreement/the-paris-agreement

Chapter 5
Historical Development of Chinese SMEs

Fenfang Lin
University of Southampton, UK

Alasdair Marshall
University of Southampton, UK

Wendy Wu
Edinburgh Napier University, UK

ABSTRACT

The importance of the SME is well established in the literature. These account for the majority of economic contribution in many economies. In the case of emerging markets, SMEs make significant contributions to the local income generation, employment support, and innovation development. The aim of this chapter is to provide an overview of how the world's largest emerging economy—China—helps promote its SMEs. This chapter provides a brief history of Chinese SMEs throughout the Great Economic Reform that started in 1978. Next, the SMEs' achievements and current constraints are outlined. Last, this chapter discusses how the SMEs in China upgrade through innovation and branding to embark on future pathways. Through this timeline approach, the experience of Chinese SMEs development will provide some insights for other emerging regions.

DOI: 10.4018/978-1-5225-9377-5.ch005

INTRODUCTION

Small- and medium-sized enterprises (SMEs) have been at the forefront of the economic development in most countries, and their importance to the economic development is well documented in the literature. SMEs serve as the engine of economic growth to generate innovation and employment, and provide social stability (Pistrui, Huang, Oksoy, Jing & Welsch, 2001). They account for the majority of economic contribution in the developed markets; i.e. over 99% of businesses in the US, the UK and Europe are SMEs (OECD, 2016). In emerging markets, SMEs contribute significantly to the regional and national economy development; for instance, over 95% of total business units in India are in the small-scale sector (Singh, Garg, & Deschmukh, 2009), and the United Arab Emirates (UAE) SMEs account for the same percentage[1]. In the case of the world's largest emerging market—China, SMEs accounts for more than 98% of the total businesses in China, over 65% of gross industrial output value, and more than 77% of employment (Singh et al., 2009). The majority of SMEs in China are privately owned enterprises, and, they are the sources of generating innovation, employment and wealth, and also advance the economic growth of the country (Malik, 1997; Poutziouris, Wang and Chan, 2002).

This chapter discusses the development of Chinese SMEs where the UAE SMEs can use as benchmark for development process. It first sets out a brief background of Chinese SMEs by applying the great Open Door Policy as the main timeline to divide the contemporary history of Chinese SMEs. This chapter then turns its attention to the current achievements of Chinese SMEs as well as the challenges faced by Chinese SMEs. The discussion on the future direction for SMEs is outlined at the end of this chapter.

HISTORY OF ENTERPRISE DEVELOPMENT IN CHINA

This section introduces the contemporary history of Chinese SMEs' development to understand how the modern Chinese enterprises formed and developed. The discussion follows the important historical cornerstone of the launch of China's Open Door Policy in 1978 led by the great economic reformer Deng Xiaoping, when China opened up to foreign investment and encouraged the development of regional small enterprise. This has transformed the Chinese economic system from a central-planned economy to a market-based economy and brought great changes to Chinese SMEs' developmental system (Ahlstrom & Ding, 2014). Since the introduction of the policy, China has transformed from a poor country to the world's second largest economy (behind the USA). Two sub-sections follow: the situation pre-1978 and the situation since the introduction of the Open Door Policy.

Before 1978

China was once the world's major economic power dating back to the Qing Dynasty (prior to the 1820s), and contributed over 32% of the world's total GDP (Maddison, 1998). However, the Chinese economy began to stagnate from 1820 onwards, particularly after the 1860s, when the economy's growth rate was less than 1% annually; and it continued to decline until 1949 (Maddison, 1998; Thomas, 2006). Prior to the establishment of the People's Republic of China (PRC) in 1949, China was fully occupied with the second Sino-Japanese War and the civil war between the Communist Party of China and the Kuomintang-led government. By 1949, China was regarded as one of the world's poorer nations, with annual income of about US$50 per capita (Naughton, 2007). Scholars have listed various reasons that contributed to the decline of the Chinese economy prior to 1949, such as the failure to follow up the Western industrialisation in the nineteenth century; the foreign-imposed impediments; corrupt domestic official systems; the traditional Confucian ideology; and/or the family tie business structures lead to various restrictions (Richardson, 1999; Thomas, 2006).

In 1949, the Communist government took on full sovereignty and established the People's Republic of China. To improve the economic development, the modern Chinese government encouraged enterprise and observed a gradual annual growth of about 4% from 1953 to 1978, amongst the highest in the developing countries at that time (Thomas, 2006; World Bank, 1997). Nevertheless, China was also experiencing a number of national-level campaigns that were against private entrepreneurs, thereby hindering its further development. During 1951 and 1952, China launched the 'Three and

Five Antis' Campaign, which started with clearing up corruption, waste and bureaucracy among the state's officials—the "Three Antis". It then extended to private enterprise by focusing on bribery, tax evasion, theft of state assets, cheating in labour and material, and stealing state economic intelligence (Chan & Gao, 2008). Due to ideological and political causes, entrepreneurs were discouraged. Private business activities were banned, as they were linked with theft of state property and cheating on state contracts, and their owners were fined for bribery and tax evasion (Malik, 1997).

From 1966 to 1976, China was also in the grip of the great chaos of the Cultural Revolution that slowed down the economy with no significant progress for another decade (Poutziouris et al., 2002). Many Chinese firms distrusted the government and encountered political and market turbulence with no immediate foreseeable end in sight (Malik, 1997). The number of firms in the private economy continued to decline until 1977, after which the private enterprise was again allowed to flourish (Poutziouris et al., 2002).

Post- 1978 Growth

In 1978, China began the post-Mao economic reform. Led by Deng Xiao Ping, the Open Door policy helped China gradually transform from a planned economy into a market economy (Yang, Liu, Gao., & Li, 2012). To stimulate economic growth, the Chinese government opened the country's doors to foreign trade and investment, released the market price that used to be controlled by the state, and encouraged the reformation of private enterprises in the rural regions (Hu & Khan, 1997). The Chinese Constitution promoted and endorsed entrepreneurship, leading to the flourishing of private entrepreneurship, and a dynamic Chinese entrepreneurial spirit was revived (Dana, 1999; Poutziouris et al., 2002). In 2001, China joined the World Trade Organization (WTO) and embraced trade liberalisation policies; a number of official policies were launched to promote innovation and catch up with the advanced technologies that already existed elsewhere (Wonglimpiyarat, 2015). The importance of SMEs in the nation's economic development was acknowledged and SMEs were revolutionised and encouraged in the post-1978 years.

States regard SMEs as the backbone to a country's economy and the vehicle for market advancement (Gibb, 2006). The promotion of entrepreneur development started within rural regions to boost the regional economy growth, during the 1980s. At the time, the majority of enterprises were clustered in the coastal regions. Regions such as Guangdong have enjoyed historical industrialisation, and it was the first region to embrace the Open Door policy; Jiangsu, the east coastal region, was driven by Foreign Direct Investment (FDI); and Zhejiang was designated for promotion of its small- and medium-sized enterprises (SMEs). Together with Shanghai and Shandong, these regions collectively contribute to nearly half of all private enterprises in China (Atherton & Smallbone, 2010).

The rebirth of Chinese private enterprises was formed in the 'cottage-type' activities, referring to the individual or family-oriented business activities (Dana, 1999); and constitutes the 'diaspora entrepreneurship' model, which is exemplified as 'armies of family-owned firms who attribute their success to manufacturing excellence, innovative cultures and growth orientation towards niche-exports' (Poutziouris et al., 2002, p. 386). Academic scholars refer to such a development model as the '*Industrial Cluster*' (Marshall, 1920; Zeng, 2012), which is formed by villages or towns that function as production hubs to accommodate a large quantity of 'cottage-type' small businesses that are engaged in a single product supply chain. The concept of 'one village, one product', or 'one town, one industry' was particularly popular in the 1980s and 1990s, resulting in a number of industrial hubs, as demonstrated in 'Ningbo-costumes', 'Shenzhen-textiles', 'Wenzhou-shoes', and Yiwu-small commodities', to name a few (Hung, 2008; Liu, 2008).

Clustering is an essential strategy for SMEs to gain their competitiveness. Many small enterprises clustered under one single industry to form a specialised division which helps to enhance business flexibility and specialisation, and establish economies of scales, and this is beneficial for both small enterprises and the host town (Liu, 2008). SME clusters help to facilitate the exchange of knowledge, disseminate new ideas, generate innovation, and attract talent and new entries (Li, 2006). For small firms, the cluster creates a commercial network that reduces the operational costs, enhances small firms' efficiency and, overall, enhances SMEs' competitive power. From the host town's perspective, the specialised cluster boosts local economic development by offering specialised competitiveness. The township enterprises system released large numbers of rural agricultural labour forces and transferred them to the industrial workforce. This delivered the solution to laying a solid foundation for economic reform and development; it further increased the farmers' income and work skills, and generated great impetus to the private enterprise development (Hall, 2007). The regional infrastructure and other new services industries are encouraged to develop to best facilitate the existing enterprises (Liu, 2001).

Since 1978, the development of Chinese small enterprises has achieved unprecedented success; and this development involves three key actors: the state, industry and firms. The state promoted the township and village enterprise policies and encouraged the establishment of SMEs clusters. Various townships were established at the industrial levels, supplied by cheap labour resources and local policy support. Small enterprises grew rapidly driven by various motivators. The desire for higher income and wealth is the primary driver for the individual entrepreneurs (Hessels, Van Gelderen & Thurik, 2008). Other motivations which represent key driving forces include the desire for family security and well-being, a strong desire for learning and practicing, achieving a personal sense of accomplishment, and a longing for success (Kolvereid, 1992; Wiklund et al., 2003). These motivations align with the cultural values that underlie the social systems (i.e. the Confucianism) and support self-improvement, dedication and hard work (Dana, 1999; Pye, 2000; Pistrui et al., 2001).

Small firms take advantage of cheap labour resources linked with the global commodity chain by offering undifferentiated commodities at low prices to meet the overseas demand (Steinfeld, 2004; Singh et al., 2009). Overall, small enterprises form industrial clusters and contribute significantly to the regional and national economy growth (Chen, 2017). The interplays of state, industry and companies have successfully transformed China into the world's second largest economic power and the world's largest manufacturing hub (The State Council, 2017).

To sum up, the Chinese market experienced a long period of stagnation prior to 1949 due to wars and an unstable social and political environment; and it has shown a slow recovery after the establishment of the Communist political power; however, the unstable social environment discouraged the development of entrepreneurship, and many small enterprises were punished for their capitalist ideology. The small and private enterprise was virtually non-existent prior to 1978 (Ahlstrom & Ding, 2014). The contemporary history of Chinese enterprises' development expanded significantly following the market reform in 1978 and, with the support of the Government, Chinese enterprises entered a rapid development era.

CURRENT ACHIEVEMENT AND CHALLENGES

The definition of SMEs is complex and varies from country to country. The most widely accepted definition in the entrepreneurship literature is defining the size of enterprises according to the number of employees within the firm. Table 1 compares definitions of SMEs in terms of the number of employees in different countries. According to the American Small Business Administration (SBA), a SME stands for an enterprise with fewer than 500 employees (Xie, Zeng, & Tam, 2010), while the European Standard definition is a firm with a cut-off point of 250 employees. This definition of SMEs has been adopted worldwide, including in the UAE. The definition for the Chinese SME, nevertheless, according to the Chinese Bureau of Statistics (CBS)[2], is the firm with up to 2000 employees and other indicators include annual income below RMB 300 million, and total assets of less than RMB 40 million. The concept of SMEs in China is that they are relatively large, and in other contexts and countries, would actually be considered large firms.

Since the reform of the Chinese economy, the number and size of SMEs have undergone significant growth. The number of SMEs has increased from almost zero in 1980 to over 40 million in 2004[3]. If we only consider the small-sized enterprise, by the end of 2013, the statistics results from the Chinese Industry and Commerce Bureau (2014) showed that there were more than 55 million firms classed as the small, macro and privately or individually-owned enterprises, accounting for over 94% of the total number of enterprises.

The Chinese economy has also experienced unprecedented growth along with the development of small enterprises. Since the early 1980s, the annual GDP has grown continuously at a high rate (averaged over 9.0%) for 30 years (with a slight slow-down below 7% since 2015), ranking among the highest growth rates in the history of economic development (Woo, 1997). By 2011,

Table 1. SME definitions across the world

Country/Region	Employment-Based
China	<2,000 (manufacturing sector)
USA	<500
EU	<250
UAE	<250
Australia	<200

Source: Adapted from European Commission (2015); Wolff and Pett (2000); SMEs in Dubai (2013)

China had surpassed Japan by GDP and became the world's second largest economic nation, and global economy observers predict that by 2020, China will be surpass the United States to become the world's largest economy (Ikenberry, 2008).

With decades of efforts invested in the country's industrial development, China has earned the title of 'World Factory'. Small firms participate in the international exporting by teaming up with large exporting firms to deliver 'Made in China' goods worldwide. Chinese enterprises positioned themselves as the suppliers of massive volumes of cheap products to meet international demands for cheap Chinese goods. Chinese products offer the world's consumers ultra-low prices and benefit global consumers with millions of product options. Nevertheless, the rapid industrial development is not without costs. China has to pay the price by sacrificing the image of 'Made in China' as a number of Chinese product quality scandals developed along with the booming exporting business; some of these scandals involved recalled products in toothpastes, drugs, toys and tyres that contained poisonous chemicals (Chinen & Sun, 2011). The global customers perceive Chinese goods as cheap but low in quality (Loo & Davies, 2006), and the overall negative image of the Chinese product impedes Chinese firms from developing their own brands in the overseas market.

Chinese officials made great efforts to repair the 'Made in China' image. During the 2008 Beijing Olympic Games, China showed its great economic and political power, and presented a platform from which to challenge the existing negative perceptions of China (Blair et al., 2010). In 2011, Chinese officials composed a first 'Made in China' advert and broadcasted it on CNN International and other worldwide media, deliberately advocating China's collaborative role with foreign companies in producing high-quality and high-tech goods. The Chinese government refurbished its nation brand image, hoping to ensure a positive image worldwide of Chinese products.

Nevertheless, the key competitiveness of cheap labour resources has been challenged by the increasing labour costs in China, and the development of other emerging countries that are able to offer even cheaper resources, such as Cambodia, Vietnam and Indian (Li, 2017). China drove up its economic power from the low value-added, mass production to the high value-added and high technology production. Most recently, the Chinese government called for industrial upgrading, and promoted a number of new policies in a hope to push Chinese industries to upgrade to higher value-added production. Promotions such as '2010s' strategic emerging industries', 'Made in China 2025' and 'China 2030' encourage firms to move away from the labour-intense competition, and join the technology- and innovation-driven production (Tian et al., 2012; Wubbeke & Conrad, 2015; Li, 2017).

Large firms, including the state-owned enterprises, have actively answered the upgrading calls and have successfully transferred from labour-reliant to technology- and innovation-advanced global players, such as Lenovo, Huawei, Haier, and Alibaba. For SMEs, the upgrade pathway to technology- and innovation-advanced firms bring great challenges. The existing studies on barriers to SMEs upgrading are widespread (i.e. Orser, Hogarth-Scott, & Riding, 2000; Gill & Biger, 2012). The following content discusses two key aspects of SMEs' upgrading challenges: internal and external challenges.

The Internal Challenges

Like most SMEs in other countries, Chinese SMEs suffer from insufficient financial resources; they are weak in the technology and innovation, and lack competencies in human capital and expertise knowledge. The majority of Chinese SMEs are family owned, and built with a flat organisational structure that is unable to create an open communication environment. Furthermore, the traditional assembly and Original Equipment Manufacturer (OEM), business model impedes firms's upgrading intentions (Ahlstrom, Young, Chan, & Bruton, 2004; Singh et al., 2009).

The financial issue is perceived as one of the key internal challenges to a SME upgrading (Gill & Biger, 2012), and it underpins a firm's ability to engage in innovation, R&D activities and other capability development (Xie, Zeng, & Tam, 2010; Zhang et al., 2016). The majority of Chinese SMEs do not have sufficient capital to feed their business development, leading to limited investment in R&D (Baas & Schrooten, 2006). Most also do not have a supporting legal and regulatory environment to provide financial resources, limiting a company's desire to achieve growth (Hussain, Millman, & Matlay, 2006). Xie, Zeng and Tam (2010) investigated the innovation activities in Chinese SMEs and found that the majority of enterprises allocated very little expense (i.e. less than 10% of R&D expenditures) on R&D activities due to lack of financial capital. The majority of SMEs have to depend on owners' personal capital, and/or business revenues. Self-financing drives firms to be more short-sighted for quick profit return, and underpins the unwillingness to invest in brand, R&D and other innovative activities that require a long-term investment without a quick financial return (Ahlstrom et al., 2004).

SMEs are also weak at developing core technology and innovation. Since the successful economic reform, China as the world's factory is renowned for the sheer volume of products it has produced, rather than how innovative its outputs are (Tylecote & MacDonald, 2008). Literature has revealed a few barriers to the innovation in China, including the inadequate access to the key technology; limited interests in investing in innovation due to an unregulated market environment relating to the implementation of intellectual property rights (IPR) (Ernst & Young, 2006); and limited capability with little willingness to cultivate an innovation culture (Mitussis, 2010). Most recently, China showed its abilities in developing high-tech and innovative products; nevertheless, these achievements are associated with large firms. The majority of SMEs lack technological competencies, are weak in accessing core technology due to insufficient technical expertise, and lack funds to fill in the gaps between marketing and product function (Gunasekara et al., 2001; Hashim & Wafa, 2002; Xiong et al., 2006; Singh et al., 2009), and these deficits hinder small enterprises' technology upgrading and innovation (Berrell & Wrathall, 2007).

There are a number of approaches that Chinese SMEs take to practice technological innovation, including internal R&D, imitation, licensing of know-how, and research institution-led R&D (Liu, 2008). Internal R&D is the most popular practice to generate technological innovation; and the imitation practice contributes to the highest income generation. Licensing core technologies requires support from sufficient resources and appropriate manufacture infrastructure, and only limited SMEs are able to participate in such practices. The external-led R&D has the lowest participation in SMEs (Liu, 2008). Despite an official effort in fostering an innovative culture at the industrial level—i.e. building universities-business collaborative project and science parks—the participation from SMEs with research-institution-led R&D is still very limited (Liang, 2007). This is partially due to the complex and uncertain business relationships that hinder SME owner-managers in developing an innovative culture within the firm (Mitussis, 2010).

Human capital deficiency such as lack of skilled employees and low levels of management expertise are other barriers to SMEs' development (Singh et al., 2005). Human resources and capabilities reflect a firm's ability to 'renew, augment and adapt its competencies over time and are closely linked to the skills embodied in the firm' (Xie et al., 2010, p. 303). Research found that the deficiency in technical experts—i.e. engineers, R&D expertise—underpins the barriers that SMEs experience when trying to engage with activities in innovation and R&D (Zeng et al., 2009).

Predominantly, Chinese private SMEs are owned and managed by families (Chen, 2001; Eddleston, Kellermanns, & Sarathy, 2008) which rely on the owner's personal skills to determine the business success, and this has brought internal challenges for SMEs (Ahlstrom et al., 2004; del Brio, Junquera, & Ordiz, 2008; Xie, Zeng, & Tam, 2010). To some extent, the family business structure has its advantages in the developing market environment. By hiring family members in the top management team, a close business tie helps firms to cope with the turbulent market; protects firms from the risks associated with unacquainted business partners (Yeung, 2006; Deng, Hofman, & Newman, 2013); reduces agency cost (Gedajlovic & Carney, 2010); and promotes the information exchange within the top management team (Sirmon, Arregle, Hitt, & Webb, 2008).

Nevertheless, family ownership also results in insufficient collaboration with external parties. The family ownership structure reveals that often the close family members retain the top management positions. Such flat structure lacks transparency with no proper monitoring systems and the information tends to circulate within the small group (Ahlstrom et al., 2004); so operations and finance are unknown to externals (Kotey & Folker, 2007). Employees are often excluded from the company's strategic decision making, and are unable to engage in the discussion on short- or mid-term goals (Deng et al., 2013).

Research found that the background of the SME's owner determines the firm's success, such as the owner's education background (Robson & Obeng, 2008) and personal interests (e.g., to obtain financial benefits, personal achievement, and social status) (Jennings & Beaver, 1997; Jarvis et al., 2000; Walker & Brown, 2004; Simpson, Padmore, & Newman, 2012). The individual top management's personal impetus ties up the business development and determines the directions of the firm. A flat and centralised family ownership may aid a start-up firm but, as the firm grows, external knowledge becomes essential; thus, the family-owned business model becomes an impediment to the business growth.

Last but not least, a traditional model in assembly and OEM also impedes SMEs' motivations to upgrade. Traditionally, Chinese SMEs participate in the component producing, assembly and OEM practices, but they are yet to show their ability in producing innovative and branded products. This is partly due to the reliance on the traditional business model whereby the contracting brands provides products specification, design, quality controls, and proper distribution channels. Chinese SMEs are only responsible for production; thus they are used to the business model of passively receiving the product specification from the branded company. However, this requires them to actively go out and research the international market. The majority of Chinese SMEs focus on developing the domestic market and building the home-based network resource to facilitate their internationalisation efforts. Subsequently, their knowledge of the foreign buyer's market is very limited (Zhang et al., 2016).

The External Challenges

External environment relates to the competition, deregulation and market demands that form external challenges and significantly affect a firm's business performance (Damanpour, Walker, & Avellaneda, 2009; Ng et al., 2015). One of the key external challenges is the availability of institutional support for SMEs (Zhu, Wittmann, & Peng, 2012). Research on Chinese state-owned firms' internationalisation (Child & Rodrigues, 2005) shows that firms like Haier Group (Liu & Li, 2002) and Huawei (Sun, 2009) have enjoyed institutional support in access to finance and resources and have garnered much attention in the global market as a result. The availability of state support for SMEs' development is scarce. Zhu et al. (2012) stated that less than 10% of Chinese private enterprises are able to obtain loans from banks, and external financing from capital markets is only available for less than 1% of private firms. Chinese SMEs experience significant impediments to accessing financial information and understanding the availability of financial sources (Orser et al., 2000) due to the fact that most financial providers are state-owned and centrally controlled, and are more likely to favour large firms (Zhang et al., 2016).

The negative image of 'Made in China' in the global market also discouraged Chinese SMEs from upgrading. China has been well known for its cheap and abundant labour resources which enable it to manufacture 'Made in China' goods worldwide. The reputation of 'Made in China' products as formed by the low quality and low price image has been implanted in the international buyers' minds (Ha-Brookshire and Yoon, 2012). This unfavourable country-of-origin image does not encourage a friendly environment for SMEs' growth. Despite the great efforts from small firms in promoting their own products, the association of mass production of low quality and extra cheap price commodities is deeply rooted in the buyers' mind-set and may hinder a firm in its attempts to upgrade (Papadopoulos & Heslop, 2002; Uddin, Parvin, & Rahman, 2013).

The development of an industry cluster shaped by small firms with a strong tie that intend to participate in the supply chain has generated intense competition in the market. Industry clusters helped the regional and national economy development, but also led to a concentrated and unfair competitive environment (Zeng, 2012), particularly in the local economies of those rural and undeveloped regions that were highly dependent on the contributions from SMEs. The local government, thus, reduced the entry barriers to attract more small firms to join the cluster, and the resulting price competition among the firms led to an intensive price war (Porter, 2000).

Over decades of development, medium-sized enterprises have grown into large sized concerns; these large firms and state-owned firms receive privileged support from the government, and play a dominant role in the market (Zhu et al., 2012). China may have enacted SME Promotion Laws [4] to ensure fair market competition, but the concrete regulations and comprehensive guidelines at the practice level were missing (Zhu & Sanderson, 2009). The implementation of Promotion Laws still favours the large firms; small firms are disadvantaged from being unable to access the support from the financial institutions. The Chinese government may have implemented a number of supporting systems for SMEs to undertake R&D and encourage SMEs to engage in innovative activities, services including providing capital and subsidies for firms to develop technology (Zhu et al., 2012) but, to date, a very limited number of SMEs has benefited from these programmes. The majority of SMEs do not have sufficient internal resources, i.e. expert knowledge and skills, to support external market research; thus, they have to rely on a third party to supply the external knowledge about the market and public to complement their business practices (Zhu et al., 2012).

Overall, Chinese SMEs have achieved phenomenal success after the economic reform, but the tradition and historical influences still pose barriers, and hinder SMEs as they strive for further development. The existing studies reveal the barriers that Chinese firms face (Yang, Liu, Gao, & Li, 2012). Internally, insufficient financial support, lack of relevant human resources, weakness in core technological innovation development and management models all affect the upgrading of Chinese firms. External factors relating to market environment, government policies and institutional support, and country-of-original impact have been important influencers on Chinese SMEs' development (Li, Liu, & Zhao, 2006).

PATHWAY FOR FUTURE DEVELOPMENT

Literature has generated various upgrading pathways from the developed economies' experiences, and a list of paradigms was developed to explain the upgrading process. In the case of Japan, the 'flying geese' paradigm was delineated to explain the Japanese industrial upgrading process (Kojima, 2000; Ozawa, 2005). This was followed later by the transformation from 'imitation to innovation' to describe the technology capability development in South Korea (Kim & Nelson, 2000; Kale & Little, 2007). One of the most popular pathways to illustrate the manufacturing upgrading is the trajectory from Original Equipment Manufacturer (OEM) to Original Design Manufacturer (ODM) and Original Brand Manufacturer (OBM), and that has been applied to explain Taiwan's and China's manufacturing upgrading (Lee, 2005; Chu, 2009; Eng, 2009; Yan, 2012).

The progress of industrial upgrading is complex; it requires firms to acquire relevant knowledge and know-how skills and capabilities in the developmental pathway, including learning capabilities, creativity and innovation capabilities, design capabilities, R&D capabilities and marketing capabilities (Eng & Spickett-Jones, 2009; Liu, Tsou, & Chen, 2013). The development of Chinese SMEs started from the assembly production model, and took advantage of cheap labour resources available as a stepping-stone. Chinese SMEs established the production capabilities that are essential for OEM — by cooperating in a subcontracting relationship (Hobday, 1995). China produces goods that are often seen as components or ingredients of the final goods, but these are often marketed and branded to the consumer market by the contracting firms (Chu, 2009).

'Learning by doing' is part of the subcontracting process, where Chinese SMEs obtained relevant skills and knowledge in addition to simple assembly tasks (Azadegan et al., 2008). Individual firms started seeking further involvement in the manufacturing production process, such as acquiring design capability to step into the ODM model. To practice their design capability, firms have to engage in other activities, such as market research and R&D (Liu, Liu & Lin, 2008). Upgrading to the ODM model happens when a subcontractor can provide specific designs and services to the buyers. Nevertheless, firms still have to obtain capabilities in product design, R&D, creativity and innovation to accommodate buyers' needs (Fritsch & Meschede, 2001; Malerba & Nelson, 2011; Fossas-Olalla, Minguela-Rata, López-Sánchez, & Fernández-Menéndez, 2015).

To further advance SMEs' upgrading, more advanced knowledge in terms of branding and marketing capabilities is required in the future (Eng, 2009). Marketing capabilities refers to "a firm's 'know-what' knowledge resources and its complementary 'know-how' development capabilities" (Morgan, Vorhies, & Mason, 2009, p. 911). Firms with marketing capabilities become more market-oriented and are able to explore the market by collecting, disseminating, and applying market information relating to consumers and competitors to their internal applications (Jaworski & Kohli, 1993). A market-oriented firm is in a better position to understand consumers' needs, and forecast market trends and competitor behaviour (Kaufmann & Roesch, 2012). According Narver & Slater (1990), being market-oriented is to be customer-oriented, competitor-oriented and inter-functional coordinated. Chinese SMEs need to actively explore the customer's expected and latent needs, and learn the competitor's behaviour and strategies (Rakthin, Calantone, & Wang, 2016). Obtaining, absorbing and transferring market information internally helps SMEs develop effective strategies to manage the market competition against international rivals (Zahra & Gorge, 2002; Kuester & Rauch, 2016).

Marketing capability, including branding capability, is essential to building own brands; nevertheless, such capabilities are currently lacking in the Chinese SMEs. Having a powerful brand helps SMEs to realise financial return and form a sustainable business relationship with buyers (Marquardt, 2013). Industrial branding further builds industrial barriers against the competition (Michell, King, & Reast, 2001). However, gaining branding capability is a complex journey for SMEs; firms have to obtain skills in marketing communication and knowledge in strategic branding development (Leek & Christodoulides, 2012), and they also need to acquire sufficient knowledge about the market (Glynn, 2012). Unlike the original business models that Chinese SMEs used to practice, building a successful industrial brand requires sufficient recourses; it needs long-term investment and accumulation of capabilities to realise the financial return. It also requires firm to actively explore the buyer's market in order to understand the buyer's needs. Currently, the OEM business model plays a significant role in financially supporting SMEs' capabilities development, but undertaking a branding decision is likely to have a negative impact on a small firm.

CONCLUSION

In this chapter, we have introduced the historical development and the current achievement of Chinese SMEs. Since the market reforms that came into play in 1978, China has witnessed rapid improvement in economic and social aspects and has successfully lifted herself from a centrally-planned economy to a market-based economy. The current achievements, however, are also accompanied by some key internal and external challenges that prevent SMEs from upgrading. Internally, Chinese SMEs face challenges from the financial and human capital deficiencies, weak core technological innovation, unfavourable business model, and family management structure. Externally, the market environment relates to institutional policies and support, and country-of-origin image negatively affects SMEs' upgrading. By describing the internal and external challenges that SMEs face when they wish to upgrade, future research is outlined to explore how to remove the current obstacles that SMEs in China face in order for them to flourish (Lerner, 2009; Ahlstrom & Ding, 2014). A future pathway towards obtaining more marketing-related capabilities can lead a firm to upgrade to high value-added creation and innovation.

The overview of SMEs' development in China suggests that although China has achieved great economic success since the Open Door policy was introduced, the transition of Chinese SMEs from the traditional assembly and OEM business model that relies on labour resources can no longer achieve sustainable competitiveness. SMEs, particularly those small-sized enterprises, have to acquire relevant capabilities for upgrading to high value-added creation and innovation, and this requires firms to gain skills and knowledge in the core value of know-how. Many researchers have discussed the successful transition of Chinese large firms towards high value-added production, but the reality for the small firm remains to be unpacked.

REFERENCES

Ahlstrom, D., & Ding, Z. (2014). Entrepreneurship in China: An overview. *International Small Business Journal, 32*(6), 610–618. doi:10.1177/0266242613517913

Ahlstrom, D., Young, M. N., Chan, E. S., & Bruton, G. D. (2004). Facing Constraints to Growth? Overseas Chinese Entrepreneurs and Traditional Business Practices in East Asia. *Asia Pacific Journal of Management, 21*(3), 263–285. doi:10.1023/B:APJM.0000036463.20310.de

Atherton, A., & Smallbone, A. (2010). State promotion of SME development at the local level in China: An examination of two cases. *Journal of Chinese Entrepreneurship, 2*(3), 225–241. doi:10.1108/17561391011078721

Azadegan, A., Dooley, K. J., Carter, P. L., & Carter, J. R. (2008). Supplier innovativeness and the role of interorganizational learning in enhancing manufacturer capabilities. *The Journal of Supply Chain Management, 44*(4), 14–35. doi:10.1111/j.1745-493X.2008.00070.x

Baas, T., & Schrooten, M. (2006). Relationship banking and SMEs: A theoretical analysis. *Small Business Economics, 27*(2-3), 127–137. doi:10.100711187-006-0018-7

Berrell, M., & Wrathall, J. (2007). 'Between Chinese culture and the rule of law: What foreign managers in China should know about intellectual property rights. *Management Research News, 30*(1), 57–76. doi:10.1108/01409170710724304

Blair, T. C., Chen, K., Shieh, M. D., & Chiou, S. C. (2010). Brand a Nation: What is being Brand? The Impact of Olympics on China. *International Journal of the Humanities, 7*(10), 57–66. doi:10.18848/1447-9508/CGP/v07i10/42752

Chan, H. S., & Gao, J. (2008). Old wine in new bottles: A country-level case study of anti-corruption reform in the People's Republic of China. *Crime, Law, and Social Change, 49*(2), 97–117. doi:10.100710611-007-9096-y

Chen, H. (2017). *The institutional transition of China's township and village enterprises: market liberalization, contractual form innovation and privatization*. New York: Routledge. doi:10.4324/9781315211305

Chen, M. J. (2001). *Inside Chinese business*. Boston: Harvard Business School Press.

Child, J., & Rodrigues, S. B. (2005). The Internationalization of Chinese Firms: A Case for Theoretical Extension? *Management and Organization Review*, *1*(3), 381–410. doi:10.1111/j.1740-8784.2005.0020a.x

Chinen, K., & Sun, Y. (2011). Effects of Country-of-Origin on Buying Behavior: A Study of the Attitudes of United States Consumers to Chinese-brand Automobiles. *International Journal of Management*, *28*(2), 553–563.

Chinese Industry and Commerce Bureau. (2014). The development of Small and macro enterprises. *The State Council of The People's Republic of China*. Retrieved November 27, 2018, from http://www.gov.cn/xinwen/2014-03/31/content_2650031.htm

Chu, W.-W. (2009). Can Taiwan's second movers upgrade via branding? *Research Policy*, *38*(6), 1054–1065. doi:10.1016/j.respol.2008.12.014

Damanpour, F., Walker, R. M., & Avellaneda, C. N. (2009). Combinative Effects of Innovation Types and Organizational Performance: A Longitudinal Study of Service Organizations. *Journal of Management Studies*, *46*(4), 650–675. doi:10.1111/j.1467-6486.2008.00814.x

Dana, L. (1999). Small business as a supplement in the People's Republic of China (RPC). *Journal of Small Business Management*, *37*(3), 76–80.

del Brío, J. A., Junquera, B., & Ordiz, M. (2008). Human resources in advanced environmental approaches–a case analysis. *International Journal of Production Research*, *46*(21), 6029–6053. doi:10.1080/00207540701352094

Deng, Z., Hofman, P. S., & Newman, A. (2013). Ownership concentration and product innovation in Chinese private SMEs. *Asia Pacific Journal of Management*, *30*(3), 717–734. doi:10.100710490-012-9301-0

Dubai SMEs. (2013). The state of Small & Medium Enterprises (SMEs) in Dubai: a report by Dbuai SME. *An agency of the Development of Economic Development*. Retrieved from http://www.sme.ae/studiesandresearchdocument/sme_report_english.pdf

Eddleston, K. A., Kellermanns, F. W., & Sarathy, R. (2008). Resource configuration in family firms: Linking resources, strategic planning, and technological opportunities to performance. *Journal of Management Studies*, *45*, 26–50.

Eng, T.-Y. (2009). Manufacture upgrade and interfirm relationship development: The case of electronics firms in the Pearl River Delta. *Asia Pacific Business Review*, *14*(4), 507–525. doi:10.1080/13602380802461419

Eng, T.-Y., & Spickett-Jones, J. G. (2009). An investigation of marketing capabilities and upgrading performance of manufacturers in mainland China and Hong Kong. *Journal of World Business*, *44*(4), 463–475. doi:10.1016/j.jwb.2009.01.002

Ernst & Young. (2006). *Progressions 2006. Capturing global advantage in the pharmaceutical industry*. New York: Ernst & Young Global Pharmaceutical Centre.

European Commission. (2015). *User guide to the SME definition*. Retrieved from https://ec.europa.eu/regional_policy/sources/conferences/state-aid/sme/smedefinitionguide_en.pdf

Fossas-Olalla, M., Minguela-Rata, B., López-Sánchez, J.-I., & Fernández-Menéndez, J. (2015). Product innovation: When should suppliers begin to collaborate? *Journal of Business Research*, *68*(7), 1404–1406. doi:10.1016/j.jbusres.2015.01.022

Fritsch, M., & Meschede, M. (2011). Product innovation, process innovation, and size. *Review of Industrial Organization*, *19*(3), 335–350. doi:10.1023/A:1011856020135

Gedajlovic, E., & Carney, M. (2010). Markets, hierarchies and families: Toward a transaction cost theory of the family firm. *Entrepreneurship Theory and Practice*, *34*(6), 1145–1171. doi:10.1111/j.1540-6520.2010.00418.x

Gibb, A. (2006). Making markets in business development services for SMEs: Taking up the Chinese challenge of entrepreneurial networking and stakeholder relationship management. *Journal of Small Business and Enterprise Development*, *13*(2), 263–283. doi:10.1108/14626000610665962

Gill, A., & Biger, N. (2012). Barriers to small business growth in Canada. *Journal of Small Business and Enterprise Development, 19*(4), 656–668. doi:10.1108/14626001211277451

Glynn, M. S. (2012). Primer in B2B brand-building strategies with a reader practicum. *Journal of Business Research, 65*(5), 666–675. doi:10.1016/j.jbusres.2011.03.010

Gunasekaran, A., Marri, H. B., Mcgauahey, R., & Grieve, R. J. (2001). Implications of organization and human behavior on the implementation of CIM in SMEs: An empirical analysis. *International Journal of CIM, 14*(2), 175–185.

Ha-Brookshire, J., & Yoon, S.-H. (2012). Country of origin factors influencing US consumers' perceived price for multinational products. *Journal of Consumer Marketing, 29*(6), 445–454. doi:10.1108/07363761211259250

Hall, C. (2007). When the dragon awakes: Internationalisation of SMEs in China and implication for Europe. *CESifo Forum, 8*(2), 29–34.

Hashim, M. K., & Wafa, S. A. (2002). *Small and Medium Sized Enterprises in Malaysia –Development Issues*. Prentice-Hall.

Hessels, J., Van Gelderen, M., & Thurik, R. (2008). Entrepreneurial aspirations, motivations, and their drivers. *Small Business Economics, 31*(3), 323–339. doi:10.100711187-008-9134-x

Hobday, M. (1995). East-Asian Latecomer Firms - Learning the Technology of Electronics. *World Development, 23*(7), 1171–1193. doi:10.1016/0305-750X(95)00035-B

Hu, Z. F., & Khan, M. S. (1997). Why Is China Growing So Fast? *Staff Papers, 44*(1), 103–131. doi:10.2307/3867499

Hung, C. T. (2008). The Articulated Process of Small Commercial Market Town and Spatial Capital Restruction: Case Study of Yiwu, Zhejiang Province, China. *Journal of Architecture and Planning, 9*(1), 1–20.

Hussain, J., Millman, C., & Matlay, H. (2006). SME financing in the UK and in China: A comparative perspective. *Journal of Small Business and Enterprise Development, 13*(4), 584–599. doi:10.1108/14626000610705769

Ikenberry, G. J. (2008). The Rise of China and the Future of the West - Can the Liberal System Survive. *Foreign Affairs*, *87*(1), 23–37.

Jarvis, R., Curran, J., Kitching, J., & Lightfoot, G. (2000). The use of quantitative and qualitative criteria in the measurement of performance in small firms. *Journal of Small Business and Enterprise Development*, *7*(2), 123–134. doi:10.1108/EUM0000000006834

Jaworski, B. J., & Kohli, A. K. (1993). Market orientation: Antecedents and consequences. *Journal of Marketing*, *57*(3), 53–70. doi:10.1177/002224299305700304

Jennings, P., & Beaver, G. (1997). The performance and competitive advantage of small firms: A management perspective. *International Small Business Journal*, *15*(2), 63–75. doi:10.1177/0266242697152004

Kale, D., & Little, S. (2007). From Imitation to Innovation: The Evolution of R&D Capabilities and Learning Processes in the Indian Pharmaceutical Industry. *Technology Analysis and Strategic Management*, *19*(5), 589–609. doi:10.1080/09537320701521317

Kaufmann, L., & Roesch, J.-F. (2012). Constraints to Building and Deploying Marketing Capabilities by Emerging Market Firms in Advanced Markets. *Journal of International Marketing*, *20*(4), 1–24. doi:10.1509/jim.11.0116

Kim, L., & Nelson, R. R. (2000). Introduction: technology and industrialisation in newly industrialising countries. In L. Kim & R. R. Nelson (Eds.), *Technology, Learning and Innovation: Experiences of Newly Industrialising Economies* (pp. 1–9). Cambridge, UK: Cambridge University Press.

Kojima, K. (2000). The "flying geese" model of Asian economic development: Origin, theoretical extensions, and regional policy implications. *Journal of Asian Economics*, *11*(4), 375–401. doi:10.1016/S1049-0078(00)00067-1

Kolvereid, L. (1992). Growth aspirations among Norwegian entrepreneurs. *Journal of Business Venturing*, *7*(3), 209–222. doi:10.1016/0883-9026(92)90027-O

Kotey, B., & Folker, C. (2007). Employee Training in SMEs: Effect of Size and Firm Type—Family and Nonfamily. *Journal of Small Business Management*, *45*(2), 214–238. doi:10.1111/j.1540-627X.2007.00210.x

Kuester, S., & Rauch, A. (2016). A job demands-resources perspective on salespersons' market intelligence activities in new product development. *Journal of Personal Selling & Sales Management, 36*(1), 19–39. doi:10.1080/08853134.2016.1142793

Lee, K. (2005). Making a Technological Catch-up: Barriers and opportunities. *Asian Journal of Technology Innovation, 13*(2), 97–131. doi:10.1080/19761597.2005.9668610

Leek, S., & Christodoulides, G. (2012). A framework of brand value in B2B markets: The contributing role of functional and emotional components. *Industrial Marketing Management, 41*(1), 106–114. doi:10.1016/j.indmarman.2011.11.009

Lerner, J. (2009). *Boulevard of Broken Dreams: Why Public Efforts to Boost Entrepreneurship and Venture Capital Have Failed – and What to Do About it*. Princeton, NJ: Princeton University Press. doi:10.1515/9781400831630

Li, L. (2017). China's manufacturing locus in 2025: With a comparison of "Made-in-China 2025" and "Industry 4.0". *Technological Forecasting and Social Change, 135*, 66–74. doi:10.1016/j.techfore.2017.05.028

Li, Y. (2006). Review and experience of mode of SME clusters in Guangdong. *Business Economics (Cleveland, Ohio), 7*, 58–59.

Li, Y., Liu, Y., & Zhao, Y. B. (2006). The role of market and entrepreneurship orientation and internal control in the new product development activities of Chinese firms. *Industrial Marketing Management, 35*(3), 336–347. doi:10.1016/j.indmarman.2005.05.016

Liang, G. (2007). Policy System on promoting SME innovation and entrepreneurship in China. *Torch High Technology Industry Development Center, Ministry of Science and Technology, China*. Retrieved October 10, 2018, from http://www.insme.info/documents/06_INSME2007_Liang.ppt

Liu, F.-H., Liu, H.-Y., & Lin, T.-L. (2008). The competence and constraints of brand building for contract manufacturers. *Journal of Brand Management, 15*(6), 412–432. doi:10.1057/bm.2008.8

Liu, F.-H., Tsou, H.-T., & Chen, L.-J. (2013). The impact of OEM supplier initiatives on buyer competence development: The moderating roles of collaborative relationship and competitive environment. *Asia Pacific Journal of Management*, *30*(4), 1285–1303. doi:10.100710490-011-9266-4

Liu, H., & Li, K. (2002). Strategic Implications of Emerging Chinese Multinationals: The Haier Case Study. *European Management Journal*, *20*(6), 699–706. doi:10.1016/S0263-2373(02)00119-6

Liu, Q. (2001). Review of mode of Sunan, Wenzhou, Pearl River. *China Situation and National Power*, *4*, 23–24.

Liu, X. (2008). SME development in China: A policy perspective on SME industrial clustering. In SME in Asia and Globalization. ERIA Research Project Report, 2007-5.

Loo, T., & Davies, G. (2006). Branding China: The Ultimate Challenge in Reputation Management? *Corporate Reputation Review*, *9*(3), 198–210. doi:10.1057/palgrave.crr.1550025

Maddison, A. (1998). *Chinese economic performance in the long run*. Paris: Development Centre of the Organisation for Economic Co-Operation and Development.

Malerba, F., & Nelson, R. (2011). Learning and catching up in different sectoral systems: Evidence from six industries. *Industrial and Corporate Change*, *20*(6), 1645–1675. doi:10.1093/icc/dtr062

Malik, R. (1997). *Chinese Entrepreneurs in the Economic Development of China*. London: Praeger.

Marquardt, A. J. (2013). Relationship quality as a resource to build industrial brand equity when products are uncertain and future-based. *Industrial Marketing Management*, *42*(8), 1386–1397. doi:10.1016/j.indmarman.2013.07.017

Marshall, A. (1920). *Principes of Economics* (8th ed.). London: Macmillan.

Michell, P., King, J., & Reast, J. (2001). Brand values related to industrial products. *Industrial Marketing Management*, *30*(5), 415–425. doi:10.1016/S0019-8501(99)00097-8

Mitussis, D. (2010). SME innovation in Zhejiang, China: Potential constraints to development of widespread innovation. *Journal of Knowledge-based Innovation in China*, *2*(1), 89–105. doi:10.1108/17561411011032007

Morgan, N. A., Vorhies, D. W., & Mason, C. H. (2009). Market orientation, marketing capabilities, and firm performance. *Strategic Management Journal*, *30*(8), 909–920. doi:10.1002mj.764

Narver, J. C., & Slater, S. F. (1990). The Effect of a Market Orientation on Business Profitability. *Journal of Marketing*, *54*(4), 20–35. doi:10.1177/002224299005400403

Naughton, B. (2007). *The Chinese economy: Transitions and growth*. Cambridge, MA: The MIT Press.

Ng, S. C. H., Rungtusanatham, J. M., Zhao, X., & Ivanova, A. (2015). TQM and environmental uncertainty levels: Profits, fit, and firm performance. *International Journal of Production Research*, *53*(14), 4266–4286. doi:10.1080/00207543.2014.994076

OECD. (2016). *Financing SMEs and Entrepreneurs 2016- An OECD Scoreboard*. Paris: OECD Publishing.

Orser, B. J., Hogarth-Scott, S., & Riding, A. L. (2000). Performance, firm size, and management problem solving. *Journal of Small Business Management*, *38*(4), 42–58.

Ozawa, T. (2005). *Institutions, industrial upgrading, and economic performance in Japan: the 'flying-geese' paradigm of catch-up growth*. Cheltenham, UK: Edward Elgar. doi:10.4337/9781845425678

Papadopoulos, N., & Heslop, L. (2002). Country equity and country branding: Problems and prospects. *Journal of Brand Management*, *9*(4), 294–314. doi:10.1057/palgrave.bm.2540079

Pistrui, D., Huang, W., Oksoy, D., Jing, Z., & Welsch, H. (2001). Entrepreneurship in China: Characteristics, Attributes, and Family Forces Shaping the Emerging Private Sector. *Family Business Review*, *XIV*, 2, 141–152.

Porter, M. E. (2000). Location, competition, and economic development: Local clusters in a global economy. *Economic Development Quarterly*, *14*(1), 15–20. doi:10.1177/089124240001400105

Poutziouris, P., Wang, Y., & Chan, S. (2002). Chinese entrepreneurship: The development of small family firms in China. *Journal of Small Business and Enterprise Development*, *9*(4), 383–399. doi:10.1108/14626000210450568

Pye, L. (2000). Asian values: From dynamos to dominoes? In L. Harrison & S. Huntington (Eds.), *Culture matters how values shape human progress* (pp. 244–255). New York: Basic Books.

Rakthin, S., Calantone, R. J., & Wang, J. F. (2016). Managing market intelligence: The comparative role of absorptive capacity and market orientation. *Journal of Business Research*, *69*(12), 5569–5577. doi:10.1016/j.jbusres.2016.03.064

Richardson, P. (1999). *Economic change in China, c. 1800-1950*. Cambridge, UK: Cambridge University Press. doi:10.1017/CBO9781139171229

Robson, P. J., & Obeng, B. A. (2008). The barriers to growth in Ghana. *Small Business Economics*, *30*(4), 385–403. doi:10.100711187-007-9046-1

Simpson, M., Padmore, J., & Newman, N. (2012). Towards a new model of success and performance in SMEs. *International Journal of Entrepreneurial Behaviour & Research*, *18*(3), 264–285. doi:10.1108/13552551211227675

Singh, R. K., Garg, S. K., & Deshmukh, S. G. (2009). The competitiveness of SMEs in a globalized economy: Observations from China and India. *Management Research Review*, *33*(1), 54–65. doi:10.1108/01409171011011562

Sirmon, D. G., Arregle, J.-L., Hitt, M. A., & Webb, J. W. (2008). The role of family influence in firms' strategic responses to threat of imitation. *Entrepreneurship Theory and Practice*, *32*(6), 979–998. doi:10.1111/j.1540-6520.2008.00267.x

SME Dubai. (2014). *The state of Small & Medium Enterprises (SMEs) in Dubai – a Report by Dubai SMEs- An agency of the Department of Economic Development*. Retrieved December 1, 2018, from http://www.sme.ae/studiesandresearchdocument/sme_report_english.pdf

Steinfeld, E. S. (2004). China's shallow integration: Networked production and the new challenges for late internationalisation. *World Development*, *32*(11), 1971–1987. doi:10.1016/j.worlddev.2004.04.003

Sun, S. L. (2009). Internationalization Strategy of MNEs from Emerging Economies: The Case of Huawei. *Multinational Business Review*, *17*(2), 129–156. doi:10.1108/1525383X200900013

The State Council. (2017). *China remains world's largest manufacturer and major network power the people republic of China*. Retrieved October 23, from http://english.gov.cn/state_council/ministries/2017/02/17/content_281475570357858.htm

Thomas, S. C. (2007). China's Economic development from 1860 to the present: the roles of sovereignty and the global economy. *Forum on Public policy: A Journal of the Oxford Round Table. Academic OneFile*. Retrieved October 23, from https://link.galegroup.com/apps/doc/A244026614/AONE?u=googlescholar&sid=AONE&xid=64fb8a7d

Tian, M., Li, D., & Yin, X. (2012). Literature Review about Strategic emerging industries for China. *Interdisciplinary Journal of Contemporary Research in Business*, *4*(7), 42–48.

Tylecote, A., & Macdonald, S. (2008). *Information for innovation in Chinese firms: personal relationships versus personal networks*. Paper presented at 1st Asian Management and Entrepreneurship Workshop: New and Old Chinese, Indian and Japanese Firms, European Institute for Advanced Studies in Management (EIASM), Brussels, Belgium.

Uddin, J., Parvin, S., & Rahman, M. L. (2013). Factors Influencing Importance of Country of Brand and Country of Manufacturing in Consumer Product Evaluation. *International Journal of Business and Management*, *8*(4), 65–74. doi:10.5539/ijbm.v8n4p65

Vos, J. P. (2005). Developing strategic self descriptions of SMEs. *Technovation*, *25*(9), 989–999. doi:10.1016/j.technovation.2004.02.014

Walker, E., & Brown, A. (2004). What success factors are important to small business owners? *International Small Business Journal*, *22*(6), 577–594. doi:10.1177/0266242604047411

Wiklund, J., Davidsson, P., & Delmar, F. (2003). What do they think and feel about growth? An expectancy-value approach to small business managers' attitudes toward growth. *Entrepreneurship Theory and Practice*, *27*(3), 247–270. doi:10.1111/1540-8520.t01-1-00003

Wolff, J. A., & Pett, T. L. (2000). Internationalization of small firms: An examination of export competitive patterns, firm size, and export performance. *Journal of Small Business Management*, *38*(2), 34–47.

Wonglimpiyarat, J. (2015). New economics of innovation: Strategies to support high-tech SMEs. *The Journal of High Technology Management Research*, *26*(2), 186–195. doi:10.1016/j.hitech.2015.09.006

Woo, W. T. (1997). Chinese economic growth: sources and prospects. In M. Fouquin & F. Lemoine (Eds.), *The Chinese Economy*. London: Economica.

World Bank. (1997). *China 2020: development challenges in the New Century*. Washington, DC: World Bank.

Wubbeke, J., & Conrad, B. (2015). 'Industrie 4.0': Will German Technology Help China Catch Up with the West? *MERICS China Monitor*. Retrieve December 2, from https://www.merics.org/sites/default/files/2017-09/China_Monitor_23_Industrie40_EN.pdf

Xie, X. M., Zeng, S. X., & Tam, C. M. (2010). Overcoming barriers to innovation in SMEs in China: A perspective based cooperation network. *Innovation, Management. Policy & Practice*, *12*(3), 298–310. doi:10.5172/impp.12.3.298

Xiong, M. H., Tor, S. B., Bhatnagar, R., Khoo, L. P., & Venkat, S. (2006). A DSS approach to managing customer enquiry stage. *International Journal of Production Economics*, *103*(1), 332–346. doi:10.1016/j.ijpe.2005.08.008

Yan, H.-D. (2012). Entrepreneurship, Competitive Strategies, and Transforming Firms from OEM to OBM in Taiwan. *Journal of Asia-Pacific Business*, *13*(1), 16–36. doi:10.1080/10599231.2012.629877

Yang, J., Liu, H., Gao, S., & Li, Y. (2012). Technological innovation of firms in China: Past, present, and future. *Asia Pacific Journal of Management*, *29*(3), 819–840. doi:10.100710490-010-9243-3

Yeung, H. (2006). Change and continuity in Southeast Asian Chinese business. *Asia Pacific Journal of Management*, *23*(3), 229–254. doi:10.100710490-006-9007-2

Zahra, S. A., & George, G. (2002). Absorptive capacity: A review, reconceptualization, and extension. *Academy of Management Review*, *27*(2), 185–203. doi:10.5465/amr.2002.6587995

Zeng, D. Z. (2012). China's Special Economic Zones and Industrial Clusters: The Engines for Growth. *Journal of International Commerce. Economic Policy*, *3*(3), 1–28.

Zhang, X., Ma, X., Wang, Y., Li, X., & Huo, D. (2016). What drives the internationalization of Chinese SMEs? The joint effects of international entrepreneurship characteristics, network ties, and firm ownership. *International Business Review*, *25*(2), 522–534. doi:10.1016/j.ibusrev.2015.09.001

Zhu, Y., Wittmann, X., & Peng, M. W. (2012). Institution-based barriers to innovation in SMEs in China. *Asia Pacific Journal of Management*, *29*(4), 1131–1142. doi:10.100710490-011-9263-7

Zhu, Y. M., & Sanderson, J. W. (2009). The key obstacles and countermeasure against development of innovative SMEs in China. *China Soft Science*, *9*, 23–31.

ENDNOTES

1 SME Dubai (2014). The state of Small & Medium Enterprises (SMEs) in Dubai – a Report by Dubai SMEs- An agency of the Department of Economic Development. Available at http://www.sme.ae/studiesandresearchdocument/sme_report_english.pdf

2 Source of definition for Chinese SMEs: http://www.stats.gov.cn/statsinfo/auto2073/201310/t20131031_450691.html

3 China Bureau of Statistics: http://www.stats.gov.cn/english/statisticaldata/AnnualData/

4 For instance, in 2002, the National People's Congress Standing Committee passed the SME Promotion Law (source: Zhu et al., 2012).

Chapter 6
Survey of Financing Options and Key Challenges Faced by SMEs in the UAE:
Economic Environment, Finance, and Regulatory Landscape

Abderazak Bakhouche
Higher Colleges of Technology, UAE

Randa Elchaar
Higher Colleges of Technology, UAE

Manal Emam
Higher Colleges of Technology, UAE

ABSTRACT

Innovation has an essential impact on SME creation, and governments are concerned with stimulating adoption of innovation by SMEs to strengthen growth and development and adapt to the ever-changing business environment. Innovation by SMEs requires operating within a generally embracing economic and financial environment. The availability of various formal and informal financing options and a growing economy encouraging consumer spending, innovation-driven investment spending and export, and a policy favoring enhancing private equity, economic diversification, and market competition are incipient factors contributing to a culture of private initiatives by entrepreneurs and SMEs.

DOI: 10.4018/978-1-5225-9377-5.ch006

INTRODUCTION

Policymakers highly celebrate the role of entrepreneurship and Small and Medium Enterprises (SMEs) in the economy due to the impact on employment, innovation, and social stability. It has become essential for governments to promote an entrepreneurship culture among individuals and innovation among SMEs to seek to strengthen financial position on a global level. As a result, SMEs constitute the mainstay of most economies in the world. SMEs represent more than 95% of registered firms and 50% of employment worldwide and contribute more than 35% of GDP in many emerging markets (Alibhai et al, 2017).

In recent years, driven by the necessity of economic diversification, the UAE government has recognized the multiplier effect of SMEs, and embarked upon a program enhancing the capabilities of the SME sector, particularly in the field of innovation (Issac, 2015). The UAE vision 2021 aims to boost SMEs' contribution to GDP to reach 70%. A report on SMEs in the MENA region suggests that for every ten successful new enterprises, about $1.5 billion in current valuations and more than 2,500 jobs creation (Alkasmi et al, 2018). This "multiplier effect" of entrepreneurship in the economy showcases the contribution of entrepreneurs and SMEs in achieving a policy's economic and social objectives such as economic stability and development. Flourishing SME ecosystem is essential for a thriving economic and social structure, characterized by better allocation of resources driven by inherent innovation, efficiency, and competitiveness. Entrepreneurship is recognized as an essential factor of innovation and employment, hence leading to economic growth and increased well-being.

SMEs generate most of the new jobs and help diversify a country's economic base through the promotion of innovation, new goods and services, and integrating women and youth into the economic mainstream. Despite all these benefits, SMEs remain significantly underserved by financial institutions. Research indicates that the credit gap that formal SMEs confront is about $1 trillion (Alibhai et al, 2017). Over ten million of population mostly youth, and a GDP approaching half a trillion USD, the UAE has developed to become a hub of innovation and entrepreneurship in the MENA region. It is increasingly and rapidly embracing the digitisation and digitalisation with evolving institutional, infrastructure, and regulatory framework.

The United Arab Emirates (UAE) has increased its propensity for digital adoption and access to and use of technology. The whole population owns a smartphone device, and 90% of the population connect daily and connects online an average of three hours. The high smartphone penetration rates in the UAE has increased the number of active social media users. More than a third of the population are active social media users (Alkasmi et al, 2018). The demand for digital content and services has resulted from the increase in smartphone penetration and online accessibility.

The oil price slump in 2014 has led decision-makers to re-think growth and development towards increasing the share of the non-oil sector in the economy. The policy is increasingly relying on introducing institutional facilities and promoting the entrepreneurship culture among the youth to move towards a post-oil economy. The SMEs sector employs 42% of Dubai workforce and contributes 40% of the emirate's GDP. However, the performance of the SME sector seems to lag as reported by Dubai SME's where access to funding coupled with promoting risk-taking culture (introducing the bankruptcy laws). Policy efforts have looked at reducing unnecessary red tape and regulations concerning setting-up the enterprises with clear post signs. Statistics show that less than 25% of surveyed SMEs used bank finance in the last five years. Personnel money/savings are the dominant source of finance, as 80% of the respondents indicated personal money as a means of financing. In the UAE, SMEs play a pivotal role in the development and restructuring of the economy which leads this fundamental underpinning the economic, private equity, and banking environment describing first, the economic structure of the UAE and surveys the recent trends in economic conditions about SMEs in an economic expansion. Second, a brief analysis of banking performance as a primary source of finance for SMEs. Third, financing options for SMEs in the UAE. There are three central public microfinance schemes available in the UAE: Khalifa Fund for Enterprise Development, Mohammed Bin Rashid Fund for SMEs, and Ruwad Sharjah Entrepreneurship Foundation.

BRIEF SURVEY OF ECONOMIC STRUCTURE

The UAE is a high-income country with a GDP per capita of USD 40,700 (USD11,300 in PPP terms) and a population of 9.3 million in 2017. The UN classifies the UAE as being a high-ranking country in many areas, including human development, doing Business report, economic freedom, and governance. The UAE has launched a program of economic development that aims at shifting the structure of the economy away from oil dependency. Many measures have been adopted to overcome the institutional and structural impediments to create an economic system that sustainably creates value through private initiatives and innovation. The UAE economy is the most diversified economy in the Oil producing countries club and MENA region.

Table 1 shows the monetary contribution of economic sectors and industries, both oil and non-oil, in the UAE from 2010 to 2017. Table 2 shows the percentage share of economic sector and industry in the economy. Tables 1 and 2 show that UAE has achieved higher levels of economic diversification less than a decade. The non-oil sector had increased from about 60% in 2011 to about 80% in 2016-19. The economy becomes reliant on the non-oil sector with almost 80% of production stemming. It includes wholesale and retail trade, transport, and government, financial, professional, and personal services such as education, health care, and real estate services. The manufacturing sector accounts for 16%, with machinery and electronics being its most important component (Table 2). Tourism sector became dominant particularly for Dubai accounting about 10% of GDP in 2017, 15% employment, and is a source of foreign exchange. Tourist arrivals by the increase in critical indicators such as occupancy rates, and tourism overall receipts with continuous investment in infrastructure including accommodation, entertainment and culture sites, shopping malls, sun-related sites, and services. The role of the aviation sector in transporting tourists support. The UAE is now the tourist destination in the MENA region, with relatively the highest per capita spending per tourist, well ahead of competitors such as Turkey and Egypt. Investment in the sector has increased, implying a better quality of service and facilities (European Investment Bank, 2015).

OVERVIEW OF BANKING

Financial system, including financial market and financial institutions, plays a significant role in the economy by ensuring efficient allocation of resources, especially when providing finance to the real sector. Many studies provided evidence for the role of finance and financial deepening and breadth on economic growth and development.

With assets representing about 200% of GDP compared to 60% financial market capitalisation to GDP, the UAE banking sector is the second largest,

Table 1. Distribution of Gross Domestic Product by economic activities, 2010 – 2017 (in millions of AED)

Economic Sectors/ Activities	2010	2011	2012	2013	2014	2015	2016	2017
Non-Financial Corporations	935,739	1,152,044	1,226,010	1,257,324	1,284,246	1,105,990	1,090,929	1,171,448
Agriculture, Forestry and Fishing	8,125	8,653	8,789	9,223	9,468	9,746	10,176	10,721
Mining and Quarrying (inc. crude oil and natural gas)	331,042	501,453	537,337	528,820	505,157	286,970	253,148	313,052
Manufacturing	84,803	99,402	105,690	108,085	115,141	116,380	117,808	123,422
Electricity, gas, and Water Supply; Waste Mngt	26,472	30,934	34,763	35,705	38,825	46,471	48,719	53,315
Construction	116,939	115,806	112,728	115,646	122,268	127,693	123,820	122,749
Wholesale and Retail Trade; Repair of Motor Vehicles and Motorcycles	126,794	130,089	137,178	150,680	155,774	160,969	170,458	172,288
Transportation and Storage	61,790	72,094	75,824	79,598	84,260	89,983	80,434	82,461
Accommodation and Food Service Activities	18,902	22,027	24,375	28,564	31,968	32,402	31,631	32,357
Information and Communication	30,988	31,199	31,937	32,875	36,182	37,929	40,162	41,347
Financial and insurance activities	73,237	77,536	83,747	100,537	115,541	125,221	131,646	134,773
Real Estate Activities	52,660	56,711	65,148	66,070	74,400	81,184	89,357	89,432
Professional, Scientific and Technical Activities	32,486	33,031	34,033	36,686	39,118	40,783	42,238	43,425
Administrative and Support Service Activities	18,385	19,788	21,242	23,643	25,871	27,377	29,814	31,453
Public Admin; Defense; Compulsory Social Security	55,268	58,242	65,926	74,809	80,735	84,040	88,673	98,786
Education	9,147	11,388	13,193	14,000	15,648	16,237	18,312	18,836
Human Health and Social work Activities	6,546	8,923	12,014	14,866	16,012	16,629	18,162	19,298
Arts, Recreation and Other Service Activities	6,010	5,442	6,307	6,075	6,545	7,012	7,836	8,136
Activities of Households as Employers	4,651	5,104	5,451	6,788	7,608	8,225	8,854	9,156
Total	**1,064,244**	**1,287,821**	**1,375,684**	**1,432,670**	**1,480,521**	**1,315,251**	**1,311,248**	**1,405,007**
Total Non-oil	**733,202**	**786,369**	**838,347**	**903,850**	**975,364**	**1,028,280**	**1,058,101**	**1,091,955**

Table 2. Percentage distribution of Gross Domestic Product by economic activities, 2010 – 2017 (in %)

Economic Sectors/ Activities	2010	2011	2012	2013	2014	2015	2016	2017
Non-Financial Corporations	87.9	89.5	89.1	87.8	86.7	84.1	83.2	83.4
Agriculture, Forestry and Fishing	0.8	0.7	0.6	0.6	0.6	0.7	0.8	0.8
Mining and Quarrying (inc. crude oil and natural gas)	31.1	38.9	39.1	36.9	34.1	21.8	19.3	22.3
Manufacturing	8	7.7	7.7	7.5	7.8	8.8	9	8.8
Electricity, gas, and Water Supply; Waste Mngt	2.5	2.4	2.5	2.5	2.6	3.5	3.7	3.8
Construction	11	9	8.2	8.1	8.3	9.7	9.4	8.7
Wholesale and Retail Trade; Repair of Motor Vehicles and Motorcycles	11.9	10.1	10	10.5	10.5	12.2	13	12.3
Transportation and Storage	5.8	5.6	5.5	5.6	5.7	6.8	6.1	5.9
Accommodation and Food Service Activities	1.8	1.7	1.8	2	2.2	2.5	2.4	2.3
Information and Communication	2.9	2.4	2.3	2.3	2.4	2.9	3.1	2.9
Financial and insurance activities	6.9	6	6.1	7	7.8	9.5	10	9.6
Real Estate Activities	4.9	4.4	4.7	4.6	5	6.2	6.8	6.4
Professional, Scientific and Technical Activities	3.1	2.6	2.5	2.6	2.6	3.1	3.2	3.1
Administrative and Support Service Activities	1.7	1.5	1.5	1.7	1.7	2.1	2.3	2.2
Public Admin; Defense; Compulsory Social Security	5.2	4.5	4.8	5.2	5.5	6.4	6.8	7
Education	0.9	0.9	1	1	1.1	1.2	1.4	1.3
Human Health and Social work Activities	0.6	0.7	0.9	1	1.1	1.3	1.4	1.4
Arts, Recreation and Other Service Activities	0.6	0.4	0.5	0.4	0.4	0.5	0.6	0.6
Activities of Households as Employers	0.4	0.4	0.4	0.5	0.5	0.6	0.7	0.7
Total	100	100	100	100	100	100	100	100
Total Non-oil	68.9	61.1	60.9	63.1	65.9	78.2	80.7	77.7

within the GCC and large MENA regions, managing more than USD710bn of assets, USD400bn of deposits and USD500bn. The overall banking sector shows adequate levels of liquidity and capitalisation, and sound quality of assets and a positive record of profitability.

As of 2018, there were 22 locally incorporated banks, six banks from GCC and 21 foreign banks. Increasing consolidation activities characterize the sector. The year 2017 witnessed the merger of the First Gulf Bank with the National Bank of Abu Dhabi, resulting in a decline in the number of branches of locally incorporated banks from 810 in of 2017 to 751. The sector is highly concentrated at the top, but fragmented at the bottom, with the top three largest banks accounting for about half of the sector's assets, and 92% of GDP in 2017. However, the HHI index, a measure of concentration, has remained at levels below 1,100 n 2013-17 in terms of assets, loans, and deposits. The score is one of the lowest in the MENA banking markets. Studies have shown that banking in the UAE exhibits a higher degree of competition in regional comparison. However, the high concentration ratio may suggest less competitive pressure since banks still enjoy relatively high net interest margin (NIM)M.

The Central Bank of the UAE (CBUAE has the mandate of supervising and regulating banking in the country. Recently, the focus of the CBUAE is to improve the soundness and stability of the system by adopting and implementing internationally recognised prudential norms, to make supervision a more risk-based. Recent data show (Table 5) that despite the impact of the global economic slowdown and plunge in oil price impacting overall growth, the UAE banking sector has remained mostly resilient and in good shape.

Reports have indicated that default in lending has remained at similar levels in recent years. However, the default rates were relatively higher for the Small and Medium Enterprises (SME) and retail sectors compared with the other sectors (Central Bank of the UAE, 2017). Table 7 shows that banks have reduced their lending exposure to SMEs between 2014 and 2018. Table 8 shows the non-performing loans in the UAE and selected MENA countries. Table 8 shows that non-performing loans is higher in the UAE compared to MENA countries and World average. Recently, regulation has focused on shielding quality of assets and increasing bank stability, but this may have increased running costs and capital requirements for lenders, creating pressure in risky assets.

Table 7 shows that banks continue to be the primary source of external financing for the UAE private sector, as a credit to the private sector represents

Table 3. Selected banking sector statistics (various sources)

	2014	2015	2016	2017
Total Bank Assets (AED bn)	2,233,310	2,405,777	2,534,627	2,614,062
Total assets growth	8.7%	7.4%	5.2%	3.1%
Loan to deposits	97%	99.7%	99.4%	
Capital ratios				
Regulatory capital to risk-weighted assets	18.4%	18.3%	18.9%	18.6%
Tier 1 capital ratio	16.2%	16.5%	17.4%	16.6%
Assets quality				
NPLs (AED, bn)	96.01	92.77	100.45	117.29
NPLs ratio	6.7%	6.0%	6.1%	6.7%
Provision coverage ratio	102.0%	109.8%	110.2%	107.1%
Profitability and earnings				
ROE	17.4%	17.3%	10.7%	10.8%
ROA	2.4%	1.6%	1.7%	1.5%
NIM	2.7%	2.7%	2.5%	2.4%
The cost to income ratio	34.2%	34.8%	34.6%	39.1%
Noninterest expenses to gross income (%)	36.4	38	38	39.1
Liquidity				
Eligible Liquid Assets Ratio (ELAR)	15.7%	17.4%	16.2%	18.2%
Advanced to stable resources ratio		87.1%	86.2%	84.5%
Liquid domestic and foreign assets to total assets	15.85%	17.49%	15.89%	17.12%
Liquid domestic and foreign assets to demand deposits ratio	96.89%	108.77%	100.86%	108.58%
Domestic Credit facilities to total domestic liabilities ratio	62.73%	63.01%	63.08%	61.65%
Domestic Loans to domestic deposits ratio	102.25%	107.98%	108.27%	102.76%
Domestic and foreign Credit to assets ratio	59.79%	59.92%	60.25%	58.66%
Credit to the private sector to total assets ratio	40.74%	41.10%	41.15%	40.33%
Credit to private sector to total domestic credit	73.50%	73.74%	73.95%	74.79%

about 75% of total credit in 2014-2018. However, bank lending to SMEs remains limited in UAE, with a share of SMEs lending to total lending of only about 15%. This compares favourably to Morocco, which has a much lower share of lending to SMEs of about 10% but favourably to Egypt (5%) or Jordan (10%).

Table 4. Bank Credit to Residents by Economic Activity

	In Millions of AED					In Percentage				
Year	**2014**	**2015**	**2016**	**2017**	**2018**	**2014**	**2015**	**2016**	**2017**	**2018**
1) Agriculture	2,698	1,559	1,374	2,127	1,984	0.21%	0.11%	0.09%	0.15%	0.13%
2) Mining and Quarrying	9,181	11,922	13,550	12,101	14,734	0.72%	0.86%	0.93%	0.83%	0.98%
3) Manufacturing	65,140	69,110	69,300	75,236	76,921	5.10%	5.00%	4.76%	5.18%	5.10%
3.1 Food, Beverages and Tobacco	6,463	6,516	5,817	7,043	6,252	0.51%	0.47%	0.40%	0.48%	0.41%
3.2 Textile and Leather Products	1,100	1,477	1,365	1,284	1,459	0.09%	0.11%	0.09%	0.09%	0.10%
3.3 Furniture and Other Wood Products	1,789	2,528	2,403	2,786	2,538	0.14%	0.18%	0.17%	0.19%	0.17%
3.4 Paper And Paper Products	1,341	1,992	1,958	2,374	2,368	0.10%	0.14%	0.13%	0.16%	0.16%
3.5 Chemicals, petroleum & Petro-Chemicals	12,693	17,480	17,266	16,123	19,881	0.99%	1.27%	1.19%	1.11%	1.32%
3.6 Basic Metal Products (inc Aluminium)	15,428	12,524	13,683	14,501	15,306	1.21%	0.91%	0.94%	1.00%	1.01%
3.7 Fabricated Metal, machinery& equipment	6,724	6,869	6,857	13,245	11,230	0.53%	0.50%	0.47%	0.91%	0.74%
3.8 Other Manufactured Products	19,602	19,724	19,951	17,880	17,887	1.53%	1.43%	1.37%	1.23%	1.19%
4) Electricity, Gas and Water	18,937	20,482	18,455	16,735	16,998	1.48%	1.48%	1.27%	1.15%	1.13%
5) Construction and Real Estate	212,550	235,010	264,762	298,126	315,415	16.64%	17.02%	18.20%	20.52%	20.90%
5.1 Construction	59,119	60,501	66,861	68,686	71,781	4.63%	4.38%	4.60%	4.73%	4.76%
5.2 Real Estate	153,431	174,509	197,901	229,440	243,634	12.01%	12.63%	13.61%	15.79%	16.14%
6) Trade	155,761	161,689	155,821	152,769	154,048	12.19%	11.71%	10.71%	10.52%	10.21%
6.1 Wholesale	106,160	114,877	108,703	103,243	106,306	8.31%	8.32%	7.47%	7.11%	7.04%

continued on the following page

Table 4. Continued

Year	In Millions of AED 2014	2015	2016	2017	2018	In Percentage 2014	2015	2016	2017	2018
6.2 Retail	49,601	46,812	47,118	49,526	47,742	3.88%	3.39%	3.24%	3.41%	3.16%
7) Transport, Storage and Communication	56,494	59,155	63,507	54,935	51,496	4.42%	4.28%	4.37%	3.78%	3.41%
8) Financial Institutions	131,824	135,599	145,561	127,499	129,781	10.32%	9.82%	10.01%	8.78%	8.60%
9) Government	135,982	157,493	162,727	168,251	186,851	10.64%	11.40%	11.19%	11.58%	12.38%
10) Personal Loans for Business Purposes [1]	102,988	95,812	94,799	79,991	86,384	8.06%	6.94%	6.52%	5.51%	5.72%
11) Personal Loans for Consumption Purposes [2]	289,889	320,700	339,234	326,648	325,831	22.69%	23.22%	23.32%	22.49%	21.59%
12) All Others [3]	96,176	112,649	125,323	138,278	148,851	7.53%	8.16%	8.62%	9.52%	9.86%
Total	**1,277,620**	**1,381,180**	**1,454,413**	**1,452,696**	**1,509,294**	**100.00%**	**100.00%**	**100.00%**	**100.00%**	**100.00%**

Source: Central Bank of the UAE, 2019.

Table 5. Bank nonperforming loans to total gross loans (%)

	2009	2010	2011	2012	2013	2014	2015	2016	2017
Algeria	21.14	18.31	14.40	11.73	10.56	9.21	9.81	11.44	
UAE	4.18	5.27	6.09	7.13	6.74	5.64	5.20	5.30	6.44
Kuwait	11.46	8.95	6.98	5.19	3.64	2.89	2.37	2.22	1.95
Lebanon			3.76	3.79	3.97	4.01	4.20	4.88	5.67
Saudi Arabia	3.29	2.97	2.22	1.67	1.31	1.08	1.24	1.38	1.61
UK	3.51	3.95	3.96	3.59	3.11	1.65	1.01	0.94	0.73
USA	4.96	4.39	3.78	3.32	2.45	1.85	1.47	1.32	1.13
World	4.29	4.01	3.78	3.74	4.09	4.16	4.01	3.92	3.45

Source: World Bank, 2019.

In addition, the superior position of the UAE in regional finance is incipient in the Global Financial Centre Index, which places Dubai and Abu-Dhabi as the leading financial powerhouses in the MENA region. Both cities are home

Figure 1. Number of days required to starting a business (Source: World Bank, 2019)

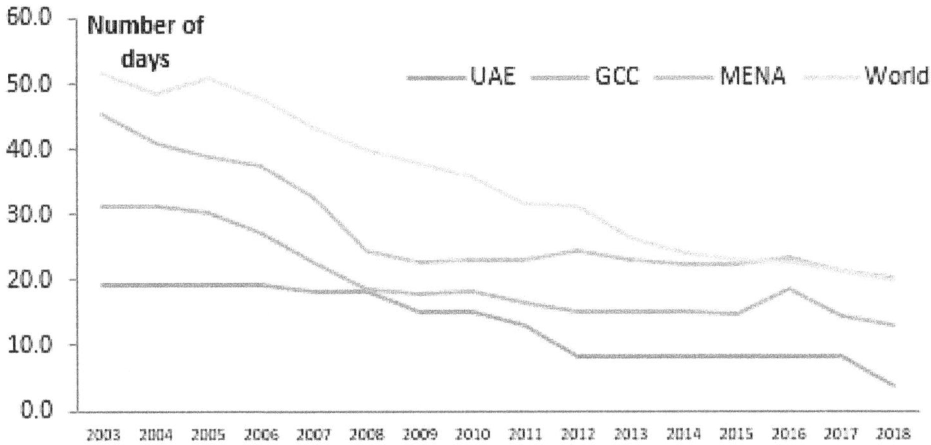

Figure 2. Number of procedures required for starting a business (Source: World Bank, 2019)

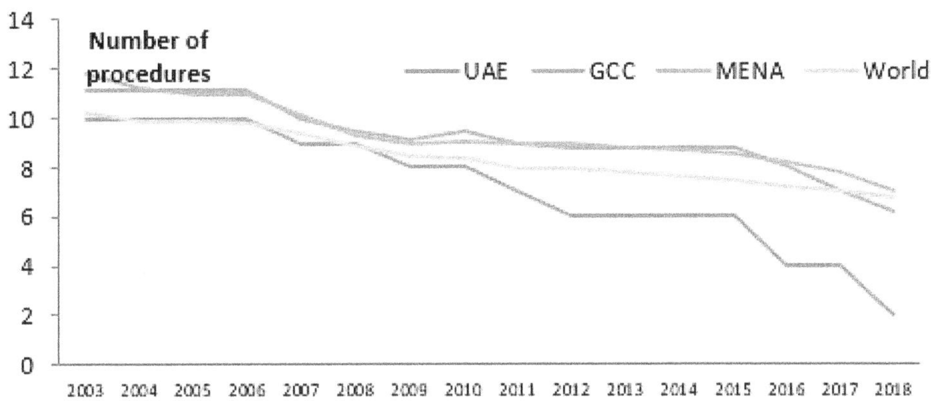

to other combined largest stock markets in terms of capitalization, following the Saudi Tadawul. Similarly, both cities are homes to commercial free zones: Dubai International Financial Centre (DIFC), and Abu Dhabi Global Market (ADGM). The DIFC promotes finance, banking, and insurance by attracting international financial institutions through independent regulation, law courts, and tax-friendly regime. The ADGM aims to become an international financial business hub. With an ecosystem of around 1,800 firms, DIFC provides an enabling platform for region-wide investment banking, M&A, commercial banking and innovative project finance, including securitization and asset-backed financing, insurance, and reinsurance providers, across the Middle East, Africa and South Asia (MEASA) region.

OVERVIEW OF BUSINESS ENVIRONMENT

The UAE has been improving the business environment to attract, and orient the public and private, both domestic and foreign investments, especially in the SME sector, towards increasing the contribution of non-oil economic activities in GDP (Smart SME MENA, 2019). On the other hand, the development and growth of SMEs are propelled by the progress in the business environment which hampers red tape, corruption, complex entry regulations, and transparency. The better the business environment, the more SMEs will be established and prospered. It is the leading region in terms of doing business, occupying the 11th position in the World Bank's Ease of Doing Business in 2019 compared to the 21st position in 2018, followed by Morocco at 60th. The UAE is far ahead in GCC: Bahrain (62), Oman (78), Qatar (83), Saudi Arabia (92), and Kuwait (97).

The World Bank report ranks 190 countries based on ease of doing business. A high ease of doing business ranking indicates that the regulatory environment is more conducive to the starting and operation of a firm. Ten topics determine the rankings, each consisting of several indicators, giving equal weight to each topic. The UAE shows superiority in many areas, including getting an electricity connection, paying taxes, dealing with construction permits, registering property, enforcing contracts, and protection of minority investors. Available statistics from the World Bank show that setting up a business in the UAE takes only 3.7 days only and two procedures.

Global Entrepreneurship Index assembled by the Global Entrepreneurship & Development Institute (GEDI) is an annual index that measures the quality and the scale of the entrepreneurial process in 137 countries worldwide and captures the strength and weakness of the entrepreneurial ecosystem. The UAE is ranked 26th globally and third in the MENA region in 2018. The UAE has world-leading scores (full score) in Networking and product innovation.

Biggest jumps in scores were in 4 pillars; Networking (+0.31), Product innovation (+0.17), Process innovation (+0.17) and Internationalization (+0.32). UAE scores in most of the pillars reflect its financial wealth and its high-quality human capital (Federal Competitiveness and Statistics Authority, 2019). The high ranking reflects that the UAE has made significant progress in nurturing and enhancing the business environment manifested by sound and efficient business regulation where entrepreneurs and SMEs can thrive.

SME FEDERAL LAW

The UAE issued Federal Law No 2 of 2014 on SMEs seeks to empower entrepreneurs, create a distinct legislative environment, and regulate the evolution of its national economy (Issac, 2015). It a legislative framework that supports and encourages entrepreneurship and initiating business ventures, and recognizes the prominent role of SMEs in the UAE's economic structure. The law defines an SME, which is "a firm or an individual venture engaged in small economic activity, including micro and medium." The law provides a unified definition of SMEs and classifies the SMEs community into three categories: micro, small, and medium enterprises. Each category is defined based on two or more criteria, including the size of employment, turnover, and capital investment. The law stipulates that definition may cater to the nature and type of the economic activities of the enterprise. The objectives of the law are:

- Nurturing of SMEs as a contributor to the economic development.
- Dissemination of information about the law and encouragement of research - Innovation, creativity, and fostering a culture that stimulates entrepreneurship.
- Coordinating the efforts of various entities involved in the development of SMEs.
- Boosting the competitiveness of SMEs to provide employment opportunities.
- Creating programs and initiatives aimed at the development of SMEs.
- Stimulating and supporting citizens to enter the SME's labour market to contribute to the country's GDP.

- Strengthening the country's position as an entrepreneurial hub.

The law offers incentives to SMEs in finance, marketing and promotion, provided associating. It embodies the following:

- Commitment of Federal Government entities to contract with local SMEs by not less than 10% of the total contracts of these entities towards meeting their purchasing; servicing and consulting needs (article 10).
- Commitment of companies in which the Federal Government owns more than 25% of capital, to contract with local SMEs by at least 5% of the total contracts of these companies.
- Reducing licensing costs.
- Enabling them to benefit from land granted to them for industrial or agricultural purposes, by relevant legislations and in coordination with the concerned authorities.
- Allocation of adequate space in the exhibitions that the UAE participates in abroad, to showcase products made by national SMEs, and providing necessary information to them about international markets by the regulations prescribed by this law.
- Organising local, specialized exhibitions for small and medium enterprises or facilitating their participation in domestic exhibitions to promote and market their products.
- Permissibility of exempting SMEs, for production purposes, from customs tax for equipment, raw materials, and intermediate goods.
- Exempting SMEs from bank guarantees that companies must pay per new worker.

Article (12) of the law protects the copyrights of inventors and patent owners. Article (17) addresses the methods of facilitating credit and funding services for activities undertaken by small and medium enterprises and establishments. The law state that the "Emirates Development Bank" helps in setting procedures for credit and funding facilitation for SMEs. The Bank is obligated to contribute no less than 10% of its total annual financing facilities to SMEs.

Conventional lenders are sometimes unwilling or unable to support SMEs given their limited assets or lack of a proven record of company operations. This makes it difficult for SMEs to make business and finance provisions can

Figure 3. Definition of SMEs

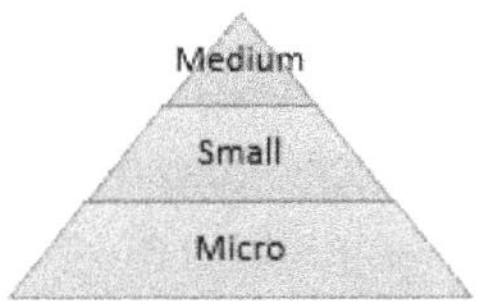

Trading		Manufacturing and services	
Employees	Sales	Employees	Sales
<= 75	<=AED 250mn	<= 250	<=AED 250mn
<= 35	<=AED 50mn	<= 100	<=AED 100mn
<= 9	<=AED 9mn	<= 20	<=AED 10mn

be expensive or inflexible (UAE Government, 2018). Article 18 stipulates that the CBUAE is to establish procedural and technical standards for providing commercial loans to SMEs, the role of the CBUAE is to increase institutional support so that SMEs will be in a better position to deal with market forces and have better access to marketing channels, domestic as well as for exports, increase capacity building at SMEs to help them offer better documentation to banks, consistent with internationally accepted accounting practices, and finally set up a well-designed and credible credit guarantee scheme in order "to decrease risks of default for potential lenders that may jeopardise financial stability (Issac, 2015).

SURVEY OF SMES

Government Efforts to Sustain SMEs

With SMEs markedly playing a pivotal role in UAE economy, the government has increasingly concentrated on developing the SME sector through various schemes, initiatives and policies, and improving the regulatory and institutional environment within which the SME sector is operating. Recent efforts towards understanding the profile, needs, and preferences of SMEs, streamlining the literature, and identifying the key challenges.

The definition of SMEs separates firms operating in the Trading sector and those operating in the manufacturing and services sector. The figure shows the SME definition in Dubai according to the sector, number of employees, and sales. For the Trading sector, SMEs are firms that have between 9 and

75 employees. On the other hand, Dubai considers SMEs operating in the manufacturing and services sectors as firms with several employees between 21 and 250. At the lower end, embraces another segment of SMEs, which accommodates the smaller "micro" enterprises with several employees of up to 9 in the trading sector, and up to 20 in the manufacturing and services sector.

SMEs tend not to have assets to pledge, and others do not maintain proper account books. Kilani also noted the problem of some expatriates fleeing the country if they find themselves in financial troubles, leaving unsettled debts. The UAE has taken steps to remedy some of these broader issues:

- In March 2016, after increasing levels of default in the SME corporate sector, banks agreed to halt criminal prosecutions for bounced checks drawn by SMEs immediately and, instead, work with individuals to restructure their debts.
- In September 2016, the UAE announced a new bankruptcy law that, according to Fitch rating agency, could encourage banks to increase lending to SMEs because it sets out a framework for insolvency proceedings and debt restructuring.

The SME ecosystem in the UAE consists of trading, manufacturing, and services sector activities. The large share of SMEs is active in the trading and services sector, spanning from a variety of sub-sectors from a trade, technical activities, real estate services, catering, and hospitality. Recent SMEs and start-ups are mostly-related to scientific and technical innovation-related activities. This broad range of sector-related SME activities may underline the role envisioned by policymakers that SMEs can play within the broad economic diversification strategy, and reducing dependence on the oil-export sector. The growing active of entrepreneurship in innovation and technology-related sector highlights the critical role that SMEs in creating new sources of value added, productivity and therefore, future prosperity.

In the UAE, there are about 400,000 SMEs, representing more than 94% of the total number of companies operating in the country, and 86% of the private sector's workforce. SMEs contribute nearly 60% of GDP, and this is estimated to grow to 70%by 2021. To compare, SME contribution to a GDP was 59% in Indonesia, 47% in Singapore, 37% in Thailand, 35% in the Philippines and 33% in Malaysia (Deloitte, 2015).

Table 6. Key Business Challenges (SMEs): 2001-2012

	2011	2012	2013	2014	2015	2016	2017	2018
Cost of operations	28%	30%	13%	26%	14%	7%	11%	23%
Increase in operational expenses			1%			3%	10%	14%
Impact of oil prices				2%	2%	2%		3%
Availability/cost of materials	6.60%	2%	1%	1%	2%		1%	3%
Availability/ cost of labour	5.40%	3%	1%	3%	5%			3%
Cost of rental/leasing	6.40%	13%	10%	20%	5%	2%		
Cost of utilities	9.30%	11%						
Cost of fuel		1%						
Competition	41.30%	17%	11%	20%	10%	8%	26%	46%
Delay in payments/ receivables	7.50%	9%	1%	2%	4%	6%	9%	34%
Demand/market conditions	40.70%	1%	1%	7%	5%	4%	9%	27%
Inflation				6%			2%	
VAT implementation							12%	18%
Government regulation/fees	18%	35%	5%	5%	7%	1%	4%	9%
Government regulation	7.70%	13%						
Government fees	10%	22%						
Delay/ no new project								8%
Availability of Bank finance/cost of finance	9%	5%	1%	1%	3%	2%	2%	5%
Global/regional economic conditions					1%	1%	1%	5%
No negative factors			64%	38%	55%	72%	37%	12%
Currency fluctuations	2.50%		1%	1%	1%			1%
Other	1.90%		3%	1%		1%	1%	1%

Source: Data are obtained from the quarterly publication by SME Dubai: "SMEs Business \Optimism Survey." All data are for Quarter 4 in each year. www.sme.ae

The majority of SMEs in the UAE (73%) operate in the wholesale and retail trade sector, 16% are engaged in the services sector, and 11% in the manufacturing sector (Issac, 2015). In Dubai, 95% of firms established belong to the SME sector. Micro firms account for 72% of the overall business count in Dubai, followed by Small and Medium firms accounting for 18% and 5% of the business count, respectively. In terms of a sector-wise split of the number of establishments, the Trading sector accounts for a majority (57%) of SMEs in Dubai, followed by the Services sector (35%), and subsequently followed by the Manufacturing sector (8%). Business licenses issued in Dubai reached 15,203 in 2008; however the number fell significantly to 11,743 in 2009, at the peak of the global financial crisis. As recovery set in 2010, the number of licenses issued increased to 14,406 and reached 16,688 in 2012. 5 Commercial licenses account for the majority of licenses issued in Dubai (75% of licenses issued from 2009 to 2012), followed by Professional licenses (23% of licenses issued during the same period). Of all the licenses issued (post economic crisis in 2009), Tourism licenses6 have witnessed the highest growth rate between 2009 and 2012 (CAGR of 24%), followed by Professional licenses (CAGR of 17%).

Economic Performance of the SME Sector measured by gross Value-added shows that SMEs contributes around 40% to the total value-added generated by Dubai's economy. Contribution of SMEs is estimated is distributed as 8% (micro), 14% (small) and 17% (medium), respectively. To sector-wise contributions, Trading SMEs account for 47% of the total value-added by SMEs; the share of Service SMEs is around 41%, and that of Manufacturing SMEs is estimated at around 13%. Also, SMEs account for 42% of the total workforce in Dubai. In the trading sector, Micro, Small, and Medium firms account for approximately 14.6%, 16.4% and 11% of the total workforce, respectively.

SMEs account for 51% of the total workforce employed within the services sector, followed by Trading with 33%. The Manufacturing sector is estimated to contribute another 16% to the total employment within the SME sector. However, data show that conventional banks reject approximately 50-70% of the (SMEs) applications for funding. Loans to SMEs account for just 3.8% of the outstanding bank credit in the UAE, below the MENA average of 9.3% (Issac, 2015).

Small and Medium Enterprises (SMEs) are the backbone of Dubai's economy, representing 95% of all establishments in the Emirate. These SME businesses account for 42% of the workforce and contribute around 40% to the total value added generated in Dubai's economy. The Government has a high focus on enhancing the contribution and performance of the SME sector to make these businesses comparable to their counterparts in other developed and high-income nations. Against this backdrop, the initiatives aimed at the development of SMEs and enhancing support for them have to be formulated on detailed research on their current state and development needs.

Survey of Key Challenges for SME's

SMEs Dubai conducted a survey asking SMEs to identify their primary concerns and challenges quarterly.

Growth opportunities for UAE-based SMEs propelled by alleviating obstacles related to access to finance. Businesses consider access to finance (and to electricity) as the most critical challenge. Already established SMEs may benefit from specific financial measures during the setup phase, but they may lack finance instruments supporting their growth. Among business economists, this lack of focus has been named "the missing middle." Over time, the survey shows that the significant challenges impacting the SMEs community in Dubai remained the same as different.

1. The high cost of operations.
    a. Cost of utilities (electricity, water, telecom and internet charges).
    b. The high cost of rentals & leasing.
    c. Volatility in the cost of raw materials, cost of skilled labor, rental costs and lack of accessibility to bank finance coupled with the rising cost of finance are the other challenges that have been highlighted by respondents. A few of the respondents also reported an inability to manage internal overhead costs.
2. Reduced demand for products and services. The surveys reveal that a decline in demand was experienced by SMEs that were highly dependent on construction activity & government projects. Also, the current economic climate in the US and Europe, coupled with political instability in the region has created ripple effects impacting businesses engaged in Transportation & Logistics, and Trading & Manufacturing companies focusing on exports.
3. Competition (cited by 40% of the respondents). The surveys reveal that competition from international and local players has impacted revenues and profit margins, especially in sectors such as Firms in manufacturing (cement, food & beverage, garments), services (construction & travel) and trading (auto parts, computers) and electronics. Respondents have said that the severity of this challenge stayed high.
4. Government fees, duties, and regulation. Rising government fees (employee visa, license renewal, and municipality) and duties (custom, import, and port charges) have been cited as a challenge amongst the businesses in Dubai. Also, frequent changes in business regulations

(relating to business licensing procedures, import-export procedures, and municipality and traffic rules). The formalities and paperwork (particularly in customs), leading to trans-shipment delays was also voiced as a critical challenge by respondents.

5. Delays in payment receivables. The surveys reveal that businesses faced challenges in collecting money from clients, making timely payments to suppliers, and negotiating better credit terms.
6. Currency fluctuations as of concern.

In 2011, the challenges for SMEs were similar to those faced by large companies. However, for the latter, the availability and cost of skilled labour figure among the challenges, just after the demand for products & services, and competition (SME, 2011).

In 2012, in terms of differences across business categories, it can also be observed that challenges cited by SMEs were similar to those faced by the overall business community. On the other hand, the cost of utilities is the most challenge affecting large companies (SME, 2012).

In 2013, terms of factors impacting businesses by firm size, the top three challenges for SMEs were competition, cost of rental/leasing and government regulations, while for large companies the leading challenges are the cost of rental/leasing, competition, and cost of labor. As for exporters, the top challenges are the same as the overall economy (SME, 2013).

In 2014, the first challenges for both SMEs and large companies remained the same, with competition and rising costs of rental/leasing emerging as most prominent in terms of severity. (SME, 2014).

In 2015, large companies indicated their top three concerns as competition, the impact of oil prices and demand/market conditions. For SMEs, the obstacles are competition, government regulations/fees, and the rising cost of rental/leasing (SME, 2015).

In 2016, for critical hurdles faced by large companies were competition, demand/market conditions and increase in expenses. The top hurdles for SMEs were competition, delays in payments, and weak demand/market conditions (SME, 2016).

In 2017, the critical challenges reported by large companies were competition, VAT implementation, and reduced market/demand conditions (SME, 2017).

In 2018, the critical challenges reported by large companies were competition, delay in payments/receivables, and VAT implementation (SME, 2018).

Characteristics of Access to Finance by SME's

SMEs borrow for numerous reasons including financing growth of noncurrent assets such as equipment; and funding working capital such as late payments. Therefore, availability and the degree to which access to finance by SMEs is recognized as a factor necessary to SMEs' growth. SMEs are usually associated with the significant borrower when it comes to external financing because of their small size, a low degree of financial sophistication and information asymmetries. Since SMEs access to capital markets is limited, they rely significantly on bank finance, which faces limitation as lending rates may become less favorable. High lending rates faced by SMEs can be attributed to information asymmetries and banks' funding costs.

Volatile economic conditions coupled with inherent risk stemmed from information asymmetries are two main factors behind the difficulty of accessing bank funding for the recent evolvement of bank capital regulation focusing on financial stability has increased pressure on financial lenders to solidify cushion against systematic stress and distress. Financial institutions tend to reduce their vulnerability to systematic adverse outcomes by reducing exposure to the riskier items on the balance sheet, which include lending to SMEs.

A 2016 report by the OECD on entrepreneurship and SMEs in Abu Dhabi reported that SMEs faced high bank rejection rates and limited "optimal" access to credit due to strict lending requirements, and high-interest rates on business loans, due to lack of collateral and information asymmetries.

Dubai SME assesses the level of access survey (Dubai SME, 2019) to bank finance for SMEs in Dubai based on the following factors:

1. Source of finance for commencing the business is 80% of the respondents indicated personal money/savings as the primary source of finance for commencing their business operations. This indicates the limited availability of externally sourced start-up financing in Dubai.
2. Source of finance for business operations and expansion 10% of the SMEs (i.e., 41% of the 23% of the SMEs that had access to finance) have accessed long-term financing for capital investment in their business.
3. Type of bank finance accessed (long-term versus short-term finance). 23% of respondents indicate that they have accessed bank finance in the last five years. This suggests limited availability of bank finance for

growth and operations. 59% of survey respondents point out that the fundamental purpose indicated by businesses for accessing external debt from banks is to meet their working capital requirements. Moreover, 37% of businesses indicated that they have accessed term loans for capital expansion/investment in their business. 4% mentioned that they had accessed a combination of long-term and short-term financing.
4. The average value of long-term and short-term finance and frequency of accessing short-term finance.

The long-term financing requirements of SMEs are typically found to be in the range of AED 1 to 5 million, while the short-term financing requirements are primarily up to AED 1 million per year. These could be in the form of short term loans, revolving credit, and/or trade financing facilities. The reduced access to bank credit can be attributed to enterprise size and operating sector. Access to bank finance is the highest in the case of trading SMEs and from an enterprise size perspective; it is the most prevalent amongst Medium-sized firms. Because of the strategic importance of SMEs diversifying the economy of the UAE, and given the various hurdles that SMEs face, access to finance remains a current issue that needs addressing as means to developing the SMEs sector and enhance its growth, and enlarge its contribution in the various indicators of the economy.

SME'S NON-BANK PRIVATE FINANCING

In the SMEs sector, financing needs differ per sector, and as the entity immigrates from a sub-segment to another. Generally, three segments may be distinguished. First, more informal microenterprises, household- or family-owned and managed, second, small enterprises often called the "missing middle", and third is the medium-size enterprises that are aspiring export-oriented.

The UAE financial systems may be characterized by large size, bank-based, short-term-driven, high NIMs, and lower concentration. Private equity and venture capital markets are growing in the UAE. The institutional and regulatory framework for private equity investments has led to a rise in the establishment of many investment vehicles. This financing segment has benefited from a clear legal and regulatory framework.

The microfinance sector in the UAE has changed substantially in the last two decades. We can distinguish between two types of microfinance and finance for SMEs providers: (1) public and government-funded agencies, lending to both individuals and micro-firms at no or administratively set interest rates; (2) Private providers of finance including financial intermediaries and private funds. The terms "angel capital," "venture capital," and "private equity" tend to be used interchangeably when referring to obtaining credit from non-bank private sources. Although these sources of finance often overlap in practice, they have different characteristics.

PUBLIC-SECTOR LENDING: GOVERNMENT-BASED FUNDING SCHEMES

The UAE oriented efforts to diversify the economy in preparation for its transition to a post-oil period has added to the impetus for SMEs to be a key pull of government-led investments. The government, central and local, has developed numerous financing schemes to make finance available to entrepreneurs in the start-up and SME sector. The financing initiatives put in place by the governments cares for the activity sector, size, and the stage of development of the firm.

The UAE government has put in place a variety of SME development agencies to provide funding specifically to Emirati entrepreneurs and small businesses (figure 4).

In 2003, Dubai SME was created to provide support to local SMEs in Dubai. Then, in 2007, the Khalifa Fund for Enterprise Development was launched in Abu Dhabi, being endowed with an original investment capital of 2 billion AED ($540 million) to enhance access to credit for local SMEs and new entrepreneurs. Sharjah has also formed a similar scheme in 2005, called the "Ruwad Establishment." The standard features among these funds are the following:

- Fund new and innovative business ideas that contribute to the strategic goals of the UAE. They nurture the sense of innovation and creativity of local entrepreneurs. Innovation may be done by adopting leading digital and smart technologies and rebooting operations.

Figure 4. Financing options in the UAE

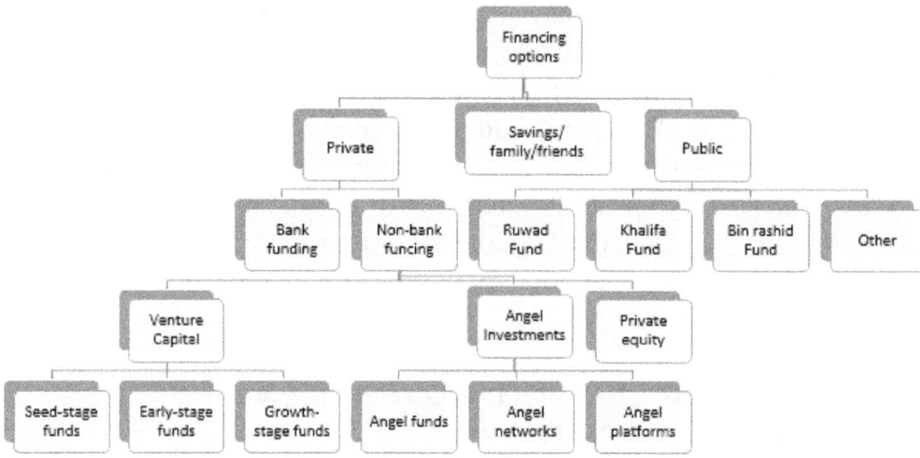

- Funds act as an incubator to innovative projects through in-house incubators or in cooperation with external incubators such as Hamdan Innovation Incubator.
- They finance different stages and sizes of businesses.
- Funds cooperate with other government agencies to provide further financing and non-financial facilities.
- Asking applicants to contribute between 10% and 20% of total project costs.
- Operating model ensures sustainability through re-investing the loan settlement to finance new projects.
- Funds allow for a grace period through which no accumulating interests apply.
- Funds monitor the funded projects through reviewing its business reports and field visits and offering advice to entrepreneurs as and when needed.

Ruwad- Sharjah Entrepreneurship Foundation

Sharjah Entrepreneurship Foundation "Ruwad" was introduced in 2005 to expand the SMEs network in Sharjah by financially supporting local entrepreneurs (Ruwad Establishment, 2019).

It is tasked with "providing financial and technical support and paving the way for a suitable environment for the establishment and development of these projects, and creating an encouraging climate for all Emiratis' individual and collective entrepreneurial projects, through an innovative and entrepreneurial spirit for a positive development of projects."

The fund provides two types of financing programs: direct and indirect. First, the right financing program is called the "microfinance program" helps to incorporate new enterprises. The ceiling for micro-credits is AED 300,000, accompanied by other facilities which include the exemption from paying the instalments of the financing during the first year of incorporation, the exemption from paying interest and bank charges, and the amount of financing is paid back three years after the end of the first year of incorporation.

The other financing program is implemented in cooperation with banks. It is intended for projects which cost more than AED300,000. Beneficiaries are also granted the following privileges, Ruwad bears 25% of the total guarantees determined by the Bank, Ruwad bears the percentage of bank profits on financing for the first year from establishing the project, and granting a General grace period for the payment of principal instalments of the Bank's financing.

The fund required that the applicant finance the project by at least 20% of the total costs. Second, the indirect financing program grants support in the form exemptions and facilitate to entrepreneurs by cooperating with the concerns public organisations. It aims at simplifying government and business regulation at the executive level. The following facilities may be highlighted:

1. The fund exempts entrepreneurs from paying licensing fees for three years to the following government organizations (Sharjah Economic Development Department, Sharjah Chamber of Commerce and Industry, Sharjah City Municipality, Sharjah Electricity and Water Authority, and Sharjah Directorate of Public Works).
2. the fund waives bank warranty required by the Ministry of Human Resources & Emiratisation.
3. help to increase the visibility of these projects, such as participating in the Sharjah Expo.
4. supporting projects to obtain legal, financial, and administrative consulting services at reduced costs through accredited bodies and institutions from "Ruwad" Foundation.

Khalifa Fund for Enterprise Development

Abu Dhabi Government set up an entrepreneurial fund through the Khalifa Fund for Enterprise Development in 2007 with an initial capital of AED 300 million (USD 81.6 million) which was increased to AED 2 billion (USD 544.5 million). This fund was established to spread entrepreneurship culture, encourage innovation, and provide support to small to medium-sized investments (Khalifa Fund, 2019). This scheme targets are channelling creative ideas and enhancing the administrative and managerial skills of fresh graduates and those already in business. The creation of the fund enters within the overall framework of making the SEMS contributing to the social and economic development of the UAE. The fund provides support services that include:

- Business Counselling.
- Financial support & financial advice.
- Business monitor and support for funded projects.
- Technical support and guidance.
- Participate in Khalifa Fund marketing campaign and network.
- Government support and exemptions.

The fund offers seven funding programs depending on the size of the loan and sector of activity. The minimum micro-credit is AED50,000 for micro-enterprises which do not require significant capital, which can be started from home through licenses granted for this purpose. The ceiling is AED10,000,000 for projects promoting growth and industrial diversification. The fund grants grace periods and relaxed repayment period, with fees waived in five financing programs. However, the applicant will have to make a financial contribution to the business of a minimum of 10%.

Mohammed Bin Rashid Fund for SMEs

Mohammed Bin Rashid Fund for SME was launched in 2015 to fund innovative pilot projects owned by local investors in the SME sector (Dubai SME, 2019). It leads efforts to finance and support the business establishment and entrepreneurship spirit. Statistics show that more than 23,000 local entrepreneurs took benefit from its business consultancy services. Over 4,000 projects have also received support from the agency. Investments supporting Emirati entrepreneurs through incentive packages have reached more than AED 290 million. In terms of financing, the Mohammed bin Rashid Fund has provided at least AED 600 million funds for company start-ups, with 56 new businesses have secured a total of AED 48 million. The fund has three fund schemes:

- **Seed Capital Loan** (non-profit), which ranges from AED100,000 to AED 1,000,000, is intended to help to fund the establishment of new projects or to fund the expansion costs or working capital for the existing ones. As an advantage, Seed Capital Loan is a non-profit loan that aims to reduce the initial costs on the borrowers. It offered directly to start-ups requiring funding of more than Dh50,000 but not exceeding Dh500,000. The Credit Scheme Loan, offered through banking partners and guaranteed by the fund, to both start-ups and existing businesses requiring funding of more than Dh1m but not exceeding AED3m.
- **Credit Bank Scheme** proposes finance between AED 1 and AED3 million for business seeking growth and enhancing competition in the market. The loan is facilitated by a grace period which enables beneficiaries to cover the costs and make profits other than the reasonable interest rate.
- **Invoice/Lpo Finance** is a receivable finance facility between AED 10,000 - AED 1,000,000 that addresses a significant obstacle for SME growth in Dubai. This product aims at improving cash flows by extending a cash advance facility for payments due in the future.

Bank Lending

Banks view the SME market as niche and risk-inherent segment. The presence of the stock market in the country has made banks to focus on large corporate. The SME loan size remains small despite the significant contribution of SMEs to GDP and employment. SMEs are considered by banks as risk-inherent compare to lathe corporate. Many reasons explain the trend depending on industries and region, including information about lack of credit history, the absence of financial backing or collateral, reduced business and managerial experience or financial knowledge, and low business diversification. However, recent developments show that SME banking is expanding. The Dubai-based Gulf Finance Corporation (GFC), was set up to serve the SME sector through small business loans and other financing solutions. The National Bank of Abu Dhabi (NBAD), which merged with FGB, had an SME team that helps provide tailored products and services to start-ups. Several UAE banks have been accommodative toward SMEs. Arabian Business granted "SME Bank of the Year" accolade to many large banks such as Mashreq Bank, Emirates NBD, and most recently First Gulf Bank.

Credit reports include personal identity information, details of credit cards, loans and other credit facilities, along with payment and bounced cheque history. Plan to include court data, rents, and even salaries in its credit reports, to ensure a resident's payment obligations are fully transparent to lenders. The introduction of credit bureau will help banks increase exposure to lending to SMEs with low default risk, and will make SMEs take more a discipline-based approach in management and use of funds. It will help both parties forging a lending relationship, and therefore, solidifying the entrepreneurship culture.

CONCLUSION

Since innovation, entrepreneurship, and SMEs are the mainstays of any country's economy; government policies are allocating adequate support of various layers and levels in materialising an entrepreneurial idea, vision or proposition into productive business activity, adding value to the economy. The UAE is placing a higher priority to SMEs as it emerging in policies and initiatives, in order to expand the contribution of the non-oil sector in the economy to unprecedented levels by 2021. However, SMEs face multitude of challenge, and one important challenge is limited access to finance. The main concern is how to make banking firms seen as enabling SMEs and entrepreneurs to secure the external financial support they need. This issue can be alleviated by nurturing a transparent SME-bank relationship stemming from expanding entrepreneurship spirit and environment.

In addition to access to finance, numerous other challengers are identified by SME and entrepreneurs including the absence of governance structure, lack of appropriate industry training requirements, innovation capabilities, and business experience. Also, we can list challenges associated with cash flow and pricing policies, limited access to technology, insufficient knowledge of the industry and market, and failure to secure effective negotiations with external stakeholders were identified as roadblocks.

Efforts to enhancing the UAE financial infrastructure, and improving the general lending environment and lending quality include the establishment of a credit bureau in 2010, which started operating in 2014. To reduce information symmetries, a Credit Bureau was set up to regularly collect credit information from financial and non-financial institutions in the UAE. The bureau aggregates and analyse collected data and issues credit scores and produce credit reports, showing the quality of the borrower.

A healthy entrepreneurship environment requires greater transparency in the relationship between providers of finance and entrepreneurs and finance. There is already a law in place to regulate the relationship between all government institutions and SME entrepreneurs. The law is a turning point in empowering people and realizing the aspirations of our younger generation. Another move is the setting up of a council to drive the growth of SMEs and entrepreneurs in the country.

REFERENCES

Alibhai, S., Bell, S., & Conner, G. (2017). What's Happening in the Missing Middle?: Lessons from Financing SMEs. *World Bank*. Retrieved from: https://openknowledge.worldbank.org/handle/10986/26324

Alkasmi, A., El Hammsy, O., Khoury, L., & Syed, A. (2018). Entrepreneurship in the Middle East and North Africa: How investors can support and enable growth. *McKinsey Digital*. Retrieved from: https://www.mckinsey.com/~/media/mckinsey/featured%20insights/Middle%20East%20and%20Africa/How%20investors%20can%20support%20entrepreneurship%20in%20the%20Middle%20East%20and%20North%20Africa/Entrepreneurship-in-the-Middle-East-and-North-Africa.ashx

Central Bank of the UAE. (2017). *Financial Stability 2017*. Retrieved from: https://www.centralbank.ae/sites/default/files/2018-09/FinancialStabilityReport2017.pdf

Central Bank of the UAE. (2019). Retrieved from: https://www.centralbank.ae/en/statistics/monthly-statistics

Deloitte. (2015). *Digital banking for small and medium sized enterprises: Improving access to finance for the underserved*. Retrieved from: https://www2.deloitte.com/content/dam/Deloitte/sg/Documents/financial-services/sea-fsi-digital-banking-small-medium-enterprises-noexp.pdf

DubaiS. M. E. (2019). *The Fund*. Retrieved from: https://www.thefund.ae/

Dubai, S. M. E. (2019). *The State of Small & Medium Enterprises (SMEs) in Dubai*. Retrieved from: http://www.sme.ae/studiesandresearchdocument/sme_report_english.pdf

Establishment, R. (2019). *Who we are*. Retrieved from: http://www.ruwad.ae/en/index.php/about-us/

European Investment Bank. (2015). *Tunisia Neighbourhood SME financing*. Retrieved from: https://www.eib.org/attachments/efs/economic_report_neighbourhood_sme_financing_tunisia_en.pdf

Federal Competitiveness and Statistics Authority. (2019). Retrieved from: http://fcsa.gov.ae/en-us/Pages/Competitiveness/Reports/Global-Entrepreneurship-Index-by-GEDI.aspx

Issac, J. (2015). SMEs' GDP input set to hit 70% by 2021. *Khaleej Times*. Retrieved from: https://www.khaleejtimes.com/business/local/smes-gdp-input-set-to-hit-70-by-2021

Khalifa Fund. (2019). Retrieved from: https://www.khalifafund.ae/

Smart S. M. E. MENA. (2019). *SME Sector & GCC*. Retrieved from: https://smartsmemena.com/smart-sme-mena-sme-and-gcc/

The Official Portal of the UAE Government. (n.d.) *Crowdfunding in the UAE*. Retrieved from: https://www.government.ae/en/information-and-services/business/crowdfunding

The World Bank. (2019). Retrieved from: https://data.worldbank.org/indicator/ic.reg.durs

Chapter 7
The Characteristics of SMEs in Dubai and Their Impact on Innovation

Mercy Veronica Chaita
Higher Colleges of Technology, UAE

ABSTRACT

This chapter explores the extent and characteristics of small and medium enterprises (SMEs) in Dubai and their innovative practices. Within this context, considerable emphasis is placed on evaluating the propensity of these SMEs to adopt new technology. SMEs are significant to the local entrepreneurship and innovation activities as well as improving competitiveness. Furthermore, these enterprises play a crucial role in job creation and are fundamental to economic growth. The connection between economic success in SMEs is fundamental since these firms are able to incorporate innovation into their operations and organizational practices.

DOI: 10.4018/978-1-5225-9377-5.ch007

INTRODUCTION

This chapter explores the extent and characteristics of Small and Medium Enterprises (SMEs) in Dubai, and their innovative practices. Within this context, considerable emphasis is placed on evaluating the propensity of these SMEs to adopt new technology. SMEs are significant to the local entrepreneurship and innovation activities as well as improving competitiveness. Furthermore, these enterprises play a crucial role in job creation and are fundamental to economic growth. The connection between economic success in SMEs is fundamental since these firms are able to incorporate innovation into their operations and organisational practices, (Bravo-Biosca et al., 2016). This chapter is divided into three sections and section one sets the scene by exploring the breadth of the definition of SMEs and the concept of innovation, while section two examines the impact of SMEs on economic development in Dubai. Section three concentrates on the nature of infrastructure and support mechanisms for SMEs. Of the seven states in the UAE, the state of Dubai is the focus of this chapter because is the first to implement major reforms, achieve high economic and market growth and form a strong position in the business world.

In Dubai, SMEs comprise the majority of firms operating in, both, the service and manufacturing industry sectors and making significant contributions to the local economy (DCCI 2010). As an emerging market and fastest growing economy in the Middle East and North Africa, Dubai has attained important levels of modernisation, industrialisation, and rapid economic growth. It is considered to be in a transitional phase between a developing and a developed market economy. The progress towards becoming an advanced market economy include forming market exchange and offering opportunities in foreign direct investment and adapting international technological knowledge. Hence, SMEs are supported and stimulated to revive the market and initiate new products and services, (UAE MFT 2012). However, in order for SMEs to establish in the Dubai market, the firms must have a minimum of 51% UAE national ownership. Dubai reflects the features of the UAE economy in areas such as infrastructure, business activities, investment, competitiveness, economic and social changes. This is achieved through a strategic plan which is knowledge-driven and competitive, (UAE MFT 2012). Furthermore, Dubai has designed a consistent strategy to promote large scale innovation with great potential for becoming an innovation hub for the region.

Figure 1. Source: Agency of the Department of Economic Development – Government of Dubai

	Trading		Manufacturing		Services	
	Employee	Turnover	Employee	Turnover	Employee	Turnover
Micro	<= 9 &	<= AED 9	<= 20 &	<= AED 10	<= 20 &	<= AED 3
Small	<= 35 &	<= AED 50	<= 100 &	<= AED 100	<= 100 &	<= AED 25
Medium	<= 75 &	<= AED 250	<= 250 &	<= AED 250	<= 250 &	<= AED 150

PART I: BREADTH OF THE DEFINITION OF SMES AND INNOVATION

Defining an SME

There is lack of homogeneity within the SME definition, beyond that of being different to large organisations. Furthermore, size classifications within SMEs are not the sole differentiating factor, but they represent a key factor and initial starting point for studying SMEs, ILO (2017). What constitutes an SME depends on country, the enterprise, number of employees, annual sales, assets, or any combination of these. For instance, in Canada the term SME refers to businesses with fewer than 500 employees, while in the EU, a business employing less than 250 is classified as medium-sized; a business with less than 50 employees is classified as small, while a business with less than 10 employees is considered a micro-business, (EU/OECD, 2016).

SME Definition from Dubai Perspective

According to the Agency of the Department of Economic Development – Government of Dubai (2018), an SME leads to convergence of multiple stakeholders engaged in various business activities. Thus, an SME enables efficient coordination and collaboration amongst stakeholders and serves as a baseline and framework for implementing multiple initiatives directed towards the development of the firm. Apart from creating a framework for determining the eligibility of establishments for various SME development programs, the definition ensures a reliable basis for monitoring the impact of these initiatives as indicated below.

Table 1. Gross value add by SME size of firms

		Percentage (%)
1.	Large	60
2.	Medium	16
3.	Small	15
4.	Micro	9

Source: Dubai Statistics Center (2016)

Table 2. Sector-wise split of value add by SMEs

		Percentage (%)
1.	Manufacturing	13
2.	Services	40
3.	Trading	47

Source: Dubai Statistics Center

Conceptualizing Innovation

Innovation is a complex and elusive concept, which can be given different meaning in different contexts. According to OECD (2010) innovation involves making fundamental or radical changes comprising transformation of a new idea or technological invention into a marketable product or process. Furthermore, Xie, et al. (2013) defined innovation as a significant technical advancement within a given industrial context. Thus, innovation can be defined as an introduction of newness into an organisation, by application of a new idea or process. However, Yongyoon, (2012) emphasised that the main characteristic of innovation is novelty. Hence, another central dimension for the definition of innovation is reflected by the questions "new to whom?" and "new in which context?" Similarly, different levels of meaning were distinguished by (OECD 2017g) which highlighted that a product or organisational process might be:

- New to the firm.
- New to the market.
- New to the entire economy.

Table 3. Contribution of Employment by size of SME size

		Percentage (%)
1.	Large	58
2.	Medium	11
3.	Small	16
4.	Micro	15

Source: Dubai Statistics Center

Table 4. Sector-wise split of workforce employed by SMEs

		Percentage (%)
1.	Manufacturing	16
2.	Services	51
3.	Trading	33

Source: Dubai Statistics Center

It follows from this analysis that if a firm starts to produce a new product, which is already produced by other firms, this would be an innovation for the firm, but not for the economy as a whole.

PART II: THE IMPACT OF SMES ON ECONOMIC DEVELOPMENT IN DUBAI

This section presents an overview of the performance of the SME sector in Dubai on SMEs contribution to economic development and employment. The economic performance is assessed based on contribution of SMEs by size, sector value-added and employment in Dubai's economy. These indicators have been analyzed based on data captured and supplied by the Dubai Statistics Center.

Dubai SME, the agency of the Department of Economic Development (DED, 2018) in Dubai, has revealed that small and medium-sized businesses make up 47 percent of the emirate's GDP and more than half of its workforce. Furthermore, the following contributions to the economy were highlighted.

- SMEs count for 95% of the total enterprise population in Dubai
- SMEs employ around 42% of Dubai's workforce
- SMEs contribute 40% of Dubai's value add

According to Dubai SME, the agency of the Department of Economic Development, SME contribution to Dubai's economy rose from 40% in 2009 to 47% in 2016, while their contribution to job creation rose from 42% to 52.4% during the same period in spite of slow global economic growth. Younger start-ups make up nearly 50% of the companies registered in Dubai and it validates the emirate's appeal as a global center for entrepreneurship, knowledge transfer and innovation. The SMEs are supported by state-of-the-art infrastructure and flexible legislative framework conducive to investment. Overall, across UAE, the sector accounts for more than 86% of the total private sector workforce as well as more than 60% of the country's current GDP, which is estimated to go up to 70% by 2021.

SMEs Prevalence on Innovation

A comparative innovation study conducted by UK Innovation Survey through the Department of Business, Innovation and Skills, (2011) highlighted the prevalence of innovation amongst Dubai SMEs. The study indicated that 42% of the total prevalence of innovation comes from product and service development, as compared to innovation within internal processes which make up 30% while distribution and delivery contributes 28% of innovation activities. The study confirmed that the key objective of implementing innovation in SMEs was to create a competitive advantage through product and service differentiation. (UK Innovation Survey (conducted by Department of Business, Innovation and Skills, 2011). The Global Competitiveness Index by World Economic Forum, (2013) also analyzed the following key parameters:

Comparative Analysis of Innovation Competitiveness

See Table 5.

Comparative Analysis of SMEs Export Orientation

The survey conducted by Internationalization of European SMEs, European Union (2016) revealed that SMEs in Dubai are highly export-oriented with 51% of the SMEs indicating that they have some part of their revenues coming from regional and international markets (as compared to 44% in EU-27 and 18% in New Zealand)18. Moreover, a high proportion of SMEs for instance, 60% of the SME exporters have more than 20% of their sales

Table 5.

Key Parameters	Key Findings
Innovation Input: Allocation of annual budget for R &D	▪ 8% of SMEs surveyed maintain an annual budget for R&D and product development (compared to 18% in New Zealand and 24% in the UK. ▪ Manufacturing SMEs are the most oriented towards R&D (17%)
Innovation Input: Innovation at product or process level	▪ Only 13% of the surveyed SMEs were found to have implemented innovation compared to both 23% in New Zealand and EU 27% and 25% in Malaysia. ▪ A higher focus on R&D by manufacturing SMEs has translated into higher levels on innovation output for these firms (29%).
Type and objective for implementing innovation:	▪ The major prevalence of innovation amongst Dubai SMEs is at the level of product/service level (42%) compared to innovation within internal processes (30%) and distribution and delivery formats (28%). ▪ The key objective for implementing innovation by businesses is to differentiate their products/services from competitors offering (38%).
International orientation and innovation amongst SMEs:	▪ There is higher prevalence of innovation amongst exporting businesses (75%), as compared to non-exporting SMEs (48%)

Source: Global Competitiveness Index by World Economic Forum, (2013).

Table 6. UAE Ranking on key indices

Index	Ranking	Number of countries
Innovation	28	144
Global Innovation	37	141
Use of IT	30	144
Technological readiness	32	144

Source: Global Competitiveness Index by World Economic Forum, (2013).

revenues emanating from international markets. The survey reflects that export-orientation is the highest amongst Medium-sized firms, followed by Small and Micro enterprises. Furthermore, 66% of the Medium firms indicated that they earn revenues from international markets as compared to 55% and 39% of the Small and Micro firms, respectively.

PART III: INFRASTRUCTURE AND SUPPORT MECHANISMS FOR SMES

As per the Global Competitiveness Index by World Economic Forum, (2013) the entrepreneurship ecosystem comprises four layers of enablers – Personal Enablers, Financial Enablers, Business Enablers and Environment

Table 7. Level of Technology Adoption amongst SMEs in Dubai

Key Parameters	Key Findings
Level of IT usage:	▪ 21% of SMEs indicated deployment of advanced IT systems such as (ERP, CRM) to manage their business operations. ▪ 26% of services firms deploy IT more intensely than manufacturing and trading firms.
Level of dedicated employee/department:	▪ Overall, 26% of SMEs have a dedicated IT employee or full-fledged IT department as compared to 20% in the EU. ▪ The dedication of IT employee tends to be more prominent amongst manufacturing and service SMEs.
Allocation of an annual budget for IT Expenditure:	▪ Even though 70% of SMEs use basic (software for specific functions) or advanced IT systems, only 35% make an accounting provision for IT expenses in their annual budgets. The tendency for provision for an IT budget is highest amongst service firms (40)
Presents of website and online ordering capabilities:	▪ Overall, half of the SMEs surveyed has a website, however, only 6% has online ordering capabilities as compared to 25% of SMEs in the EU and 31% of SMEs in New Zealand.
International orientation and IT adoption amongst SMEs	▪ Export orientation SMEs have a higher rate of IT adoption as compared to non-exporters (across all enterprise size classes). For instance, 46% of the medium sized SME exporters deploy advanced IT systems compared to 37% within the non-exporting category.

Table 8. Key Strategic initiatives are grouped under 4 Dimensions

Dimension 1 Entrepreneurship Promotion	▪ Partnering with regional and int'l stakeholders to promote entrepreneurship ▪ Establishing university entrepreneurship centres
Dimension 2 Ecosystem Development (policy & regulation)	▪ Advocating on innovation, IP, and productivity policies ▪ Advocating on assessing the impact of new regulation on SMEs ▪ Establishing a platform to voice concerns of SMEs ▪ Advocating policies to increase SME access to finance
Dimension 3 Business Development Programs	▪ Setting up sector based startup advisory services ▪ Setting up sector based capability development programs ▪ Developing an SME professionalization program ▪ Establishing sector focused incubators ▪ Promoting an equity financing culture ▪ Establishing IP awareness / support program ▪ Expanding the Dubai SME 100 Initiative & offering targeted growth support ▪ Developing and Executing an SME EXPO2020 Plan ▪ Promoting SME products domestically and abroad
Dimension 4	▪ Developing a Strong internal database and statistical reports ▪ Developing Internationally comparable statistics and macro data on SMEs ▪ Establishing an Entrepreneurship Research Network

Source: An Agency of the Department of Economic Development – Government of Dubai (2018)

Table 9. Supporting Initiatives

1. SME Definition	6. Dubai SME 5-Year Plan
2. SME Policy Needs	7. Foreign IP Attraction Program (Entrepass Scheme)
3.IP and Innovation Plan	8. Academic – Business Linkages
4.SME Sector studies	9.SME capability development programs
5.SME Development Council	10.Dubai SME 100

Table 10. Incubation

	Pre Incubation	Incubation Process		Graduation
Duration	1 Year or less	**1- 3 years**		3rd year
Incubation Stages	Idea to plan	Early stage	Classic incubation	Graduation

Enablers. The Government has a high focus on enhancing the contribution and performance of the SME sector in Dubai to enable these businesses to become comparable with their counterparts in other developed and high income nations. In this context, the Government has implemented a number of policies and programs across various levels of the ecosystem to provide support and impetus to the SME sector.

The Agency of the Department of Economic Development – Government of Dubai (2018), highlighted that a number of Dubai SME's initiatives are focused on enhancing the overall business environment in order to make it more conducive for SMEs in Dubai to thrive and grow. Dubai SME's role and support for SMEs spans across three facets, namely:

- Advocacy (advocating key policy issues, related to SMEs, to other relevant Dubai government entities).
- Seeding (promoting entrepreneurship amongst individuals as well as supporting establishment of new businesses).
- Grooming (enhancing and supporting the existing SMEs in Dubai).

The agency further indicated the key strategic initiatives as follows:

CONCLUSIONS

The chapter investigated characteristics of SMEs innovative practices and capabilities in Dubai. SMEs comprise the majority of firms in the economy of Dubai which is the fastest growing market in the Middle East. The SMEs count for 95% of the total enterprise population in Dubai and they account for more than 86% of the total private sector workforce as well as more than 60% of the country's current GDP. Hence, Dubai is ranked as the most innovation-driven economy in the Arab world and ranked 37 in global innovation competitiveness. SMEs adopt technology with export orientation companies indicating a higher rate of IT adoption as compared to non-exporters

Different support mechanism and initiatives were examined and these include collaborative relationships with universities and incubation centers.

FURTHER RESEARCH

Having examined SME innovative activities in Dubai, further research is needed to other environmental and organisational determinants of incremental and radical innovation, for example (Bravo-Biosca et.al, 2016), suggested other types of inter-organisational relationships that may accelerate radical innovation such as strategic alliances and external contracts. The external environment is generally outside the scope of the manager's duties. But the decision makers can further increase innovation potential, whether incremental or radical, by fostering intra-firm linkages: cross project communications, the mixing of team members, or other creative ideas (OECD, 2017g).

In addition, having considered some innovation constructs and models, there are some commonalities that do exist. While it is often assumed that the entire innovative process is carried out within a single firm, innovating firms in fact draw from a much broader range of knowledge and activities. Thus, it will be important to examine whether SMEs display unique characteristics on how to manage knowledge, particularly given the economic considerations of innovation and the potential lack of knowledge management research focused in the area?

Furthermore, interest in the nature and relevance of organisational innovations within firms and in business networks is increasing. Therefore further research could include how to define and quantify organisational innovations as well as examining how they in turn, relate to technological innovations. In particular, evidence on the objective of innovative efforts may shed new light on the process by which firms select innovations. More attention should also be devoted to the information that can be gathered on the objectives and priorities of innovative efforts and how they relate to major current problems such as the diffusion of information technology, their impact on employment and environment protection.

REFERENCES

Bravo-Biosca, A., Criscuolo, C., & Menon, C. (2016). What drives the dynamics of business growth? *Economic Policy*, *31*(88), 703–742. doi:10.1093/epolic/eiw013

Dubai Statistics Center. (2016). *Climate and environment*. Dubai: Government of Dubai.

EU/OECD. (2016). Policy Brief on Scaling the Impact of Social Enterprises. *European Union and OECD*. Retrieved from http://www.oecd.org/cfe/leed/Policy-brief-Scaling-up-social-enterprises-EN.pdf

ILO. (2017). *World Employment and Social Outlook 2017: Sustainable enterprises and jobs: Formal enterprises and decent work*. Geneva: International Labour Office.

OECD. (2010). *SMEs, Entrepreneurship, and Innovation*. Paris: OECD.

OECD. (2017g). *Small, Medium, Strong. Trends in SME Performance and Business Conditions*. Paris: OECD Publishing.

UAE MFT. (2012). *Why UAE: Unlimited Opportunity Yearbook 2012*. Ministry of Foreign Trade Publications.

Xie, X., Zeng, S., Peng, Y., & Tam, C. (2013). What affects the innovation performance of small and medium-sized enterprises in China? Innovation: Management. *Policy & Practice*, *15*(3), 271–286. doi:10.5172/impp.2013.15.3.271

Yongyoon, S., & Kim, M. S. (2012). Effects of SME collaboration on R&D in the servicesector in open innovation, Innovation: Management. *Policy & Practice*, *14*(3), 349–362. doi:10.5172/impp.2012.14.3.349

Chapter 8 Entrepreneurship in the United Arab Emirates

Ahmad A. Okasha
Canadian University Dubai, UAE

ABSTRACT

The United Arab Emirates (UAE) has developed a young, vibrant, and innovative economy. The UAE is ranked 11th in the ease of doing business globally according to the 2018 world bank report on the ease of doing business. The UAE is ranked the first in the Arab World in terms of ease of doing business. The UAE has achieved this amazing ranking and is approaching the top 10 global economies in terms of ease of doing business. According to Arab Youth Survey, the UAE was selected as the top country Arab youth wish to live in. The UAE became even more attractive than the USA for Arab youth. The survey explores where young aspiring individuals in the Arab countries would like to live and work. Historically, many young individuals in the Arab region, excluding gulf countries, fancy immigrating and working in the US, Canada, Europe, or Australia. They were aspiring for a better live and better economic conditions. In the recent survey, Dubai and the UAE topped the traditional immigrant attractive countries.

DOI: 10.4018/978-1-5225-9377-5.ch008

INTRODUCTION

The UAE leaders have realized that they cannot heavily depend on oil and gas revenues. They have been investing to diversify the UAE economy. Also, they have been opening the economy and connect it with the global economy. The UAE is becoming a magnet for business and dreamers as well. The leaders of the country have turned deserts and sands into a world-class city that more than 200 nationalities call home. The UAE has become an amazing entrepreneurial environment.

Dubai competed to host the world Expo 2020. Dubai won the global race and is hosting the 2020 Expo. The UAE as a whole is behind Dubai and eager to welcome more than 20 million expected visitors.

These chapters address entrepreneurship in the UAE. The first part of this chapter describes the UAE economy, Gross Domestic Product (GDP), key characteristics, and major government initiatives. The second part discusses the contributions of small and medium businesses (SMEs) to the UAE Economy. The third part emphasizes the role of women SMEs in the UAE. The fourth part tells the story of successful SMEs in the UAE. The fifth part summarizes the regulation and IP rules in the UAE. The sixth part discusses the financing fields for entrepreneurs. The final part forecasts the future of entrepreneurship in the UAE.

The UAE Economy

The International monetary fund estimated that the UAE economy is valued at $455 billion in 2018 (IMF, 2019). The UAE gross national product (GNP) rose by 0.8% in 2017 compared to 2016 accounting for price change (UAE Ministry of Economy, Annual Economic Report 2018, 2018). The Oil and Gas contribution to the overall economic activities is estimated at 23%. The UAE government has established a 2021 vision which maintained that “The UAE will benefit from a sustainable and diversified economy, flexible in adopting new economic models, and capitalizing on global economic partnerships to guarantee long-term prosperity for current and future generations of Emiratis” (UAE Ministry of Economy, Annual Economic Report 2018, 2018).

The UAE government has identified 12 key performance indicators to track and measure the transformation of economy:

- Increase non-oil real GDP growth
- Increase Gross National Income (GNI) per capita
- **Increase Net Inflow of Foreign Direct Investment as a percentage of GDP**
- Improve Global Competitiveness Index
- Enhance the share of UAE nationals in the workforce
- **Improve the Ease of Doing Business Index**
- Increase Emiratization Rate in the private sector
- **Enhance the SME's contribution to non-oil GDP**
- **Improve the Global Entrepreneurship and Development Index (GEDI)**
- **Improve the Global Innovation Index**
- **Share of 'knowledge workers' in the labor force**
- **Increase the research and development expenditure as a percentage of GDP**.

The KPIs above foster the development of entrepreneurship environment. Furthermore, the KPIs which are bolded are directly related to developing a prosperous entrepreneurship economy.

The characteristics of the UAE economy summarized as:

- Having a strategic location in the middle between Asia, the Middle East, and Africa. Which enable it to serve more than 2 billion individuals in the neighboring countries.
- Strong financial reserves. The UAE has a robust banking sector and a current account surplus that is forecasted to continue to grow.
- Large sovereign wealth fund. The UAE has the fifth largest sovereign wealth fund globally valued at 792 billion in 2016 (UAE Ministry of Economy, 2019).
- Consistent government spending. The government of the UAE is continuing to support the economy and maintain government spending in infrastructure projects, security, health, and education. For instance,

Dubai is investing in infrastructure projects related to hosting the Expo 2020. While the UAE as a whole is planning to spend AED six billion on significant infrastructure developments across the UAE.

- The progressive policy of economic diversification. As indicated above in the vision of the government, the UAE government is maintaining a strategy of diversification.
- Free Zones. There are 45 free zones in the UAE according to a report by Gulf News Paper (GulfNews, 2017). The free zones around the country offer 100 percent foreign national ownership of a firm with no requirement of local sponsor or local service agent. Also, free zones offer 100 percent repatriation of revenue and profits. The availability of free zones in the UAE especially Dubai has contributed to the growth of entrepreneurship in the UAE. Many of the successful technology companies that grew out of the UAE started in the free zones. Many companies attracted international attention and were acquired by global firms such as Uber and Amazon. Uber recently acquired Careem for a value of $3.1 billion (Alkhaleejtimes, 2019), and Amazon acquired Souq.com for a value of $580 million (Kim, 2019). Both companies started in Dubai.
- Increased foreign direct investment (FDI). According to the United Nation Conference on Trade and Development (UNCTAD) World Investment Report 2018, the United Arab Emirates saw their inflows of FDI increase by 8% between 2016 and 2017 (UNCTAD, 2019). The value of FDI in 2017 was $10 billion ranking the UAE in 30th place of FDI receipt global ranking (Santander, 2019).

The UAE Ministry of Economy is also focusing on the following growth accelerators:

Islamic Economy: Individuals who follow the Islamic faith is expected to grow to 1.8 billion individuals (WorldAtlas, 2019). The growth of Muslim populations around the world triggered the UAE to recognize the importance of the Islamic Economy. That includes Islamic finance and halal products. The global Islamic economy is estimated at around $4.2 trillion in 2014 (Thomson Reuters, 2015).

Green Economy for Sustainable Development: The UAE government has published a state of a green economy. In 2012, His Highness Sheikh Mohammed bin Rashid Al Maktoum, Vice President and Prime Minister of the UAE and Ruler of Dubai, established a long-term national strategy to build the green economy of the UAE under the slogan 'A Green Economy for Sustainable Development".

The Green Economy initiative includes six major fields covering a wide range of legislation, policies, programs, and projects which are (The UAE Government, 2019):

- Promote the production and use of renewable energy.
- Encourage investments in the green economy and to facilitate the production, import, export, and re-export of green products and technologies.
- Preserve the environment and to raise the efficiency of housing and buildings environmentally.
- Promote organic agriculture, maintain biodiversity and protect the ecological balance.
- Promote rationalizing the use of water resources, electricity, and natural resources and recycle waste.
- The development and promotion of green technology.

In 2016, the UAE Government established a ministry for climate change. The mission of the Ministry of Climate Change is to Work with partners to protect the environment, preserve and develop their resources and invest them efficiently to ensure their sustainability (Ministry of Climate Change, 2019).

Contributions of Small Medium Businesses to the UAE Economy

A significant part of the UAE 2021 vision is related to entrepreneurship and SME development. The UAE Government has the ambition to enhance the contribution and performance of the SME sector. The UAE government is taking a major role in establishing initiatives and programs to help with sources for funding SMEs. Initiatives include:

- Mohammed Bin Rashid Establishment for SME Development
- Khalifa Fund.

Back in 2002, the Dubai Department of Economic Development established a special SME department (SmallandMediumEnterprises, 2018). One of the major goals of Dubai SME is to promote innovation and leadership across all segments of the small and medium enterprise sector. With that in mind, Dubai seeks to turn ideas and creativity into successful businesses.

In Abu Dhabi, the Khalif Fund provide similar services to the SME development office in Dubai.

The Dubai government has established a specialized center, Mohammed Bin Rashid Establishment for SME Development. The center is responsible for facilitating SME development in Dubai and the UAE. The center works in partnership with the Dubai Chamber.

The center is focusing on removing the obstacles to the growth of the SME in Dubai. The center unifies the definition of what we mean by SME. The SME definition facilitates a 'common language' that is understood by multiple stakeholders engaged in various SME development roles and activities.

According to SME.ae (2018), SME defined according to the following:

- A micro business is an enterprise with less than or equal to 20 employees AND a turnover of less than or equal to AED 3 million.
- A small business is an enterprise with less than or equal to 100 employees AND turnover of less than or equal to AED 25 million.
- A medium business is an enterprise with less than or equal to250 employees AND turnover of less than or equal to AED 150 million.
- Any enterprise with greater than 250 employees OR turnover greater than 150 million will be considered 'large.'

Dr. Karim El Solh, CEO of Gulf Capital, maintained that in the UAE, SMEs makeup 95 percent of all enterprises, employ 42 percent of the workforce and contribute over 60 percent to the country's GDP. SMEs are the engine of growth for the local economy, and we need to actively support and encourage them and celebrate their achievements," said Dr. Karim El Solh, CEO of Gulf Capital. (Times, SMEs key to drive UAE's economic growth, 2017).

Dr. Karim El Solh, CEO of Gulf Capital, maintained that in the UAE, SMEs makeup 95 percent of all enterprises, employ 42 percent of the workforce and contribute over 60 percent to the country's GDP. SMEs are the engine of growth for the local economy, and we need to actively support and encourage them and celebrate their achievements," said Dr. Karim El Solh, CEO of Gulf Capital.

According to the intelligentsme.com there are around 300,000 small and medium enterprises in the UAE, contributing more than 60% of the region's GDP.

A 2016 study by the Organization for Economic Co-operation and Development (OECD) found that in the UAE, the survival rate was 83% after year one for the manufacturing sector, falling to 69% after two years and 55% after three years. In services, the figures were slightly lower: around 80%, 70%, and 50% respectively. These figures dovetail with the latest quarterly business confidence survey from Dubai SME, which in general finds manufacturing to be a sector that is more confident about prospects than trading or services. (Petch, 2018)

Globally with related to small and medium enterprises and according to Meredith Wood, the most profitable businesses in the US are the following:

- Mobile businesses functioning to customers needs.
- Child-oriented businesses. As the government is spending less on schools, parents are spending more on their children education.
- Sharing-oriented economy businesses.
- Online education businesses.
- Freelance B2B businesses. (Wood, 2018).

In Germany for instance, we can cite a couple of profitable businesses such as sandwich shops and snack shops, transportation businesses, online marketing, and advertising, freelance writing, appliance repairing, and janitorial and cleaning businesses. (profitableventure.com, 2018).

In Dubai, Keith Perena, the Khaleej Times maintained the following profitable small businesses in Dubai:

- Photographer.
- Teacher/Tutor.
- Social media influencer.
- Vlogger.
- Graphic designer/Web developer.

Okasha (2017) believed that the best businesses in Dubai are:

- Consulting and coaching businesses.
- Training and online education businesses.
- Adventure tourism businesses.

- Import/Export businesses.
- Health and Medical businesses.
- Children-oriented businesses.
- Rental businesses.
- Sandwich/snack shops.
- Entertainment/Sports event management businesses.

Prof. Muhammad Yunus, a pioneer in microfinancing and social businesses, maintained that jobs are not the destiny of individuals. It is a false destiny that was fabricated by the capitalistic businesses to serve their interests. Which would make individuals slaves to large companies. He maintained that the interests of capitalistic businesses are selfish. He proposed social businesses. Social businesses are both selfish and selfless. The social business fundamental purpose is to solve problems. Social businesses invest in solving problems, and their investments have mutual benefits for them and society. He proposed to empower individuals to solve problems and be entrepreneurs. He believes that entrepreneurship is the way to go. Humans are creative beings with entrepreneurship; they may fail and then succeed again. Social businesses encourage people to use their imaginative powers. (Yunus, 2018).

Women Entrepreneurs

The UAE has several initiatives to empower women in various sectors including business and entrepreneurship. Speaking at the UAE's first Women's Economic Empowerment Global Summit (WEEGS), Shaikha Jawaher maintained that productivity in the workforce increases by more than 50 percent with the active inclusion of women. (Times, How the UAE is empowering women, 2017). "The UAE is an example of a country that takes the education and empowerment of women seriously. Around 70 percent of university students are girls, and 46.6 percent of the labor market today is made up of women. Also, 66 percent of all government employees are women. Over 30 percent of managerial positions across various industries are taken up by women, and 15 percent of expert positions in the private sector are held by women," Shaikha Jawaher informed.

Today more than 70 percent of Emiratis in federal higher education institutions are women. (GulfNews, Why women graduates outnumber men in the UAE?, 2011). This percentage is expected to continue for the next couple of years. Women pay in the UAE is equal to their male counterparts.

A study titled 'United Arab Emirates female entrepreneurs: Motivations and Frustrations' by Hanifa Itani, Yusuf Sidani and Imad Baalbaki, " The UAE is witnessing an increasing trend of women's participation in business and entrepreneurial activities." The UAE also offers equal opportunities for men and women. The current UAE young nation's Cabinet has more women in ministerial positions than some of the most developed countries in the world as a major achievement for women empowerment for the UAE. The UAE offers a promising business landscape for women entrepreneurs to explore and flourish. Women in the UAE can own 100 percent of their businesses will motivate them by addressing the safety and security concerns when starting a new business (Shamuzova, 2018).

The UAE has recently announced a 10-year visa rule. This rule is likely to encourage more people, women, in particular, to commence and pursue business in the UAE. The new visa regulations will hopefully bring about a healthy influx of women entrepreneurs in the UAE which will, in turn, fuel the country's vision to become one of the world's top 25 countries for gender equality by 2021. (Shamuzova, 2018).

In March 2018, UAE-based female-focused angel investment group "Women" announced their women empowerment plan, "Momentum." "Momentum" is an early-stage accelerator program for female-led startups. Another program by a consultancy company grow.ME established an annual entrepreneurship program called Women-able. The program empowers women-focused SMEs by guiding business skills and confidence building (Hopkins, 2018).

Successful SMEs in the UAE

Many successful entrepreneurs made the UAE their home. Entrepreneurship is deep-rooted in the history and culture of the UAE. The success stories about entrepreneurs in the UAE is not exhaustive. One of the legacy entrepreneurship stories in the UAE is the story of Al Ghurair family. The Al Ghurair family legacy can be traced back to Ahmad Al Ghurair who founded Al Ghurair Group in 1960. At that time Dubai was undergoing significant economic and commercial growth. The family name has been well known across the UAE business community ever since. Ahmad Al Ghurair passed on his legacy to his sons Saif, Abdulla, Majid, Marwan, and Jomaa. (ArabianBusiness, 2010). The family was the first to start a cement factory in addition to a flour mill, a sugar refinery and an aluminum smelter. It also built the country's first shopping mall in 1981. The Group's business philosophy has been to build strong foundations in attractive markets, and to focus was primarily on activities that would grow the economy of Dubai and UAE. (Al GhurairGroup, 2018)

Saif Ahmad Al Ghurair and Abdulla Al Ghurair decided to form two unique yet complementing diversified industrial groups led to the creation of Saif Ahmad Al Ghurair Group and Abdulla Al Ghurair Group. Abdullah Al Ghurair started Mashreq from scratch with $1.6m worth of investment capital 40 years ago. Abdullah's son Abdul Aziz is the current CEO of Mashreqbank. Al Ghurair group has interests in food, construction, and real estate; a non-family member is the group CEO. Besides, Al Ghurair Foods claims to have the biggest pasta factory in the Middle East. Its pasta products are sold under the Jenan brand.

The online business in Dubai has witnessed tremendous growth. Many online startup companies have grown to medium size companies. A couple of companies such as Souq.com was the target of acquisition by Amazon.

Cobone

Paul Kenny, 33 years of age has set up cobone an e-commerce company selling vouchers online. Paul Kenny's company was not the first in the Dubai market; it was the second company to launch an online discount voucher. The first company was called GoNapit.com. Paul Kenny realized that he needed to differentiate his company. Otherwise they will become statistics. He launched a guerilla public relation announcement which was very successful in attracting more than 1000 customers in less than 12 hours (Arabian Business, 2016). Kenny indicated that his journey in building the company at age 25 was challenging. However, the journey was fun as well (Arabian Business, 2016). Kenny's entrepreneurship journey was built on his family business back in Ireland. His family owned Kenny's Bookshop and Gallery. Kenny confessed that he did not complete his higher education in Ireland. He moved to Dubai at the age of 22 and started as an intern in the Jumeirah Group (Uowdubai, 2013).

Paul Kenny indicated that he has focused on the long terms goal of building his company. He maintained that it was very difficult to raise capital. He said that he had spoken to 100 potential investors before he secures acceptance from two of them (Uowdubai, 2013).

Paul Kenny is one of the highly respected young businessmen in the region. Forbes has listed Paul as one of 2018's most influential expats in the UAE (PaulKenny, 2019). In 2013 he was named as the 10th most influential person under the age of 30 in the Middle East, and one of the 25 most important people in technology in the region. In 2012, he won the Gulf Business Middle East Entrepreneur of the Year and the Ernst & Young Emerging Entrepreneur of the Year awards (Uowdubai, 2013). Cobone has witnessed a significant growth of more than 50% growth. His company was quickly reporting a profit.

E-commerce is an interesting area for a small startup. Dubai attracted many high tech e-commerce companies. The government of Dubai has set up a couple of free zones encouraging internet companies. This has led to many successful online businesses such as Cobone, Bayt.com, Souq.com, Dubizzle.com, and Careem.

Careem.com

The sharing economy segment is growing at an increasing rate globally. Uber.com has re-wrote the principles of how to start and grow businesses. Uber has become a billion-dollar company providing taxi services to move people around. The company does not own a single taxi. The company does not pay salaries to drivers. Uber.com has invested in a high tech e-commerce platform that enables a person using their mobile phone to order a taxi anywhere anytime they choose. Similar to Uber, Careem is a regional Uber.

Recently, Uber has acquired Careem for a value of $3.1 billion (Alkhaleejtimes, 2019).

Careem is an e-commerce Dubai based company. Careem provides hired rides throughout the Middle East. The company is similar to Uber which is based on the shared economy concept. Careem has provided a nice ride to the people of the Middle East. Similar to Uber, customers may trust that young adult to ride a Careem car. The customer trust that drivers registered with Careem. With a registered credit card and a mobile application. The customer can order a car anywhere Careem provides services. A driver will come to the chosen pick location. There is no need to go outside to the street and wait for a taxi . Careem is distributing the local taxi companies by providing limousine services at the cost of local taxis.

Careem is not investing in buying cars or hiring drivers. However, they have invested in a high tech online system. HoIt provides an e-commerce system that links drivers to individuals who want to travel locally from one place to another.

Using Careem, payment is automated online. The customer registers their credit card and orders a Careem car by a few clicks on the mobile phone. In short time, a driver will accept the order and the application will show the driver location and how long it will take the driver to reach location with the price of the service and traffic update rationalizing the pricing strategy.

NMC

NMC is a unique healthcare company who gained international recognition. It all started with a young ambitious Indian national who made the UAE his second home. BR Setty came with a clinical degree in pharmacy to Abu Dhabi back in 1973. He started a couple of business ventures. In 1975 he set up a healthcare venture and called it New Medical Center (NMC) (Shetty, 2019). The center grows rapidly. NMC experienced significant and miraculous growth. It grows to several hospitals and many clinics. It was the first healthcare company to be listed in the London Stock Exchange. In addition to NMC, Mr. Setty established UAE Exchange and Neo Pharma which became very successful in their own.

Kcal

People are more aware and conscious of the importance of healthy eating. Entrepreneurs are individuals who spot a need and build a business around fulfilling this need. One day, after finishing their workout at the gym, Mark and Andreas were very hungry and were looking for healthy food. They could not find anything healthy. That is when they got the idea to start a healthy food company. That is how Kcal was started by Mark Carroll and Andreas L Borgmann in Dubai back in 2010. (Kcal, 2018).

Kcal is operating out of its Dubai headquarters. The company received People's Choice Award at the SME Stars of Business Awards, SME of the year and franchise of the year. Kcal has pursued an ambitious outlet growth. Kcal has opened eight restaurants within the UAE and planning to expand to Kuwait and Qatar.

Kcal provided individuals in Dubai healthy menus that consider both the calories count and the quality of food. In the nutrition world, they consider calories, micro, and macronutrients. Macronutrients are carbohydrate, protein, and fat. Micronutrients are needed vitamins and minerals.

Bayt.com

A group of individuals in their twenties in Dubai wanted to tackle unemployment in the Middle East started the idea of Bayt.com. Mr. Ataya obtained a degree in electrical engineering at Stanford University (Hill, 2015). Rabea Ataya started his job career in investment banking when he was 21. After working in the US for four years later, he identified record management as a growing area and a solution that he can take back to Dubai. He validated the need in Dubai market form his family constructing a business. He started his own company info for which is a record management company. One of the main challenges that he faced while trying to grow InfoFort was hiring the right talent. This was surprising to him considering the high percentages of unemployed people in the Middle East (Anserson, 2015). Mr. Ataya maintained that he was traveling a lot in the Middle East region and he was meeting many people who were complaining that they could not jobs (Hill, 2015). Mr. Ataya realized that the problem was related to the disconnect between people seeking jobs and the opportunities available in the market. He further indicated that the Internet was being available in the Middle East. He started Bayt.com in InfoFort warehouse in Al Qoze area in Dubai. Mr. Ataya said that "It was a pretty crazy time to start an internet business and in hindsight, I often wonder – if I knew back then what I know now, would I have embarked on that journey? Probably not. However, my naivety helped to be brave, and we felt very strongly that we would be a compelling solution to help people to improve their lives." (Hill, 2015)

Since 2000, Bayt.com has grown in the region along with the growth and the adoption of the Internet. In 2001 Bayt.com expanded by opening offices in Abu Dhabi and the Eastern region of Saudi Arabia. In 2002, Mr.

Ataya was awarded the "e-Entrepreneur of the Year" by His Highness Sheikh Mohammed Bin Rashid Al Maktoum. (Al-Assi, 2019). In 2005 the Bayt.com reached 1 million subscribers, and in 2011 the company was selected as one of the ten best companies to work for in the Middle East. In 2014, the World Economic Forum added Bayt.com to their list of 28 global growth companies (Al-Assi, 2019).

Ataya maintained that Bayt.com is adding more than 15000 resumes daily. Later Bayt.com started providing solutions to employers in salary benchmarking, surveys, and recruitments.

Rabea Attaya laster sold InfoFort to Aramex (Anserson, 2015). Mr. Ataya has invested in several e-commerce companies such as GoNapit.com, Yallamotor.com, and Doctorona.com (Hill, 2015). Mr. Ataya's sister, Mona Ataya who was a marketing manager at Bayt.com started in her own Mumzworld.com.

At the age of 19, Mahmoud started an e-commerce site. He was one of probably hundreds of thousands of young entrepreneurs throughout the world whose first business idea is built around a web site. Mahmoud's first company, Xeswar, selling accessories and jewelry break-even analysis was negative. He realized that the business market size would not turn the break-even analysis to a positive number, so he launched ShuGeek, an online store based in ThinkGeek. (MacBride, 2016). ShuGeek also failed. He was frustrated, but was also inquisitive. He found that in the Middle East, more than 300 e-commerce sites are being set up every quarter. He set up another e-commerce site which indexed shopping sites in the UAE.

Okasha (2017) in his book titled "How to be Successful in Dubai: 12 Lessons that I Learnt running a small business in Dubai" described his entrepreneurship journey in Dubai. Okasha started a couple of healthcare companies in Dubai. He started his entrepreneurship journey by founding a company that was focusing on outsourcing physiotherapy services to private hospitals in Dubai. He summarized his experience in 12 lessons:

1. Being authentic, not wearing a social mask because this is what the society expects of us. Okasha (2017) maintained that entrepreneurs would not be truly successful and realized their potential unless they are true to themselves. Entrepreneurs need to identify their true talent, aspirations and interest. Then, they need to act according to their true passion and interests.

2. Avoiding conflicts, discomforts, stepping up will not make the entrepreneur's life easy. The entrepreneurship journey is encountered with obstacles. Expect failure and plan for success. True entrepreneurs need to manage their discomfort, pain, and emotional obstacles for growth.
3. Conducting local market research, feasibility and understand risks are not theoretical leads. Lack of this action will lead to disasters. Okasha (2017) brings scenarios from his entrepreneurship journey about the value and significance of doing local market research.
4. Being careful not to rush and blindly trust "the experts" finance, a legal consultancy.
5. The importance of picking the right team. The team is essential for success and sustainability. Jim Collins maintained "First Who …Then What" (Collins, 2001).
6. Keep exercising as a source of energy. Okasha (2017) tells the story of how he did not realize the value of exercising and how it affects his ability to make better and wiser decisions. He mentioned that the lack of exercise contributed for him to make high-risk decisions. The caused severe impacts on the financial situations and his family.
7. People will chana ge loyalty even if they promise.
8. Be aware of your mind under stress. Okasha (2017) indicated that the ability of entrepreneurs to decide pressure is risky. In a time of stress, the brain activates the survival mode limit the ability to make wiser decisions.
9. Running your own race. Do not run more than you can handle. The importance of being patient and do not a comparison for others.
10. Competition is always there, and you always have competitors. Okasha (2017) maintained that consumers had limited tolerance to be ready to exceed their expectations within a short timeframe. The assumption that businesses are unique, and the business do not have competition is not valid.
11. Being careful with cash flow, watch the overspending. There is a difference between profit on paper and cash in the bank. A business can be profitable and at the same time run out of cash. Entrepreneurs need to keep a watchful eye on their cash flow.
12. Relying on one or two strategic alliances, customers. Okasha (2017) discussed the importance of balancing the need for big strategic customers and having a continuous steady stream of revenues is coming from small and medium customers.

Abdulla Jengan, an Emirati, is a second generation entrepreneur, he succeeded his in managing their trading business and moving it towards manufacturing. He maintained: "We design, fabricate, assemble and test low-voltage diesel generator sets and sell them to different countries in the Middle East and North Africa," he said. "We design water pumping systems, too, that can be used to transfer water in buildings and pump water and wastewater inside commercial buildings like hospitals, villas, and malls. The generator sets are a power back-up." (Malek, 2018). Mr. Jengan's started in trading, and he is planning to shift the focus of the family business to manufacturing.

Regulations and IP in the UAE

The UAE has enacted special laws to protect intellectual properties. The Intellectual property legislation of the UAE includes Patents and Industrial Design Law number 44 of 1992, Trademarks law number 37 as of 1992, Copyright and Neighboring Rights Law number 40 of 1992. (stalawfirm, 2018)

The UAE joined the Berne Convention (Literary and Artistic Works) officially on July 14, 2004. Also, the UAE joined the Rome Convention as of January 14, 2005. The UAE is also a member and signatory to TRIPS Agreement since April 1996. The Ministry of Finance has established a special office to administer trademarks and patents.

The Patents Law of UAE provides that a patent is valid for a term of twenty (20) years.

The UAE Ministry of Finance has established the following sections about Intellectual property and trademarks (UAE Ministry of Finance, 2018):

Trade Mark Department. The department is responsible for the implementation of the federal low No. 37 for the year 1992 regarding the trademarks and its variations, and the protection of the owners of the trademarks. The Department of Trade Mark Department also:

- Receive and manage the applications to register the trade;
- Receive the complains and follow up on the cases related to the trademarks in the specialized courts; and
- Follow up on all international agreements and coordinate with the international organizations specialized in trademarks.

International Center for Patent Registration

The center is responsible for implementing federal law no. 31 for the year 2006 and related laws federal law no. 17 for the year 2002, regarding regulating and protecting the industrial property of the patents, the designs, prototypes, know-how, and the contractual licenses.

- The center is also responsible for receiving and managing the applications for the patents.
- Receive and manage complains, and aggrieving related to patents, and dealing with it as per the law and follow up the cases in the courts.
- Establishing a database for the international patents and coordinate the communication and the relations with the international centers that certify the patents.

Copy Right Department

The copyright department is responsible for implementing federal law no. Seven for the year 2002 regarding the copyrights and its variations, and protecting the innovators as stated in the law.

- The center is also responsible for receiving and managing the applications to register the rights and deposit the records of the ordinary people and the recognized people.
- Receive and manage complaints and follow up the cases in the courts.
- The communication, the participation, and the coordination with the international organizations specialized in the copyrights and intellectual property and followed up on the new legislation.
- Ministry of Finance Intellectual Property Sector http://www.economy.gov.ae/english/Ministry/MinistrySectors/Pages/CopyRightSector.aspx
- Dubai Custom Intellectual Property Rights https://www.dubaicustoms.gov.ae/en/IPR/Pages/WeAreIPR.aspx

Financing Entrepreneurs in the UAE

According to Statiscal.com, a statistical portal, the global transaction value in the crowdfunding segment amounts to US$9,370 million in 2018. This value is expected to grow at a rate (CAGR 2018-2022) of 29.0% resulting in the total amount of US$25,919.3m by 2022. (Statistica, 2018).

Peer to Peer Lending in the UAE

In the UAE, the UAE Central Bank regulates financial activities regarding the granting of loans – financial institutions and intermediaries require approval from the UAE Central Bank to operate. Also, under the UAE Penal Code, private individuals are prohibited from providing loans with interest based on Sharia laws which can be a hurdle to crowdfunding.

DIFC and the ADGM may provide the flexibility for creative structures with regards to peer-to-peer lending. Beehive, an online peer to peer lending platform. Using Beehive, investors can contribute funds to businesses and earn interest – funds raised by the platform are managed by a third party fund administrator based in the DIFC and is, therefore, DFSA regulated. Beehive is also certified by the Shariyah Review Bureau (SRB) to be Sharia compliant (fichtelegal.com, 2018).

In Dubai, many local banks are providing loans to existing businesses. Local banks can provide loans to existing SME business that have been operating for more than one year.

Banks are reluctant to loan money for a new startup. For startups, the founders have to personally take a loan from a bank using personal collateral such an existing home or any other related assets. There is a new company that was founded to help SME with loans. The company is called the Beehive. The company operates on the principles of peer to peer lending which is similar to crowdfunding. More about this company is the crowdfunding section.

With the establishment of free zones in the UAE and the business-friendly government of the UAE, the UAE has attracted many venture capital enterprises. Investors in the UAE have begun to come in all shapes and sizes - from family offices to MNCs to growth stage capital getting involved in earlier stages. (KhaleejTimes, 2018)

TechStars Dubai, in partnership with Ginco, is the first US accelerator and venture capital fund to establish an office in the UAE. It has invested in over 1,300 startups globally alongside top global companies such as Sony, Barclays, Amazon and now Ginco. (KhaleejTimes, 2018)

Beehive.ae. Beehive is an online peer to peer (P2P) lending platform providing finance to creditworthy, UAE based small and medium-sized enterprises (SMEs).

Beehive business finance ranges from AED 100k to AED1 million. The loan terms are 6-36 month loan terms. Beehive can support finance requests for working capital, growth & expansion capital and re-financing.

Future of Entrepreneurship in the UAE

We are living in a century of abundance. This is the century in which entrepreneurship is the key to resolve human capital global economic challenges.

We are living in a time where resources are accessible that are similar to what presidents of greatest nations have 30 years ago. We have google.com search engine that will have thousands of related information at the press of a keyboard. Do it yourself skill support, learn a new language by listening to tutorials free of charge set to step by step in an engaging application. Every day, there are discoveries in science and technology. Scientists and engineers are highly skilled in finding solutions to the many problems and challenges that we have. However, these solutions, findings, and technologies available users are created by entrepreneurs working within a vision, purpose, resource, and strategies to make it available online. Take these technologies to learn from them, differentiate your vision, and enjoy your entrepreneurship journey in solve or improve a market gap or human need.

The UAE government understood that the promising future is for those who view the greatest human challenges as opportunities for growth. For instance, global warming, poverty, unemployment, education, the need for clean water. The UAE leaders have started global programs to tackle these challenges.

In January 2016, the UAE government held a retreat on the post-oil phase of industry six at Bab Al Shams Resort in Dubai. Federal and local government officials participated in the retreat and discussed ideas and initiatives that would contribute in moving the UAE's economy away from being dependent on oil revenues and ensuring its sustainability with an emphasis on human capital, knowledge, and innovation. (Emirates247.com, 2016)

The UAE strategy for after oil includes ideas and initiatives concluded in the retreat. It will work to strengthen the competitiveness of the current economic sectors as well as gradually introduce new sectors, which will achieve a giant leap in the UAE's economy by the highest international standards (Emirates247.com, 2016).

In 2015, the UAE government invested AED300 billion to transform the UAE economy to a knowledge economy. An economy is driven by innovation to move UAE from being heavily dependent on oil revenues. The Emirates Science, Technology and Innovation Higher Policy launch 100 initiatives with initial investments in education, health, energy, transport, space, and water. The policy targets fields such as robotics, solar power, developing intellectual property, stem cell research and biotechnology (MOei.gov.ae, 2019).

H. H. Sheikh Mohammed bin Rashid Al Maktoum, Vice-President and Prime Minister of the UAE and Ruler of Dubai launched Centennial Plan 2071. The plan is built on the previous 2021 UAE vision. The plan is a long-term, full-vision plan that extends for five decades after 2021. The plan forms a clear map for the long-term government work to fortify the country's reputation and its soft power (UAE Government, 2019).

Also, H. H. Sheikh Mohammed bin Rashid Al Maktoum declared a very ambitious goal to establish the first inhabitable human settlement on Mars by 2117 (UAE Government, 2019). The UAE Mars 2117 project includes devising a program to prepare Emiratis for Mars and space exploration. The project aims to build the first city on Mars in 100 years (Emirates247.ae, 2019). This ambitious project will be achieved through various scientific alliances and partnering with global CEOs who have a similar plan such as Elon Musk (Thenational.ae, 2017).

The UAE Mars plan and various initiatives listed in the UAE government's future web site will provide entrepreneurs in the UAE with massive opportunities to participate in building and realizing these initiatives. The UAE will create a friendly environment for entrepreneurs to realize these goals. Realizing these goals requires the joint efforts of thousands of entrepreneurs. The steady growth to achieve these goals will create and develop solutions and technologies that do not exist now. These technologies and solutions will benefit the world, let alone the UAE society.

REFERENCES

Al-Assi, R. (2019). *The Story of Bayt.com: A Tale of Love, Hard Work, and Success*. Retrieved from bayt.com: https://www.bayt.com/en/blog/3967/the-story-of-bayt-com-a-tale-of-love-hard-work-and-success-infographic/

Al GhurairGroup. (2018). *Our History*. Retrieved August 28, 2018, from Al Ghurair Group: http://www.alghurair.com/about-us/our-history

Alkhaleejtimes. (2019, March 26). *Uber acquires Dubai-based Careem for $3.1 billion*. Fretrieved from Alkhaleejtimes.com: https://www.khaleejtimes.com/business/uber-acquires-dubai-based-careem-for-31-billion

Anserson, R. (2015, November 15). *Bayt.com founder on Middle East's job market*. Retrieved from Arabian Business: https://gulfbusiness.com/bayt-com-founder-middle-easts-job-market/

Arabian Business. (2016, January 16). *PR stunt kick-started our business, says Cobone founder*. Retrieved from Arabian Business: https://www.arabianbusiness.com/pr-stunt-kick-started-our-business-says-cobone-founder-620003.html

ArabianBusiness. (2010). *Arabian Business Rich List 2010The Al Ghurair Family*. Retrieved August 28, 2018, from Arabian Business: https://www.arabianbusiness.com/arabian-business-rich-list-2010-367763.html?itemid=367814

Baldwin, D. (2018, May 8). *UAE chosen top country for young people says the Arab Youth Survey*. Retrieved rom Gulfnews.com: https://gulfnews.com/going-out/society/uae-chosen-top-country-for-young-people-says-arab-youth-survey-1.2218208

Collins, J. (2001). *Good to Great*. Harper Business.

Emirates247.ae. (2019). *UAE starts on a 100-year plan to settle planet Mars*. Retrieved from emirates247.ae: http://www.emiratesnews247.com/uae-starts-on-100-year-plan-to-settle-planet-mars/

Emirates247.com. (2016, January 31). *UAE Ministerial Retreat at Bab Al Shams*. Retrieved from Emirates247.com: https://www.emirates247.com/news/emirates/uae-ministerial-retreat-at-bab-al-shams-2016-01-31-1.619243

fichtelegal.com. (2018). *Crowdfunding in the UAE – An Opportune Time For Regulatory Certainty*. Retrieved 2018 from fichtelegal.com: https://fichtelegal.com/wp-content/uploads/2017/02/2017.02-executive-insights-crowdfunding-1.pdf

GulfNews. (2011). *Why women graduates outnumber men in the UAE?* Retrieved August 28, 2018 from Gulf News: https://gulfnews.com/gn-focus/why-women-graduates-outnumber-men-in-the-uae-1.790849

GulfNews. (2017, August 14). *There are 45 free zones in the UAE: Find the right one for your new business*. Retrieved from Gulfnew.com: https://gulfnews.com/lifestyle/community/45-free-zones-in-the-uae-find-the-right-one-for-your-new-business-1.1716197

Hill, J. (2015, December 14). *How Bayt.com proved to be just the job for entrepreneur Rabea Ataya*. Retrieved from The national.ae: https://www.thenational.ae/business/how-bayt-com-proved-to-be-just-the-job-for-entrepreneur-rabea-ataya-1.104680

Hopkins, A. (2018). *Calling Female Entrepreneurs: Why The UAE Is The Place To Be*. Retrieved from entreprenuer.com: https://www.entrepreneur.com/article/320548

IMF. (2019). The *United Arab Emirates*. Retrieved August 28, 2018 from International Monetary Fund: http://www.imf.org/en/Countries/ARE

KCAL. (2018). *How it all started*. Retrieved August 28, 2018 from Kcal: https://www.kcalextra.com/about-us/

KhaleejTimes. (2018, April 9). *Dubai is the best place for venture capitalists*. Retrieved from Khaleej Times: https://www.khaleejtimes.com/20180409/46/no-title

Kim, E. (2019, January). *Amazon plans to launch a new Middle East marketplace, two years after buying Souq for $580 million*. Retrieved from CNBC: https://www.cnbc.com/2019/01/29/amazon-new-middle-east-marketplace-rivals-souq.html

MacBride, E. (2016, January 31). *Forbes*. Retrieved August 29, 2018 from Lessons From Startup Success In Dubai: To Win As An Entrepreneur, Do This One Thing, Fast: https://www.forbes.com/sites/elizabethmacbride/2016/01/31/dubai-based-adrelated-draws-attention-from-google-and-elsewhere-for-its-innovation/#6e56d58a3140

Malek, C. (2018). *Meet the young Arab entrepreneurs paving the way for the region's future*. Retrieved from The National: https://www.thenational.ae/uae/meet-the-young-arab-entrepreneurs-paving-the-way-for-region-s-future-1.693816?videoId=5716439907001

Ministry of Climate Change. (2019, March 25). *Mission & Vision & Values*. Retrieved from the Ministry of Climate Change: https://www.moccae.gov.ae/en/about-ministry/about-the-ministry/missionvision-and-values.aspx

MOei.gov.ae. (2019). *Innovation Science Technology & Innovation Policy*. Retrieved from moei.gov.ae: https://www.moei.gov.ae/en/innovation/innovation-science-technology-and-innovation-policy.aspx

Okasha, A. (2017). *How to be Successful in Dubai: 12 Lessons that I Learnt running a small business in Dubai*. Amazon Kindle Publishing.

PaulKenny. (2019). *Paulkenny.com*. Retrieved from About Paul: https://www.paul-kenny.com/#contact

Petch, N. (2018). *Startup success by the numbers – battling the odds*. Retrieved August 29, 2018 from Virtuzone: https://vz.ae/startup-success-by-the-numbers-battling-the-odds/

profitableventure.com. (2018). *50 Best Small Business ideas in Germany for 2018*. Retrieved August 28, 2018 from profitableventure.com: https://www.profitableventure.com/business-ideas-in-germany/

Santander. (2019, March 25). *United Arab Emirates: Foreign Investment*. Retrieved from Santander.com: https://en.portal.santandertrade.com/establish-overseas/united-arab-emirates/foreign-investment

Shamuzova, S. (2018). *t's action time for female entrepreneurs in the UAE.* Retrieved from Khaleejtimes.com: https://www.khaleejtimes.com/business/local/its-action-time-for-female-entrepreneurs-in-the-uae

SmallandMediumEnterprises. (2018). *About Us.* Retrieved 2018 from SME.ae.

stalawfirm. (2018). *Intellectual Property Guide.* Retrieved August 30, 2018 from stalawfirm.com: https://www.stalawfirm.com/public/uploads/downloads/UAE-Intellectual-Property-Guide.pdf

Statistica. (2018). *Crowdfunding.* Retrieved 2018 from Statistica: https://www.statista.com/outlook/335/100/crowdfunding/worldwide

SuccessHarbor. (2017). *What Percentage of Businesses Fail – The Real Number.* Retrieved August 28, 2018 from Success Harbor: https://www.successharbor.com/percentage-businesses-fail-09092015/

The national.ae. (2017). *Elon Musk launches Tesla in the UAE.* Retrieved from The national.ae: https://www.thenational.ae/arts-culture/elon-musk-launches-tesla-in-the-uae-1.30459

The UAE Government. (2019, March 25). *Green Economy for Sustainable Development.* Retrieved from Government.ae

Thomson Reuters. (2015). *State of the Global Islamic Economy.* Dubai, UAE: Thomson Reuters.

Times, K. (2017, December 4). *How the UAE is empowering women.* Retrieved August 28, 2018 from Khaleej Times: https://www.khaleejtimes.com/business/local/how-the-uae-is-empowering-women

Times, K. (2017, October 14). *SMEs key to driving UAE's economic growth.* Retrieved August 28, 2018 from Khaleej Times: https://www.khaleejtimes.com/smes-key-to-drive-uaes-economic-growth

TradingEconomics. (2019, March 25). *Ease of Doing Business in the United Arab Emirates.* Retrieved from Tradingeconomics.com: https://tradingeconomics.com/united-arab-emirates/ease-of-doing-business

UAE Government. (2019). *The future.* Retrieved from government.ae: https://www.government.ae/en/about-the-uae/uae-future

UAE Ministry of Economy. (2018). *Annual Economic Report 2018*. Abu Dhabi: UAE Ministry of Economy.

UAE Ministry of Economy. (2019, March 25). *Economy*. Retrieved from government.ae: https://www.government.ae/en/about-the-uae/economy

UAE Ministry of Finance. (2018). *Intellectual Properties Sector*. Retrieved August 30, 2018 from UAE Ministry of Finance: http://www.economy.gov.ae/english/Ministry/MinistrySectors/Pages/CopyRightSector.aspx

UNCTAD. (2019, March 25). *World Investment Report 2018*. Retrieved from UNCTAD.org: https://unctad.org/en/pages/PublicationWebflyer.aspx?publicationid=2130

Uowdubai. (2013). *Cobone CEO inspires entrepreneurs of the future*. Retrieved from uowdubai.com: https://www.uowdubai.ac.ae/news/cobone-ceo-inspires-entrepreneurs-future

Wagner, E. T. (2013, September 12). *Five Reasons 8 Out Of 10 Businesses Fail*. Retrieved August 28, 2018 from Forbs: https://www.forbes.com/sites/ericwagner/2013/09/12/five-reasons-8-out-of-10-businesses-fail/#4b1d35ad6978

Wikipedia. (2019, March 25). *Ease of doing business index*. Retrieved from Wikipedia.org: https://en.wikipedia.org/wiki/Ease_of_doing_business_index#Ranking

Wood, M. (2018, July 27). *The 5 Most Profitable Small Businesses in 2018*. Retrieved August 28, 2018 from Fundera.com: https://www.fundera.com/blog/most-profitable-industries

WorldAtlas. (2019, March 25). *Muslim Population By Country*. Retrieved from WorldAtlas: https://www.worldatlas.com/articles/countries-with-the-largest-muslim-populations.html

Chapter 9
The Impact of Entrepreneurship Education on Entrepreneurs' Skills

Fatima Fouad Almahry
Ahlia University, Bahrain

Adel Sarea
https://orcid.org/0000-0001-6154-4261
Ahlia University, Bahrain

Allam Mohammed Hamdan
Ahlia University, Bahrain

Muneer M. S. Al Mubarak
Ahlia University, Bahrain

ABSTRACT

This study aimed to measure the impact of entrepreneurship education on entrepreneurs' skills, which are technical, business management, and personal entrepreneurial skills. A survey method was chosen to measure the impact of entrepreneurship education on entrepreneurs' skills. Respondents were required to rank their perceptions on the impact of entrepreneurship education on entrepreneurs' skills based on a five-point Likert scale.

DOI: 10.4018/978-1-5225-9377-5.ch009

INTRODUCTION AND LITERATURE REVIEW

The development of any economy in the world is the result of human development. It is achieved by using the available resources and creating new ways of production, leading to the issue of entrepreneurship in creating new businesses and new job opportunities. A growing existence of entrepreneurs can have a significant impact on different aspects of the economy as it can reduce the unemployment, increase the level of creativity and productivity (Memba et al., 2012; Aremu and Adeyemi, 2011).

In the recent years, it has become clear that entrepreneurship is a key driver of economic growth (Marcotte, 2012). For this reason, the governments around the world created ways to encourage entrepreneurship, including entrepreneurs financing, and suitable governance and legal protections for contracts (Armour and Cumming, 2006). One of the instruments to encourage and support entrepreneurship is entrepreneurship education (Fayolle et al., 2006). In US, the number of entrepreneurship programs and investment in entrepreneurship programs has increased significantly (Goldin and Katz, 2008). In addition, the European Commission supports this kind of education since they believe that the primary purpose of entrepreneurship education is to "develop entrepreneurial capacities and mindsets" (European Commission, 2008: 11).

The interest in entrepreneurship education started around the 1980's (Barucic and Umihanic 2016). Gibb (2009) defines entrepreneurship education as a process where an individual develops skills, behaviors and attributes, to create, bear and enjoy the changes and innovation in a larger level of uncertainty and complexity. Previous studies measured and analyzed the impact of entrepreneurship education, out of 41 studies 39 indicated a positive or mixed result (Lorz et al., 2011) while only two recent studies find a negative impact of entrepreneurship education (Oosterbeek et al., 2010; von Graevenitz et al., 2010). Although previous studies focused on the importance of entrepreneurship education on several aspects, but the impact of entrepreneurship education on building substantial skills in entrepreneurs has not been sufficiently examined. Therefore, this study aims to measure the impact of entrepreneurship education on entrepreneurs' skills.

The model is designed based on the literature review. In general, this study proposes the conceptual framework as shown in Figure 1.

The study hypotheses are designed based on the literature review.

Hypothesis one:

$H1_0$: The entrepreneurship education has no impact on technical skills.

H1a: The entrepreneurship education has impact on technical skills.

Hypothesis two:

$H2_0$: The entrepreneurship education has no impact on business management skills.

H2a: The entrepreneurship education has impact on business management skills.

Hypothesis three:

$H3_0$: The entrepreneurship education has no impact on personal entrepreneurial skills.

$H3_a$: The entrepreneurship education has impact on personal entrepreneurial skills.

Research Methodology

In order to find out appropriate answers for the research aim and assess better understanding for the research problem, the quantitative method been selected to measure the impact of entrepreneurship education on entrepreneurs' skills. To calculate a suitable sample size, sample size calculator was used as follows:

$$\frac{s = Z^{2*}(p)*(1-p)}{c^2}$$

Figure 1. Conceptual Framework

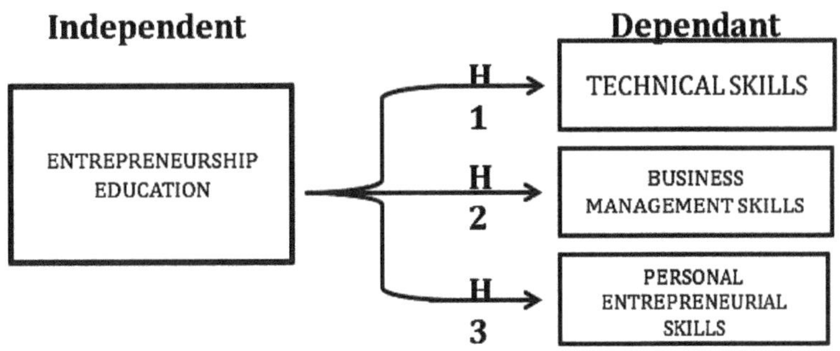

where:

Z = "Z value (e.g. 1.96 for 95% confidence level)"
p = "percentage picking a choice, expressed as decimal (.5 used for sample size needed)"
c = "confidence interval, expressed as decimal (e.g., .04 = ±4)"
*The confident level= 95%, the confidence interval= 6%, the population size unknown, the sample size found: 96

The suitable sample size for the current study are 96 entrepreneurs with 95% confident level and 10% margin error, these would give a fair representation of the whole population. The questionnaires were distributed among 110 entrepreneurs in Bahraini market, total of 104 completed questionnaires were received back.

Data Analysis and Discussion

The questionnaire gathered information from participants through many statements; the following table summarizes the frequencies and percentages along with the mean and standard deviation, see Table 1.

Entrepreneurship Education

The first variable is the entrepreneurship education which is the independent variable that is measured through ten statements. Measurement of the education role in encouraging entrepreneurship in the Kingdom of Bahrain shows that most of the respondents strongly agree (37.5%) and agree (32.7%) that the education has a role in encouraging entrepreneurship. The mean is (3.885) and standard deviation is (1.1849) which point out the high reliability level of the responses.

When measuring the important role of entrepreneurial education could play in the development of the entrepreneurship, it was found that the majority agree (45.2%). The mean is (3.827) and standard deviation (.9994) which show that the entrepreneurial education has an important role in the development of entrepreneurship. Similarly, the majority of the responses agreeing (45.2%) that the entrepreneurship education builds awareness and knowledge to the students. Having the mean of (3.923) and standard deviation of (.9316), (41.3%) of the respondents agree on the importance of the entrepreneurship education.

Table 1. Descriptive Analysis

Questions		Answers						Mean	Std. Deviation
		Strongly Agree	Agree	Neutral	Disagree	Strongly Disagree	Missing		
Entrepreneurship Education									
1. Bahrain encourages entrepreneurship through education	Freq.	39	34	19	4	8		3.885	1.1849
	%	37.5	32.7	18.3	3.8	7.7			
2. Entrepreneurship education plays an important role in entrepreneurship development	Freq	26	47	23	3	5		3.827	-.9994
	%	25	45.2	22.1	2.9	4.8			
3. Effective entrepreneurship education can build awareness and knowledge of students	Freq	29	47	22	3	3		3.923	-.9316
	%	27.9	45.2	21.2	2.9	2.9			
4. Entrepreneurship education is essential for all entrepreneurs	Freq	27	43	28	5	1		3.865	-.8929
	%	26	41.3	26.9	4.8	1.0			
5. Entrepreneurship education relevant and responsive to the complex economic situation	Freq	25	35	32	6	6		3.644	1.0876
	%	24	33.9	30.8	5.8	5.8			
6. Entrepreneurship education is diversified to meet needs of different level of students and entrepreneurs	Freq	42	41	15	3	3		4.115	.9584
	%	40.4	39.4	14.4	2.9	2.9			
7. Entrepreneurship education is a high quality education in Bahrain	Freq	16	60	22	3	3		3.798	.8405
	%	15.4	57.7	21.2	2.9	2.9			
8. Entrepreneurship education gives equal opportunities for both genders	Freq	45	40	14	3	2		4.183	.9113
	%	43.3	38.5	13.5	2.9	2.9			
9. Bahrain needs to increase the number of institutions offering entrepreneurship education	Freq	41	45	13	3	2		4.154	.8897
	%	39.4	43.3	12.5	2.9	1.9			
10. Universities in Bahrain should introduce entrepreneurship education programs	Freq	40	35	17	4	8		3.913	1.1833
	%	38.5	33.7	16.3	3.8	7.7			

continued on the following page

Table 1. Continued

Questions	Answers						Mean	Std. Deviation
	Strongly Agree	Agree	Neutral	Disagree	Strongly Disagree	Missing		
Technical Skills								
11. Enhance the ability to deliver the idea clearly with confidence in both oral and written form.	**Freq.**	38	36	18	4	8	3.885	1.1767
	%	36.5	34.6	17.3	3.8	7.7		
12. Implementation of technology to save time and money, and to improve the quality of work	**Freq.**	31	40	23	4	6	3.827	1.0833
	%	29.8	38.5	22.1	3.8	5.8		
13. Use and manage time and recourses probably.	**Freq.**	23	47	26	3	5	3.769	.9876
	%	22.1	45.2	25.0	2.9	4.8		
14. The ability to use the information from surrounding environment to guide the business probably (information about market, competition… Etc)	**Freq.**	30	48	19	5	2	3.952	.9178
	%	28.8	46.2	18.3	4.8	1.9		
15. Able to identify and analyze problems in complex situations and make justifiable evaluation.	**Freq.**	29	51	18	3	3	3.962	.9129
	%	27.9	49.0	17.3	2.9	2.9		
16. Able to develop relationship with others for business success purpose.	**Freq.**	22	41	31	7	3	3.692	.9762
	%	21.2	39.4	29.8	6.7	2.9		
Business Management Skills								
17. Estimating and designing business plan.	**Freq.**	28	44	23	7	2	3.856	.9596
	%	26.9	42.3	22.1	6.7	1.9		
18. Set and achieve business goals.	**Freq.**	24	44	25	7	4	3.740	1.0144
	%	23.1	42.3	24.0	6.7	3.8		
19. Make decision in uncertain situations.	**Freq.**	22	42	22	15	3	3.625	1.0629
	%	21.2	40.4	21.2	14.4	2.9		
20. Managing human and financial recourses probably to develop the business.	**Freq.**	21	28	23	25	7	3.298	1.2297
	%	20.2	26.9	22.1	24.0	6.7		

continued on the following page

Table 1. Continued

Questions		Answers						Mean	Std. Deviation
		Strongly Agree	Agree	Neutral	Disagree	Strongly Disagree	Missing		
21. Read and interpret to financial statements.	Freq.	25	41	21	13	4		3.673	1.0923
	%	24.0	39.4	20.2	12.5	3.8			
Personal Entrepreneurial Skills									
22. Identify new ways to combine recourses to achieve goals.	Freq.	42	41	15	3	3		4.115	.9584
	%	40.4	39.4	14.4	2.9	2.9			
23. Brainstorm (always coming up with new ideas).	Freq.	35	50	13	3	3		4.067	.9166
	%	33.7	48.1	12.5	2.9	2.9			
24. Manage and face risk in uncertain situations.	Freq.	33	47	14	7	3		3.962	.9944
	%	31.7	45.2	13.5	6.7	2.9			
25. Building great self-confidence	Freq.	40	49	7	5	3		4.135	.9457
	%	38.5	47.1	6.7	4.8	2.9			
26. Responding flexibly to changing situations.	Freq.	37	49	11	3	3.1		4.107	.9173
	%	35.6	47.1	10.6	2.9	2.9			
27. Organize, motivate, and share ideas.	Freq.	33	46	19	3	3		3.990	.9399
	%	31.7	44.2	18.3	2.9	2.9			
28. The ability of leading a team.	Freq.	53	40	7	1	1.2		4.402	.7481
	%	51	38.5	6.7	1	1.9			
29. Taking a positive attitude to failure.	Freq.	39	52	10	1	2		4.202	.8051
	%	37.5	50	9.6	1.0	1.9			

The responses show that (33.7%) agree and (30.8%) have neutral opinion to the statement with the mean of (3.644) and standard deviation of (1.0876). This finding indicates that the entrepreneurship education is slightly relevant and responsive to the complex economic situation. Also, the findings show that (40.4%) of the respondents strongly agree and (39.4%) agree that the entrepreneurship education is diversified to meet different needs of entrepreneurs. (57.7%) agree on the high quality of entrepreneurship education in Bahrain with the mean of (3.798) and standard deviation of (.8405).

(43.3%) of respondents strongly agree that the entrepreneurship education does not discriminate between genders where only (1.9%) strongly disagree, with the mean of (4.183) and standard deviation (.9113). With regard to the need of increasing the institutions that offer entrepreneurship education in

Bahrain, the majority of the respondents agree and strongly agree with (43.3%) and (39.4%) respectively, with a mean of (4.154) which indicates the high demand for increasing these institutions. Moreover, (38.5%) strongly agree and (33.7%) agree to introduce entrepreneurship education in the universities with the mean of (3.913) and standard deviation of (1.1833).

Technical Skills

The second variable is the technical skills which is tested by six statements. The first statement measures the impact of entrepreneurship education on communication ability to confidently and clearly deliver an idea whether it is in an oral or a written form. The majority strongly agree and agree with the statement by (36.5%) and (34.6%) respectively, while only (3.8%) of the respondents disagree with the statement. The statement has a mean of (3.885) and standard deviation of (1.1767) which on average shows a high level of agreement with high level of reliability of the responses.

The second statement tests the technology implementation benefits in saving time, money and quality of work. Most of the respondents agree with the statement by (38.5%) and few disagree by (3.8%) of the total respondents. The statement has a mean of (3.827) and standard deviation of (1.0833) where it shows that the majority agree with the role of entrepreneurship education in enhancing the implementation of technology. The third statement illustrates that the majority (45.2%) agree that entrepreneurship education enhances the management skill, (25%) of respondents have neutral opinions and only (2.9%) disagree with the statement. This result shows a mean of (3.769) and standard deviation of (0.9876).

The fourth statement shows (46.2%) and (28.8%) of respondents agree and strongly agree respectively and they support the ability to use information to business benefit, and only (1.9%) strongly disagree with the statement. That concludes a mean of (3.952) and standard deviation of (0.9178). Similarly, the fifth statement, the majority of the respondents have voted to agree and strongly agree by (49%) and (27.9%) with a mean of (3.962) and standard deviation of (0.9129). This outcome indicates that the entrepreneurship education improves the skill of identifying and analyzing problems and at the same time coming up with a solution regardless how difficult the situation is.

The final statement measures the ability to build a relationship that can be beneficial to the business. (39.4%) of respondents agree on this statement and only (2.9%) strongly disagree. This shows that entrepreneurship education encourages such skills since the mean for this statement is (3.692) with a standard deviation of (0.9762).

Business Management Skills

The third variable, business management skills has five statements to measure. The first statement shows that (42.3%) agree that the entrepreneurship education helped them in estimating and designing their business plan and only (1.9%) of the respondents strongly disagreed with the statement. The statement has a mean of (3.856) and standard deviation of (0.9596). The second statement, setting and achieving goals that are considered part of business management skills, the results show that the majority agree (42.3%), while only (3.8%) strongly disagree, with a mean equal to (3.740) and standard deviation (1.0144) showing a high level of reliability. This result indicates that the majority agree that education helps developing goal setting and achieving skills by the entrepreneur.

Moving on to the third statement which is about decision-making skill, an important skill for every entrepreneur, (40.4%) of the participants agree with the statement, with a mean of (3.625) and standard deviation (1.0629). Therefore, the results show that participants believe that decision-making skill can be improved by education. Regarding the fourth statement, the skill or techniques of managing human or financial resources, the result shows a slightly higher in agreement than disagreement, which indicates that not all the participants believe in the impact of education in building this kind of skill but still the majority do believe in that. The final statement which mentions reading and interpreting financial statements skills, (39.4%) agree and (24%) strongly agree. The mean equal to (3.673) and standard deviation (1.092), the result indicates that education is the best way to build this kind of skill.

Personal Entrepreneurial Skills

Moving on to identifying new ways to combine resources and brainstorming which are the first two skills to measure the personal entrepreneurial skills, these two statements are close in results, the majority agree with almost

(39.4%) and (48.1%) respectively, while less than (3%) disagree. This result illustrates that education helps the entrepreneur in conducting the best way of combining resources and brainstorming skills.

The third statement measures the impact of education in risk management skill, (45.2%) agree with the statement with a mean equal to (3.962) and standard deviation (0.994) indicating that respondents agree with the importance of education in building risk management skills. Regarding self-confidence and responding effectively to changing situations, both statements are close in results, almost (47.1%) agree indicating the important role of education in enhancing these types of skills. The last three statements measure leadership skills in terms of sharing ideas, ability to lead the team, and taking positive attitude to failure. In these three statements the majority agree, which show that leadership skills can be built through education.

Hypotheses Testing

The hypotheses of the study are related to measuring the impact of entrepreneurship education on three types of entrepreneurs' skills (Technical, Business Management and Personal Entrepreneurial). A model is developed for each type of the skill as follows:

Model 1: Technical Skills= $\beta_0+\beta_1$ Education+e_i
Model 2: Business Management Skills= $\beta_0+\beta_1$ Education+e_i
Model 3: Personal Entrepreneurial Skills= $\beta_0+\beta_1$ Education+e_i

Where

β0: Represents the consistent level of each group of skills without the impact of education.
$\beta_{1:}$ Represents the impact of education
$e_{i:}$ Represents the other factors that affect each group of skills.

For hypothesis testing the simple regression is used based on the non-parametric results of the data gathered. As shown in Table 2., the simple regression was measured based on the relations between the independent variable and the dependent variables.

Technical Skills

$H1_0$**:** The entrepreneurship education has no impact on technical skills.
$H1_a$: The entrepreneurship education has impact on technical skills.

As Table 2. illustrates, the impact of entrepreneurship education on the technical skills of an entrepreneur shows that there is a positive and significant impact since T-test=34.293 and the Sig=.000, which is considered statistically significant.

This result supports hypothesis 1, we accept **H1a** and reject **H.**

Referring to Table 2., the "R" for the level of correlation between education and technical skills shows that a 100% increase in the level of education impacts the level of technical skills by (95.9%) which indicates that they are highly correlated. The "R -Square" value of (.920) shows that the independent variable (Entrepreneurship Education) predicts (92%) change in the dependent variable (Technical Skills).

Business Management Skills

$H2_0$: The entrepreneurship education has no impact on business management skills.
$H2_a$: The entrepreneurship education has impact on business management skills.

As Table 2. illustrates, the impact of entrepreneurship education on business management skills of an entrepreneur, shows that there is a positive and significant impact since T-test=12.089 and the Sig=.000, which is considered statistically significant.

This result supports hypothesis 2, we accept **H2a** and reject $\mathbf{H2_0}$

Referring to Table 2, the "R" for the level of correlation between education and business management skill shows that a (100%) increase in the level of

Table 2. Hypotheses Testing

Model	R	R^2	Adjusted R^2	T-test	Sig	Accepted/ Rejected
Technical Skills	0.959	0.920	0.919	34.293	.000	Accepted
Business Management Skills	0.767	0.589	0.585	12.089	.000	Accepted
Personal Entrepreneurial Skills	0.774	0.599	0.595	12.335	.000	Accepted

education impacts the level of business management skills by (76.7%) which indicates that they are highly correlated. The "R -Square" value of (.589) shows that the independent variable (Entrepreneurship Education) predicts (59%) change in the dependent variable (business management skills).

Personal Entrepreneurial Skills

$H3_0$: The entrepreneurship education has no impact on personal entrepreneurial skills.

$H3_a$: The entrepreneurship education has impact on personal entrepreneurial skills.

As Table 2. illustrates, the impact of entrepreneurship education on personal entrepreneurial skills of an entrepreneur shows that there is a positive and significant impact since T-test=12.335 and the Sig=.000, which is considered statistically significant.

This result support hypothesis 3, we accept **H3a** and reject **$H3_0$**

Referring to Table 2., the "R" for the level of correlation between education and business management skill shows that a (100%) increase in the level of education impacts the level of business management skills by (77.4%) which indicates that they are highly correlated. The "R -Square" value of (.599) shows that the independent variable (Entrepreneurship Education) predicts (60%) change in the dependent variable (Personal Entrepreneurial Skills). The "Adjusted R^2 values of the three dependent variables show that entrepreneurship education impacts the technical skill more than the other two types of skills by (91.9%).

CONCLUSION AND RECOMMENDATIONS

Based on the objective of this research, and after reviewing the findings of this study, we can present a conclusion. From the results that have gathered, the objective of the study has been successfully tackled. In addition, it has further validated previous studies' findings and accordingly provide greater confidence on the recommendation. Regarding the descriptive analysis for statements of the questionnaire, all statements had a high level of reliability considering the mean and standard deviation. For hypotheses testing, a simple regression was applied and the results showed that entrepreneurship education has a positive and significant impact on technical, business management and personal entrepreneurial skills. In this regard, any improvement in entrepreneurship education will also mean increasing and improving the level of those skills.

The research results presented in this study show that not all skills are equally affected by entrepreneurship education, the most effected kind of skills are technical skills. Based on the results of this study, we can conclude that the hypotheses are correct and proven. Hence, we can recommend improving the entrepreneurship education in order to play a crucial and important role in providing the necessary skills for entrepreneurs to operate their daily business requirements, and enable them to face obstacles and challenges that might come across during their entrepreneurial live.

REFERENCES

Aremu, M. A., & Adeyemi, S. L. (2011). Small and medium scale enterprises as survival strategy for employment generation in Nigeria. *Journal of Sustainable Development*, *4*(1), 200–206.

Armour, J., & Cumming, D. J. (2006). The legislative road to Silicon Valley. *Oxford Economic Papers*, *58*(4), 596–635. doi:10.1093/oep/gpl007

Barucic, A., & Umihanic, B. (2016). Entrepreneurship education as a factor of entrepreneurial opportunity recognition for starting a new business. *Management*, *21*(2), 27–44.

Boyles, T. (2012). 21 century knowledge, skills, and abilities and entrepreneurial competencies: A model for undergraduate entrepreneurship education. *Journal of Entrepreneurship Education*, *15*, 41–55.

European Commission. (2008). *Entrepreneurship in higher education, especially in nonbusiness studies: Final report of the expert group*. Retrieved from http://europa.eu.int/comm/enterprise/entrepreneurship/support_measures/index.htm

Fayolle, A., Gailly, B., & Lassas-Clerc, N. (2006). Assessing the impact of entrepreneurship education programmes: A new methodology. *Journal of European Industrial Training*, *30*(9), 701–720. doi:10.1108/03090590610715022

Gibb, A. (2009). Meeting the Development Needs of Owner Managed Small Enterprise: A Discussion of the Centrality of Action Learning. *Journal Action Learning: Research and Practice*, *6*(3), 209–227. doi:10.1080/14767330903299415

Goldin, C., & Katz, L. F. (2008). *The Race Between Education and Technology*. Boston: Harvard University Press.

Haynie, M. J., Shepherd, D., Mosakowski, E., & Early, C. P. (2010). A situated metacognitive model of the entrepreneurial mindset. *Journal of Business Venturing*, *25*(2), 13.

Lorz, M., Müller, S., & Volery, T. (2011). Entrepreneurship Education: A Meta- Analysis of Impact Studies and Applied Methodologies. *FGF G Forum 2011*.

Marcotte, C. (2013). Measuring entrepreneurship at the country level: A review and research agenda. *Entrepreneurship and Regional Development*, *25*(3-4), 174–194. doi:10.1080/08985626.2012.710264

Memba, S. F., Gakure, W. R., & Karanja, K. (2012). Venture capital (VC): Its impact on growth of small and medium enterprises in Kenya. *International Journal of Business and Social Science*, *3*(6), 32–38.

Oosterbeek, H., Van Praag, M., & Ijsselstein, A. (2010). The impact of entrepreneurship education on entrepreneurship skills and motivation. *European Economic Review*, *54*(3), 442–454. doi:10.1016/j.euroecorev.2009.08.002

Von Graevenitz, G., Harhoff, D., & Weber, R. (2010). The effects of entrepreneurship education. *Journal of Economic Behavior & Organization*, *76*(1), 90–112.

Chapter 10
Using Health Psychology to Inspire Entrepreneurial Innovation in Dubai

Nada Okasha
East London Foundation Trust, UK

ABSTRACT

Being an entrepreneur encompasses a number of traits. Used as an "umbrella term," it constitutes self-motivation, leadership, resilience, proactivity, creativity, and a sense of light-hearted preparation to deal with potential failure in different aspects of the startup. These individual traits are prevalent in most people; however, it is the combination of them, alongside sound physical health and access to social resources that allows an entrepreneur to enjoy success in due time. Psychological theory and practice may inform techniques in developing and facilitating what it takes to succeed as an entrepreneur. Specifically, health psychology explains how individuals' unique biological, psychological, and social factors, as informed by biopsychosocial theory, together produce adaptive or maladaptive behaviors. To translate this for the context of entrepreneurship, only an individual, who is physiologically healthy or otherwise manages their physical condition well, might enjoy entrepreneurial success.

DOI: 10.4018/978-1-5225-9377-5.ch010

INTRODUCTION

Being an entrepreneur encompasses a number of traits. Used as an "umbrella term", it constitutes self-motivation, leadership, resilience, proactivity, creativity, and a sense of light-hearted preparation to deal with potential failure in different aspects of the startup. These individual traits are prevalent in most people, however it is the combination of them, alongside sound physical health and access to social resources that allows an entrepreneur to enjoy success in due time.

Psychological theory and practice may inform techniques in developing and facilitating what it takes to succeed as an entrepreneur. Specifically, health psychology explains how individuals' unique biological, psychological, and social factors, as informed by biopsychosocial theory (Engel, 1997), together produce adaptive or maladaptive behaviors. To translate this for the context of entrepreneurship, only an individual, who is physiologically healthy or otherwise manages their physical condition well, might enjoy entrepreneurial success. In addition, having the cognitive capacity to motivate oneself and not be defeated by inevitable failures in life and business, and is assertive in receiving social support or is surrounded by emotionally supportive and resourceful peers, will facilitate success in a business start up.

While psychological factors such as resilience, cognitive capacity to process competing cues and tasks, self-efficacy, and ability to motivate oneself on a regular basis may be obvious trait requirements for a successful entrepreneur, biological and social aspects are less obvious. Nevertheless, a significant proportion of our population is living with a long-term condition today, and comorbidity with a number of conditions is similarly prevalent. As for social factors, research has demonstrated a significant benefit of social support on quality of life, happiness, and longevity.

This represents one aspect of how health psychology can be used to support entrepreneurship in Dubai: by directly considering the individual behind the start up. The alternative approach is to use health psychology to inspire novel ideas in Dubai's pool of business start-ups, specifically with the intention of maintaining and improving biopsychosocial health and quality of life in Dubai. Both of these avenues for intervention will be discussed in this chapter.

It seems to be the responsibility of academics, educators, national healthcare systems and professionals, and ultimately governments to facilitate a biopsychosocially healthier community for the benefit of a more prosperous economy, higher success rates for entrepreneurs, and greater national economic growth. Psychoeducation appears to be the beginning of a solution – followed by cognitive-behavior based therapies for individuals who require more comprehensive intervention. By up-skilling citizens with the necessary tools to manage their physical conditions (or maintain their physical health), strengthen psychological capacity and resilience, and be assertive in their social support needs and utilizing existing social resources effectively.

In the interest of economic development, a governmental body might decide to delegate different aspects of such a biopsychosocial intervention unto senior figures across the economy, rather than appointing multiple health and occupational psychologists, whose services may be costly. This includes educators, from primary school to degree-level; business owners; national campaigners; community representatives; consulates; stakeholders. There is potential for a vast impact on residents of Dubai.

Still, preventative and secondary interventions must be distinguished. For instance, in considering obesity as a rising national crisis in the Gulf area, and the lack of entrepreneurs in sport-related enterprise; school psychoeducation of mindful eating, recommended daily physical activity levels and calorific intake might be useful as a preventative intervention for obesity.

However, given that there are already overweight residents, a secondary intervention will be required to address obesity in Dubai (Hussain, 2015). This in turn lowers further increases in healthcare costs related to comorbidities and health complications associated with a high BMI, such as hypertension and Type 2 Diabetes (Hall et al., 2018). This may involve a self-managed, digitally delivered mindfulness course on healthy eating and exercise behaviors. Alternatively, healthcare professionals, and senior figures of everyday life may be trained in cognitive-behavioral therapy techniques for weight loss and increased exercise, to incorporate a social support aspect. Perhaps even a family-based intervention may help. Such measures will surely encourage community-based sporting activities, and encourage entrepreneurs to consider a startup in this area.

Obesity-focused and physical activity businesses provide just some examples. There are multiple enterprises for budding entrepreneurs to consider, such as a digital learning platform or higher education program for individuals with learning disabilities; increasing physical accessibility for wheelchair users to allow all citizens to work; a restaurant chain to target food waste in the UAE, and more. The economic growth of the UAE has potential to reach new heights if all citizens were to contribute to entrepreneurship, despite any biological, psychological, or social difficulties. Health psychology theory can inform national interventions for the UAE. This chapter will propose new avenues for psychological intervention to facilitate a healthier, happier, more inclusive, thus stronger entrepreneur-spirited community.

BACKGROUND: WHAT IS HEALTH PSYCHOLOGY?

Grounded in Engel's biopsychosocial theory, health psychology investigates the psychological mediators and moderators in physical health and illness ("Division of Health Psychology I BPS", 2018). Its framework considers an individual's' health status to be an interactional result of biological, psychological, and social factors (Figure 1) (Engel, 1997). This also suggests that, to intervene on an individual or national level, these factors must be assessed on their individual effects and how they create new effects when combined.

Biological factors consist of ethnic, genetic, and purely physical biomarkers such as blood composition, hormonal activity, deoxyribonucleic acid (DNA) profile, and other cell-level biomarkers unique to each individual (de Lacy Costello et al., 2014).

Psychological factors include any mental and cognitive processes that either detriment or protect overall health. On the adaptive end of the spectrum, reasonable or informed optimism, resilience or mental toughness, a sense of personal control (referred to as self-efficacy in most psychological literature), and other such positive beliefs may be protective to health. They are said to be psychological "resources" that buffer one against adversity (Taylor, Kemeny, Reed, Bower & Gruenewald, 2000). In support of this, there is systematic review evidence that self-efficacious and optimistic traits explained up to 39% of the variance in participants' health-related quality of life (HRQoL), where more positively minded individuals reported a greater quality of life (Huang et al., 2017). This therapeutic effect extends upon individuals affected by a physical health condition as well; a systematic review found that optimism and positive affect were prospectively correlated with better clinical outcomes in cardiovascular disease patients, even after controlling for the adverse effects of depression or negative affect (DuBois et al., 2015).

On the other end of the spectrum, individuals at times develop maladaptive psychological processes such as negative filtering of personal experiences, catastrophizing, holding inaccurate beliefs that maintain inaccurate schemas, therefore allowing unhealthy behaviors (Barnard & Teasdale, 2014). A Large-scale longitudinal study found that participants with higher levels of negative affectivity developed a greater number of chronic conditions ten years later. Daily stressors are inevitable, however individual ability to recover from daily stressors and manage negative affectivity was found to explain different proportions of variance in future physical health outcomes. Negative emotions individuals experience from daily stressors were demonstrated to be impactful enough to cause more negatively-minded individuals to develop more chronic conditions later in their lives (Leger, Charles & Almeida, 2018). Interestingly, there evidence that the effect of mood on health may be mediated by behaviors, in alignment with cognitive-behavioral theory (Gonzalez-Prendes & Resko, 2011). It was found that participants who experience self-compassion and other positive emotions in daily life were more likely to engage in health-promoting behaviors, potentially reducing the risk of future chronic condition development. More positively minded individuals are said to regulate their mood more effectively, and avoiding self-defeating behaviours such as overeating or avoiding exercise (Sirois, Kitner & Hirsch, 2014).

Finally, social factors are modelled to influence our health directly and indirectly. Social support is largely researched for its positive impact on human life in general, and it can be defined as the perceived or actual experience of receiving functional or emotional social resources (Uchino, Bowen, de Grey, Mikel & Fisher, 2018). Feeney & Collins (2015) modelled social support to influence health through the phenomenon of thriving; referring to growth, development, and prosperity. The nature of our relationships are said to either facilitate or hinder “thriving”, by supporting an individual in their experience of adversity, and in promoting adaptive participation in life opportunities that may improve quality of life. Functional and emotional social support were also distinguished. Emotional support refers to providing psychological comfort and refuge to individuals experiencing adversity, and providing encouragement and positive appraisal and feedback to individuals experiencing general life successes. Functional social support however refers to tangible offerings of help to individuals in order to alleviate adverse experiences or encourage participation in positive opportunities. This may include lending money to an individual in need, helping a new neighbor move into their home, or driving someone to an important interview that has potential to improve their quality of life (Feeney & Collins, 2014).

The biopsychosocial approach can explain health phenomena in a holistic way. Consider obesity; its biological influences may include a genetic predisposition or sedentary lifestyle, its psychological influences may include the attentional sensitivity to an obesogenic environment or tendency to consume highly caloric foods as snacks to comfort one's emotional distress, and its social influences may include being raised in an environment that normalises the over-consumption of caloric foods or guardian obesity (Ravussin & Ryan, 2017, Stryjecki, Alyass & Meyre, 2017, Stok et al., 2015). The biopsychosocial approach posits that, in order to truly understand the causes of obesity-maintaining and inducing behaviors, all the mentioned factors must be considered holistically for intervention, otherwise there is risk of adopting a reductionist approach (Engel, 1997).

HEALTH IN DUBAI

When assessing population health, it is important to consider psychological and physical health, as well as the nature and degrees of social integration. Dubai as a city of interest is unique in its combination of traditional cultures and modern technological advances. The climate in Dubai, with temperatures reaching up to 45 degrees Celsius and humidity averaging at 60%, is also significant as it does influence lifestyles.

The most urgent population health issue in Dubai today appears to be weight-related. It is concerning that 34% of Dubai males were reported as being overweight with a BMI greater than 25, and 20.6% classified as obese. Similar statistics appeared for women; 36% of them reported being overweight, with 30% being obese. Interestingly, those younger than the age of 15 had higher prevalence rates of overweight and obesity than older citizens (Hussain, 2015). The following predictors were found to significantly correlate with overweight and obesity in this study: eating fast food regularly and having a family history of obesity, already reflecting the influence of perhaps emotionally-lead eating behaviors and social factors (Hussain, 2015). Since younger individuals demonstrated a greater prevalence of overweight and obesity compared with those older than 15, perhaps more modern lifestyles associated with Dubai's technological advances might explain this difference. This will be explored further when considering national intervention techniques (Hussain, 2015).

Hypertension, or high blood pressure, is another physical condition of interest that is mostly unnoticeable to the layperson, however it has grave consequences such as stroke and heart attack when untreated. The only way to diagnose hypertension is to check blood pressure ("High blood pressure (hypertension)", 2018). 3.2% and 5.1% of UAE male and female residents respectively were reported to knowingly have hypertension in a prevalence study. As for citizens who are of Emirati nationality, the prevalence rates of hypertension increase to 18.9% for females and 20% for males (Taryam et al., 2017). While 18.9-20% are in fact high prevalence rates, one would expect them to be higher given the relatively high rates of overweight and obesity. A study found excess weight gain in Dubai adolescents to significantly predict 65-75% of the risk of hypertension, once again highlighting a concern for younger UAE citizens (Afra, Musaiger & D'Souza, 2010).

Type 2 diabetes (T2D), a metabolic disorder characterized by the body's lack of sufficient insulin, and inability to use the insulin released by the pancreas efficiently ("Diabetes", 2018). Similarly to the prevalence rates of hypertension and obesity, those of T2D are also relatively high. Interestingly, 25% of Dubai residents are affected by T2D, and it is mostly poorly controlled. This is due to issues with adherence to medication and lifestyle recommendations. While Dubai citizens with T2D demonstrate higher rates of screening among younger individuals compared with benchmark rates in the United States of America, rates of adherence to medication and lifestyle recommendations are still lower (Szabo et al., 2015).

Obesity's role in increasing the risk of developing T2D is one of the reasons why it is such a pressing concern in Dubai's health, especially for young citizens. It was found that overweight individuals are less responsive to insulin and likely to develop insulin resistance. At first, the pancreas responds by over-secreting insulin, however this insufficient overcompensation will eventually develop T2D (Choi & Cohen, 2017).

Lower back pain is also highly prevalent in the UAE, with 32.9% of residents reporting it (Al Saleh, Manal, Monsef & Darwish, 2016). This may be explained by sedentary lifestyle and a lack of physical activity.

While there is limited evidence on exercise patterns and physical activity or lifestyle characteristics of Dubai citizens, the literature does suggest those as very likely predictors of lower back pain. A study suggests that sitting for prolonged periods during work and leisure time is positively associated with an increased risk of developing back pain (Heneweer, Vanhees & Picavet, 2009).

Long-term conditions are of interest when developing national interventions as more individuals are expected to be affected by them as they age. This is relevant to the UAE population as its elderly population is expected to increase by 23.6% by 2025 (Alshaali & Al Jaziri, 2015). Dubai's ageing population is a result of improved healthcare services and successful prevention of infectious diseases. While this is a positive improvement for Dubai and means that citizens are living longer, it does not guarantee that those older than 65 live in good health. In fact, 11.7% of Dubai's elderly live with two chronic conditions, 18% live with three chronic conditions, and a considerable 70.3% of them live with four or more chronic conditions (Alshaali & Al Jaziri, 2015).

As for mental health, there are limited resources available regarding prevalence rates of psychological difficulties or psychiatric conditions, which is an area of improvement within itself.

RELATIONSHIP BETWEEN NATIONAL HEALTH AND ENTREPRENEURSHIP AND INNOVATION

Given that obesity, hypertension, and diabetes are some of the most common physical long-term conditions in Dubai today, it is important to consider their impact on residents' lives and the national healthcare system. In 2017, the UAE was reported to have spent 62.2 billion Dirhams for healthcare services, and this amount is expected to increase to 83.1 billion Dirhams in 2022, perhaps due to the country's ageing population ("Healthcare Resource Guide: United Arab Emirates", 2018). As for the residents, it might be very time consuming to pursue recommended behavior changes, such as a regular exercise routine in a year-round hot and humid city, or incorporating a strict diet and eating routine to manage T2D. Therefore, living with long-term conditions is costly on a national as well as individual level.

If less time and money were invested in secondary treatment methods for long term conditions, and more time and money were to be invested in preventive and primary intervention techniques instead, perhaps a smaller proportion of citizens would be affected by obesity, hypertension, and diabetes. This might allow the government to invest in education, national campaigns, and entrepreneurial grants in the interest of boosting Dubai's economy with the funding saved from fewer Emiratis requiring healthcare services for their conditions. Governmental bodies may decide to invest in encouraging and empowering self-management among Emiratis living with the long-term conditions of interest.

Less time and money invested into healthcare services for long-term conditions might also allow both governmental bodies and individuals to invest in school and higher education programs. This is an important consideration since higher levels of educational attainment among citizens correlate to a more prosperous economy due to increased availability of skills and services, and more money being circulated within the community's businesses (Perna, 2005).

Applying biopsychosocial intervention in Dubai may also benefit the economy through citizens becoming psycho-educated through exposure to national campaigns and such. Therefore budding entrepreneurs, with the appropriate financial or physical support from government funding (which is supposed to become more readily available from saving on healthcare expenditure), may become inspired by the biopsychosocial approach. For instance, there is a demand and lack of supply for self-sustaining health-promoting services. This may include a digital social support platform for individuals living with or in remission from different types of cancer, where they are able to advise one another, organize social events, or simply feel relieved from learning of others' experiences of successful treatment. Digital provision of a medication adherence program, or self-paced cognitive behavioral therapy modules are more examples of enterprises that might benefit Dubai's economy in the long-term.

HOW HEALTH PSYCHOLOGY MIGHT INTERVENE

There have been previous attempts of biopsychosocial national interventions in Dubai. One example is the Dubai Residency Training Program (DRTP), which is a postgraduate educational program that launched in 1992 with the intention of improving UAE healthcare by improving health literacy. This program succeeded in bridging the gap between medical school training and hospital based care, however resulted in becoming a service provider rather than an education provider (Abdulrahman, AlSharief, Khansaheb, Abdulghafoor & Ahmed, 2018).

Another attempt was made in which the intervention reduced obesity by 1% in the primary care setting, and 1.5% through a school strategy (HY et al., 2017). However it was unclear from the paper how the intervention was designed and therefore it is not possible to distinguish the intervention's successful aspects. In any case, a 1-1.5% reduction in obesity is relatively low and there is a further need for intervention research in Dubai.

Perhaps it would be useful to address the health literacy in Dubai, which refers to the ability to obtain, process and understand health information and services in order to make appropriate health decisions (Gerich & Moosbrugger, 2018). This means that an individual with high health literacy should be able to recognize a common health presentation, use online resources to reinforce or correct one's understanding of it, then understand how to address it.

High population health literacy is important for a number of reasons including reducing health inequalities between groups within a population, allowing for early intervention of a health presentation due to early detection (which would not be possible if health literacy were low), and generally improving healthcare services) (Batterham et al., 2016). It is also worth noting that increased health literacy has been linked to greater empowerment, making it a useful tool for developing self-efficacy in a community (Gerich & Moosbrugger, 2018).

Mental health literacy is an important consideration for Dubai given the previously discussed high prevalence rates of chronic physical health conditions. It has been widely reported that those individuals have an increased vulnerability to mental health problems such as anxiety and depression (Taryam et al., 2017; Szabo et al., 2015).

Therefore, it is important that healthcare professionals demonstrate sufficient mental health literacy, such they can provide information to the individual and make referrals to appropriate services. A study of health literacy in Dubai found a limited recognition of mental health disorders, ranging from 47% for Post-Traumatic Stress Disorder to 54.3% for psychosis. Approximately half the participants were unable to correctly identify the disorders descriptions provided to them (Al-Yateem et al., 2017).

ISSUES

It is essential to anticipate potential issues when implementing such interventions.

Firstly, a mental health taboo exists in most communities, and indeed prevails in Dubai, UAE. This stigma is collectively influenced by culture, religion, and a lack of mental health literacy (Alkhanbashi, 2018). Psychological treatments only became available in Dubai in the 1970s, and even then were not practiced properly. The title "Psychologist" was not protected, meaning that practitioners who did not necessarily receive sufficient clinical training or had insufficient qualifications were able to practice. This means it was likely that unqualified healthcare professionals designed and delivered treatments that are not evidence-based (Haque, Thompson, and Bassuni, 2015).

While not qualified in counseling, some pharmacists in Dubai are expected to provide counseling services to their patients. A structured observation study found these counseling services to be lacking in contextual relevance and expertise. 72% of the observed pharmacist-patient interactions demonstrated very basic, brief, and generic mental health information being taught to patients by pharmacists. Less than 1% of the observed interactions actually involved patient-pharmacist discussions or mental health information that is personalized to the patient's unique needs. When asked about their perception of what requires improvement, the pharmacists only identified the non-availability of counseling rooms and did not recognize their lack of qualification or sufficient training in counseling as a problem (Hussain et al., 2013). This study provides an estimation of the need for increased accessibility to qualified mental health support in Dubai.

The influence of religion on Dubai is also noteworthy in the discussion of mental health practice. Interestingly, a study of nurses' perception of the most helpful way to intervene for depression found religious intervention to score as one of the most helpful approaches for depression. Religious practices such as reading the Quran or the Bible were rated as more helpful than psychotherapy focusing on social relationships or problems that stem from the past, or talking about the problem with a friend or family member. Receiving support from religious leaders such as priests or sheikhs were also rates as more helpful than consulting a doctor, or receiving telephone counseling (Al-Yateem et al., 2017).

It is evident those religious leaders are highly influential in Dubai, and that residents feel a strong sense of trust when approaching them with mental health concerns. Despite large investments being made in Dubai's healthcare services, traditional healers (Mutawa) have maintained popularity for mental health support (Thomas, Al-Qarni & Furber, 2015). Upon qualitative investigation of the healers' perceptions of mental health problems, it emerged the belief that individuals who frayed from observing religious duties were more susceptible to developing psychological conditions. The healers also reported believing that formal prayer is the appropriate treatment for such conditions (Thomas, Al-Qarni & Furber, 2015).

Therefore, it is not completely unexpected that there is a mental health "taboo" in Dubai, whereby residents may not feel comfortable discussing mental health concerns with healthcare professionals nor their peers. Instead, it seems relatively commonplace for residents to consult religious leaders regarding mental health problems (Thomas, Al-Qarni & Furber, 2015). The combination of a lack of mental health literacy, a lack of qualified therapists and psychologists, and finally the tendency for residents to consult religious leaders in lieu of designated healthcare professionals results in an uninformed approach to mental health care.

From once perspective, it is positive that residents are consulting their religious leaders for mental health needs, as there are multiple barriers to accessing mental health treatment. These barriers, such as low perceived need for mental health treatment and the desire to handle the issue independently are some of the most common reasons individuals do not initiate mental health treatment. Therefore, it is positive that some individuals at least recognize their need for treatment, and understand the importance of seeking help from a trusted and supposedly expert source (Arndale et al., 2014). However, there is room for concern regarding the accuracy and helpfulness of the information shared with emotionally vulnerable individuals seeking mental health support.

The rapid growth of technological innovations in Dubai is worth considering in the discussion of national health. On one hand, Dubai's modern metropolitan nature is adaptive, however it is simultaneously problematic. For instance, recent advances in technology have been associated with an increase in global rates of obesity. Mass marketing targeted at children is partly to blame for the increase in daily caloric intake among young people today. Technological advancements have also resulted in decreased physical activity and an increase in sedentary behavior (Cooper & Morton, 2018).

At the same time however, technological advancements are capable of being integrated into behavior change interventions to target health issues such as obesity, by providing up-to-date and instant biometric data to aid one's progress in an exercise program for weight loss. This includes digitally administered interventions that can offer service users access to information and healthcare professionals' expertise quickly and conveniently (Cooper & Morton, 2018). It is therefore essential to consider both the potential benefits and setbacks of using technological integration when designing national health interventions.

There is also an obesity stigma among healthcare professionals that serves as a barrier for individuals seeking weight loss advice. An "anti-fat" bias is prevalent among healthcare professionals, which results in patients with obesity receiving poorer treatment from them in the form of unhelpful "fat-shaming" (Tomiyama et al., 2018). This is a significant area for improvement if the Dubai government were to implement a national intervention targeted at weight loss in the obesity demographic. Obesity interventions must address changing the attitudes of healthcare professionals, perhaps through medical training by educating future practitioners about the harmful effects of weight bias on patients (Tomiyama et al., 2018).

Solutions for the discussed issues have in fact been attempted in the past, however it is important to recognize there is an "intention-behaviour" gap. This gap refers to the consistent evidence that education programs are insufficient to change behavior; there is an unbridged area between one's intention to make a change and taking first steps to actually make the change. For instance, it is unlikely that a smoker is not informed that smoking is harmful for the health and is a direct cause of lung cancer, however this information is not enough to facilitate smoking cessation. It is therefore essential that national health interventions provide residents with access or knowledge of the appropriate tools and resources to change their behavior (Sniehotta, Scholz, & Schwarzer, R., 2005).

USING HEALTH PSYCHOLOGY MODELS

Leventhal et al.'s (1992) Self-Regulation model (SRM) and Miche et al.'s (2011) COM-B model are attempts to conceptualize the influential factors of and decision-making process behind a health behavior (Leventhal, Diefenbach

& Leventhal, 1992; Michie, van Stralen & West, 2011). There are theoretical and application similarities and differences between the models, which will be investigated for their effect on the models' predictive power of health behaviors.

The SRM model was developed according to previous theory on memory and problem solving, and assumes that health behaviors are the product of a dynamic and bidirectional deliberation between three constructs: representation, coping, and appraisal. These three constructs also follow two simultaneous pathways, as people problem solve how to deal with a health threat using cognitive and emotional interpretations of the constructs. The model suggests that, in response to a health threat such as a symptom or an illness diagnosis, a person will (in no specific order) create a representation of the health threat, perform a health behavior as a coping procedure, and then appraise the success of the behavior which either reinforces the behavior or goes back to attempting new coping procedures that may work (Leventhal et al., 1992).

Similarly to SRM, COM-B was also based on previous theory, however while the SRM is a social cognition model based on problem solving theory, the COM-B model was developed by integrating the most predictive and valid constructs of previous models and theories to create one, all-encompassing model. The COM-B model suggests that behavior is a result of the interaction between capability, opportunity, and motivation such that the three constructs can either directly cause a behavior or that motivation can mediate the relationship between capability and behavior and between opportunity and behavior. COM-B maps onto the Behavior Change Wheel (BCW) as an extension of the model, which suggests appropriate interventions respective of a health behavior's specific capability, opportunity, and motivation interaction (Michie et al., 2011). Since capability, opportunity, and motivation are large constructs, they have later been specified into domains that make up the taxonomy of health behaviors' facilitators and barriers.

COM-B, which stands for Capability, Opportunity, Motivation, and Behaviour (Figure 1) is a useful model for designing and implementing national health interventions.

COM-B also explicitly models automatic and reflective motivation as constructs in performing health behaviors. Intention as an aspect of reflective motivation is not clearly mentioned in SRM as a predictor of behavior. While

Figure 1.

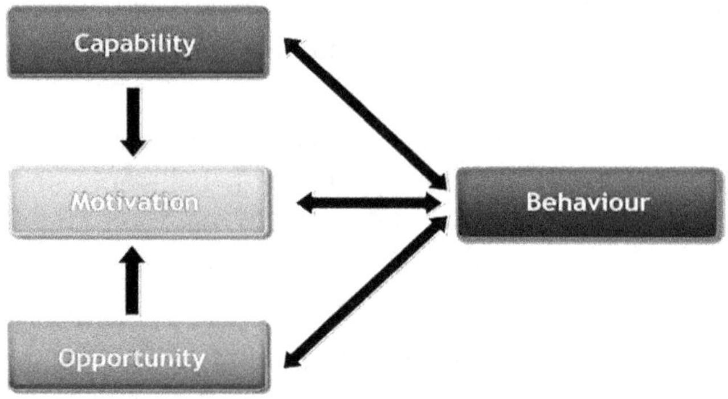

this may be a limitation, SRM's dismissal of intention can be due to the previously documented intention-behavior gap. A meta-analysis on health behavior models found intention alone to be insufficient to guide a health behavior, as other factors may make it difficult for one to bring their intentions for behavior into fruition (Sheeran, 2002).

However, COM-B's placement of intention (reflective motivation) in between capability and opportunity accounts for the intention-behavior gap, as the model recognizes that intention can moderate or mediate the influences of capability and opportunity on behavior (Michie et al., 2011). A longitudinal study explored the mediating effects between exposure variables and the outcome of physical exercise. The exposure variables are translatable to TDF domains and constructs, making them valid predictors of health behavior and suitable representatives of COM-B constructs. The study found psychological capability constructs such as task self-efficacy, outcome expectancies, and risk awareness (TDF constructs of the beliefs about capabilities, beliefs about consequences, and information domains respectively) to be significant predictors of intentions for physical exercise. Intentions were found to have a negligible direct effect on exercise behaviors, further supporting the mediating effect of intention between psychological capability and exercise. A direct causation cannot be guaranteed however this study intends to suggest mediation rather than causation. The participants scored generally high in motivation measures, which could be explained by that the participants were sampled from a cardiac rehabilitation clinic, where service users are expected to already have a notable intention to change their behaviors. This may be a sampling bias, however it can be argued that high levels of motivation across the participants is irrelevant to the results' validity as the researchers were more concerned with exploring the motivational constructs, or third variables, that explain the true association between intention and exercise (Sniehotta, Scholz & Schwarzer, 2005).

Besides reflective motivation, COM-B has also accurately identified automatic motivation, or habit, as a mediator that accounts for the intention-behavior gap (Michie et al., 2011). When a health behavior becomes habitual, a person develops an automatic association between a cue and a behavior. Reflective motivation has a smaller or diminished effect compared with automatic motivation. An intervention study investigated the effect of repeatedly pairing contextual cues with healthy eating behaviors such that a habit is formed, and intervention participants would develop an automatic motivation to perform the healthy eating behavior when presented with the cue. Contextual cues in this study can be referred to as aspects of opportunity in the COM-B model. The cues in this study are event-based, such as during mealtime. The TDF's knowledge of task environment construct of the environmental context and resources domain is translatable to mealtime as cue. This means that participants' knowledge that mealtime is associated with being given an extra portion of fruit and vegetables can, over repeated pairings, develop the habit of consuming healthy foods. The intervention strengthened habit immediately, thus resulting in sustained healthy eating behaviors across different time points in the intervention group compared with the control group (Gardner, Sheals, Wardle & McGowan, 2014).

This study was not tailored for the COM-B model, however TDF constructs help in mapping relevant variables into the COM-B framework, and given the validity of the TDF taxonomy, it is sensible to translate the event-based cue mealtime into COM-B's opportunity construct. Therefore COM-B's explicit modeling of motivation as a facilitator or barrier construct is an advantageous strength over SRM, which is more reductionist for solely focusing on the cognitive and emotional interpretations of a stimulus and disregarding our habit-forming nature (Michie et al., 2011; Miche et al., 2005; Leventhal et al., 1992). COM-B, on the other hand, places behavior as the focus of the model. The BCW extension further supports this idea, as it suggests multiple ways in which behavior change can be implemented. It appears as though

COM-B emphasizes on intervention by identifying case-specific facilitators and barriers of a health behavior rather than simply predicting behavior. This is also evident in that most of the research on COM-B is intervention-based (Han, Middleton, Bubner & Crowther, 2015; Rubinstein, Marcu, Yardley & Michie, 2015). This is a strength of the model in that it accounts for the next step of intervening after a health behavior's predictors have been identified. The model's structure and the BCW extension provide guidance on the tailored and appropriate intervention for a defined health behavior. However it can be considered a weakness as the main emphasis on intervention makes it difficult to test the model's validity and predictive power. This makes it difficult for researchers to obtain confirmatory, quantitative results, hence the mostly qualitative nature of COM-B research (Leventhal et al., 1922; Michie et al., 2011). Whether this is truly a result of the models' application differences or due to COM-B being a relatively new health behavior model in the field is unclear. Still, it is a difference worth considering in evaluating the models' predictive power of health behaviors.

COM-B still appears to be valid. A non-intervention prospective study investigated the construct and predictive validity of the model for physical activity. The model explained 77% of variance in motivation and 50% variance in the moderate to vigorous physical activity (MVPA) measure. Capability and opportunity were found to be significant predictors of motivation, and the greatest predictor of MVPA was capability. These results support the validity of COM-B's constructs and the predictive powers of capability, opportunity, and motivation. Physical capability and opportunity were not found to be significant direct predictors of MVPA. However this is may be a sampling bias rather than a theoretical flaw as the participants were healthy, with high baseline activity levels and belonged to a high socioeconomic status group. Perhaps if the participants were overweight and had limited physical resources to perform exercise, physical capability and environmental opportunity would have predicted MVPA directly (Howlett, Schulz, Trivedi, Troop & Charter, 2017).

To conclude, there are a few similarities between SRM and COM-B, including their dynamic conceptualization of the pre-health behavior process and consideration of bias as a significant influence on behavior. Both of these similarities are validity strengths of the models. They are also differences in the way constructs are modeled; appraisal is an explicit construct of SRM while COM-B demonstrated it using arrows, and the placement and different emphasis on the stimulus and behavior constructs. The similarities advantage both models by making them reliable and valid, which may be why they were included in both models in the first place. However the models have separate advantages depending on the intention of using the model. SRM is highly predictive of behaviors, while COM-B is very useful for informing behavior change and behavior-specific interventions (Michie et al., 2011; Leventhal et al., 1992).

For the example of weight bias among healthcare professionals; a motivational interviewing style can be trained to clinical trainees. This involves adopting a reserved, patient, and non-judgmental approach when identifying a problem area with a patient. Motivational interviewing is a gentle approach in guiding patients to recognize their maladaptive habits and behaviors independently, allowing them to take ownership and responsibility for themselves such that they can feel empowered to make lifestyle changes (Miller & Rollnick, 2012).

Entrepreneurs in the information and technology field in Dubai may also be interested in telehealth for long-term conditions. This includes the delivery of personalized healthcare without requiring the service user to come into a clinic if it is inconvenient for them. Electronically, patients may provide data such as recordings, electrocardiography, or oxygen saturation that provides information about their physical health. After reviewing the information, the healthcare professional will be able to feedback personalized medical recommendations. This is a useful idea for patients experiencing limited mobility or chronic pain, and benefits the Dubai's national healthcare system by reducing unnecessary visits to medical centers (McLean, Protti & Sheikh, 2011).

CONCLUSION

There are a number of ways in which health psychologists or health psychology theory can inspire entrepreneurial development in Dubai. The COM-B model is an appropriate template when applying ideas in behavior change to national settings. If agreed reserves of governmental funding contributed to the discussed national interventions, it would be a long-term investment in that the national health and quality of life of Dubai's residents will improve, making room for diversification in the world of entrepreneurship. National efforts to improve health literacy through psycho-education are a realistic way to begin intervening in Dubai's biopsychosocial issues. This can then be followed by further intervention pathways using the BCW and the COMB-B model to address more specific areas of potential change (Michie, van Stralen & West, 2011; Michie et al., 2011).

REFERENCES

Abdulrahman, M., AlSharief, W., Khansaheb, H., Abdulghafoor, S., & Ahmed, A. (2018). Evolution of family medicine residency training program in Dubai Health Authority: A 24-year review, challenges, and outcomes. *Journal of Family Medicine and Primary Care*, *7*(2), 425. doi:10.4103/jfmpc.jfmpc_183_17 PMID:30090788

Afra, B., Musaiger, A., & D'Souza, R. (2010). The Association between Obesity and Blood Pressure among Adolescents in Dubai, UAE. *Pakistan Journal of Medical Sciences*, *26*(2), 271–276.

Al Saleh, J., Manal, E., Monsef, N., & Darwish, E. (2016). The Prevalence and the Determinants of Musculoskeletal Diseases in Emiratis Attending Primary Health Care Clinics in Dubai. *Oman Medical Journal*, *31*(2), 117–123. doi:10.5001/omj.2016.23 PMID:27168922

Al-Yateem, N., Rossiter, R., Robb, W., Ahmad, A., Elhalik, M., Albloshi, S., & Slewa-Younan, S. (2017). Mental health literacy among pediatric hospital staff in the United Arab Emirates. *BMC Psychiatry*, *17*(1), 390. doi:10.118612888-017-1556-z PMID:29216871

Alkhanbashi, S. O. (2018). *Barriers to Delivering and Accessing Mental Health and Family Therapy Services in the United Arab Emirates: Perspective of Mental Health Clinicians* (Doctoral dissertation). Alliant International University.

Alshaali, A., & Al Jaziri, A. (2015). Health Profile of Elderly Patients Registered in the Elderly Home Based Primary Care, Dubai, United Arab Emirates. *Middle East Journal Of Age And Ageing*, *12*(1), 13–19. doi:10.5742/MEAA.2015.92609

Andrade, L. H., Alonso, J., Mneimneh, Z., Wells, J. E., Al-Hamzawi, A., Borges, G., ... Florescu, S. (2014). Barriers to mental health treatment: Results from the WHO World Mental Health surveys. *Psychological Medicine*, *44*(6), 1303–1317. doi:10.1017/S0033291713001943 PMID:23931656

Barlow, J., Singh, D., Bayer, S., & Curry, R. (2007). A systematic review of the benefits of home telecare for frail elderly people and those with long-term conditions. *Journal of Telemedicine and Telecare, 13*(4), 172–179. doi:10.1258/135763307780908058 PMID:17565772

Barnard, P., & Teasdale, J. (2014). *Affect, Cognition and Change*. Hoboken, NJ: Taylor and Francis. doi:10.4324/9781315804750

Batterham, R. W., Hawkins, M., Collins, P. A., Buchbinder, R., & Osborne, R. H. (2016). Health literacy: Applying current concepts to improve health services and reduce health inequalities. *Public Health, 132*, 3–12. doi:10.1016/j.puhe.2016.01.001 PMID:26872738

Choi, C., & Cohen, P. (2017). How does obesity lead to insulin resistance? *eLife*, 6. PMID:29239299

Cooper, M., & Morton, J. (2018). Digital Health and Obesity: How Technology Could Be the Culprit and Solution for Obesity. In Digital Health (pp. 169-178). Springer.

de Lacy Costello, B., Amann, A., Al-Kateb, H., Flynn, C., Filipiak, W., Khalid, T., ... Ratcliffe, N. M. (2014). A review of the volatiles from the healthy human body. *Journal of Breath Research, 8*(1), 014001. doi:10.1088/1752-7155/8/1/014001 PMID:24421258

De Wit, J., & Ridder, D. (2006). *Self-regulation in health behavior*. Chichester, UK: Wiley.

Diabetes. (2018). Retrieved from https://www.nhs.uk/conditions/diabetes/

Division of Health Psychology. (2018). Retrieved from https://www1.bps.org.uk/networks-and-communities/member-microsite/division-health-psychology

DuBois, C., Lopez, O., Beale, E., Healy, B., Boehm, J., & Huffman, J. (2015). Relationships between positive psychological constructs and health outcomes in patients with cardiovascular disease: A systematic review. *International Journal of Cardiology, 195*, 265–280. doi:10.1016/j.ijcard.2015.05.121 PMID:26048390

Engel, G. (1997). From Biomedical to Biopsychosocial: Being Scientific in the Human Domain. *Psychosomatics, 38*(6), 521–528. doi:10.1016/S0033-3182(97)71396-3 PMID:9427848

Feeney, B., & Collins, N. (2014). A New Look at Social Support. *Personality and Social Psychology Review, 19*(2), 113–147. doi:10.1177/1088868314544222 PMID:25125368

French, D., Vedhara, K., Kaptein, A., & Weinman, J. (2010). *Health psychology* (2nd ed., p. 17). Chichester, UK: BPS Blackwell.

Gerich, J., & Moosbrugger, R. (2018). Subjective Estimation of Health Literacy—What Is Measured by the HLS-EU Scale and How Is It Linked to Empowerment? *Health Communication, 33*(3), 254–263. doi:10.1080/10410236.2016.1255846 PMID:28033479

Gonzalez-Prendes, A., & Resko, S. (2011). Cognitive-Behavioral Theory. In S. Ringel & J. Brandell (Eds.), Trauma: Contemporary Directions in Theory, Practice, and Research (pp. 14-33). Academic Press.

Hall, M. E., Wang, Z., do Carmo, J., Kamimura, D., & Hall, J. E. (2018). Obesity and Metabolic Syndrome Hypertension. In *Disorders of Blood Pressure Regulation* (pp. 705–722). Cham: Springer. doi:10.1007/978-3-319-59918-2_42

Han, S., Middleton, P. F., Bubner, T. K., & Crowther, C. A. (2015). Women's views on their diagnosis and management for borderline gestational diabetes mellitus. *Journal of Diabetes Research.* PMID:25785278

Haque, A., Thompson, M., & El Bassuni, F. (2015). *Clinical psychology in United Arab Emirates: Prospects and challenges in private practice.* Academic Press.

Healthcare Resource Guide: United Arab Emirates. (2018). Retrieved from https://2016.export.gov/industry/health/healthcareresourceguide/eg_main_108626.asp

Heneweer, H., Vanhees, L., & Picavet, S. (2009). Physical activity and low back pain: A U-shaped relation? *Pain, 143*(1), 21–25. doi:10.1016/j.pain.2008.12.033 PMID:19217208

High Blood Pressure (Hypertension). (2018). Retrieved from https://www.nhs.uk/conditions/high-blood-pressure-hypertension/

Howlett, N., Schulz, J., Trivedi, D., Troop, N., & Chater, A. (2018). *Examining the constructs and predictive validity of the COM-B for physical activity*. Academic Press.

Huang, I., Lee, J., Ketheeswaran, P., Jones, C., Revicki, D., & Wu, A. (2017). Does personality affect health-related quality of life? A systematic review. *PLoS One*, *12*(3), e0173806. doi:10.1371/journal.pone.0173806 PMID:28355244

Hussain, H. (2015). Obesity and Overweight among Dubai Population, Prevalence and Associated Risk Factors. Cross Sectional Analytical Study. *International Journal of Epidemiology, 44*(S1), i133-i133.

Hussain, S., Hussain, A., Hussain, K., Asif, M., Khalil, M., Rahman, D., ... AlKhani, R. (2013). Pharmacist–patient counselling in Dubai: Assessment and reflection on patient satisfaction. *European Journal of Hospital Pharmacy. Science and Practice*, *20*(4), 241–247. doi:10.1136/ejhpharm-2012-000263

HY, H., MMO, T., W, A., Abdulla, A., N, A., & N, M. (2017). Targeting Parents and Children at Schools in the Treatment of Childhood Obesity: Short-Term Results, Dubai 2016. *Academic Journal of Pediatrics & Neonatology, 3*(3).

Leger, K., Charles, S., & Almeida, D. (2018). Let It Go: Lingering Negative Affect in Response to Daily Stressors Is Associated With Physical Health Years Later. *Psychological Science*, *29*(8), 1283–1290. doi:10.1177/0956797618763097 PMID:29553880

Leventhal, H., Diefenbach, M., & Leventhal, E. (1992). Illness cognition: Using common sense to understand treatment adherence and affect cognition interactions. *Cognitive Therapy and Research*, *16*(2), 143–163. doi:10.1007/BF01173486

McLean, S., Protti, D., & Sheikh, A. (2011). Telehealthcare for long term conditions. *BMJ, 342*(2), d120-d120.

Michie, S., Johnston, M., Abraham, C., Lawton, R., Parker, D., & Walker, A. (2005). Making psychological theory useful for implementing evidence based practice: A consensus approach. *Quality & Safety in Health Care*, *14*(1), 26–33. doi:10.1136/qshc.2004.011155 PMID:15692000

Michie, S., van Stralen, M., & West, R. (2011). The behaviour change wheel: A new method for characterising and designing behaviour change interventions. *Implementation Science; IS*, *6*(1), 42. doi:10.1186/1748-5908-6-42 PMID:21513547

Miller, W. R., & Rollnick, S. (2012). *Motivational interviewing: Helping people change*. Guilford Press.

Perna, L. (2005). The Benefits of Higher Education: Sex, Racial/Ethnic, and Socioeconomic Group Differences. *The Review Of Higher Education*, *29*(1), 23–52. doi:10.1353/rhe.2005.0073

Ravussin, E., & Ryan, D. (2017). Three New Perspectives on the Perfect Storm: What's Behind the Obesity Epidemic? *Obesity (Silver Spring, Md.)*, *26*(1), 9–10. doi:10.1002/oby.22085 PMID:29265770

Salter, A., & Martin, B. (2001). The economic benefits of publicly funded basic research: A critical review. *Research Policy*, *30*(3), 509–532. doi:10.1016/S0048-7333(00)00091-3

Sirois, F., Kitner, R., & Hirsch, J. (2014). Supplemental Material for Self-Compassion, Affect, and Health-Promoting Behaviors. *Health Psychology*.

Sniehotta, F. F., Scholz, U., & Schwarzer, R. (2005). Bridging the intention–behaviour gap: Planning, self-efficacy, and action control in the adoption and maintenance of physical exercise. *Psychology & Health*, *20*(2), 143–160. doi:10.1080/08870440512331317670

Stok, F., De Vet, E., Wardle, J., Chu, M., De Wit, J., & De Ridder, D. (2015). Navigating the obesogenic environment: How psychological sensitivity to the food environment and self-regulatory competence are associated with adolescent unhealthy snacking. *Eating Behaviors*, *17*, 19–22. doi:10.1016/j.eatbeh.2014.12.003 PMID:25528719

Stryjecki, C., Alyass, A., & Meyre, D. (2017). Ethnic and population differences in the genetic predisposition to human obesity. *Obesity Reviews*, *19*(1), 62–80. doi:10.1111/obr.12604 PMID:29024387

Szabo, S., Osenenko, K., Qatami, L., Korenblat Donato, B., Korol, E., Al Madani, A., ... Levy, A. R. (2015). Quality of Care for Patients with Type 2 Diabetes Mellitus in Dubai: A HEDIS-Like Assessment. *International Journal of Endocrinology*, *2015*, 1–8. doi:10.1155/2015/413276 PMID:26089885

Taryam, M., Al Faisal, W., Hussein, H., Suliman, E., Al Janahi, T., Al Salaq, A., & Wasfy, A. (2017). Hypertension among Dubai Population, Prevalence and Patterns, Reflected in Dubai Household Health Survey 2014. *American Journal Of Food Science And Health*, *3*(1), 14–17.

Taylor, S., Kemeny, M., Reed, G., Bower, J., & Gruenewald, T. (2000). Psychological resources, positive illusions, and health. *The American Psychologist*, *55*(1), 99–109. doi:10.1037/0003-066X.55.1.99 PMID:11392870

Thomas, J., Al-Qarni, N., & Furber, S. (2015). Conceptualising mental health in the United Arab Emirates: The perspective of traditional healers. *Mental Health, Religion & Culture*, *18*(2), 134–145. doi:10.1080/13674676.2015.1010196

Tomiyama, A., Carr, D., Granberg, E., Major, B., Robinson, E., Sutin, A., & Brewis, A. (2018). How and why weight stigma drives the obesity 'epidemic' and harms health. *BMC Medicine*, *16*(1), 123. doi:10.118612916-018-1116-5 PMID:30107800

Uchino, B., Bowen, K., de Grey, R., Mikel, J., & Fisher, E. (2018). Social Support and Physical Health: Models, Mechanisms, and Opportunities. In Principles and Concepts of Behavioral Medicine (pp. 341-372). Springer.

Chapter 11
Quality Management Obsession:
Drive Out Fear, Create Innovative Climate in a Quality Culture

Eman A. Zabalawi
https://orcid.org/0000-0003-4948-7684
Higher Colleges of Technology, UAE

ABSTRACT

Entrepreneurship is a driving force to modern economies if organizational excellence is achieved. High-quality outputs are important at the local, regional, and international level due to e-commerce evolution in business industries. Therefore, factual approach to solve managerial challenges toward quality at the micro and macro level is on demand to outreach global markets. Even local companies selling locally will have to compete globally with high quality and cost-cutting strategies to gain customer loyalty. The quality challenge is to have consistency in all products and services sold anywhere in the world; this can only be achieved if standardized processes, systems, and training are adopted in a quality culture. As an entrepreneur, acquiring "Quality Strategic Management" approach helps prevention of poor outcomes by keeping failure and appraisal costs to the minimum through quality planning and quality training, quality testing, and quality auditing to avoid factors preventing competitive advantage strategies promptly.

DOI: 10.4018/978-1-5225-9377-5.ch011

INTRODUCTION

Three factors inhibit business competitiveness in becoming an entrepreneur. Firstly, family related factors in upbringing to develop soft skills and, hence, application to knowledge areas. However, a person could learn entrepreneurship through family and community, so it may be possible to teach relevant content and application from youth in a contained scale to offer a service or product. Secondly, education-related factors such as a weak curriculum leads to a poorly skilled workforce. Accordingly, the education sector has been focused on research in entrepreneurship in recent decades (Bager, 2011). Thus, research on entrepreneurship has become an important aspect to the higher education decision makers due to the significant economic surplus Additionally, its relation of behavioral sciences including quality management, economics, sociology, and psychology in a hybrid approach have presented many success stories in the market. Thirdly, business-related factors that focus on a variety of knowledge areas such as internships or summer jobs support successful outcomes. Specifically, as what will be shown below, acquiring knowledge from a quality management system perspective correlates a positive outcome for entrepreneuras through the "Do" and "Act" of quality continual improvement.

Quality is a relative term. It is more concerned with the end use of a product or service. Therefore, quality definition reference to Juran views quality as "the fitness for use or purpose at the most economical level." (Bryce & Troy, 2018) Customers select the quality grade of product from the market as well as from what one can afford. With that in mind, as an entrepreneur, one has to then ensure the quality process in order to achieve positive, revenue impact outcome.

Background

Late 20th century was the emergence of the new management of principles labeled "quality management." The term "Quality" was given importance and had in its fold in introducing concepts such as support, business improvement, waste minimization, customer satisfaction feedback, and risk management (9000:2005, 2005). The term 'quality' differs from person to person when a product is perceived as good quality, but perceived to be of bad quality by another. In such situations, the leadership phase is crucial to determine quality as a focus and orient their actions and production level. Organizations strategically then develop plans in order to meet customer requirements, and strive to exceed customer expectations through continouse improvemtn which should increase revenue and market share. Thus, in order to enhance customer satisfaction, it becomes systematic management in relation to customer relationships. The evolution of TQM has emerged in industries starting with Inspection, followed by Quality Control, Quality Assurance. It begins with the knowledge provided by gurus of quality: Shewhart, Deming, Juran, Feigenbaum, and Crosby (Bryce & Troy, 2018) These gurus contributed to the development of principles and practices, the tools, and techniques. Therefore, this chapter will enlighten discussion on how SME's start-up utulizing a quality management system based on the ISO 9000: 2015.

The United Arab Emirates has increased awareness towards achieving business excellence in quality management by launching quality awards such as the Sheikh Khalifa Excellence Award, and the Dubai Quality Awards in full adoption excellency management (Manna, Adebanjob, Laosirihongthong, & Punnakitikashem, 2011). The awards have became the drivers of business excellence as well as created a positive reflection of organizations focused on TQM. Also, while organizations that have implemented TQM have found it to be beneficial, more needs to be done to improve awareness, particularly among small-to-medium enterprises (SMEs). Thus, the implications for more mature organizations to facilitate more sharing of quality best practices increases the competencies of both the organization and the country through innovative problem solving toward excellence (Fonseca L., 2015) .

TQM IMPLEMENTATION

TQM implementation from a holistic perspective (Deming, 1993) is a dynamic process that brings about organizational change in-order or trasformation of business outcomes to reduce operational pitfalls by applying Plan, Do, Ceck, and Act is known as Demming cycle which is the foundation of the International Organization for Standardization standards for quality management systems (ISO 9000)., ten categories implenetation in four stages reference to ISO manual (9000:2005, 2005) . "Plan" stage the inclueds scope, normative references, and terms and definitions, and organizaitonal context,leadership commitment to customer focus, and quality management system, support of recourses planing. The "Do" stage were product and service are developed. "Check" stage is the performance evaluation for management review with records and evidence to outcomes. The final stage is the "Act" stage that implies provesions for reasons of non conformance, act on improvement during mangerial review briefing, propose an enhansment to the quality management syestem and appraise employees according to outcomes sumarized in table 1.

In order for SMEs to succeed in the transformation process, top management must take full responsibility in implementing, nurturing and empowering all employees in TQM activities. The impact of quality management will be evaluated to include reduced errors and improved quality while intangible factors will include improved employee loyalty and motivation.

An organization's guiding principles establish an organization's value quality system for possible franchise either locally, regionally, or international upon successful implementation. The guiding policies, processes, and procedures support a systematic approach, with relatable job descriptions with clarification of risk and opportunities to maximize outputs according to the best understanding of consequences. Specific targets help to measure

Table 1. ISO 9001:2015 Setup Manual (Boiral, 2012)

(PLAN)Scope	
(PLAN) Normative references	
(PLAN) Terms and Definitions	
(PLAN) Organizational Context	(Polices, Management System Processes, Procedures)
(PLAN) Leadership	(Commitment to Customer Focus, Roles, Responsibilities, Authorities, Internal and External Communication)
(PLAN) Quality Management System Planning	(Addressing Risks, Opportunities, Quality Objectives, Planning for Change)
(PLAN) Support	(Resources availability, People, Infrastructure, Operational Environment, Monitoring & Measurement Tools, Organizational Knowledge)
(DO) Product & Service Development	(Operational Planning & Control, Customer Requirements, Design & Development, Control of Suppliers & External Processes, Production & Service Provision)
(CHECK) Performance Evaluation	(Customer Satisfaction, Analysis, and evaluation to Internal Audit, Management Review, Inputs solutions, Outputs corrective action and documentation update)
(ACT) Improvement	(Non-conformity & Corrective Action, Product, Policy, Procedure, Process, Communicate corrective documentation)

operation, and performance attainment to grow creative environment assuring sustainability, involvement, and sense of ownership within the synergic effect to quality outcomes (Buch, 2001).

Business Startup Considerations

Starting a business requires consideration to the internal and external issues that can impact its strategic objectives and the business plan. The context of the organization requires the organization to evaluate itself and its context within the market. In addition, one has to study the influences of various elements on the business and how they are reflected on a business system, culture, objectives, and goals, products, size of the organization and market, customers to detect opportunities and threats regarding the business context. Applying SWOT and PESTEL analysis supports the use of analytical tools to understand the business context (Qualsys, 2018) in understanding internal and external issues, needs and expectations of interested parties (government regulations, customers and shareholders expectations, employees talent and culture, and competition supports successful operational execution within a focused scope and objectives (Adebanjo, 2010). Knowing the context of the business, and the expectations of all business stakeholders are the start point to successful planning. SWOT analysis in table 2 identify and assess strengths, weaknesses, opportunities, and threats analysis to yield strategic

Table 2. SWOT analysis- business context (Valentin 2001)

<table>
<tr><td>Internally: Examples of Strengths:
• Financial strength
• High-quality product
• Talented workforce
• Characteristics and attitudes of ALL employees (Self-image, Education, Social cooperation and willingness to work together, Respect for authority, Attitude toward work, Loyalty).
• Management accounting and control (Overall reporting strategy, Planning, and control, Measurements, Investment justification)
• Planning a competitive focus on SMART policies, processes, and procedures to achieve conformance of outcomes such as (Operating strategy, Inventory, and other resources, Quality control, Vendors and customers, Equipment, Production)</td><td>Externally: Examples of opportunities:
• Availability of new suppliers
• Availability of new markets
• Failure of competitors</td></tr>
<tr><td>Internally: Examples of weaknesses:
• Obsolete facilities
• Weak management team
• Products with decreasing demand</td><td>Externally: Examples of threats:
• Entry of new competitors
• Changing needs of consumers</td></tr>
</table>

insights in quality management culter into ways of realizing the desired alignment (Ansoff 1965; Andrews 1987; Porter 1991; Mintzberg, Ahlstrand, and Lampel 1998).

SCOPE APPROACH

Scope and context setup is followed by six quality management approachs because with an ongoing business operation, managers are bound to deal with challenges. Through leadership, organizations aim for gaining sustainable competitive advantage leadership strategies focusing on efficiency and cost-control (supplier activity cost, in-house activity cost, and distribution activity cost) differentiation strategies through technological superiority, continuous outperformance in the area of quality, offering better support services. Moreover, market-niche strategies are focusing on a narrowly defined segment of the market and becoming a leader for that niche.

Strategic approach and commitment to achieve business scope include the formulation of a strategic plan that integrates quality as a core component to develop, deploy and execute the strategic plans. When an organization chooses to make quality a competitive edge (differentiation), it becomes the central issue in strategic planning reflected on policy guidelines, the process used to outreach quality outcome in every action.

Leadership

The five major components of leadership are commitment,customer ocuse, policy, communication, and finally roles, responsibilities and authorities clarified across the business. It is the process where business develops guiding policies driven to maximize customer focus outcomes through clear communication to roles and hierarchy by authorities and employees responsibilities through clear job descriptions, tasks process, and procedures. Leaders aspire to "To make people happy" describes what a business is all about by clear communication to who we are, who are our customers, what do we do and how do we do it. Reference to His Highness Sheikh Mohammed bin Rashid Al Maktoum, UAE Vice President, Prime Minister and Ruler of

Dubai, upon the launch of the Mohammed bin Rashid Government Excellence Award as part of Sheikh Khalifa Government Excellence Progamme as the most prestigious award for corporate excellence in the UAE. The award encourages employees and federal government entities to serve and achieve happiness and wellbeing for all society segments (SKGEP, 2019). Leaders have spearheaded international excellence frameworks, recognition programs to achieving international standards, with quality-focused with associations to improving competitiveness of UAE's. Although challenges remain, there is an optimism and passion for quality and the journey towards excellence continues for both government and private sector.

The benefits of participating in the Mohammed bin Rashid Government Excellence Award are the usage of the award criteria, which are based on the criteria of government excellence as a guidance to achieve outstanding performance as a recognition of the efficient performance. For example. Sheikh Khalifa Excellence Award (SKEA) established in year 2001 by Abu Dhabi Chamber of Commerce and Industry, Abu Dhabi for private and public sector. SKEA uses framework based on European Foundation Quality Management. At the other hand, Dubai Quality Award was born out of vision of His Highness Sheikh Mohammed Bin Rashed Al Maktoum, Ruler of Dubai and current Vice President and Prime Minister of UAE with establishment of Dubai Quality Award in 1994for the private sector organizations, as a means of improving the standards of businesses operating in Dubai. Thus boosting external and internal trade. Dubai Quality Award is awarded to those companies that have demonstrated a consistent commitment to best practices in their respective fields and to promote organizational excellence in business model based on the European Quality Model to till date and operating from Dubai Champers of Commerce to improve quality, productivity and competitiveness of Dubai-based businesses (Dubai Economic Department, 2012)

Given the context that UAE's economy was gradually becoming a service and knowledge based economy, UAE's leaders realized the need for organizations to improve quality and customer service to become competitive. To accomplish this, they instituted a number of strategic and far reaching macro level quality and excellence initiatives for all sectors of the economy namely the government departments, public and private sector across all UAE emirates adopting best practices, international standards on Quality and Business Excellence frameworks and investing in people development (Thawani, 2014).

Planning to develop operation quality management, leaders are required to have the ability to create or change organizational culture expecting barriers to successful quality implementation. Many have found that changing a company's culture to reflect TQM is difficult and requires much time. Reference to quality gurus W. Edwards Deming who stated that it takes three to five years to implement TQM into an organization fully (Buch, 2001). First, trust through clarity of purposeful procedures, and the company's focus is cruisal. Unfortunately, organizations are impatient and often focus on the quick solutions obtaining results. For an organization's culture to change the effort must be targeted restructuring with a defined purpose and explicitly expected outcomes: communication through policies for performance evaluation, procedures clarifying responsibilities and authorities, and tasks processes to how to expectations of tasks processes and procedures released at the start of the change period. Regular updates to those documents and excessive follow up will confuse the employees and cause a distraction to expected outcomes.

To emphasize that improvement is an ongoing process. It takes place after feedback of employees, analysis of performance review, and customers satisfaction. The findings should be used to corrective actions to update policies, processes, and procedures, followed by communication in an appropriately timely manner that does not negatively effect the flow of production. For example, new policy affects safety and security procedures communication upon need, and quarterly if its an improvement to other policies and procedures needed along with the updated procedures, and an updated task related workflow clarified further in the continual improvement section. Management commitment shall be accompanied by a written quality policy, stating that each person is expected to perform precisely like the processes and tasks workflow requirements, to output what the customers and stakeholders need in a smart timeframe alignment with the support and resources set in the task flow. Simply, managers must become the role model for quality improvement to their prospective employees for customer-focused leadership approach determines the level of quality specified in the scope according to the outcome of context analysis.

It is the executive leaders' role to understand customer needs before planning and execution to support and operation phase. Setting the context that meets the future needs of the customers. Leaders need to ask themselves questions such as: "whom will the customers be?" will the customer base change?" and "what will they want?" Followed by customer positioning to determine where the business wants to retain, reduce, or expand the customer base.

The organization needs to concentrate its efforts on areas of excellence. The product factors will determine the extent of quality to a customer. In today's buyers' market, the customer is demander emphasizes the customer requirements due to customer satisfaction to service to repeat the purchase of the product or service which recognizes that customer needs and business goals are inseparable. It ensures maximum efficiency and effectiveness within a business. Employees at all levels in the business must understand who the customer is, and how to satisfy them. Without the buyer/user, the whole process becomes meaningless. Hence, the organization should focus on quality as what customer perceives it to be. However, as customers go on changing their needs, the quality level needs are to be improved continuously to meet the customer's demand by updating the business scope and objectives. That is why the basic concept of TQM philosophy is continuous process improvement that guarantees to improve the business out of policies, processes, services, costs, and the product in an economically and environmentally system.

QUALITY-RELATED COSTS

Quality-related costs are costs incurred by the planning stage of the project to the sum of money spent on developing quality management system ensuring that stakeholders requirements planned to discuss in a factual approach as a preventive to costs wasted through failing to achieve the desired level of economy of scale within controlled technical and allocative efficacies:

1. Cost of prevention (or cost of conformance), includes the cost of planning that includes the costs of creating an overall quality plan, market research, and product development. Cost of documenting manuals, procedures, policies, and processes that could yield profit upon the success of business operation " the case for franchising" where process control cost association to allocative plans and procedures to achieve the stated purpose with prevention to recurring defects. The cost of analysis, and correction of causes of defects that leaders to quality awareness and quality culture.

2. Cost of appraisal includes the insurance costs that are assessing the products/services conformance to the requirements. Which relate to testing, execution, and examination to assess whether specified quality is being maintained with calibration of testing and inspecting, followed by analysis to institution performance results and suppliers rejects.
3. Cost of internal failures (or cost of non-conformance) due to correcting mistakes before delivery the product/service.
4. Cost of external failures arises from the rejection of the products/ services by the customer due to poor on non-match to regulations such as repair costs, expenses, and replacement costs, lost goodwill of customer loyalty or business reputation.

TQM SURVIVAL

TQM becomes a question of survival in the intense competitive environment. Increasing customer consciousness all over the world as a need for earning a profit. Moreover, the crucial role played by organizational success, such as the context of the organization, leadership, planning, support, operation, performance evaluation, and improvement process. As markets have become competitive with the revolution technology, quality has become a pivotal aspect of sustaining performance and customer satisfaction through the suggested integrative quality management planning, Leadership commitment to customer focus approach, support of recourses to fulfill conforming outcomes by all stakeholders, performance appraisal to the operation effectiveness, and finally continues improvement.

Quality Management System Planning

The management should design a clear scope which shall be apparent to apply. Popularize the scope statement among everyone in the organization to make effective achievement. Followed by designing policies, procedures, and tasks aligned with a timeframe, workflow, and expected outcomes suitable to the *monitoring* system to check whether day to day activity is fulfilling the scope for the developments taking place around the organization. Checking at regular interval is also important to motivate, appreciate, and appraise every employee to own the scope statement and to persuade until it is attained. At that stage, innovative actions start to evolve.

Table 3. Workflow checklist (Petra, 2013)

From the Management point of view	From the employee's point of view	From the products/Service angle
☐ **Providing World Class Company.** ☐ **Providing high productivity.** ☐ **Providing quality award-winning.** ☐ **Cost cutting.** ☐ **Within time frame profit** ☐	☐ Clarity of procedures. ☐ Excellent teamwork. ☐ Accuracy of data ☐ Adequate support of resources ☐ Empowerment. ☐ Within timeframe appreciation	☐ The product must conform to specifications. ☐ The products' utility value. ☐ The products' affordable cost. ☐ The products' longer life. ☐ The products' reliable performance ☐ The products' ease of maintenance. ☐ The products' prompt after-sales service, etc. ☐ Providing environment-friendly. ☐ Creative design. ☐ Within time frame service

Plan execution is to put the policies, procedures, and tasks workflow to execution followed by measurable actions by regularly checking performance outcome in another five to ten years. It provides the commitment, the motivation toward the projects, and tasks necessary. Tactics (how) are well-defined activities carried out to achieve specific desired results in support of the written work of process and flowchart procedures. By this situational analysis, the executive staff proposed business roles, responsibilities that should cover six major areas: leading staff, production staff, product design, customer satisfaction, cost, and speed to market for the proposed objectives across the division, and the feedback-driven to develop the final business scope. Employee's input could be as a professional input before finalizing the plan, due to well-skilled employees selection, they will be able to provide insight into issues, challenges, concerns, and opportunities which may not have been known. Ensure their "buy-in" during the Strategic Implementation Stage which will integrate the quality planning into attainable operational actions. The operational effectiveness starts with the development of detailed action plans required to meet the scope. Performance phase measures will ensure that it is clear when each task procedure and related objective achievement, an appraisal to the team takes place to encourage quality outcome followed by innovative outcome due to the constructive feedback set in each process.

Writing quality policies to express the directive of the top management concerning quality is a strategic item. Policies must be fully integrated with task procedures and time frame expectations. Periodically reviewed for suitability of outcomes. Policies are linked to performance indicators and targets, scope, and KPIs. The policy must cover the internal and external issues that affect the company, and the parties involved, clarifying the desired path of progress for the organization as a whole to reach a desired, measurable result regarding quality planned. Followed by Identifying realization processes which add value upon execution. Promoting policies and objectives to increase awareness, motivation, and involvement of people, predicting the future, put preventive action within the policy and making it happen. Having a concise policy provides criteria for sound decision making. The scope, policies, procedures, and task workflow could focus on below checklists:

Writing procedures will help identify the roles or activities to which an individual is committed, and provides the overall direction for achieving the scope. The main focus is on what the business wants to achieve and how contributions to achievements are evaluated and appraised. Each process should indicate the roles by priority, and the methodologies followed for fulfilling each process by set targets in each responsibility area. This procedure will carry information that is fulfilled with actions to successful outcomes. Time factor should be brought in, to make it more systematic. Among other things, the process answers all questions related to the outcome "what we do, and how we do it." It provides a clear integrative solution for employees, customers, and management. The process consists of the specific and measurable expected target outcome reference to the scope and available support of resources to cut waste.

Lack of management commitment shall cause barriers to quality management successful implementation: All types of organizations, including schools, manufacturing companies, health care organizations, and public organizations, experience low employee participation and interest in their quality management when management commitment is missing or minimal support at any level. For example, TQM will not succeed if upper management is motivating by pressures or threat, such as needing to please the board of directors or meet an accrediting agency's standards within a short timeframe. Thus, if employees see discrepancies in what management says and what it does, they will lose interest and faith in quality management. For successful implementation, the administrative team must have a communicated awareness campaign to quality management, be consistent in its application, and not treat it as management fad or blame culture on change. Alternatively, they should create and maintain the internal environment in which people can become fully involved in achieving the organization's scope by creating and sustaining shared values, fairness, and ethical role models at all levels of the organizations toward continues improvement supported by systematic procedures. Pitfalls in strategic planning and execution adopted from (Ghemawat, 1991) are:

- Failure to focus on differentiation of the business context and scope
- Unrealistic policies that lack reality or specialty outcome
- excessive short-run updates
- lack of procedures to follow by employees
- Require tasks that are not supported by policy or a procedure that lacks timeframe
- conflict outcomes due to cross-division management
- Inadequate data or time to process

Support

Organizations determine knowledge necessary for the operation of processes and to achieve conformity of products and services internal and external resource needs. Determined and project resources needed to establish, implement, maintain, and improve the system, consider the capabilities, and constraints on existing internal resources, and external providers. Therefore, the competence of personnel, and job descriptions identifying the qualifications, experience, and responsibilities for each position that affects product and system conformity.

Selection to the industry related certified employees supports resources availability, cost less, and produce to meet the scope with high competence. All employees are made aware of the relevance and importance of their activities and how they contribute to the achievement of policies and objectives. Providing the person necessary for the effective operation of the quality management system and its needed processes. Ensure the organization can consistently meet customer and applicable legal requirements.

The selection of suppliers and dealers to contribute to the planning process. Employees' involvement and customers' satisfaction are evidence to partnership input. Give teams what they need to understand the root causes of problems, develop solutions and establish controls to maintain continues gains as an emerging competency needs during management reviews. Emergent competency needs become job descriptions through internal or external recruitment depending on the competency availability in-house that could lead to job enlargement and potential career advancement with training support.

Monitoring and measuring resources to demonstrate products and services conform to requirements. It must make sure that it provides the necessary resources to ensure that it is monitoring and measuring results. Retaining appropriate documented information as evidence of competence, employees awareness toward quality policy, quality objectives, how they contribute to the effectiveness of the quality management system and the implications for not conforming to the quality management system requirements.

When documented information is created, the organization must ensure that it is appropriately identified, and described and reviewed and approved for suitability and adequacy with relevant access, retrieve and use documented information.

Leadership structure requires a communication structure that considers internal and external outreach for what, whom, and how to communicate. For example, what documented information is necessary for the effectiveness of the quality management system? Such documentation is required by the standards to identify necessities for the effective operation of their quality management system.

Organizational knowledge is a valuable resource that supports the quality management activities and ensures continual product and service conformity. Due to a strong link between organizational knowledge and the competence of people reflects the ability to apply knowledge to assigned work that is embedded in the process, and retained and transferred to products or services. Examples of Organizational knowledge include documented information regarding a process previous specifications and work instructions; the experience of skilled people and their processes and operations; knowledge of technologies and infrastructure available in the organization. Sources of internal knowledge also include intellectual property; knowledge gained from experience and coaching; lessons learned from failures and successes; capturing and sharing undocumented knowledge and experience; the results of improvements in processes, products, and services. Sources of external knowledge often include standards; research papers; conferences; or knowledge gathered from customers, stakeholders or other external parties.

During times of organizational change, or implementation to quality management, effective communications play a significant success factor in maintaining morale, and in motivating employees at all levels. Communications involve strategies, method, and timeliness. Management must optimize the efforts of teams, workgroups, and staff areas to achieve the aims and purpose of the organization by establishing a long-term win-win relationship with business partners such as suppliers, employees based on mutual trust and teamwork, and on sharing of both risks and rewards. The objective is to focus on what each party does best, by establishing specific roles for each participant. The purpose of partnering is to enhance competitiveness. Health communication with partners allowed access to knowledge through reducing risk and potential mistakes by a greater understanding of the operational context that is relying on a wider pool of technical expertise, experience, skills, labor, and networks. It creates more appropriate products and services to reduce costs and delivery systems and avoiding duplication. The partnership supports innovation by developing unexpected/new ways of addressing old issues and complex challenges and enhances professional skills and competencies in the workforce. It results in Long-term stability and impact by being efficient and effective Reputation and credibility.

Operation and Control

Business leaders establish and implement documented plans and procedures that describe the processes, and the controls required for the provision of services in awareness of the objectives in risks and opportunities. Identifying processes considering parameters of verification, validation, monitoring, inspection, and test requirements helps to meet objectives, and requirements; followed by documented information to demonstrate conformity to demonstrate process effectiveness; resources availability and related controls matches product/service acceptance. Within the control process, potential consequences and mitigation to change affecting input requirements, and resources necessary to support the ongoing operation of the service are planned within the procedures to follow with an ending to each procedure that conformity manager role and responsibility of what actions need to be taken in accordance with the leadership commitment to exceed the element of delivering customer satisfaction. Appropriate handling of customer communication helps to reduce customer dissatisfaction and in many cases turn a dissatisfying scenario into a satisfying experience is captured and understood before the acceptance of an order.

Changes in Requirements ensure that all relevant documented information; relating to changes in product or service requirements, is authorized and amended where necessary and that all relevant personnel is made aware of the documented requirement changes to grant specification conformity and approvals according to the industry regulations and conform with specified requirements.

It is the responsibility of the compliance manager to evaluate and select suppliers based on their ability to supply services by requirements. Additionally, other internal resources may be called on to assist as required. The criteria for the selection, evaluation, and reevaluation are defined in the Purchasing & Procurement Procedure, while evaluation records and any necessary actions arising from the evaluation is subject to continual improvement. Purchased items checked against the purchase order to confirm identity and quantity. If items get rejected on a receipt, a non-conformance report should be raised, and the supplier contacted to arrange replacement or credit within the process timeframe. This is a time-consuming process that delays to outputs, sourcing and establishing a partnership with quality oriented suppliers speeds the process of inspection to ensure that purchased products conform to purchase orders and delivery specifications either on a national or international standards level. Quality awareness must be raised by understanding the importance of product conformance and the costs of non-conformance risks and opportunities among customers, employees, and suppliers.

Performance Evaluation

Monitoring, Measurement, Analysis & Evaluation methods for determining which aspects of the quality management system and its processes are to be monitored, measured and evaluated. The frequency and methods by which our processes are monitored, measured and evaluated is determined and informed by regulatory requirements; Customer feedback and specification requirements; Process and QMS requirements; Process performance and audit results; Level of risk and types of control measure; and Trends in nonconformities or corrective actions (Chuan, 2000). All monitoring, measuring and evaluation outputs are documented and analyzed to determine process effectiveness and to ensure their effectiveness in achieving in-tolerance results and to identify opportunities for improvement. Where applicable, records are retained as documented information for a minimum of three years. This documented information includes details of the final inspection authority to confirm that all critical parameters were by established requirements and specifications. Additionally, product samples shall be available for a minimum of five years. Services are not delivered until all compliance have been checked, and that documented information exists to provide evidence of conformity with acceptance criteria and to identify the person(s) authorizing the release according to the procedure.

Compliance Manager who initiates appropriate corrective actions shall review survey data, written or verbal customers feedback and complaints. The level of customer satisfaction is monitored using various sources of customer data to gain trends that support higher market share; analysis of customer complaints and customer satisfaction surveys to feedback to the production team and management team; finally recognition and consumer awards is the closing phase.

Ref. Title & Description

A process is effective if the desired results are measurably achieved, the effectiveness of the system is measured regarding product quality, process accuracy, delivery schedule performance, cost and budgetary performance, employee function performance against established objectives and levels of customer satisfaction. In order to identify strengths, weaknesses, threats and opportunities in our quality management system, businesses monitors and analyses trends using quality data points such as Characteristics of processes, services and their trends; Conformity to product, customer and legal requirements; Customer satisfaction and perception data; Supplier and external provider performance data; Results of actions taken to address risks and opportunities; Effective implementation of QMS planning; and Improvement opportunities identified during internal audits and management reviews.

Control limits the process and product performance, monitoring, and measures to conformity through planned internal audit undertakes corrective action when the data shows a trend toward the defined control limit. Employees, who utilize statistical tools to analyses; measure and verify outputs, are sufficiently competent to ensure proper deployment of these techniques. Results of internal audit are critical inputs to assess the effectiveness of quality management system using risk-based thinking and the notion of continual improvement as the main drivers. Internal audits are conducted at planned intervals to determine whether the quality management system conforms the planned arrangements and to the requirements of standards that considers the status and importance of each process that comprises our quality management system. The audit frequency is based upon process performance trends, results from previous audits, levels of customer satisfaction, rates of non-conformity and corrective action. To ensure that our organizations focus on the aspects that affect product and process conformity the most. The criteria, scope, frequency, and methods of each audit are defined in the audit plan. The selection of trained auditors and their subsequent impartial conduct ensures objectivity throughout the audit process, ensuring that results are reported to the compliance in charge, corrective action is undertaken where required; retain documented information such as audit checklists and audit reports as evidence of the effective implementation of the audit programme in respect of each audit.

To ensure the continuing suitability, adequacy, and effectiveness in meeting the business strategies, top management conducts formal management review meetings at planned internals to review comprise data from conformance and performance measurements that are gathered at key quality data points from various processes (McFarland D., 2013). Subsequent recommendations for improvement are based on the evaluation of such measurements to detect, correct, and prevent nonconformity. Performance then demonstrates the ability to achieve desired results.

Corrective action: Opportunities for correction are generated by measuring quality and evaluating the cost of quality, as well as by discussion among employees. These ideas should be brought to the supervisory level and resolve there, people at all levels are the essence of business, and their full involvement enables to maximize abilities outputs for mutual benefit.

Performance Effectiveness

Information must be gathered continually to identify and understand problems and to develop and implement solutions. It must be made available to people who can use it to improve quality and performance. Most crucial is not to be used to judge individual performance as this will defeat the purpose of the quality management system and continual improvement process because employees' outcomes are dependent on the accuracy of policies, procedures, and processes put in place for effectiveness. Management understands that the purpose of the inspection is to improve the process and reduce its cost, mass or regular inspection is costly and unreliable. Where appropriate, it should be replaced by never-ending improvement using statistical techniques to reduce defect samples prevention. Employees who are responsible for work must also have the authority to act by information about performance improvement to achieve quality. They must be empowered to control their activities rather than wait for orders but within a detailed process set by leaders. At the same time, employees must be able to use their empowerment successfully by applying their knowledge, skills, and tools due to the caliber employed with experience in assigned tasks, it is crucial to involve employees in feedback, amendment, and corrective actions put to serve the organizational success.

Achievements must be recognized, and employees must be rewarded for their results according to the measures set in the leadership phase. These rewards must be given for improved quality and problem-solving to challenging process gaps. The rewards may be both symbolic and material. Employees will probably expect material rewards, but regardless of the form of the reward, it is essential for them to share in the success achieved in the factual approach appreciate that is decided upon statistical results. Employees must know that their jobs are securely based on company performance rather than individual assessment. Proactive improved processes and procedures cut the cost of training, alternatively will cause low morale which leads to a high retention rate of employees with the consequences not being able to make informed decisions that support high conformance rate in a culture of fairness, which must be reinforced by the actions of managers. A successful leadership plan concentrates on defect prevention rather than defect detection.

Table 4. Elements integration

Element	Traditional Org.	Empowered Org.
Organization Structure	Layered	Flat / team
Job Design	Narrow, Single-task	Whole Process / Multiple Task
Management Role	Direct / Control	Plan/ Coach / Facilitates/ Support
Leadership	Top-down	Shared with Team/ Responsibility
Information Flow	Controlled / limited	Open /Shared / role oriented
Rewards	Individual / Seniority	Team / Skill Based
Job Process	Managers Control also, feedback	Managers Plan and Support/supervisor Control and Improve / Team Produce and feedback to improve

Continual Improvement

The outputs of management review meetings are management actions that are taken to make changes or improvements to the quality management system processes to meet customer requirements applying updated procedures with provision of available support of recourses, operation possible opportunities and risks to resolve all nonconforming records. Improvement decisions made, assigned actions, responsibilities, and their due dates are recorded in the management review minutes. The overall effectiveness of continuous improvement program (including corrective actions taken as well as the overall progress towards achieving corporate-level improvement objectives) is assessed by reviewing the processes for gaps and lack of communication channels, followed by an integrated update.

Business must also ensure that opportunities for improvement from daily feedback on operational performance are evaluated by the compliance process and procedure which are typically implemented through the corrective action system. Opportunities for improvement from analysis of longer-term data and trends are evaluated and implemented through the management review process and are prioritized concerning their relevance for achieving our quality objectives. Evidence of non-conformance, product customer dissatisfaction or service, process speed, and finally policies supporting the drive to continual improvement system. Since problems may already exist, immediate correction must aim at eliminating or reducing the likelihood of its recurrence. Leaders and management are responsible for using their authority for implementing corrective action promptly of product or process. Investigating and eliminating the root cause of these failures is a critical part of the continual improvement process (Skerlavaj, 2007). Business takes action to eliminate the cause of non-conformities in order to prevent their recurrence. The documented "Corrective Action Procedure" defines the requirements for reviewing non-conformities, including customer complaints; determining the causes of product non-conformities and process deficiencies; evaluating the need for action to ensure that nonconformities do not recur; finally determining and implementing action needed and reviewing the results of actions taken and if it is appropriate to the impact and nature of the problem encountered. Results of data analysis and recommendations are presented to evaluate and updated policies and procedures in a factual approach. Organizations shall use this information, by analyzing it and ensuring that the QMS is adequate for the organization's effectiveness. Each nonconformance case reflects a gap in the processes and or procedures followed.

During management review which is the measures and effectiveness to the processes shared with employees are insufficient if nonconformance records are an indicator to how productive the team is, and possible strengths and weaknesses within the organizational capabilities relate to product design planning, policies, and procedures planning, and finally, processes followed.

A Fact-based decision making improves decision-making accuracy, achieve consensus, and allow prediction based on history — management institute methods for improvement through the developed quality management system that allow the business to integrate for successes. Applying the principle of system approach to management typically leads to achieve the organization's objectives most effectively and efficiently (Fonseca, 2015). Understanding the interdependencies between the processes ability to integrate processes. Key differences between traditional and empowered organization:

An integrated system where all functions are interconnected to achieve quality management plan aligned with a scope and the elements in table 2 (Boiral, 2012).

CONCLUSION

A quality culture drive entrepreneurship in taking the time in studying the product, the customers, stakeholders, and country strategic directions to map the business scope with the governance of the market. Few examples of the benefit of understanding the local culture to facilitate outreach techniques that are precisely tailored to the local market. Studying how other enterprises function and what might or might not be social taboos or myths in a systematic planning process begins after context and leadership are declared. The executive staff review scope, context to make sure they are aligned across all expected outcomes fulfilling all stakeholders needs. Starting by human resource section to source quality employees share the same values and believes in working together in supporting operations by cutting cost toward less nonconforming outcomes. Loyalty and trust of employees are gain through shared expectations to success measures. Leaders must forecast to plan well the future conditions that will affect the demand on the product or service using tools such as demographics studies, economic forecasts, projections to help predict the future in support initiative to state needs of employees selection, product design, resources demanded, and market trends to maximize profit within economies of scale production in the lowest risk and maximum opportunities.

Qualifications are core to support resources upon hire if any differences between the employee's qualifications and the requirements for the job description, training or other action is taken to provide the employee with the necessary competence. The results of training are then evaluated to determine if it was effective, and how the policies and procedures influence the business to perform their assigned duties in the least use of resource possible to highest conformance output.

Institutional knowledge contributes to the communication of lessons learned from non-conformities, corrective actions, and the results of improvement; gathered knowledge from customers, suppliers, and partners, benchmarking against competitors; capturing knowledge existing within the Organization.

Employee involvement is a process where employees' input and suggestions are expected and require responsibility for accomplishing task correctly. The employee becomes process owner- thus the individual is not only responsible but also accountable. Empowering, and bringing them employees with decision-making provides the opportunity for continuous process improvement. Competition is so fierce that it would be unwise not use every available tool. Mutually Beneficial Supplier Relationships can be an outstanding motivator that increases the ability to create value for both parties in a changing the market or customer needs and expectations and optimizing of costs and resources. Pooling of expertise and resources can achieve this with partners in a clear and open communication in relationships that balance short-term gains with long-term considerations.

The operation and control to compliance have overall responsibility for planning and implementing the inspection and test activities needed to verify that supplied material, customer communication and satisfaction to product outputs are met at appropriate stages of production. Service delivery does not proceed until all compliance has been satisfactorily completed and internally checked. Understand the capabilities and competencies through communicating the roles and responsibilities of each required output including suppliers. Leaders are expected that, once they have done their planning of how this can be done operationally then ensure staff have skills and understand the process of using resources to conform to the product design following clear instructions, drawings, and procedures risk assessments to enable them to do the job. Managers collect and analyze data using appropriate statistical techniques to determine the suitability and effectiveness of the quality management system to identify opportunities for improvement. At a minimum, data is analyzed to assess the achievement of the corporate level objectives and customer requirements. Internal audits monitor information and trends relating to customer perception as to whether the organizations have fulfilled the customers' requirements — customer complaints about analysis and corrective actions about both quality control and productivity checks to prevent any problems which might affect customer satisfaction.

In order to determine and select opportunities for improvement or to implement any necessary actions to meet the requirements of customers and relevant interested parties, or to enhance customer satisfaction, business drives improvement via the analysis of relevant data. The data inputs for the improvement process taken in the management review to the performance phase. Risk and opportunity evaluations; assessment of the changing needs and expectations of interested parties; the conformity of existing products and services; the effectiveness of the QMS; supplier performance; levels of customer satisfaction, including complaints and feedback; internal and external audit results; and finally corrective action to non-conformance rates; shall continually improve the effectiveness of its quality management system through the practical application of corporate policies, objectives, auditing and data analysis, corrective and preventive actions and management reviews. The continual improvement process begins with the establishment of the corporate policies and objectives for improvement, internal audit will work within the written policy to assess the areas of poor quality and its related cost, then compared against objectives or KPIs to identify additional opportunities for improvement. The overall effectiveness of continual improvement phase, including corrective actions taken, as well as the overall progress towards achieving corporate-level improvement objectives, are assessed through our management review process for continual improvement actions.

Employment to supervisors with statistical training to monitor and masseur through factual approach using relevant statistical tools is essential; Instead of focusing on a negative, fault-finding atmosphere, quality supervisors should create a positive, supportive improving culture that can flourish. All communication must be clear from top management to customers, supervisors, and operators. Each employee must be oriented to the organization's philosophy of commitment to never-ending improvements. Management must allocate resources to train employees to perform their jobs in the best manner possible to recommend improvement, the quality, and productivity of the entire business. The quality journey and change is an encouraged culture among the organization.

REFERENCES

Adebanjo, D. A. (2010). An investigation of the adoption and implementation of benchmarking. *International Journal of Operations & Production Management*, *30*(11), 1140–1169.

Bager, T. (2009). *The Camp Model for Entrepreneurship Teaching*. Paper to EFMD conference, Barcelona, Spain. Available at www.idea-denmark.dk

Boiral, O. (2012). ISO 9000 and Organizational Effectiveness: A Systematic Review. *Quality Management Journal*, *19*(3), 16-37.

Bryce, G. R., & Troy. (2018). *Quality Management Theories and Their Application.* Retrieved from ProQuest LLC: https://search.proquest.com/openview/d4123ff9b2a6da727b5d5ba05c353f9e/1?pq-origsite=gscholar&cbl=35812

Buch, K. R., & Rivers, D. (2001). TQM: The role of leadership and culture. *Leadership and Organization Development Journal*, *22*(8), 365–371. doi:10.1108/01437730110410080

Chuan, T. (2000). *A detailed trends analysis of National Quality Awards worldwide*. Academic Press.

Deming, W. E. (1993). *The New Economics*. Cambridge, MA: MIT Press.

Economy, D. (2012). *Promoting Business Excellence Award.* Dubai: Dubai Economy Department.

Fonseca, L. (2015). From Quality Gurus and TQM to ISO 9001:2015: a review of several quality paths. *International Journal of Qualitative Research*, *9*(1), 167–180.

Fonseca, L. (2015). The relationship between ISO 9001 certification maturity and EFQM Business Excellence Model results. *Quality Innovation and Prosperity*, *19*(1), 85–102. doi:10.12776/qip.v19i1.556

Ghemawat, P. (1991). *Commitment: The Dynamic of Strategy*. New York: Free Press.

ISO. (2016, November 9). *Ge2002*. Retrieved from www.docsity.com: http://dcemecha.weebly.com/uploads/5/8/0/3/58036683/ge2022_tqm_notes1.pdf

ISO 9000. (2005). International Standard, Quality management systems — Fundamentals and vocabulary. International Organization for Standardization.

Manna, R., Adebanjob, D., Laosirihongthong, T., & Punnakitikashem, P. (2011). Awareness and impact of business excellence in Asia. Routledge Taylor & Francis.

McFarland, D. A. G. (2013). *Organizational Analysis*. Stanford, CA: Stanford University.

Mintzberg, H., Ahlstrand, B., & Lampel, J. (1998). *Strategy Safari: A Guide Through the Wilds of Strategic Management*. New York: Free Press.

Petra, C. M. (2013). Document Management for the Implementation and Maintenance of Management Systems Case study - Sherlock Web. Quality - Access to Success, 14(134), 80.

Qualsys. (2018). Retrieved from Context of the organization: http://quality.eqms.co.uk/iso-9001-2015-revision-explained-context-of-the-organisation

Skerlavaj, M. S., Štemberger, M. I., Škrinjar, R., & Dimovski, V. (2007). Organizational learning culture – the missing link between business process change and organizational performance. *International Journal of Production Economics*, *106*(2), 346–367. doi:10.1016/j.ijpe.2006.07.009

SKGEP. (2019). *Sheikh Khalifa Government Excellence*. Retrieved from https://www.skgep.gov.ae/en

Thawani, S. (2014). *UAE Journey Towards Excellence*. Academic Press.

Valentin, E. K. (2001). Swot Analysis from a Resource-Based View. *Journal of Marketing Theory and Practice*, *9*(2), 54–69. doi:10.1080/10696679.2001.11501891

Vanguard, C. (2018). *vanguard-method.net*. Retrieved from systems-principles: https://vanguard-method.net/library/systems-principles/demings-seven-deadly-diseases/

APPENDIX

Evolution of Quality Management

These techniques are used in the product and service realization from internal/ external customers, or interested parties provides information to continually improve the organization's system, product, and services. Many of the 'gurus' appear to present different theories of quality management. In reality, they are all thinking the same 'language,' but they use different dialects and procedures. There are some writers whose work dominates the quality movement. Their ideas and approaches have stood the test of time and have' come to form a body of accepted knowledge, to lead and advise their movement in quality. However, it is beyond the book scope to go into great detail on each of the gurus their philosophies, teachings, and tools.

Deming PDCA Cycle

PDCA stands for Plan, Do, Check and Act. The cycle repeats for improvement of the process for higher productivity.

Deming's Seven Deadly Diseases

Freeing a company of the Deadly Diseases. Only in time will these results become apparent (Vanguard, 2018).

Juran's Quality Planning

Used to establish processes that are capable of meeting quality standards; that quality control is necessary in order to know when corrective action is needed. The entire concepts of Juran's quality trilogy can be summarized as below:

Crosby 'Zero Defects' and' Do It Right the First Time

Crosby proposed four absolutes of quality for his quality improvement process:

Absolute1: The definition of quality is conformance to requirements, not goodness.

Table 5. Deming PDCA explained

PDCA cycle	Elements for investigation
Plan	• Identify the process which requires continuous improvement: Fix the criteria for selecting the process. (It may be time, resource, result based criteria). Assess the criticality (What is the effect of this process on the overall performance of the system) • Locate the problem area: Study the constraints prevailing in the situation. Selection may be based on the frequency, severity of the problem and the constraints involved. • Define the problem: Care should be taken to define the problem, rather than stating the problem (many times problems are stated, leaving room for many options to be sorted out for a solution; but it is found that defining the problem narrows down the options and solving the problem becomes more comfortable). • Project the expected results: Think about the expected outcome of this exercise and document the same. • Identify the best method for solving: list out all the possible methods of solving the problem. Pick out the best one regarding easiness of solving and minimum resource utilization or based on any other criteria. • Set targets for solving the problem: Let the targets be specific, time-bound and measurable Finalize the metrics for measurement. • Preparing the resources: identify the requirements regarding men, material, machine, money, skill. Arrange to get everything as per the need. • Prepare a schedule: Draw the Gantt chart.
Do:	• If training is required to carry out the processes as per the plan, then it has to be taken up as the first activity. It can be need-based in-house or external training. Evaluate the training outcomes. If satisfied take up the next activity, else redo the training. • Improvement activity has to be taken up: Let it be a data-based approach. Scientific methodologies to be followed. Cross-functional teams to be involved • Commitment on the part of the personnel involved has to ensure: Commitment of top management is critical.
Check	• The methodology followed and the outcome achieved after the process is over, are compared with the plans already made. The gap is existing if any is identified.
Act	• This involves either standardization or non-conformance analysis. • If there is compliance, then steps have to be taken to ensure that solution methodologies are made a part of the regular process so that the problems do not reoccur. In other words, standardization is done to integrate the improvement methodology into the system. • If there is non-compliance, then such items are identified, and the reasons for non-compliance are analyzed — scientific basis established for such non-compliance to identify better methods of solving the problem. With this background data, it is passed on to do the revised planning, and the cycle is continued

Absolute 2: The system for causing the quality is preventive not appraisal.

Absolute3: The performance standard must be zero defect, not "that is close enough."

Absolute4: The measurement of quality is the price of nonconformance, not indexes

Table 6.

Deadly diseases	Examples
Lack of constancy of purpose	This philosophy must be widespread throughout the company. Employees require proof that the company is serious.
Emphasis on short-term profits	Profits is fed by fear of unfriendly take-over or, says Dr. Deming, the equally devastating leveraged buyout.
Evaluation of performance, merit rating, or annual review	Management by objective (MBO) and management by the numbers fall in this category. Management by fear would be a better name as suggested Dr. Deming. It discourages risk-taking, builds fear, undermines teamwork, and pits (opposes) people against each other for the same rewards.
The mobility of top management	How can a manager know a company when he is there for only two or three years?
Running a company on visible figures alone	Visible figures are important. However, the figures that are unknown are also prominent to measure the gains in quality.
Excessive medical costs	embedded in the steel that goes into an automobile (payment of wages and salaries to people under treatment for an injury on the job)
Excessive costs of liability	increased by lawyers that work on contingency fees

Table 7.

Quality Planning	• **Identify the customers** • **Determine the customer needs** • **Develop product features** • **Establish quality goods** • **Develop a process** • **Prove process capability**
Quality control	• Choose control subjects (What to control?) • Choose units of measurement • Establish measurement • Establish a standard of performance • Measure actual performance • Interpret the difference(actual vs. standard) • Take action of the difference
Quality Improvement	• Prove need for improvement • Identify specific projects for improvements • Organize to guide the projects • Organize for diagnosis- for the discovery of causes. • Diagnose to find the causes • Provide remedies • Prove that remedies are valid under the operating conditions • Prove for control to hold gains.

Crosby's Four Absolutes of Quality Management

1. Quality must be defined as conformance to written requirements, not subjective
2. The best way to ensure quality is prevention, not inspection
3. The standard for quality must be zero defects, not "close is good enough."
4. Quality is measured by nonconformance

Garvin's Eight Dimensions of Quality

A product can be excellent in one dimension and average or poor in another. Very few, if any, products excel in all dimensions. The Dimensions of quality are:

Table 8.

Dimension	Meaning and Example
Performance	primary product characteristics, such as brightness of the picture
Features	secondary characteristics, added features, such as remote control.
Conformance	meeting specifications or industry standards, workmanship
Reliability	consistency of performance over time, avg. Time for the unit to fail.
Durability	useful life includes repair.
Service	resolution of problems and complaints, ease of repair.
Response	human-to-human interface, such as the courtesy of the dealer.
Aesthetics	sensory characteristics, such as exterior finish.
Reputation	past performance and other intangibles, such as being ranked first.

Chapter 12
The Moderating Role of Public Governance on the Relationship Between the Entrepreneurship and Economic Growth:
Evidence From United Arab Emirates

Allam Mohammed Hamdan
Ahlia University, Bahrain

Reem Khamis
Brunel University, Bahrain

Anjum Razaqi
Ahlia University, Bahrain

ABSTRACT

This study aims to investigate the role played by public governance in the relation between entrepreneurship and economic growth in the United Arab Emirates (henceforth UAE). To achieve its goals, the study used a time series that extends from (1996-2015), a span of 20 years. The study came up with the following results: there was a positive impact of entrepreneurship activities on the economic growth in UAE within the framework of the public governance. Based on the previous results, the study came up with a set of recommendations that focuses on supporting entrepreneurship activities that play a significant role in the economic growth.

DOI: 10.4018/978-1-5225-9377-5.ch012

INTRODUCTION

The activity of entrepreneurship is vital to stimulant economic growth, through its environment. In the long run here is a strong relationship between job opportunities and entrepreneurship. Entrepreneurs not only offer new local job opportunities, but also achieve a fortune and new development. In fact, entrepreneurship is regarded as a critical mechanism to create new inventive ideas in the market, which powerfully correlate with economic growth. Hence, the role entrepreneurship plays in order to achieve economic progress is inevitable, considering the essential factor which lend a hand in acknowledging society's progress (Al-Sokari et al., 2014). Entrepreneurship is regarded as one of the basic pillars for economic development, as it increases prosperity of society by producing more commodities and services; and creates new job opportunities (Bourne, 2011, Yand & Li, 2011). As a result, many countries have tried to consolidate entrepreneurship activities, and as a result, look out for factors that facilitate the activities which improve, economic development/ growth. (Méndez-Picazo et al., 2012).

This information and the findings of this chapter shed light on to the diversified economy of the Gulf Council states, and particularly the United Arab Emirates (UAE). The chapter also analyzes historically entrepreneurship activities in the UAE during a period of twenty years. The aims here is to search for contributing factors for economic growth; to aid the develop of the governmental policy-based solutions. Also, to build econometric models that explain the growth phenomenon, and their relationship with entrepreneurship in the UAE.

One of the fundamental goals of entrepreneurship in an economy is its contribution to economic growth. This is a nations long-term strategy aimed towards economic diversification for an innovative knowledge-based economy. Entrepreneurship is one of the sources of economic growth as it creates new job opportunities, and new markets (Sabella et al., 2014). The UAE realized the importance entrepreneurship earlier on, hence provided support for entrepreneurship education and small and medium enterprises. Such an initiative was pivotal in its vision 2021 strategy for becoming a nation whose economy is underpinned by knowledge and fruitful competition (Abonamah, Karayim, & Thomas, 2016). The government of the UAE is aware that small and medium enterprises are central to an economic growth, and an inspiration for harnessing creativity, new job opportunities and investments. The UAE uses its present fortune to build a more sustainable and stable economy, through its social and economic development plans (such as: Emirates 2021, Dubai 2015, and Abu Dhabi 2030). Such a governmental support prepares a foundation for legislations which will encourage entrepreneurship that could secure job opportunities for the knowledge-worker citizens of the UAE. Such a contribution is manifested in the government's creation of new enterprises and developing small corporates to become bigger ones with an international weight (Al-Sokari et al., 2014).

The tripartite discussed by Al-Sokari et al., (2014) determines the basic principles for a successful activity for entrepreneurs, which depends on governmental support, political vision capable of change, and on supportive entrepreneurship-encouraging legislations. Such variables are adopted by the study, which is described in this chapter, in order to investigate the role of how entrepreneurship plays in economic growth under the auspices of good governance. This is how the UAE prospered in realizing its economic vision for diversifying by supporting entrepreneurship? In addition, what is its role in economic growth within the legislative environment that encourages entrepreneurship known as public governance? This chapter investigates for the answers for these questions. Previous research investigated such relation between entrepreneurship and economic growth in developed economies. The question that gets raised is whether such a positive relation exists in others. Additionally, we need to understand the different mechanisms which can improve such a role as presented in legislative and general policy which contribute in one way or another to improving entrepreneurship activities (Sabella et al., 204). Public governance such as: legislations, general policies, and legislative milieu has a in/direct and a positive effect on economic growth. Therefore, such a relationship supports entrepreneurship, which in turn affects economic growth (Me'ndez-Picazo, 2012).

Due to the increase in oil prices, the Gulf Cooperation Council (GCC) region composed of UAE, Kingdom of Bahrain, Kuwait, Qatar, Kingdom of Saudi Arabia, and Oman (Razzaque et al., 2019) rapidly achieved a remarkable progress in economic and human fields. These countries now occupy a distinguished position, with regard to individual income and human development (Al-Abbas, 2012). According to World Monetary Fund the

UAE was ranked number 23 worldwide in the average individual income index (WorldData.info, 2019), and ranked first as a Middle Eastern country and 32nd as in the world ranking as per the index of human development report by the UN development program (Ismail, 2010), with a very low level of unemployment. Despite such figures the GCC region staggers with its sustainable economic growth. Hence, this chapter aims to explore the potential of the scope of effect of entrepreneurship for development the GCC economy, particularly taking under consideration the environmental challenges of UAE; conspiring the uncertain future of oil and substitution energy, which led the GCC pass through a decline of its income as compared to the rapid growth observed in the Asian countries, which. in general, and the UAE has had to reconsider the oil-revenue-dependent-development model to diversify the sources of income, and to achieve a sustainable development for the next generations. The significance of this study arises from its inspiration to assess the development experiment observed in the UAE, as well as the other countries whose economies need to diversify, and the sense of diversification springs from the phenomenon of entrepreneurship which hence leads to an economic growth and a knowledge-based economy.

LITERATURE REVIEW

The economic activity in general requires a sound legislative environment which allows individuals to practice economic activities freely and safely. Therefore, the public governance is considered a fundamental corner in economic progress. This role played by the institutional and public governance in the economic growth could be achieved through the following conditions: First, the need to impose royalty rights as such a thing secures these rights and encourages individuals to take initiatives for investment. Second, to stop the interference of influential political groups to avoid anything that might affect royalties. Third, to secure equal opportunities for a large section of the society so that a large number of individuals can participate in economic activities (Acemoglu, 2003). More than that North (1990) sees that several historical, cultural, social, and political factors should be taken into consideration as they influence entrepreneurship activities, besides economic policies that establish a kind of relation between governance and institutions.

Good governance can be judged by the considerable institutions in any country; such institutions play a major role in economic activity and lay down rules which determine the mechanism of economy in various fields. The impact of entrepreneurship on economic growth is a complicated and controversial issue, according to many studies. Contrary to other factors, establishing a direct relationship between entrepreneurship and economic growth has various interactive factors difficult to be measured (Sabella et al., 2014). Previous scholars tackled two trends relating entrepreneurship and economic growth. The first trend reported that entrepreneurship has an ascending impact on economic growth through increasing job opportunities and production. The second trend denies first trend's claim while both trends are empirically justified.

Entrepreneurship Positively Affect Economic Growth Within Public Governance

Previously, research indicated a positive relation between entrepreneurship and economic growth: such that the more active the entrepreneurship is, the more positive is its impact on economic growth (Schumpeter, 1911; Kirzner, 1973; Carree and Thurik, 2003; Martinez, 2005).

Schumpeter (1911) sees the relation between entrepreneurship and economic growth from the perspective of its role to produce new ideas that transform to new products/services contributing to new jobs and achieving more organizational gains, hence contributes towards the economic growth. According to Acs (1992) entrepreneurs are agents for transforming ideas to new products, thus creating new jobs that improve the economy (Sabella et al., 2014). When assessing the impact of entrepreneurship on economic growth in thirteen European countries, Carree and Thurik (1998) confirmed a positive relation between entrepreneurship and economic growth and stressed on that fact that countries with active entrepreneurship achieved far better economic growth than those which do not possess such activities. The relation between entrepreneurship and economic growth resonates from the newly created jobs, which makes it easier for enterprises to attain loans, raise market competition, and introduce the market with higher quality production; making all these positively influencing factors for economic growth (Naude, 2008). Carree and Thurik, also indicated that entrepreneurs improve economies through increased productivity, and this is evident when investments are created from new entrepreneurship activities. As per Minniti and Lavesque, (2g06), the significance of entrepreneurship stems from its creativity which taps into under-utilized resources for making economies grow.

Literature that prove the existence of relationships between entrepreneurship and economic growth, for instance, Wong, Ho, and Autio, (2005) concluded that entrepreneurs may contribute to economic growth through: improving the level of economic diversification, creativity in presenting commodities and services, opening new markets, and improving competitive ability in this field. In such form of entrepreneurship and economic growth one can distinguish supply and demand of entrepreneurship. The demand refering to the opportunities available for economic activity, while the supply refers to the required skills and available resources (Audretsch, et al., 2002).

It is questionable if there exists a relation between entrepreneurship and economic growth. Carree et al. (2007) is an example of a study that indicates that entrepreneurship differs in countries according to GDP and according to the economic growth level in that country. The relation between establishing entrepreneurship corporates and individuals' share in the national income is not a linear one, but of a "U" shape. Countries with per capita income have a rise in entrepreneurship activities as the individuals attempt to improve such income; countries with high per capita also have a rise in entrepreneurship activities due to the availability of financial resources, technology, and governmental support. But entrepreneurship may differ in these two types of countries for one kind of entrepreneurship is necessity entrepreneurship activity while the other is opportunity entrepreneurship (Minniti, Bygrave, and Autio 2005). Therefore, general policy makers in any country should care for suitable stimulants which lead to the ideal entrepreneurship that copes with the country's economic status and plays a role in economic growth (Valliere and Peterson, 2009). Institutions are considered an active factor in economic growth as they are the major motive for those concerned with economy in the society, investment, technology and capita which are usually influenced by the institutions (Me'ndez-Picazo et al., 2012). Institutions might be formal such as: lists, contacts, procedures, etc. or informal such as: culture, values, or social criteria of a particular society (Aparicio et al., 2016).

As for this study, it builds its alternative hypothesis of the UAE on entrepreneurship activity and its relation to economic growth under auspices of public governance which can be explained in the following: "There is a moderating role of public governance on the relationship between the entrepreneurship and economic growth".

Wong, Ho, and Autio, (2005) provided theoretical evidence on the relation between entrepreneurship and economic growth. The evidence indicates that there is an influence of active corporates on economic growth; this emerges from various types of behavior including inventiveness, combining resources and increasing competition. Anyway, previous studies found that various circumstances, economic variables, and general policies may play a role in activating entrepreneurship and its role in economic growth. There are three theories and evidences which support this kind of relation and put down frameworks to activate this role.

These are: First, the new economic environment: this theory is based on internal growth theory and on the national system of inventiveness. Such theories explain the performance of economic role of the country in relation to factors such as: infrastructure, human capital, and cultural factors. These local differences can be a factor of disagreement between developing and developed countries concerning economic growth (Valliere and Peterson, 2009). From this perspective, one can see that geographic and internal factors play a significant role in economic development (Krugman 1991a, 1991b, 1991c). Second, the theory of internal growth aims to determine the role played by local inventiveness in economic growth (Romer, 1990; Nijkamp and Poot 1998). Contrary to the modern classical theory which stresses that technological change might be of external origin, the local theory of development stresses that technological change stems from the local environment (Valliere and Peterson 2009).

Consequently, countries with inventiveness grow faster (Suarez-Villa 2000). This growth comes from local investments that help create knowledge which serves local environment even if it were from some who aim at profit. These innovations could not be available at a large scale in countries within a short period of time, but the interaction can be between the close parties to create this knowledge of local innovation system (Valliere and Peterson 2009; Glaese et al., 1999; Sternberg and Wennekers, 2005, Anselin Varga, and Acs 2000; and Varga 2005). Technology activation in business can be through entrepreneurship activity which benefits from such inventions in commodity production for unusual services and through opening new markets and creating job opportunities which lead to improvement of economic growth (Audrestch and Kleibach, 2004). According to this theory, the country's concentration on economic activity emerges from three criteria: increasing individuals' participation in economic activity, reducing transportation costs, and increasing demand for local products (Valliere and Peterson 2009). The third concept of economic growth depends on the collective national system of inventiveness as presented in: the roles of government and institutions, learning and technology systems, administration and institutional frameworks which motivate entrepreneurship (Freeman 1988; Lundvall 1988; Nelson 1988). Institutions or public governance play a central role in this system for this role is important in development and in correlated various resources to achieve this development. This system leans on royalties and authority of law (Gwartney Halcombe, and Lawson 1999).

The institutions functioning in a suitable investment environment are necessary to encourage development, entrepreneurship, and economic growth (Boettke and Coyne 2003). Thus, institutions are not enough for active functioning of this system; economic and social factors also play an important role in this field. Individual entrepreneurship is the constructive fabric of the country's economy (Audretsch et al., 2002).

Entrepreneurship Has No Impact on Economic Growth

Economic growth has been of an important increasing concern by decision makers and researchers, especially after the rise in the level of unemployment in the world. Despite the extensive studies and evidence which found a relation between entrepreneurship and economic growth, yet on the other hand, there are some who argue against this issue on the ground that entrepreneurship exploits surplus revenues (Minniti and Lavesque, 2006). Consequently, results of past experimental studies on this relationship between entrepreneurship, inventiveness and economic growth were different. Most of those studies did not have control factors on entrepreneurship activities and their motives (Valliere and Peterson 2009). New knowledge contributes to economic growth, but mechanism through which this knowledge is practically applied, and its role in the economic development is arguable. For instance, why didn't big investments in research and development affect economic growth in Japan and Sweden? Contrary to European countries, why didn't entrepreneurship activities play a big role in economic growth in the United Kingdom? Or why does such an impact vary from time to time? In general, why doesn't new knowledge incessantly lead to economic growth? (Carlsson et al., 2009). Acs (2006) study went beyond that when it came to the conclusion that there was a negative impact of some entrepreneurship activities on economic growth. This study, therefore, adopts the null hypothesis on the relation between entrepreneurship activities and economic growth under auspices of general public governance. This relationship can be illustrated in the following: "There is no moderating role of public governance on the relationship between the entrepreneurship and economic growth".

Experimental studies didn't precisely determine any causal relationship between entrepreneurship expansion and economic growth. Many studies hypothesized a relation between the average of registering new corporates as an indication of such a relation, but never took into consideration other factors affecting entrepreneurship (Carree et al., 2007) Fritsch, (2007) argues that the rise in the newly founded enterprises in any economy could not necessarily have a positive relation with creating new jobs in that economy. There are two types of entrepreneurships: necessity-entrepreneurship activity and hypothesis-based one. The first type emerges when the individual has no available options, but the second gets involved in searching for available opportunities in a specific market. The first has a negative impact on economy but the second a positive one. In Palestine (Sabella et al., 2014), study found that the necessity entrepreneurship had no impact on economic growth; it also found that 40% of entrepreneurships in Palestine was non-official; thus, the role of entrepreneurship in achieving economic growth in the complicated Palestinian environment was of great doubt. Fritsch, (2007) sees that the necessity entrepreneurship activity does not necessarily create new jobs. Tang and Koveos, (2014) study discussed two types of entrepreneurship: Voluntary and Creative and their role in economic growth. The study concluded that voluntary entrepreneurship has an influence of direct proportion on economy in countries with high income than those of medium ones and finally those of low, while the creative one plays a negative role.

The different influences of entrepreneurship on the growth of economy lie in the type of work: official and non-official. The difference in results may go back to data sources on entrepreneurship. Data derived from International Bank measure entrepreneurship by the officially registered enterprises, but those derived from GEM measure the first stage of Entrepreneurship (Sabella et al., 2009), noting that enterprises serving the society should not necessarily be officially registered; this imposes restrictions on the data used in many studies and on the ability of monitoring the relation between economic growth and Entrepreneurship.

Contributions of Current Study

At Present, the UAE undergoes an economic growth paralleled with legislations and regulations on several economic and social aspects of life. Thus, it aims at a more sustainable economy through diversification of economic resources in moving toward knowledge economy which encourages creative entrepreneurship to exploit resources. As discrepancy was apparent in literatures on the relation between entrepreneurship and economic growth with regard to economic, administrative, cultural, and social factors, the current study focuses on UAE entrepreneurship activity for the purpose of analyzing economic and administrative environments related to the activity in order to determine the best administration practices that contribute to activation of entrepreneurship. The study also investigates the range of contribution entrepreneurship plays in the economic growth in UAE to know which of them affects such a growth.

This study provides two contributions: the theoretical level and the practical one. At the theoretical level, the study adds up to the literature of economy concerned with the impact of entrepreneurship on economic growth in one of the developing countries that have different economic and social environments and depend on oil revenues to finance their general expenditures to reinforce economic growth. As for the practical level, the study is expected to provide results which contribute to understanding of the nature of entrepreneurship in UAE and to what extent that contributes to economic growth. It will also determine the adequate type of entrepreneurship that suits the social and cultural environments which will actively contribute to the growth in UAE.

In addition, the study will provide its vision on the role of public governance in creating a suitable entrepreneurship environment that will give decision makers a clear picture of the role governance plays in the relation between entrepreneurship and economic growth in the Emirates.

RESEARCH METHODOLOGY

Based on various entrepreneurship and economic growth under public governance theories as presented by past scholars in various countries, this study's model and express such roles, followed by secondary data analysis to test the model and hypotheses.

Time Series and Sources of Data Collection

This study investigates entrepreneurship activity in the UAE and its role in achieving economic growth within public governance. To achieve its goals, the study covered a time series of (20) twenty years between (1996-2015). It depended on secondary sources for collecting data presented in World Bank database, General statistics of UAE, and GEM.

Study Models

The preliminary goal of this study is to evaluate entrepreneurship activity in the UAE between 1996-2015. Then it endeavors to test its influence upon economic growth within this period under the auspices of public governance. To achieve the second goal, it adopts an extensive neoclassical product function of growth stemming from the following function:

$$EconGrowth_t = \alpha + \beta_1 Labor_t + Capital_t + \ell_t \tag{1}$$

This relation will be extended by adding up some control variables to the model like oil price (oilt) and level of economic diversification at UAE (Divert), so the formula becomes:

$$EconGrowth_t = \alpha + \beta_1 Labor_t + Capital_t + Oil_t + Diver_t + \ell_t \tag{2}$$

After that the independent variable in the model will be added up to the model (Entert) to refer to entrepreneurship in the UAE, in addition to the interactive variable (PGIndex*Enter) between entrepreneurship and public governance to end up with the final model of the study:

$$EconGrowth_t = \alpha + \beta_1 Labor_t + Capital_t + Oil_t + Diver_t + Enter_t + (PGIndex * Enter) + \ell_t \quad (3)$$

As independent and control variables might later affect economic growth, for example economic diversification or oil prices, entrepreneurship needs some time to effectively influence economic growth. Therefore, time factor will be taken into consideration in the model by using one Log period (Log 1) in assessing the model which will be illustrated later.

Measuring Economic Growth and Production Function

This part of the study illustrates methods adopted in defining and measuring variables. The study used the growth in GDP and GDP from non-oil sector as a measure for economic growth, like many past studies which discussed economic growth and its relation to entrepreneurship (Audretsch and Fritsch,1996, 2002; Acs and Armington,2002; Van Stel and Storey,2004; Fritsch and Mueller, 2004).

As for the economic justification of adding variables to the model and measuring it is as follows:

Labor variable: Labor is considered one of the most important factors which determine the level of GDP and one of the most significant inputs in the production process. Thus, this variable was added to the standard model of the study to control the relation between the variable associated with "economic growth" and the independent variable "entrepreneurship". This variable will be tested through labor data in the UAE as disclosed by the department of general statistics throughout the period of the study.

Capital Variable: According to the classical and neo-classical theories, production level is related to capital and depends on investment accumulation through time after deducing consumption Therefore this variable was added to the model for being one of the influencing factors in the level of local product as it acts as a control variable between the dependent and independent ones. Data for this variable were obtained from the data disclosed by the general department of statistics in UAE through period of the study.

Oil Price: This variable is expected to leave a possible impact on the GDP. Rise in oil prices increases country's revenues which eventually lead to economy performance in general. Due to this, the variable was added for it acts as a control variable between the dependent and independent ones. West Texas price average, adopted by Gulf States, was the one used throughout the year.

Economic Diversification: Many international studies (Audretsch et al., 2002; Wong, Ho, and Autio, 2005, Hamdan, 2017) consider economy diversification one of the important factors in achieving economic development. Due to this, the factor was added to the study model as it is a control variable between economic growth and entrepreneurship. There are many measures for economic growth like (Gini coefficient) which the study adopted. This coefficient is one of the best and simplest measures which was designed by Si Gini (1912). The coefficient is used to measure degree of economy diversification. Absence of diversification is "Very high" if the rate exceeds (0.7) and "High" if the coefficient ranges between (0.5-0.7), "average" between (0.35-0.5), and "weak" if it was less than (0.35) (Twadro, 2006). The lower the Gini's coefficient is, the more economic diversification exists. The following formula illustrates the coefficient:

$$Gini_t = 1 - \sum_{K=1}^{n} (x_k - x_{k-1})(y_k + y_{k+1}) \tag{4}$$

(XK) represents the frequent ascendance of the relative accumulation of the total variable (GDP sector). (YK) represents the ascendance of relative accumulation of sector number, (n) represents the number of economic sectors constituting GDP. Gini's index ranges between zero-one. Once the coefficient is zero, then the economic diversification is complete and when it is one, diversification is nil- a case in which economic products are centered in one activity, other activities do not contribute to GDP (Al-Khatib, 2011).

Measuring Entrepreneurship Variables and Public Governance:

In measuring entrepreneurship variables and public governance, secondary databases were used as follows:

Measuring Entrepreneurship: The study, in measuring entrepreneurship, depended on two scales; the first is based on the International Bank database regarding the size and rate of creating new enterprises in the UAE, while the

Table 1. Entrepreneurship Motivation and Gender in UAE

	Mean	SD
Percentage of population who believe they have the required skills and knowledge to start a business.	59.731	9.521
Percentage of population who see good opportunities to start a firm in the area where they live.	45.087	3.635
Percentage of population perceiving good opportunities to start a business who indicate that fear of failure would prevent them from setting up a business.	34.700	11.065
Percentage of population (individuals involved in any stage of entrepreneurial activity excluded) who are latent entrepreneurs and who intend to start a business within three years.	19.986	18.215
Percentage of population who personally know someone who started a business in the past two years.	37.554	8.201
Percentage of population who agree with the statement that in their country, most people consider starting a business as a desirable career choice.	72.986	3.952
Percentage of male population who are either a nascent entrepreneur or owner-manager of a 'new business'.	9.607	4.411
Percentage of female population who are either a nascent entrepreneur or owner-manager of a 'new business'.	4.227	2.766

second is based on the investigation conducted by GEM. The size and rate of establishing new enterprises were used as an entrepreneurship substitute in the study model no. (3). The data derived from the GEM will be used in the descriptive study.

Public Governance Scale: Five variables were used to refer to the level of public governance in UAE. These variables were derived from International Bank Reports between (1996-2015) as outlined in the following: Control of Corruption, Government Effectiveness, Political Stability, Rule of Law, and Regulatory Quality.

DESCRIPTIVE STUDY

GEM investigated entrepreneurship contribution to economy through the stages of development providing several indexes of individual contributions to its activities and other factors through which these activities in UAE can best be viewed. These indexes cover four years: 2006 – 2007. 2009 and 2011 and will be discussed according to the following titles:

Table 2. Entrepreneurs in UAE

	Mean	SD
Total early-stage Entrepreneurial Activity (TEA)	7.904	4.049
Percentage of those involved in TEA who claim to be driven by opportunity as opposed to finding no other option for work	11.819	3.644
Percentage of population who have personally provided funds for a new business, started by someone else, in the past three years	6.281	2.735
Percentage of TEA who expect to employ at least five employees five years from now	65.427	15.038
Percentage of TEA who indicate that their product or service is new to at least some customers	71.060	13.734
Percentage of TEA who indicate that at least 25% of the customers come from other countries	36.568	4.330

Entrepreneurship Motivation and Differences According to Gender

Table 1 shows the attitude of a sample of population in UAE about their motives for starting business and their opinion of entrepreneurship. It was noticed that a moderate percentage of Emiratis believe that they have the skills and acquaintances necessary for starting business and there are good opportunities to start that in the area where they live. Approximately, one fifth of the population plans to start enterprises within the coming three years. A large number of them know people who have already started their enterprises. One third of Emiratis see that fear from failure prevents them from realizing their dream of having enterprises of their own. As for difference of the type of entrepreneurship, we notice that (9.6%) of the male population has become entrepreneurs at an early stage of their life, compared to (4.2%) of females are entrepreneurs at an early stage of their life. At realizing the economic and social effects of entrepreneurship, the Emiratis started a number of government programs which aim at developing and sponsoring national entrepreneurs. Within this framework, Khalifa Fund for developing enterprises was inaugurated in 2007 for the purpose of confirming entrepreneurship education, reinforcing creativity and achieving a sustained growth for small and medium Emirate corporations. Moreover, Mohammed Bin Rashid's establishment (one of Dubai's establishments for developing small and medium entrepreneurs) succeeded in preparing a suitable situation for entrepreneurship and in giving a hand to many Emirati entrepreneurs to actualize their dreams, (El-Sokari et al., 2014).

Entrepreneurs in the Emirates

GEM distinguishes between two stages of entrepreneurship: developing and new corporates. Entrepreneurs of the developing corporates indicate that owners of such corporates haven't gotten any salary for more than three months, while entrepreneurs of new corporates, wholly or partially owned, run a newly-established corporate (4-42) months without being given any salary during that period (Al-Sokari et al., 2014). Table 2 reflects some indications of new and developing corporates in Emirates and the major problems that entrepreneurs encounter during that stage. The ratio of beginners in entrepreneurship in Emirates within four years was (7.9%) of the population. The year 2009 witnessed the highest rate of entrepreneurship beginners, while early 2008 witnessed a general reduction in entrepreneurship activity which might be caused by global and financial influences that affected various economic sectors. (6.3%) of the population were personally financed to start their economic enterprise, more than (65%) expecting to hire more than five employees during the first five years, but a great portion of the participants at the early stage of entrepreneurship (11.9%) started personal enterprises because other opportunities for them were not available. It is known that this type of entrepreneurship is negative and actually never contributes to economic growth.

The Environment of Public Governance in UAE

Table 3 shows indexes of public governance in the UAE through the period of the study. The table reveals that Emirates have achieved significant results in supporting governance and institutional work in the country compared to other countries. Governmental performance was among the best indexes followed by fighting corruption which is the major obstacle in the way of any economic growth. Through political stability, law control, and good organization, the Emirates was able to achieve an index of Public governance, almost (75%) through the study period. It was noticed that the index of public governance was increasing year after another. Improving organizational and legislative environments, in addition to government performance and pubic governance indexes, are all considered a very significant factor in the economic activity of the country. The incessant improvement and development are considered an essential tributary for development in all economic and social fields.

Table 3. Public Governance Environment in UAE

Public governance and institutional indicators	Statistical indicators			
	Mean	SD	Max	Min
Control of Corruption	76.183	10.876	87.678	55.610
Government Effectiveness	79.408	5.097	91.827	72.195
Political Stability	75.461	3.377	81.159	69.712
Rule of Law	73.182	5.527	83.333	61.244
Regulatory Quality	68.132	4.972	76.442	60.287
Public Governance Index	74.473	3.254	80.728	68.838

EMPIRICAL STUDY

Modelling the Public Governance as a Moderator Variable Between Entrepreneurship and Economic Growth

Basic hypotheses of this study are based on public governance as a moderator variable between entrepreneurship and economic growth. The study hypothesizes whether there is or isn't any relation between entrepreneurship and economic growth under the auspices of public governance in UAE. The moderator variable is considered a second independent variable as it affects the direction and strength between the dependent and independent variables. To consider the variable moderator, few conditions should exist: a causal relationship between the moderator variable "Public governance" and the dependent one "economic growth". The moderator variable should play the same role of the dependent one on condition that the moderator should not relate to the independent variable (CRO, 2012). The modelling and testing of the impact of the moderator variable on the relation between entrepreneurship and economic growth pass through the following procedures:

Initially, the impact of entrepreneurship, in addition to other basic variables, are tested without taking public governance into consideration in this model:

$$EconGrowth_t = \alpha + \beta_1 Labor_t + Capital_t + Oil_t + Diver_t + Enter_t + \ell \qquad (5)$$

An interactive variable between entrepreneurship and public governance index (PGIndex*Enter) is created later and this variable is added to formula (5) according to the following model:

Table 4. Regression results, the impact of entrepreneurship on the economic growth

Variables	Model 1: GDP Growth from non-oil sector		Model 2: GDP Growth	
	β	*t*-Statistic (*p*-value)	β	*t*-Statistic (*p*-value)
Independent variable: Entrepreneurship				
Rate of creating new enterprises	0.052	2.078** (0.040)	0.013	0.734 (0.465)
Number of creating new enterprises	0.421	5.960*** (0.000)	0.209	4.169*** (0.000)
Production function variables:				
Labor	0.233	2.013** (0.047)	0.159	1.936* (0.056)
Capital	1.105	6.712*** (0.000)	0.159	1.856* (0.065)
Oil Price	0.001	1.528 (0.130)	0.001	1.477 (0.143)
Economic diversification	-1.496	-3.303*** (0.001)	1.033	-4.339*** (0.000)
Structural breaks dummy variable	-0.102	-5.943*** (0.000)	-0.032	-2.620** (0.010)
R-squared		0.641		0.390
Adjusted R^2		0.618		0.351
F-statistic		27.687***		9.927***
p-value		0.000		0.000

T - Critical: at df 19, and confidence level of 99% is 2.093 and level of 95% is 1.729 and level of 90% is 1.328. F-Critical (df for denominator n-β-1 = 20-7-1=12) and (df for numerator =β =7 and confidence level of 99% is 4.26 and confidence level of 95% is 2.92 and confidence level of 10% is 2.28. The upper value is for *t*-Statistic test and the lower value in brackets (*p*-value) is the probability value for this test. Symbols mean Significance at: *10%; **5% and ***1% levels.

$$EconGrowth_t = \alpha + \beta_1 Labor_t + Capital_t + Oil_t + Diver_t + Enter_t + (PGIndex * Enter) + \ell_t \quad (6)$$

If the interactive variable (PGIndex*Enter) shows a statistical reference and the Adjusted R2 in model two increases, this is an indication of the influence of moderator variable (Public governance) on the relation between the dependent variable (economic growth) and the independent one (entrepreneurship).

Table 5. Regression results, the impact of entrepreneurship on the economic growth under the auspices of public governance

variables	Model 3: GDP Growth from non-oil sector		Model 4: GDP Growth	
	β	t-Statistic (p-value)	β	t-Statistic (p-value)
Independent variable: Entrepreneurship				
Rate of creating new enterprises	1.077	6.506*** (0.000)	0.792	6.538*** (0.000)
Number of creating new enterprises	0.743	6.317*** (0.000)	0.000	2.959*** (0.004)
Production function variables:				
Labor	0.519	3.998*** (0.000)	0.176	1.855* (0.067)
Capital	-1.549	-5.601*** (0.000)	0.016	0.079 (0.937)
Oil Price	0.001	1.573 (0.119)	0.000	1.129 (0.262)
Economic diversification	-1.132	-4.912*** (0.000)	-1.535	-3.345*** (0.001)
(PGIndex*Enter)	0.014	6.918*** (0.000)	0.010	6.540*** (0.000)
Structural breaks dummy variable	-0.035	-2.031** (0.045)	0.005	0.376 (0.708)
R-squared		0.740		0.530
Adjusted R^2		0.720		0.494
F-statistic		37.427***		14.834***
p-value		0.000		0.000

Testing Entrepreneurship Influence on Economic Growth

In this step, model 5 on the influence of entrepreneurship on economic growth in UAE, was assessed disregarding the moderator variable "Public Governance". Economic growth was identified as the growth in the GDP first and the growth in the non-oil product sector second. Table 4 shows the results from which one notices that the two models of economic growth in the Emirates are statistically important. Fischer test revealed a statistical reference of less than (1%) for this model.

It is noticed that R-Squared and the Adjusted R2 of the first model: the growth of the product of the non-oil sector was better than the second model: the growth in the GDP indicates that entrepreneurship has a more effective role in the local product of non-oil sector. In a more detailed manner, entrepreneurship variables: index of establishing corporates of limited liability in the Emirates, and the number of corporates with statistical reference in the growth of local product in the non-oil product showed less than one percent. Entrepreneurship had no influence on the second model: growth in the GDP, except for the variable of the number of corporates with limited liability in the Emirates. To sum up, the growth model in the non-oil sector seems to better represent the relation between entrepreneurship and economic growth in the UAE.

Testing the Influence of Entrepreneurship on the Economic Growth Under the Auspices of Public Governance

In this step the interactive variable (PG Index * Enter) was infused into entrepreneurship and public governance within the model of relationship between these two. Model 6 was assessed and the results of which are shown in table 9. As noticed from the Table that the Adjusted R2 was higher for model 3 compared with 1st, and higher in model 4 compared with model 2. The interactive variable (PG Index * Enter) has a statistical reference less than (1%) in relation entrepreneurship → economic growth; reflecting the importance of the role of public governance for reinforcing entrepreneurship for economic growth in the UAE.

Hypotheses Testing

The literature review discussed various hypotheses explaining the role of entrepreneurship on economic growth in the UAE under the auspices of the state's variables of Public governance. Hence, two hypotheses were developed. The first confirmed the positive role between entrepreneurship and the second negated the role of Public governance.

Based on the results presented in table 9, one can note that the two indexes of entrepreneurship: the one on establishing corporates of limited liability and the other of corporates number, both have an influence with statistical significant at less than one percent on the economic growth in UAE in the growth from non-oil sector or the GDP growth. It is also noted that the interactive variable (PGIndex*Rate) has a significant role, with statistical significant, on economic growth in UAE. In accordance with such results, we can accept the alternative hypothesis and reject the null one. Such results also reflect success of the policies adopted by UAE to stimulate and organize entrepreneurship. This success can be seen in economic diversification and actual contribution to economic growth.

The study's findings contribute further to economic research. Valliere and Peterson, (2009) revealed that entrepreneurship, only in developed countries, contribute to economic growth through environmental organization and good governance. Such a claim seems absent in developing countries. The counter evidences of this study from developing countries, with good governance where entrepreneurship activates economic growth adds value towards the claims of Valliere and Peterson. Adusei, (2016) emphasized that entrepreneurship stimulated economic growth in twelve African countries. Hafer revealed a positive relation between entrepreneurship and economic growth in the U.S. The results of this study agree with Aparicio et al., (2016) who conducted on 43 countries, and found that non-governmental institutions stimulate economic growth in Latin American countries. The results of this study agree with Mendez-Picazo et al., (2012)'s positive relation between governance and both: entrepreneurship, and economic growth, in Spain. All these studies reveal the role institutions play to stimulate and sustaining economic activity contributing to economic growth: thus, a positive role in prosperous societies, giving credit to the economy and sustaining economic growth (Nissan et al., 2011). Public governance moderates between entrepreneurship and economic growth and enhances corporate creativity (Galindo and Mendez- Picazo, 2013). Compared with Saudi Arabia, Kayed and Hassan (2011) reported that development plans failed in reinforcing entrepreneurship activity, thus played no role in economic growth. However, some scholars suspect the role of entrepreneurship in economic growth. The results of this study differed from those of Wong et al., (2005) who indicated that only fixed and quick developing entrepreneurship positively affect economic growth. Sabella et al., (2014) did not find any influence of entrepreneurship on economic growth in Palestine; unreliable results since due to the exceptional economic and political situation in Palestine, it is difficult to measure the economic growth influencing factors.

Additional Results

Tables 8 and 9 depict a test of several basic and control factors in the model of economic growth in UAE, in addition to capital variable, essential for any economic growth. As for the influence of oil barrel in economic growth in the UAE, results of all models revealed no moral influence of this variable on any index of growth. This might be an indication of economic diversification in the UAE as oil is no more the only influential factor in the growth. The evidence is seen in the emergence of a (Gini) variable of economic diversification, statistically essential for all models of the study. This indicates that economic diversification has become important in growth formula in the UAE. This is the economic analysis of the issue. From a standard point of view, the influence of oil on growth might have disappeared when introducing the allusive variable to avoid the impact of frame differences caused by fluctuation of oil prices, as this factor showed a statistical reference in all models.

CONCLUSION

The development of societies mainly depends on the will and political ability of those in authority who regulate social and economic life through a set of laws which increases credibility and the rule of law. It also fights corruption and secures efficient governmental performance. Despite the importance of resources, yet they are not the significant factor in the development of societies when compared to rules that secure just distribution of sources and the strategic vision of investing such sources to achieve prosperity to the present generation, without affecting the sources of future ones and their right to live in prosperity and to secure ways of growth and development for those generations. One of the responsibilities of individuals to the society is to contribute to the growth and development of that society. Entrepreneurship is one of the means by which individuals can influence economic life in the country and thus contribute to its welfare.

This study aimed to investigate public governance in the UAE and its role in creating a suitable investment environment for entrepreneurs through whom entrepreneurship can achieve its goals of economic growth and diversification of sources in order to gradually move from revenue economy to a more diversified one in which many sectors and individuals can contribute to its development. To achieve such a goal, the study tested the necessary hypotheses among entrepreneurship, governance, and economic growth. Via secondary data collected from International Bank database, general statistics of UAE, and data of GEM. Data spanned from1996 to 2015. Before its use the data was tested for its validity through tests such as normal distribution test, time series Stationarity test, autocorrelation and Multicollinearity.

The empirical findings of the study are depicted under descriptive results and experimental ones. Two theories helped explain the relation between entrepreneurship and economic growth. Considering that past studies varied in their findings pertaining to the role of entrepreneurship on economic growth. Some studies expressed a positive role, while others asserted a negative role; leading to the study in this chapter to design a model based on essential variables such as: labor, capital, and environment variables like oil-barrel price, level of economic diversification, along with two variables accounting entrepreneurship. All models measured economic growth through the growth in GDP of the non-oil sector once, and growth in GDP in another. The study concludes the following results:

Experimental results presented an influence of entrepreneurship o economic growth in the UAE, whether in GDP of non-oil sector, or GDP itself. This reflects the important role of entrepreneurship, while disregarding the public governance.

The study's interactive variable that checked the influence of entrepreneurship, under public governance, on economic growth All indicated a rise in models of economic growth reflecting how significant entrepreneurship is for the growth of an economy. UAE succeed in creating the suitable environment as well as developed its economies. The goal was not to create just production and service sectors, that would contribute to diversification, but to influence national economy, to gradually be rid of oil revenues.

As entrepreneurship activity is pivotal for economic diversification in the UAE. The examined influence of diversification on growth highlighted experimental results expressing a negative relation between statistical reference and diversification index, and economic growth and that asserts a direct proportion between diversification and UAE economic development.

Economists relate a rise in oil revenues to a decrease in the level of economic diversification, due to the increase of oil sector in GDP. Through the policies adopted by the UAE, it could overcome that problem. It thus made the oil sector essential for other sectors by distributing incoming revenues to develop non-oil sectors. Interestingly, the price of oil barrel has a direct proportion with economic growth, but without any statistical references, a new model the Emirates succeeded in applying.

REFERENCES

Abonamah, A., Karayim, S., & Thomas, L. D. (2016). Delivering an Entrepreneurship-Focused MBA in the UAE. In Innovation and Entrepreneurship in Education (pp. 169 - 193). Emerald Group Publishing Limited. doi:10.1108/S2051-229520160000002010

Acemoglu, D. (2003). Root Causes. A Historical Approach to Assessing the Role of Institutions in Economic Development. *Finance & Development*, *40*(2), 27–30.

Acs, Z. J. (1992). Small Business Economics: A Global Perspective. *Challenge*, *35*, 38–44.

Acs, Z. J., & Armington, C. (2006). *Entrepreneurship, Geography, and American Economic Growth*. Cambridge, UK: Cambridge University Press. doi:10.1017/CBO9780511510816

Acs, Z. J., & Varga, A. (2005). Entrepreneurship, Agglomeration and Technological Change. *Small Business Economics*, *24*(3), 323–334. doi:10.100711187-005-1998-4

Adusei, M. (2016). Does Entrepreneurship Promote Economic Growth in Africa? *African Development Review*, *28*(2), 201–214. doi:10.1111/1467-8268.12190

Al-Sokari, H., Horne, C., Huang, Z., & Al Awad, M. (2014). *Entrepreneurship: an Emirati Perspective. The Institute for Social and Economic Research (ISER)*. Zayed University.

Andreou, E., & Ghysels, E. (2002). Detecting multiple breaks in financial market volatility dynamics. *Journal of Applied Econometrics*, *17*(1), 579–600. doi:10.1002/jae.684

Anselin, L., Varga, A., & Acs, Z. J. (2000). Geographic spillovers and university research: A spatial econometric approach. *Growth and Change*, *31*(4), 501–515. doi:10.1111/0017-4815.00142

Aparicio, S., Urbano, D., & Audretsch, D. (2016). Institutional factors, opportunity entrepreneurship and economic growth: Panel data evidence. *Technological Forecasting and Social Change*, *102*, 45–61. doi:10.1016/j.techfore.2015.04.006

Arouri, M., & Nguyen, D. (2010). Oil prices, stock markets and portfolio investment: Evidence from sector analysis in Europe over the last decade. *Energy Policy*, *38*(1), 4528–4539. doi:10.1016/j.enpol.2010.04.007

Audretsch, D. B., & Fritsch, M. (1996). Creative destruction: turbulence and economic growth. In E. Helmstader & M. Perlman (Eds.), *Behavioral Norms, Technological Progress, and Economic Dynamics: Studies in Schumpeterian Economics* (pp. 137–150). Ann Arbor, MI: University of Michigan Press.

Audretsch, D. B., & Fritsch, M. (2002). Growth regimes over time and space. *Regional Studies*, *36*(2), 113–124. doi:10.1080/00343400220121909

Audretsch, D. B., & Keilbach, M. C. (2004). Entrepreneurship and regional growth: An evolutionary interpretation. *Journal of Evolutionary Economics*, *14*(5), 605–616. doi:10.100700191-004-0228-6

Audretsch, D. B., Thurik, R., Verheul, I., & Wennekers, A. R. M. (2002). *Entrepreneurship: Determinants and policy in a European–US comparison.* Kluwer Academic. doi:10.1007/b109395

Bianchini, R. (2010). *Entrepreneurship and quality of institutions of Latin America* (Master's Thesis). Retrieved from www.wiwi.huberlin.de/professuren/vwl/fw/Dissertationen,ThesesundSeminararbeiten/dipl/MT/MTRafaelBianchini.pdf

Boettke, P. J., & Coyne, C. J. (2003). Entrepreneurship and Development: Cause or Consequence? *Advances in Austrian Economics*, *6*, 67–87. doi:10.1016/S1529-2134(03)06005-8

Bourne, L. (2011). Advising Upwards: Managing the Perceptions and Expectations of Senior Management Stakeholders. *Management Decision*, *49*(6), 1001–1023. doi:10.1108/00251741111143658

Carlsson, B., Acs, Z. J., Audretsch, D. B., & Braunerhjelm, P. (2009). Knowledge creation, entrepreneurship, and economic growth: A historical review. *Industrial and Corporate Change*, *18*(6), 1193–1229. doi:10.1093/icc/dtp043

Carree, M., van Stel, A., & Thurik, R. (2002). The impact of entrepreneurship on economic growth. In International Handbook of Entrepreneurship Research. Boston: Kluwer Academic Publishers.

Carree, M., van Stel, A., & Thurik, R. (2003). The impact of entrepreneurship on economic growth. In D. B. Audretsch & Z. J. Acs (Eds.), *Handbook of Entrepreneurship Research* (pp. 437–471). Boston: Kluwer Academic Publishers.

Carree, M., van Stel, A., Thurik, R., & Wennekers, S. (2007). The relationship between economic development and business ownership revisited. *Entrepreneurship and Regional Development*, *19*(3), 281–291. doi:10.1080/08985620701296318

Carree, M. A., & Thurik, A. R. (1998). Small Firms and Economic Growth in Europe. *Atlantic Economic Journal*, *26*(2), 137–146. doi:10.1007/BF02299356

Collier, P., & Anke, H. (2005). Resource Rents, Governance, and Conflict. *The Journal of Conflict Resolution*, *49*(4), 625–633. doi:10.1177/0022002705277551

Davis, J., Roland, O., James, D., & Seven, B. (2001). *Stabilization and savings funds for nonrenewable resources: Experience and fiscal policy implications*. New York: International Monetary Fund.

Dejardin, M. (2000). *Entrepreneurship and Economic Growth: An Obvious Conjunction?* Namur, Belgium: University of Namur.

Ewing, B. T., & Malik, F. (2010). Estimating Volatility Persistence in Oil Prices Under Structural Breaks. *Financial Review*, *45*(4), 1011–1023. doi:10.1111/j.1540-6288.2010.00283.x

Freeman, C. (1988). Japan, a new system of innovation. In G. Dosi, C. Freeman, R. Nelson, G. Silverberg, & L. Soete (Eds.), *Technical change and economic theory*. London: Pinter.

Fritsch, M. (2007). How does new business formation affect regional development? *Small Business Economics*, *30*(1), 1–14. doi:10.100711187-007-9057-y

Fritsch, M., & Mueller, P. (2004). The effects of new business formation on regional development over time. *Regional Studies*, *38*(8), 961–975. doi:10.1080/0034340042000280965

Gelb, A., & Sina, G. (2010). *How Should Oil Exporters Spend Their Rents?* Center for Global Development, Working Paper, No. 221.

Glaeser, E., Kallal, H., Sheinkman, J., & Schleifer, A. (1999). Growth in cities. *Journal of Political Economy*, *100*(1), 1126–1152.

Gwartney, J., Holcombe, R., & Lawson, R. (1999). Economic freedom and the environment for economic growth. *Journal of Institutional and Theoretical Economics*, *155*(1), 643–663.

Hafer, R. (2013). Entrepreneurship and state economic growth. *Journal of Entrepreneurship and Public Policy*, *2*(1), 67–79. doi:10.1108/20452101311318684

Hart, D. M. (2003). *Entrepreneurship policy: What it is and where it came from. In The Emergence of Entrepreneurship Policy: Governance, Startups and Growth in the U.S. Knowledge Economy*. Cambridge, UK: Cambridge University Press.

Hartog, C., Van Stel, A., & Storey, D. J. (2010). *Institutions and Entrepreneurship: The Role of the Rule of Law*. Working Paper no. H201003, EIM Research Reports.

Hitt, M. A., Ireland, R. D., Camp, S. M., & Sexton, D. L. (2001). Entrepreneurial strategies for wealth creation. *Strategic Management Journal*, *22*(1), 91–479.

Humphreys, M., Jeffrey, S., & Joseph, S. (2007). *Escaping the Resource Curse*. New York: Columbia University Press.

Ismail, M. (2010). *UAE leads region on UK human development index*. Retrieved from N UAE: https://www.thenational.ae/uae/government/uae-leads-region-on-un-human-development-index-1.530313

Kang, S. H., Cheong, C., & Yoon, S.-M. (2011). Structural changes and volatility transmission in crude oil markets. *Physica A*, *390*(23-24), 4317–4324. doi:10.1016/j.physa.2011.06.056

Kayed, M., & Hassan, K. (2011). Saudi Arabia's economic development: Entrepreneurship as a strategy. *International Journal of Islamic and Middle Eastern Finance and Management*, *4*(1), 52–73. doi:10.1108/17538391111122203

Kirzner, I. M. (1973). *Competition and Entrepreneurship*. Chicago: University of Chicago Press.

Krugman, P. (1991a). Increasing returns and economic geography. *Journal of Political Economy*, *99*(1), 99–483.

Krugman, P. (1991b). *Geography and trade*. Cambridge, MA: MIT Press.

Krugman, P. (1991c). History and industry location: The cast of the manufacturing belt. *The American Economic Review*, *81*(2), 3–80.

Kumar, D., & Maheswaran, S. (2013). Detecting sudden changes in volatility estimated from high, low and closing prices. *Economic Modelling*, *31*, 484–491. doi:10.1016/j.econmod.2012.12.021

Lundvall, B. (1988). Innovation as an interactive process: From user-producer interaction to the national system of innovation. In G. Dosi, C. Freeman, R. Nelson, G. Silverberg, & L. Soete (Eds.), *Technical change and economic theory*. London: Pinter.

Martinez, J. A. (2005). Equilibrium entrepreneurship rate, economic development and growth: Evidence from Spanish regions. *Entrepreneurship and Regional Development: An International Journal*, *17*(2), 61–145.

Méndez-Picazo, M., Galindo-Martín, M., & Ribeiro-Soriano, D. (2012). Governance, entrepreneurship and economic growth. *Entrepreneurship and Regional Development*, *24*(9-10), 865–877. doi:10.1080/08985626.2012.742323

Méndez-Picazo, M.-T., Galindo-Martín, M.-Á., & Ribeiro-Soriano, D. (2012). Governance, entrepreneurship and economic growth. *Entrepreneurship and Regional Development*, *24*(9-10), 865–877. doi:10.1080/08985626.2012.742323

Mensi, W., Hammoudeh, S., & Yoon, S. (2015). Structural breaks, dynamic correlations, asymmetric volatility transmission, and hedging strategies for petroleum prices and USD exchange rate. *Energy Economics*, *48*(1), 46–60. doi:10.1016/j.eneco.2014.12.004

Mensi, W., Hammoudeh, S., & Yoon, S.-M. (2014). Structural breaks and long memory in modeling and forecasting the volatility of foreign exchange markets of oil exporters: The importance of scheduled and unscheduled news announcements. *International Review of Economics & Finance*, *30*(1), 101–119. doi:10.1016/j.iref.2013.10.004

Minniti, M., Bygrave, W. D., & Autio, E. (2005). *Global entrepreneurship monitor: 2005 executive report*. Wellesley, MA: Babson College.

Minniti, M., & Levesque, M. (2006). *Entrepreneurial types and economic growth*. Paper presented at the international conference on entrepreneurship in emerging regions, Hyderabad, India.

Moreno, A. M., & Casillas, J. C. (2007). High-growth SMEs version non-high-growth SMEs: A discriminant analysis. *Entrepreneurship and Regional Development*, *19*(1), 69–88. doi:10.1080/08985620601002162

Naude, W. (2008). Entrepreneurship in economic development. World Institute for Development Economics Research.

Nelson, R. (1988). Institutions supporting technical change in the United States. In G. Dosi, C. Freeman, R. Nelson, G. Silverberg, & L. Soete (Eds.), *Technical change and economic theory*. London: Pinter.

Nijkamp, P., & Poot, J. (1998). Spatial perspectives on new theories of economic growth. *The Annals of Regional Science*, *32*(1), 7–38. doi:10.1007001680050061

Nissan, E., Galindo, M. A., & Mendez, M. T. (2011). Relationship between organizations, institutions, entrepreneurship and economic growth process. *The International Entrepreneurship and Management Journal*, *7*(3), 24–311. doi:10.100711365-011-0191-2

North, D. (1990). *Institutions, Institutional Change and Economic Performance*. Cambridge, UK: Cambridge University Press. doi:10.1017/CBO9780511808678

Ramsay, W. (2011). Revisiting the Resource Curse: Natural Disasters, the Price of Oil, and Democracy. *International Organization*, *65*(3), 507–529. doi:10.1017/S002081831100018X

Razzaque, A., Hamdan, A., Al-Hashimi, M., & Al-Dhaen, E. (2019). Learning readiness when sharing knowledge while e-learning. In *13th International Conference on e-Learning - MCCSIS 2019*. Porto, Portugal: MCCSIS 2019.

Ro, H. (2012). Moderator and mediator effects in hospitality research. *International Journal of Hospitality Management*, *31*(1), 952–961. doi:10.1016/j.ijhm.2011.11.003

Romer, P. M. (1990). Endogenous Technical Change. *Journal of Political Economy*, *98*(1), 71–102. doi:10.1086/261725

Rosser, A. (2007). Escaping the Resource Curse: The Case of Indonesia. *Journal of Contemporary Asia*, *37*(1), 38–58. doi:10.1080/00472330601104557

Sabella, A. R., Farraj, W. A., Burbar, M., & Qaimary, D. (2014). Entrepreneurship and Economic Growth in West Bank, Palestine. *Journal of Developmental Entrepreneurship*, *19*(01), 1450003. doi:10.1142/S1084946714500034

Sachs, D. and Andrew M. (1995). *Natural Resource Abundance and Economic Growth*. Technical Report Development Discussion, Paper no. 517a Harvard Institute for International Development Cambridge.

Schmitz, J. A. Jr. (1989). Imitation, entrepreneurship and long–run growth. *Journal of Political Economy*, *97*(3), 721–739. doi:10.1086/261624

Schultz, T. W. (1975). The value of the ability to deal with disequilibria. *Journal of Economic Literature*, *13*(3), 827–846.

Schumpeter, J. A. (1911). The Theory of Economic Development. Cambridge, MA: Harvard University Press.

Sternberg, R., & Wennekers, S. (2005). Determinants and Effects of New Business Creation Using Global Entrepreneurship Monitor Data. *Small Business Economics*, *24*(3), 193–203. doi:10.100711187-005-1974-z

Sternberg, R., & Wennekers, S. (2005). Determinants and Effects of New Business Creation Using Global Entrepreneurship Monitor Data. *Small Business Economics*, *24*(3), 193–203. doi:10.100711187-005-1974-z

Suarez-Villa, L. (2000). *Invention and the rise of technocapitalism*. New York: Rowan & Littlefield.

Tang, L., & Koveos, P. E. (2004). Venture entrepreneurship, innovation entrepreneurship and economic growth. *Journal of Developmental Entrepreneurship*, *9*(2), 161–171.

Valliere, D., & Peterson, R. (2009). Entrepreneurship and economic growth: Evidence from emerging and developed countries. *Entrepreneurship and Regional Development*, *21*(5-6), 459–480. doi:10.1080/08985620802332723

Vivian, A., & Wohar, M. (2012). Commodity volatility breaks. *Journal of International Financial Markets, Institutions and Money*, *22*(2), 395–422. doi:10.1016/j.intfin.2011.12.003

Wennekers, S., & Thurik, R. (1999). Linking entrepreneurship and economic growth. *Small Business Economics*, *13*(1), 27–55. doi:10.1023/A:1008063200484

Wennekers, S., Van Stel, A., Thurik, R., & Reynolds, P. (2005). *Nascent Entrepreneurship and the Level of Economic Development*. Discussion Paper no. 2005–14, Growth and Public Policy, Max Planck Institute of Economics.

Wong, P. K., Ho, Y. P., & Autio, E. (2005). Entrepreneurship, innovation and economic growth: Evidence from GEM data. *Small Business Economics*, *24*(3), 335–350. doi:10.100711187-005-2000-1

WorldData.info. (2019). *Average income around the world*. Retrieved from WorldData.info: https://www.worlddata.info/average-income.php

Yang, T. T., & Li, C. R. (2011). Competence Exploration and Exploitation in New Product Development: The Moderating Effects of Environmental Dynamism and Competitiveness. *Management Decision*, *49*(9), 1444–1470. doi:10.1108/00251741111173934

Compilation of References

Abdulrahman, M., AlSharief, W., Khansaheb, H., Abdulghafoor, S., & Ahmed, A. (2018). Evolution of family medicine residency training program in Dubai Health Authority: A 24-year review, challenges, and outcomes. *Journal of Family Medicine and Primary Care*, *7*(2), 425. doi:10.4103/jfmpc.jfmpc_183_17 PMID:30090788

Abonamah, A., Karayim, S., & Thomas, L. D. (2016). Delivering an Entrepreneurship-Focused MBA in the UAE. In Innovation and Entrepreneurship in Education (pp. 169 - 193). Emerald Group Publishing Limited. doi:10.1108/S2051-229520160000002010

Acemoglu, D. (2003). Root Causes. A Historical Approach to Assessing the Role of Institutions in Economic Development. *Finance & Development*, *40*(2), 27–30.

Acs, Z. J. (1992). Small Business Economics: A Global Perspective. *Challenge*, *35*, 38–44.

Acs, Z. J., & Armington, C. (2006). *Entrepreneurship, Geography, and American Economic Growth*. Cambridge, UK: Cambridge University Press. doi:10.1017/CBO9780511510816

Acs, Z. J., & Varga, A. (2005). Entrepreneurship, Agglomeration and Technological Change. *Small Business Economics*, *24*(3), 323–334. doi:10.100711187-005-1998-4

Adebanjo, D. A. (2010). An investigation of the adoption and implementation of benchmarking. *International Journal of Operations & Production Management*, *30*(11), 1140–1169.

ADGM Home. (n.d.). Retrieved from https://www.adgm.com/

Adusei, M. (2016). Does Entrepreneurship Promote Economic Growth in Africa? *African Development Review*, *28*(2), 201–214. doi:10.1111/1467-8268.12190

Afra, B., Musaiger, A., & D'Souza, R. (2010). The Association between Obesity and Blood Pressure among Adolescents in Dubai, UAE. *Pakistan Journal of Medical Sciences*, *26*(2), 271–276.

Ahlstrom, D., & Ding, Z. (2014). Entrepreneurship in China: An overview. *International Small Business Journal*, *32*(6), 610–618. doi:10.1177/0266242613517913

Ahlstrom, D., Young, M. N., Chan, E. S., & Bruton, G. D. (2004). Facing Constraints to Growth? Overseas Chinese Entrepreneurs and Traditional Business Practices in East Asia. *Asia Pacific Journal of Management, 21*(3), 263–285. doi:10.1023/B:APJM.0000036463.20310.de

Ahmadi, S., Papageorgiou, E., Yen, C., & Marin, R. (2015). Managing readiness-relevant activities for the organizational dimension of ERP implementation. *Computers in Industry, 68*, 89–104. doi:10.1016/j.compind.2014.12.009

AirLiquide Magazine. (2017). *Hydrogen mobility gains momentum in Middle East.* Retrieved from https://www.airliquide.com/magazine/hydrogen-mobility-gains-momentum-middle-east

Al GhurairGroup. (2018). *Our History*. Retrieved August 28, 2018, from Al Ghurair Group: http://www.alghurair.com/about-us/our-history

Al Saleh, J., Manal, E., Monsef, N., & Darwish, E. (2016). The Prevalence and the Determinants of Musculoskeletal Diseases in Emiratis Attending Primary Health Care Clinics in Dubai. *Oman Medical Journal, 31*(2), 117–123. doi:10.5001/omj.2016.23 PMID:27168922

Al-Assi, R. (2019). *The Story of Bayt.com: A Tale of Love, Hard Work, and Success*. Retrieved from bayt.com: https://www.bayt.com/en/blog/3967/the-story-of-bayt-com-a-tale-of-love-hard-work-and-success-infographic/

Al-Balushi, S., Sohal, A., Singh, P., Al Hajri, A., Al Farsi, Y., & Al Abri, R. (2014). Readiness factors for lean implementation in healthcare settings–a literature review. *Journal of Health Organization and Management, 28*(2), 135–153. doi:10.1108/JHOM-04-2013-0083 PMID:25065107

Alibhai, S., Bell, S., & Conner, G. (2017). What's Happening in the Missing Middle?: Lessons from Financing SMEs. *World Bank*. Retrieved from: https://openknowledge.worldbank.org/handle/10986/26324

Alkasmi, A., El Hammsy, O., Khoury, L., & Syed, A. (2018). Entrepreneurship in the Middle East and North Africa: How investors can support and enable growth. *McKinsey Digital*. Retrieved from: https://www.mckinsey.com/~/media/mckinsey/featured%20insights/Middle%20East%20and%20Africa/How%20investors%20can%20support%20entrepreneurship%20in%20the%20Middle%20East%20and%20North%20Africa/Entrepreneurship-in-the-Middle-East-and-North-Africa.ashx

Alkhaleejtimes. (2019, March 26). *Uber acquires Dubai-based Careem for $3.1 billion*. Fretrieved from Alkhaleejtimes.com: https://www.khaleejtimes.com/business/uber-acquires-dubai-based-careem-for-31-billion

Alkhanbashi, S. O. (2018). *Barriers to Delivering and Accessing Mental Health and Family Therapy Services in the United Arab Emirates: Perspective of Mental Health Clinicians* (Doctoral dissertation). Alliant International University.

Alshaali, A., & Al Jaziri, A. (2015). Health Profile of Elderly Patients Registered in the Elderly Home Based Primary Care, Dubai, United Arab Emirates. *Middle East Journal Of Age And Ageing*, *12*(1), 13–19. doi:10.5742/MEAA.2015.92609

Al-Sokari, H., Horne, C., Huang, Z., & Al Awad, M. (2014). *Entrepreneurship: an Emirati Perspective. The Institute for Social and Economic Research (ISER)*. Zayed University.

Al-Yateem, N., Rossiter, R., Robb, W., Ahmad, A., Elhalik, M., Albloshi, S., & Slewa-Younan, S. (2017). Mental health literacy among pediatric hospital staff in the United Arab Emirates. *BMC Psychiatry*, *17*(1), 390. doi:10.118612888-017-1556-z PMID:29216871

Anderson, M., Solitander, A., & Ekman, P. (2012). *Cluster branding and marketing*. Kalmar: Tendensor.

Andrade, L. H., Alonso, J., Mneimneh, Z., Wells, J. E., Al-Hamzawi, A., Borges, G., ... Florescu, S. (2014). Barriers to mental health treatment: Results from the WHO World Mental Health surveys. *Psychological Medicine*, *44*(6), 1303–1317. doi:10.1017/S0033291713001943 PMID:23931656

Andreou, E., & Ghysels, E. (2002). Detecting multiple breaks in financial market volatility dynamics. *Journal of Applied Econometrics*, *17*(1), 579–600. doi:10.1002/jae.684

Anselin, L., Varga, A., & Acs, Z. J. (2000). Geographic spillovers and university research: A spatial econometric approach. *Growth and Change*, *31*(4), 501–515. doi:10.1111/0017-4815.00142

Anserson, R. (2015, November 15). *Bayt.com founder on Middle East's job market*. Retrieved from Arabian Business: https://gulfbusiness.com/bayt-com-founder-middle-easts-job-market/

Antony, J. (2014). Readiness factors for the Lean Six Sigma journey in the higher education sector. *International Journal of Productivity and Performance Management*, *63*(2), 257–264. doi:10.1108/IJPPM-04-2013-0077

Aparicio, S., Urbano, D., & Audretsch, D. (2016). Institutional factors, opportunity entrepreneurship and economic growth: Panel data evidence. *Technological Forecasting and Social Change*, *102*, 45–61. doi:10.1016/j.techfore.2015.04.006

Arabian Business. (2016, January 16). *PR stunt kick-started our business, says Cobone founder*. Retrieved from Arabian Business: https://www.arabianbusiness.com/pr-stunt-kick-started-our-business-says-cobone-founder-620003.html

ArabianBusiness. (2010). *Arabian Business Rich List 2010The Al Ghurair Family*. Retrieved August 28, 2018, from Arabian Business: https://www.arabianbusiness.com/arabian-business-rich-list-2010-367763.html?itemid=367814

Archibald, R. D., Di Filippo, I., & Di Filippo, D. (2012). The six-phase comprehensive project life cycle model including the project incubation/feasibility phase and the post-project evaluation phase. *PM World Journal*, *1*(5), 1–40.

Aremu, M. A., & Adeyemi, S. L. (2011). Small and medium scale enterprises as survival strategy for employment generation in Nigeria. *Journal of Sustainable Development*, *4*(1), 200–206.

Arif, M., Gupta, A., & Williams, A. (2013). Customer service in the aviation industry - An exploratory analysis of UAE airports. *Journal of Air Transport Management*, *32*, 1–7. doi:10.1016/j.jairtraman.2013.05.001

Armenakis, A., Bernerth, J., Pitts, J., & Walker, H. (2007). Organizational change recipients' beliefs scale: Development of an assessment instrument. *The Journal of Applied Behavioral Science*, *43*(4), 481–505. doi:10.1177/0021886307303654

Armenakis, A., & Harris, S. (2002). Crafting a change message to create transformational readiness. *Journal of Organizational Change Management*, *15*(2), 169–183. doi:10.1108/09534810210423080

Armenakis, A., Harris, S., & Mossholder, K. W. (1993). Creating readiness for organizational change. *Human Relations*, *46*(6), 681–703. doi:10.1177/001872679304600601

Armour, J., & Cumming, D. J. (2006). The legislative road to Silicon Valley. *Oxford Economic Papers*, *58*(4), 596–635. doi:10.1093/oep/gpl007

Arouri, M., & Nguyen, D. (2010). Oil prices, stock markets and portfolio investment: Evidence from sector analysis in Europe over the last decade. *Energy Policy*, *38*(1), 4528–4539. doi:10.1016/j.enpol.2010.04.007

Artto, K., Ahola, T., & Vartiainen, V. (2015). From the front end of projects to the back end of operations: Managing projects for value creation throughout the system lifecycle. *International Journal of Project Management*, *34*(2), 258–270. doi:10.1016/j.ijproman.2015.05.003

Atherton, A., & Smallbone, A. (2010). State promotion of SME development at the local level in China: An examination of two cases. *Journal of Chinese Entrepreneurship*, *2*(3), 225–241. doi:10.1108/17561391011078721

Audretsch, D. B., & Fritsch, M. (1996). Creative destruction: turbulence and economic growth. In E. Helmstader & M. Perlman (Eds.), *Behavioral Norms, Technological Progress, and Economic Dynamics: Studies in Schumpeterian Economics* (pp. 137–150). Ann Arbor, MI: University of Michigan Press.

Audretsch, D. B., & Fritsch, M. (2002). Growth regimes over time and space. *Regional Studies*, *36*(2), 113–124. doi:10.1080/00343400220121909

Audretsch, D. B., & Keilbach, M. C. (2004). Entrepreneurship and regional growth: An evolutionary interpretation. *Journal of Evolutionary Economics*, *14*(5), 605–616. doi:10.100700191-004-0228-6

Audretsch, D. B., Thurik, R., Verheul, I., & Wennekers, A. R. M. (2002). *Entrepreneurship: Determinants and policy in a European–US comparison.* Kluwer Academic. doi:10.1007/b109395

Autio, E., Chaminade, D., & Corbett, A. (2017). *Innovation clusters: Understanding life cycles.* New York: Economist Intelligence Unit.

Ayson, S. (2011). Sustainable Management Education: A Graduate Skills Approach. In Business and Sustainability: Concepts, Strategies and Changes (pp. 293-308). Bingley, UK: Emerald Group Publishing Limited.

Azadegan, A., Dooley, K. J., Carter, P. L., & Carter, J. R. (2008). Supplier innovativeness and the role of interorganizational learning in enhancing manufacturer capabilities. *The Journal of Supply Chain Management, 44*(4), 14–35. doi:10.1111/j.1745-493X.2008.00070.x

Baas, T., & Schrooten, M. (2006). Relationship banking and SMEs: A theoretical analysis. *Small Business Economics, 27*(2-3), 127–137. doi:10.100711187-006-0018-7

Bager, T. (2009). *The Camp Model for Entrepreneurship Teaching.* Paper to EFMD conference, Barcelona, Spain. Available at www.idea-denmark.dk

Baldwin, D. (2018, May 8). *UAE chosen top country for young people says the Arab Youth Survey.* Retrieved rom Gulfnews.com: https://gulfnews.com/going-out/society/uae-chosen-top-country-for-young-people-says-arab-youth-survey-1.2218208

Ballantyne, D., & Aitken, R. (2007). Branding in B2B markets: Insights from the service-dominant logic of marketing. *Journal of Business and Industrial Marketing, 22*(6), 363–371. doi:10.1108/08858620710780127

Barlow, J., Singh, D., Bayer, S., & Curry, R. (2007). A systematic review of the benefits of home telecare for frail elderly people and those with long-term conditions. *Journal of Telemedicine and Telecare, 13*(4), 172–179. doi:10.1258/135763307780908058 PMID:17565772

Barnard, P., & Teasdale, J. (2014). *Affect, Cognition and Change.* Hoboken, NJ: Taylor and Francis. doi:10.4324/9781315804750

Bartlem, C., & Locke, E. A. (1981). The Coch and French study: A critique and reinterpretation. *Human Relations, 34*(7), 555–566. doi:10.1177/001872678103400703

Barucic, A., & Umihanic, B. (2016). Entrepreneurship education as a factor of entrepreneurial opportunity recognition for starting a new business. *Management, 21*(2), 27–44.

Batterham, R. W., Hawkins, M., Collins, P. A., Buchbinder, R., & Osborne, R. H. (2016). Health literacy: Applying current concepts to improve health services and reduce health inequalities. *Public Health, 132*, 3–12. doi:10.1016/j.puhe.2016.01.001 PMID:26872738

Beer, M., & Nohria, N. (2000a). Cracking the code of change. *Harvard Business Review, 78*, 133–141. PMID:11183975

Beer, M., & Nohria, N. (2000b). Introduction: Resolving the tension between theories E and O. In M. Beer & N. Nohria (Eds.), *Breaking the code of change* (pp. 1–33). Boston: Harvard Business School Press.

Berle, G. (1991). *The green entrepreneur: Business opportunities that can save the earth and make you money*. Blue Ridge Summit, PA: Liberty Hall Press.

Bernsau, M. (2018) Fifteen years later: A reflection on the Mass. biotech sector. *Boston Business Journal*. Available from: https://www.bizjournals.com/boston/news/2018/05/31/fifteen-years-later-a-reflection-on-the-mass.html

Berrell, M., & Wrathall, J. (2007). 'Between Chinese culture and the rule of law: What foreign managers in China should know about intellectual property rights. *Management Research News*, *30*(1), 57–76. doi:10.1108/01409170710724304

Bianchini, R. (2010). *Entrepreneurship and quality of institutions of Latin America* (Master's Thesis). Retrieved from www.wiwi.huberlin.de/professuren/vwl/fw/Dissertationen,ThesesundSeminararbeiten/dipl/MT/MTRafaelBianchini.pdf

Blair, T. C., Chen, K., Shieh, M. D., & Chiou, S. C. (2010). Brand a Nation: What is being Brand? The Impact of Olympics on China. *International Journal of the Humanities*, *7*(10), 57–66. doi:10.18848/1447-9508/CGP/v07i10/42752

Boesso, I., D'Orazio, M., & Torresan, A. (Eds.). (2012). *Supporting cluster marketing and branding*. Venezia: TACTICS.

Boettke, P. J., & Coyne, C. J. (2003). Entrepreneurship and Development: Cause or Consequence? *Advances in Austrian Economics*, *6*, 67–87. doi:10.1016/S1529-2134(03)06005-8

Boiral, O. (2012). ISO 9000 and Organizational Effectiveness: A Systematic Review. *Quality Management Journal*, *19*(3), 16-37.

Bourne, L. (2011). Advising Upwards: Managing the Perceptions and Expectations of Senior Management Stakeholders. *Management Decision*, *49*(6), 1001–1023. doi:10.1108/00251741111143658

Boyles, T. (2012). 21 century knowledge, skills, and abilities and entrepreneurial competencies: A model for undergraduate entrepreneurship education. *Journal of Entrepreneurship Education*, *15*, 41–55.

Brady, T., & Davies, A. (2010). From hero to hubris – reconsidering the project management of Heathrow's Terminal 5. *International Journal of Project Management*, *28*(2), 151–157. doi:10.1016/j.ijproman.2009.11.011

Brady, T., Davies, A., & Gann, D. (2005). Creating value by delivering integrated solutions. *International Journal of Project Management*, *23*(5), 360–365. doi:10.1016/j.ijproman.2005.01.001

Bravo-Biosca, A., Criscuolo, C., & Menon, C. (2016). What drives the dynamics of business growth? *Economic Policy, 31*(88), 703–742. doi:10.1093/epolic/eiw013

Brereton, S. J., & Papp, F. (2013). Assuring operational readiness of the National Ignition Facility. *Health Physics, 104*(6), 597–605. doi:10.1097/HP.0b013e31828d2e4c PMID:23629065

British Standards Institute (BSI). (2010). *BS6079-1: Project Management — Part 1: Principles and Guidelines for the Management of Projects*. BSI.

Bryce, G. R., & Troy. (2018). *Quality Management Theories and Their Application.* Retrieved from ProQuest LLC: https://search.proquest.com/openview/d4123ff9b2a6da727b5d5ba05c353f9e/1?pq-origsite=gscholar&cbl=35812

Buch, K. R., & Rivers, D. (2001). TQM: The role of leadership and culture. *Leadership and Organization Development Journal, 22*(8), 365–371. doi:10.1108/01437730110410080

Burke, W. W., & Biggart, N. (1997). Interorganizational relations. In D. Druckman, J. E. Singer, & H. Van Cott (Eds.), *Enhancing organizational performance* (pp. 120–149). Washington, DC: National Academy Press.

Burnes, B. (2004). *Managing change: A strategic approach to organisational dynamics*. London: Prentice Hall.

Burnett, S., Benn, J., Pinto, A., Parand, A., Iskander, S., & Vincent, C. (2010). Organisational readiness: Exploring the preconditions for success in organisation-wide patient safety improvement programmes. *BMJ Quality & Safety, 19*(4), 313–317. doi:10.1136/qshc.2008.030759 PMID:20211961

Cabezas, H., & Diwekar, U. (2012). *Sustainability: Multi-disciplinary perspectives.* Bentham Science Publishers Ltd. doi:10.2174/97816080510381120101

Carlsson, B., Acs, Z. J., Audretsch, D. B., & Braunerhjelm, P. (2009). Knowledge creation, entrepreneurship, and economic growth: A historical review. *Industrial and Corporate Change, 18*(6), 1193–1229. doi:10.1093/icc/dtp043

Carree, M., van Stel, A., & Thurik, R. (2002). The impact of entrepreneurship on economic growth. In International Handbook of Entrepreneurship Research. Boston: Kluwer Academic Publishers.

Carree, M. A., & Thurik, A. R. (1998). Small Firms and Economic Growth in Europe. *Atlantic Economic Journal, 26*(2), 137–146. doi:10.1007/BF02299356

Carree, M., van Stel, A., & Thurik, R. (2003). The impact of entrepreneurship on economic growth. In D. B. Audretsch & Z. J. Acs (Eds.), *Handbook of Entrepreneurship Research* (pp. 437–471). Boston: Kluwer Academic Publishers.

Carree, M., van Stel, A., Thurik, R., & Wennekers, S. (2007). The relationship between economic development and business ownership revisited. *Entrepreneurship and Regional Development, 19*(3), 281–291. doi:10.1080/08985620701296318

Carver, T. (2012). *The Relationship between organizational culture and readiness to change in a U. S. Army organization within japan* (PhD thesis). Northcentral University.

Cassidy, J. (1994). System analyzes readiness for integrated delivery. *Health Progress (Saint Louis, Mo.), 75*(3), 18–20, 22. PMID:10132874

Central Bank of the UAE. (2017). *Financial Stability 2017.* Retrieved from: https://www.centralbank.ae/sites/default/files/2018-09/FinancialStabilityReport2017.pdf

Central Bank of the UAE. (2019). Retrieved from: https://www.centralbank.ae/en/statistics/monthly-statistics

Chan, H. S., & Gao, J. (2008). Old wine in new bottles: A country-level case study of anti-corruption reform in the People's Republic of China. *Crime, Law, and Social Change, 49*(2), 97–117. doi:10.100710611-007-9096-y

Chartered Institute of Building. (2014). *Code of practice for project management for construction and development* (5th ed.). Wiley-Blackwell.

Chen, H. (2017). *The institutional transition of China's township and village enterprises: market liberalization, contractual form innovation and privatization.* New York: Routledge. doi:10.4324/9781315211305

Chen, M. J. (2001). *Inside Chinese business.* Boston: Harvard Business School Press.

Child, J., & Rodrigues, S. B. (2005). The Internationalization of Chinese Firms: A Case for Theoretical Extension? *Management and Organization Review, 1*(3), 381–410. doi:10.1111/j.1740-8784.2005.0020a.x

Chinen, K., & Sun, Y. (2011). Effects of Country-of-Origin on Buying Behavior: A Study of the Attitudes of United States Consumers to Chinese-brand Automobiles. *International Journal of Management, 28*(2), 553–563.

Chinese Industry and Commerce Bureau. (2014). The development of Small and macro enterprises. *The State Council of The People's Republic of China*. Retrieved November 27, 2018, from http://www.gov.cn/xinwen/2014-03/31/content_2650031.htm

Choi, C., & Cohen, P. (2017). How does obesity lead to insulin resistance? *eLife, 6*. PMID:29239299

Choi, M. (2011). Employees' attitudes toward organizational change: A literature review. *Human Resource Management, 50*(4), 479–500. doi:10.1002/hrm.20434

Choi, M., & Ruona, W. (2011). Individual readiness for organizational change and its implications for human resource and organizational development. *Human Resource Development Review*, *10*(1), 46–73. doi:10.1177/1534484310384957

Chuan, T. (2000). *A detailed trends analysis of National Quality Awards worldwide*. Academic Press.

Chu, W.-W. (2009). Can Taiwan's second movers upgrade via branding? *Research Policy*, *38*(6), 1054–1065. doi:10.1016/j.respol.2008.12.014

Coch, L., & French, J. R. P. Jr. (1948). Overcoming resistance to change. *Human Relations*, *21*(10), 512–532. doi:10.1177/001872674800100408

Collier, P., & Anke, H. (2005). Resource Rents, Governance, and Conflict. *The Journal of Conflict Resolution*, *49*(4), 625–633. doi:10.1177/0022002705277551

Collins, J. (2003, June 18). New campaign markets bay state to businesses. *Boston Globe*, p. D4.

Collins, J. (2001). *Good to Great*. Harper Business.

Cooper, M., & Morton, J. (2018). Digital Health and Obesity: How Technology Could Be the Culprit and Solution for Obesity. In Digital Health (pp. 169-178). Springer.

Cosenzo, K. a., Fatkin, L.T., & Patton, D. (2007). Ready or not: enhancing operational effectiveness through use of readiness measures. *Aviation Space and Environmental Medicine, 78*(5).

Damanpour, F., Walker, R. M., & Avellaneda, C. N. (2009). Combinative Effects of Innovation Types and Organizational Performance: A Longitudinal Study of Service Organizations. *Journal of Management Studies*, *46*(4), 650–675. doi:10.1111/j.1467-6486.2008.00814.x

Dana, L. (1999). Small business as a supplement in the People's Republic of China (RPC). *Journal of Small Business Management*, *37*(3), 76–80.

Das, D. (2018, September 24). *Dubai Govt Upgrades Payment Portal DubaiPay with Blockchain technology*. Retrieved from https://www.ccn.com/dubai-govt-upgrades-payment-portal-dubaipay-with-blockchain-technology

Davies, A., Gann, D., & Douglas, T. (2009). Innovation in megaprojects: Systems integration at London Heathrow terminal 5. *California Management Review*, *51*(2), 101–125. doi:10.2307/41166482

Davies, A., & Mackenzie, I. (2014). Project complexity and systems integration: Constructing the London 2012 Olympics and Paralympics Games. *International Journal of Project Management*, *32*(5), 773–790. doi:10.1016/j.ijproman.2013.10.004

Davis, J., Roland, O., James, D., & Seven, B. (2001). *Stabilization and savings funds for nonrenewable resources: Experience and fiscal policy implications*. New York: International Monetary Fund.

De Bruijn, H. A., & Hufen, H. A. M. (1998). The traditional approach to policy instruments. In P. B. Guy & F. K. M. van Nispen (Eds.), *Public Policy Instruments: Evaluating the Tools of Public Administration*. Cheltenham, UK: Edward Elgar.

De Bruin, A., & Lewis, K. (2005). Green entrepreneurship in New Zealand: a micro-enterprise focus. In M. Schaper (Ed.), *Green Entrepreneurship in New Zealand: A Micro- Enterprise Focus*. Aldershot, UK: Ashgate Publishing.

de Lacy Costello, B., Amann, A., Al-Kateb, H., Flynn, C., Filipiak, W., Khalid, T., ... Ratcliffe, N. M. (2014). A review of the volatiles from the healthy human body. *Journal of Breath Research*, *8*(1), 014001. doi:10.1088/1752-7155/8/1/014001 PMID:24421258

De Wit, J., & Ridder, D. (2006). *Self-regulation in health behavior*. Chichester, UK: Wiley.

Dejardin, M. (2000). *Entrepreneurship and Economic Growth: An Obvious Conjunction?* Namur, Belgium: University of Namur.

del Brío, J. A., Junquera, B., & Ordiz, M. (2008). Human resources in advanced environmental approaches–a case analysis. *International Journal of Production Research*, *46*(21), 6029–6053. doi:10.1080/00207540701352094

Del Giudice, K., Hale, K., & Johnston, M. (2015). Development of a scale for quantifying a system's human factors readiness. *Procedia Manufacturing*, *3*, 671–677. doi:10.1016/j.promfg.2015.07.580

Deloitte. (2011). *Operational excellence operational readiness assurance*. Available at: https://www2.deloitte.com/con- tent/dam/Deloitte/ca/Documents/energy-resources/ca-en-energy-resources-operations- excellence-asset-management-brochure.pdf

Deloitte. (2015). *Digital banking for small and medium sized enterprises: Improving access to finance for the underserved*. Retrieved from: https://www2.deloitte.com/content/dam/Deloitte/sg/Documents/financial-services/sea-fsi-digital-banking-small-medium-enterprises-noexp.pdf

Deming, W. E. (1993). *The New Economics*. Cambridge, MA: MIT Press.

Deng, Z., Hofman, P. S., & Newman, A. (2013). Ownership concentration and product innovation in Chinese private SMEs. *Asia Pacific Journal of Management*, *30*(3), 717–734. doi:10.100710490-012-9301-0

Diabetes. (2018). Retrieved from https://www.nhs.uk/conditions/diabetes/

Division of Health Psychology. (2018). Retrieved from https://www1.bps.org.uk/networks-and-communities/member-microsite/division-health-psychology

Doherty, S. (2008). *Heathrow's T5 history in the making*. West Sussex, UK: John Wiley & Sons.

Done, A., Voss, C., & Rytter, N. (2011). Best practice interventions: Short-term impact and long-term outcomes. *Journal of Operations Management*, *29*(5), 500–513. doi:10.1016/j.jom.2010.11.007

Dubai Green Hotel Innovation. (2018). Retrieved from http://www.dubaigreenhotelinnovation.com/

Dubai SMEs. (2013). The state of Small & Medium Enterprises (SMEs) in Dubai: a report by Dbuai SME. *An agency of the Development of Economic Development*. Retrieved from http://www.sme.ae/studiesandresearchdocument/sme_report_english.pdf

Dubai Statistics Center. (2016). *Climate and environment*. Dubai: Government of Dubai.

Dubai, S. M. E. (2019). *The State of Small & Medium Enterprises (SMEs) in Dubai*. Retrieved from: http://www.sme.ae/studiesandresearchdocument/sme_report_english.pdf

DubaiS. M. E. (2019). *The Fund.* Retrieved from: https://www.thefund.ae/

DuBois, C., Lopez, O., Beale, E., Healy, B., Boehm, J., & Huffman, J. (2015). Relationships between positive psychological constructs and health outcomes in patients with cardiovascular disease: A systematic review. *International Journal of Cardiology*, *195*, 265–280. doi:10.1016/j.ijcard.2015.05.121 PMID:26048390

Economy, D. (2012). *Promoting Business Excellence Award*. Dubai: Dubai Economy Department.

Eddleston, K. A., Kellermanns, F. W., & Sarathy, R. (2008). Resource configuration in family firms: Linking resources, strategic planning, and technological opportunities to performance. *Journal of Management Studies*, *45*, 26–50.

Elkington, J. (1998). *Cannibals With Forks: The Triple Bottom Line of 21st Century Business*. Stony Creek, CT: New Society Publishers.

Emirates Blockchain Strategy 2021. (n.d.). Retrieved from https://government.ae/en/about-the-uae/strategies-initiatives-and-awards/federal-governments-strategies-and-plans/emirates-blockchain-strategy-2021

Emirates247.ae. (2019). *UAE starts on a 100-year plan to settle planet Mars*. Retrieved from emirates247.ae: http://www.emiratesnews247.com/uae-starts-on-100-year-plan-to-settle-planet-mars/

Emirates247.com. (2016, January 31). *UAE Ministerial Retreat at Bab Al Shams*. Retrieved from Emirates247.com: https://www.emirates247.com/news/emirates/uae-ministerial-retreat-at-bab-al-shams-2016-01-31-1.619243

Engel, G. (1997). From Biomedical to Biopsychosocial: Being Scientific in the Human Domain. *Psychosomatics*, *38*(6), 521–528. doi:10.1016/S0033-3182(97)71396-3 PMID:9427848

Eng, T.-Y. (2009). Manufacture upgrade and interfirm relationship development: The case of electronics firms in the Pearl River Delta. *Asia Pacific Business Review*, *14*(4), 507–525. doi:10.1080/13602380802461419

Eng, T.-Y., & Spickett-Jones, J. G. (2009). An investigation of marketing capabilities and upgrading performance of manufacturers in mainland China and Hong Kong. *Journal of World Business*, *44*(4), 463–475. doi:10.1016/j.jwb.2009.01.002

Ernst & Young. (2006). *Progressions 2006. Capturing global advantage in the pharmaceutical industry*. New York: Ernst & Young Global Pharmaceutical Centre.

Establishment, R. (2019). *Who we are*. Retrieved from: http://www.ruwad.ae/en/index.php/about-us/

EU/OECD. (2016). Policy Brief on Scaling the Impact of Social Enterprises. *European Union and OECD*. Retrieved from http://www.oecd.org/cfe/leed/Policy-brief-Scaling-up-social-enterprises-EN.pdf

European Commission. (2008). *Entrepreneurship in higher education, especially in nonbusiness studies: Final report of the expert group*. Retrieved from http://europa.eu.int/comm/enterprise/entrepreneurship/support_measures/index.htm

European Commission. (2015). *User guide to the SME definition*. Retrieved from https://ec.europa.eu/regional_policy/sources/conferences/state-aid/sme/smedefinitionguide_en.pdf

European Investment Bank. (2015). *Tunisia Neighbourhood SME financing*. Retrieved from: https://www.eib.org/attachments/efs/economic_report_neighbourhood_sme_financing_tunisia_en.pdf

Evans, A., & Schäfer, A. (2011). The impact of airport capacity constraints on future growth in the US air transportation system. *Journal of Air Transport Management*, *17*(5), 288–295. doi:10.1016/j.jairtraman.2011.03.004

Ewing, B. T., & Malik, F. (2010). Estimating Volatility Persistence in Oil Prices Under Structural Breaks. *Financial Review*, *45*(4), 1011–1023. doi:10.1111/j.1540-6288.2010.00283.x

Faridi, A. S., & El-Sayegh, S. (2006). Significant factors causing delay in the UAE construction industry. *Construction Management and Economics*, *24*(11), 1167–1176. doi:10.1080/01446190600827033

Fayolle, A., Gailly, B., & Lassas-Clerc, N. (2006). Assessing the impact of entrepreneurship education programmes: A new methodology. *Journal of European Industrial Training*, *30*(9), 701–720. doi:10.1108/03090590610715022

Federal Competitiveness and Statistics Authority. (2019). Retrieved from: http://fcsa.gov.ae/en-us/Pages/Competitiveness/Reports/Global-Entrepreneurship-Index-by-GEDI.aspx

Feeney, B., & Collins, N. (2014). A New Look at Social Support. *Personality and Social Psychology Review*, *19*(2), 113–147. doi:10.1177/1088868314544222 PMID:25125368

fichtelegal.com. (2018). *Crowdfunding in the UAE – An Opportune Time For Regulatory Certainty*. Retrieved 2018 from fichtelegal.com: https://fichtelegal.com/wp-content/uploads/2017/02/2017.02-executive-insights-crowdfunding-1.pdf

Fiedler, J., & Wendler, A. (2016). Berlin Brandenburg Airport. In G. Kostka & J. Fiedler (Eds.), Large Infrastructure Projects in Germany: between ambitions and realities (pp. 87–145). Academic Press. doi:10.1007/978-3-319-29233-5_4

Fonseca, L. (2015). From Quality Gurus and TQM to ISO 9001:2015: a review of several quality paths. *International Journal of Qualitative Research*, *9*(1), 167–180.

Fonseca, L. (2015). The relationship between ISO 9001 certification maturity and EFQM Business Excellence Model results. *Quality Innovation and Prosperity*, *19*(1), 85–102. doi:10.12776/qip.v19i1.556

Fossas-Olalla, M., Minguela-Rata, B., López-Sánchez, J.-I., & Fernández-Menéndez, J. (2015). Product innovation: When should suppliers begin to collaborate? *Journal of Business Research*, *68*(7), 1404–1406. doi:10.1016/j.jbusres.2015.01.022

Franken, A., Goffin, K., Szwejczewski, M., & Kutsch, E. (2014). *Roads to resilience: Building dynamic approaches to risk*. Cranfield Management School.

Freeman, C. (1988). Japan, a new system of innovation. In G. Dosi, C. Freeman, R. Nelson, G. Silverberg, & L. Soete (Eds.), *Technical change and economic theory*. London: Pinter.

French, D., Vedhara, K., Kaptein, A., & Weinman, J. (2010). *Health psychology* (2nd ed., p. 17). Chichester, UK: BPS Blackwell.

Fritsch, M. (2007). How does new business formation affect regional development? *Small Business Economics*, *30*(1), 1–14. doi:10.100711187-007-9057-y

Fritsch, M., & Meschede, M. (2011). Product innovation, process innovation, and size. *Review of Industrial Organization*, *19*(3), 335–350. doi:10.1023/A:1011856020135

Fritsch, M., & Mueller, P. (2004). The effects of new business formation on regional development over time. *Regional Studies*, *38*(8), 961–975. doi:10.1080/0034340042000280965

Gardner, D. (2001). *Operational readiness—is your system more "ready" than your environment*. Project Management Institute annual seminars and symposium, Nashville, TN.

Gedajlovic, E., & Carney, M. (2010). Markets, hierarchies and families: Toward a transaction cost theory of the family firm. *Entrepreneurship Theory and Practice*, *34*(6), 1145–1171. doi:10.1111/j.1540-6520.2010.00418.x

Gelb, A., & Sina, G. (2010). *How Should Oil Exporters Spend Their Rents?* Center for Global Development, Working Paper, No. 221.

Gerich, J., & Moosbrugger, R. (2018). Subjective Estimation of Health Literacy—What Is Measured by the HLS-EU Scale and How Is It Linked to Empowerment? *Health Communication*, *33*(3), 254–263. doi:10.1080/10410236.2016.1255846 PMID:28033479

Ghemawat, P. (1991). *Commitment: The Dynamic of Strategy*. New York: Free Press.

Gibb, A. (2006). Making markets in business development services for SMEs: Taking up the Chinese challenge of entrepreneurial networking and stakeholder relationship management. *Journal of Small Business and Enterprise Development*, *13*(2), 263–283. doi:10.1108/14626000610665962

Gibb, A. (2009). Meeting the Development Needs of Owner Managed Small Enterprise: A Discussion of the Centrality of Action Learning. *Journal Action Learning: Research and Practice*, *6*(3), 209–227. doi:10.1080/14767330903299415

Gill, A., & Biger, N. (2012). Barriers to small business growth in Canada. *Journal of Small Business and Enterprise Development*, *19*(4), 656–668. doi:10.1108/14626001211277451

Glaeser, E., Kallal, H., Sheinkman, J., & Schleifer, A. (1999). Growth in cities. *Journal of Political Economy*, *100*(1), 1126–1152.

Glynn, M. S. (2012). Primer in B2B brand-building strategies with a reader practicum. *Journal of Business Research*, *65*(5), 666–675. doi:10.1016/j.jbusres.2011.03.010

Goldin, C., & Katz, L. F. (2008). *The Race Between Education and Technology*. Boston: Harvard University Press.

Gonzalez-Prendes, A., & Resko, S. (2011). Cognitive-Behavioral Theory. In S. Ringel & J. Brandell (Eds.), Trauma: Contemporary Directions in Theory, Practice, and Research (pp. 14-33). Academic Press.

Government of Dubai. (n.d.). *Solar Decathlon Middle East Dubai, 2018*. Retrieved from https://www.dubaisolarshow.com/views/sdme.aspx

Graham, A. (2009). How important are commercial revenues to today's airports? *Journal of Air Transport Management*, *15*(3), 106–111. doi:10.1016/j.jairtraman.2008.11.004

GulfNews. (2011). *Why women graduates outnumber men in the UAE?* Retrieved August 28, 2018 from Gulf News: https://gulfnews.com/gn-focus/why-women-graduates-outnumber-men-in-the-uae-1.790849

GulfNews. (2017, August 14). *There are 45 free zones in the UAE: Find the right one for your new business*. Retrieved from Gulfnew.com: https://gulfnews.com/lifestyle/community/45-free-zones-in-the-uae-find-the-right-one-for-your-new-business-1.1716197

Gunasekaran, A., Marri, H. B., Mcgauahey, R., & Grieve, R. J. (2001). Implications of organization and human behavior on the implementation of CIM in SMEs: An empirical analysis. *International Journal of CIM*, *14*(2), 175–185.

Gupta, S., & Kumar, V. (2013). Sustainability as corporate culture of a brand for superior performance. *Journal of World Business*, *48*(3), 311–320. doi:10.1016/j.jwb.2012.07.015

Gures, N., Inan, H., & Arslan, S. (2018). Assessing the self-service technology usage of Y-Generation in airline services. *Journal of Air Transport Management*, *71*, 215–219. doi:10.1016/j.jairtraman.2018.04.008

Gwartney, J., Holcombe, R., & Lawson, R. (1999). Economic freedom and the environment for economic growth. *Journal of Institutional and Theoretical Economics*, *155*(1), 643–663.

Ha-Brookshire, J., & Yoon, S.-H. (2012). Country of origin factors influencing US consumers' perceived price for multinational products. *Journal of Consumer Marketing*, *29*(6), 445–454. doi:10.1108/07363761211259250

Hafeez, K., Foroudi, P., Dinnie, K., Nguyen, B., & Parahoo, S. (2016). The role of place branding and image in the development of sectoral clusters: The case of Dubai. *Journal of Brand Management*, *23*(4), 383–402. doi:10.1057/bm.2016.18

Hafer, R. (2013). Entrepreneurship and state economic growth. *Journal of Entrepreneurship and Public Policy*, *2*(1), 67–79. doi:10.1108/20452101311318684

Hall, C. (2007). When the dragon awakes: Internationalisation of SMEs in China and implication for Europe. *CESifo Forum*, *8*(2), 29–34.

Hall, M. E., Wang, Z., do Carmo, J., Kamimura, D., & Hall, J. E. (2018). Obesity and Metabolic Syndrome Hypertension. In *Disorders of Blood Pressure Regulation* (pp. 705–722). Cham: Springer. doi:10.1007/978-3-319-59918-2_42

Han, S., Middleton, P. F., Bubner, T. K., & Crowther, C. A. (2015). Women's views on their diagnosis and management for borderline gestational diabetes mellitus. *Journal of Diabetes Research*. PMID:25785278

Haque, A., Thompson, M., & El Bassuni, F. (2015). *Clinical psychology in United Arab Emirates: Prospects and challenges in private practice*. Academic Press.

Hardison, C. (1998). Readiness, action, and resolve for change: Do health care leaders have what it takes? *Quality Management in Health Care*, *6*(2), 44–51. doi:10.1097/00019514-199806020-00006 PMID:10178159

Harris, S. G., & Cole, M. (2007). A stages of change perspective on managers' motivation to learn in a leadership development context. *Journal of Organizational Change Management*, *20*(6), 774–793. doi:10.1108/09534810710831019

Hart, D. M. (2003). *Entrepreneurship policy: What it is and where it came from. In The Emergence of Entrepreneurship Policy: Governance, Startups and Growth in the U.S. Knowledge Economy.* Cambridge, UK: Cambridge University Press.

Hartog, C., Van Stel, A., & Storey, D. J. (2010). *Institutions and Entrepreneurship: The Role of the Rule of Law.* Working Paper no. H201003, EIM Research Reports.

Hashim, M. K., & Wafa, S. A. (2002). *Small and Medium Sized Enterprises in Malaysia – Development Issues.* Prentice-Hall.

Hastings, N. (2015). *Physical asset management: with an introduction to ISO55000* (2nd ed.). Springer.

Haynie, M. J., Shepherd, D., Mosakowski, E., & Early, C. P. (2010). A situated metacognitive model of the entrepreneurial mindset. *Journal of Business Venturing*, *25*(2), 13.

Healthcare Resource Guide: United Arab Emirates. (2018). Retrieved from https://2016.export.gov/industry/health/healthcareresourceguide/eg_main_108626.asp

Heneweer, H., Vanhees, L., & Picavet, S. (2009). Physical activity and low back pain: A U-shaped relation? *Pain*, *143*(1), 21–25. doi:10.1016/j.pain.2008.12.033 PMID:19217208

Herold, D., Fedor, D., & Caldwell, S. D. (2007). Beyond change management: A multilevel investigation of contextual and personal influences on employees' commitment to change. *The Journal of Applied Psychology*, *92*(4), 942–951. doi:10.1037/0021-9010.92.4.942 PMID:17638456

Hessels, J., Van Gelderen, M., & Thurik, R. (2008). Entrepreneurial aspirations, motivations, and their drivers. *Small Business Economics*, *31*(3), 323–339. doi:10.100711187-008-9134-x

Hickey, M. (2008). *Operational readiness - making it happen. CORE 2008: rail; the core of integrated transport.* Railway Technical Society of Australasia: Engineers Australia.

High Blood Pressure (Hypertension). (2018). Retrieved from https://www.nhs.uk/conditions/high-blood-pressure-hypertension/

Hill, J. (2015, December 14). *How Bayt.com proved to be just the job for entrepreneur Rabea Ataya.* Retrieved from The national.ae: https://www.thenational.ae/business/how-bayt-com-proved-to-be-just-the-job-for-entrepreneur-rabea-ataya-1.104680

Hitt, M. A., Ireland, R. D., Camp, S. M., & Sexton, D. L. (2001). Entrepreneurial strategies for wealth creation. *Strategic Management Journal*, *22*(1), 91–479.

Hobday, M. (1995). East-Asian Latecomer Firms - Learning the Technology of Electronics. *World Development*, *23*(7), 1171–1193. doi:10.1016/0305-750X(95)00035-B

Holt, D. (2011). The Longitudinal Evolution of Environmental "Ecopreneurs" from the 1990s: Mergers and Acquisitions and the Waste Management Industry. In G. Eweje & M. Perry (Eds.), *Business and Sustainability: Concepts, Strategies and Changes* (Vol. 3). Bingley, UK: Emerald Group Publishing Limited. doi:10.1108/S2043-9059(2011)0000003013

Hong Kong Government - Legislative Council of the Hong Kong Special Administrative Region. (1999). *Report of the Select Committee to Inquire into the Circumstances Leading to the Problems Surrounding the Commencement of the Operation of the New Hong Kong International Airport at Chek Lap Kok since 6 July 1998 and Related Issues* (Vol. 1). Hong Kong: Government Printer.

Hong Kong Government - Office of the Ombudsman. (1999). *Executive Summary of the Report of the Investigation into the Commissioning and Operation of the New Airport at Chek Lap Kok.* Hong Kong: Government Printer.

Hopkins, A. (2018). *Calling Female Entrepreneurs: Why The UAE Is The Place To Be.* Retrieved from entreprenuer.com: https://www.entrepreneur.com/article/320548

Horton, B. (1998). Medicon valley: A bridge to collaboration. *Nature, 395*(6700), 412–413. doi:10.1038/26542 PMID:9759734

House of Commons: Transport Committee. (2008). *The opening of Heathrow Terminal 5.* London: House of Commons.

Howlett, N., Schulz, J., Trivedi, D., Troop, N., & Chater, A. (2018). *Examining the constructs and predictive validity of the COM-B for physical activity.* Academic Press.

Huang, I., Lee, J., Ketheeswaran, P., Jones, C., Revicki, D., & Wu, A. (2017). Does personality affect health-related quality of life? A systematic review. *PLoS One, 12*(3), e0173806. doi:10.1371/journal.pone.0173806 PMID:28355244

Humphreys, M., Jeffrey, S., & Joseph, S. (2007). *Escaping the Resource Curse.* New York: Columbia University Press.

Hung, C. T. (2008). The Articulated Process of Small Commercial Market Town and Spatial Capital Restruction: Case Study of Yiwu, Zhejiang Province, China. *Journal of Architecture and Planning*, *9*(1), 1–20.

Hussain, H. (2015). Obesity and Overweight among Dubai Population, Prevalence and Associated Risk Factors. Cross Sectional Analytical Study. *International Journal of Epidemiology, 44*(S1), i133-i133.

Hussain, J., Millman, C., & Matlay, H. (2006). SME financing in the UK and in China: A comparative perspective. *Journal of Small Business and Enterprise Development, 13*(4), 584–599. doi:10.1108/14626000610705769

Hussain, S., Hussain, A., Hussain, K., Asif, M., Khalil, M., Rahman, D., ... AlKhani, R. (2013). Pharmacist–patient counselling in Dubai: Assessment and reflection on patient satisfaction. *European Journal of Hospital Pharmacy. Science and Practice*, *20*(4), 241–247. doi:10.1136/ejhpharm-2012-000263

Hu, Z. F., & Khan, M. S. (1997). Why Is China Growing So Fast? *Staff Papers*, *44*(1), 103–131. doi:10.2307/3867499

Hvidt, M. (2009). The Dubai model: An outline of key development-process elements in Dubai. *International Journal of Middle East Studies*, *41*(3), 397–418. doi:10.1017/S0020743809091120

HY, H., MMO, T., W, A., Abdulla, A., N, A., & N, M. (2017). Targeting Parents and Children at Schools in the Treatment of Childhood Obesity: Short-Term Results, Dubai 2016. *Academic Journal of Pediatrics & Neonatology, 3*(3).

Ikenberry, G. J. (2008). The Rise of China and the Future of the West - Can the Liberal System Survive. *Foreign Affairs*, *87*(1), 23–37.

ILO. (2017). *World Employment and Social Outlook 2017: Sustainable enterprises and jobs: Formal enterprises and decent work.* Geneva: International Labour Office.

IMF. (2019). The *United Arab Emirates*. Retrieved August 28, 2018 from International Monetary Fund: http://www.imf.org/en/Countries/ARE

Isaak, R. (1997). Globalisation and green entrepreneurship. *Greener Management International.*, *18*, 80–90.

Ismail, M. (2010). *UAE leads region on UK human development index.* Retrieved from N UAE: https://www.thenational.ae/uae/government/uae-leads-region-on-un-human-development-index-1.530313

ISO 9000. (2005). International Standard, Quality management systems — Fundamentals and vocabulary. International Organization for Standardization.

ISO. (2009). *ISO 31000: Risk management – principles and guidelines.* Geneva: International Standards Organisation.

ISO. (2016, November 9). *Ge2002.* Retrieved from www.docsity.com: http://dcemecha.weebly.com/uploads/5/8/0/3/58036683/ge2022_tqm_notes1.pdf

Issac, J. (2015). SMEs' GDP input set to hit 70% by 2021. *Khaleej Times*. Retrieved from: https://www.khaleejtimes.com/business/local/smes-gdp-input-set-to-hit-70-by-2021

Janicke, M. (2008). Ecological modernisation: New perspectives. *Journal of Cleaner Production*, *16*(5), 557–565. doi:10.1016/j.jclepro.2007.02.011

Jansen, K. (2000). The emerging dynamics of change: Resistance, readiness, and momentum. *People and Strategy*, *23*(2), 53–55.

Jarvis, R., Curran, J., Kitching, J., & Lightfoot, G. (2000). The use of quantitative and qualitative criteria in the measurement of performance in small firms. *Journal of Small Business and Enterprise Development*, *7*(2), 123–134. doi:10.1108/EUM0000000006834

Jaworski, B. J., & Kohli, A. K. (1993). Market orientation: Antecedents and consequences. *Journal of Marketing*, *57*(3), 53–70. doi:10.1177/002224299305700304

Jennings, P., & Beaver, G. (1997). The performance and competitive advantage of small firms: A management perspective. *International Small Business Journal*, *15*(2), 63–75. doi:10.1177/0266242697152004

Jimenez, E., Claro, J., de Sousa, J., & de Neufville, R. (2017). Dynamic evolution of European airport systems in the context of Low-Cost Carriers growth. *Journal of Air Transport Management*, *64*, 68–76. doi:10.1016/j.jairtraman.2017.06.027

Jones, R., Jimmieson, N., & Griffiths, A. (2005). The impact of organizational culture and reshaping capabilities on change implementation success: The mediating role of readiness for change. *Journal of Management Studies*, *42*(2), 361–386. doi:10.1111/j.1467-6486.2005.00500.x

Kalakou, S., Psaraki-Kalouptsidi, V., & Moura, F. (2015). Future airport terminals: New technologies promise capacity gains. *Journal of Air Transport Management*, *42*, 203–212. doi:10.1016/j.jairtraman.2014.10.005

Kale, D., & Little, S. (2007). From Imitation to Innovation: The Evolution of R&D Capabilities and Learning Processes in the Indian Pharmaceutical Industry. *Technology Analysis and Strategic Management*, *19*(5), 589–609. doi:10.1080/09537320701521317

Kang, S. H., Cheong, C., & Yoon, S.-M. (2011). Structural changes and volatility transmission in crude oil markets. *Physica A*, *390*(23-24), 4317–4324. doi:10.1016/j.physa.2011.06.056

Kardes, I., Ozturk, A., Cavusgil, S. T., & Cavusgil, E. (2013). Managing global megapro- jects: Complexity and risk management. *International Business Review*, *22*(6), 905–917. doi:10.1016/j.ibusrev.2013.01.003

Kats, G., Alevantis, L., Berman, A., Mills, E., & Perlman, J. (2003). *The costs and financial benefits of green buildings: a report to California's sustainable building task force*. Sustainable Building Task Force. Available at https://noharm-uscanada.org/sites/default/files/documents-files/34/Build- ing_Green_Costs_Benefits.pdf

Kaufmann, L., & Roesch, J.-F. (2012). Constraints to Building and Deploying Marketing Capabilities by Emerging Market Firms in Advanced Markets. *Journal of International Marketing*, *20*(4), 1–24. doi:10.1509/jim.11.0116

Kayed, M., & Hassan, K. (2011). Saudi Arabia's economic development: Entrepreneurship as a strategy. *International Journal of Islamic and Middle Eastern Finance and Management*, *4*(1), 52–73. doi:10.1108/17538391111122203

KCAL. (2018). *How it all started.* Retrieved August 28, 2018 from Kcal: https://www.kcalextra.com/about-us/

KhaleejTimes. (2018, April 9). *Dubai is the best place for venture capitalists.* Retrieved from Khaleej Times: https://www.khaleejtimes.com/20180409/46/no-title

Khalifa Fund. (2019). Retrieved from: https://www.khalifafund.ae/

Kidd, L., & Howe, R. (2014). Operational readiness: An integral part of the facility planning process. *Healthcare Quarterly*, *17*(4), 63–67. doi:10.12927/hcq.2015.24120 PMID:25906468

Kierzkowski, A., & Kisiel, T. (2015). Functional Readiness of the Check-In Desk System at an Airport. In W. Zamojski, J. Mazurkiewicz, J. Sugier, T. Walkowiak, & J. Kacprzyk (Eds.), *Theory and Engineering of Complex Systems and Dependability* (Vol. 365). Springer. doi:10.1007/978-3-319-19216-1_21

Kim, E. (2019, January). *Amazon plans to launch a new Middle East marketplace, two years after buying Souq for $580 million.* Retrieved from CNBC: https://www.cnbc.com/2019/01/29/amazon-new-middle-east-marketplace-rivals-souq.html

Kim, L., & Nelson, R. R. (2000). Introduction: technology and industrialisation in newly industrialising countries. In L. Kim & R. R. Nelson (Eds.), *Technology, Learning and Innovation: Experiences of Newly Industrialising Economies* (pp. 1–9). Cambridge, UK: Cambridge University Press.

Kingston, J., Frei, R., Koornneef, F., & Schallier, P. (2007). *Defining operational readiness to investigate, DORI* (White Paper). The Noordwijk Risk Initiative Foundation (NRI) and the Royal Society for the Prevention of Accidents (RoSPA). Available at: http://www.nri.eu.com/WP1.pdf

Kirschenbaum, A., Mariani, M., Van Gulijk, C., Rapaport, C., & Lubasz, S. (2012). Trusting technology: Security decision making at airports. *Journal of Air Transport Management*, *25*, 57–60. doi:10.1016/j.jairtraman.2012.08.005

Kirzner, I. M. (1973). *Competition and Entrepreneurship.* Chicago: University of Chicago Press.

Kojima, K. (2000). The "flying geese" model of Asian economic development: Origin, theoretical extensions, and regional policy implications. *Journal of Asian Economics*, *11*(4), 375–401. doi:10.1016/S1049-0078(00)00067-1

Kolvereid, L. (1992). Growth aspirations among Norwegian entrepreneurs. *Journal of Business Venturing*, *7*(3), 209–222. doi:10.1016/0883-9026(92)90027-O

Kotey, B., & Folker, C. (2007). Employee Training in SMEs: Effect of Size and Firm Type—Family and Nonfamily. *Journal of Small Business Management*, *45*(2), 214–238. doi:10.1111/j.1540-627X.2007.00210.x

Kotter, J., & Schlesinger, L. (1979, March). Choosing strategies for change. *Harvard Business Review*, 106–114. PMID:10240501

Krauss, E. (2014). How does operational readiness assist in asset management : It surely is an operations function? *Australian Journal of Multi-Disciplinary Engineering*, *11*(1), 1–11. doi:10.7158/14488388.2014.11464878

Krugman, P. (1991a). Increasing returns and economic geography. *Journal of Political Economy*, *99*(1), 99–483.

Krugman, P. (1991b). *Geography and trade*. Cambridge, MA: MIT Press.

Krugman, P. (1991c). History and industry location: The cast of the manufacturing belt. *The American Economic Review*, *81*(2), 3–80.

Kuester, S., & Rauch, A. (2016). A job demands-resources perspective on salespersons' market intelligence activities in new product development. *Journal of Personal Selling & Sales Management*, *36*(1), 19–39. doi:10.1080/08853134.2016.1142793

Kumar, D., & Maheswaran, S. (2013). Detecting sudden changes in volatility estimated from high, low and closing prices. *Economic Modelling*, *31*, 484–491. doi:10.1016/j.econmod.2012.12.021

Kunzig, R. (2017, April 4). *The World's Most Improbable Green City*. Retrieved from https://www.nationalgeographic.com/environment/urban-expeditions/green- buildings/dubai-ecological-footprint-sustainable-urban-city/

Lanteri, A. (2017, November 26). *How CLEVER companies dominate the 4th Industrial Revolution*. Retrieved from https://medium.com/@alelanteri/how-clever-companies-dominate-the-4th-industrial-revolution-f250472ba93c

Larcom, S., & Swanson, T. (2013). Economics of Green Economies: Investment in Green Growth and How it Works. In P.-M. Dupuy & J. Vinuales (Eds.), *Harnessing Foreign Investment to Promote Environmental Protection*. Cambridge, UK: Cambridge University Press. doi:10.1017/CBO9781139344289.007

Lawry, K., & Pons, D. (2013). Integrative approach to the plant commissioning process. *Journal of Industrial Engineering*, *2013*, 1–12. doi:10.1155/2013/572072

Lee, E. (2000). The new Hong Kong international airport fiasco: Accountability failure and the limits of the new managerialism. *International Review of Administrative Sciences*, *66*(1), 57–72. doi:10.1177/0020852300661006

Lee, K. (2005). Making a Technological Catch-up: Barriers and opportunities. *Asian Journal of Technology Innovation*, *13*(2), 97–131. doi:10.1080/19761597.2005.9668610

Leek, S., & Christodoulides, G. (2012). A framework of brand value in B2B markets: The contributing role of functional and emotional components. *Industrial Marketing Management*, *41*(1), 106–114. doi:10.1016/j.indmarman.2011.11.009

Leger, K., Charles, S., & Almeida, D. (2018). Let It Go: Lingering Negative Affect in Response to Daily Stressors Is Associated With Physical Health Years Later. *Psychological Science*, *29*(8), 1283–1290. doi:10.1177/0956797618763097 PMID:29553880

Lerner, J. (2009). *Boulevard of Broken Dreams: Why Public Efforts to Boost Entrepreneurship and Venture Capital Have Failed – and What to Do About it*. Princeton, NJ: Princeton University Press. doi:10.1515/9781400831630

Leventhal, H., Diefenbach, M., & Leventhal, E. (1992). Illness cognition: Using common sense to understand treatment adherence and affect cognition interactions. *Cognitive Therapy and Research*, *16*(2), 143–163. doi:10.1007/BF01173486

Lewin, K. (1951). Field theory in social science: selected theoretical papers. In D. Cartwright (Ed.), Field theory in social science: Selected theoretical papers. New York: Harper.

Lewis, L., & Russell, S. (2011). Premating boundaries: Accountability at the nexus of water and climate change. *Social and Environmental Accountability Journal.*, *31*(2), 37–41. doi:10.1080/0969160X.2011.593812

Liang, G. (2007). Policy System on promoting SME innovation and entrepreneurship in China. *Torch High Technology Industry Development Center, Ministry of Science and Technology, China*. Retrieved October 10, 2018, from http://www.insme.info/documents/06_INSME2007_Liang.ppt

Li, L. (2017). China's manufacturing locus in 2025: With a comparison of "Made-in-China 2025" and "Industry 4.0". *Technological Forecasting and Social Change*, *135*, 66–74. doi:10.1016/j.techfore.2017.05.028

Liu, X. (2008). SME development in China: A policy perspective on SME industrial clustering. In SME in Asia and Globalization. ERIA Research Project Report, 2007-5.

Liu, F.-H., Liu, H.-Y., & Lin, T.-L. (2008). The competence and constraints of brand building for contract manufacturers. *Journal of Brand Management*, *15*(6), 412–432. doi:10.1057/bm.2008.8

Liu, F.-H., Tsou, H.-T., & Chen, L.-J. (2013). The impact of OEM supplier initiatives on buyer competence development: The moderating roles of collaborative relationship and competitive environment. *Asia Pacific Journal of Management*, *30*(4), 1285–1303. doi:10.100710490-011-9266-4

Liu, H., & Li, K. (2002). Strategic Implications of Emerging Chinese Multinationals: The Haier Case Study. *European Management Journal*, *20*(6), 699–706. doi:10.1016/S0263-2373(02)00119-6

Liu, Q. (2001). Review of mode of Sunan, Wenzhou, Pearl River. *China Situation and National Power*, *4*, 23–24.

Li, Y. (2006). Review and experience of mode of SME clusters in Guangdong. *Business Economics (Cleveland, Ohio)*, *7*, 58–59.

Li, Y., Liu, Y., & Zhao, Y. B. (2006). The role of market and entrepreneurship orientation and internal control in the new product development activities of Chinese firms. *Industrial Marketing Management*, *35*(3), 336–347. doi:10.1016/j.indmarman.2005.05.016

Lober, D. J. (1998). Pollution prevention as corporate entrepreneurship. *Journal of Organizational Change Management*, *11*(1), 26–37. doi:10.1108/09534819810369554

Loo, T., & Davies, G. (2006). Branding China: The Ultimate Challenge in Reputation Management? *Corporate Reputation Review*, *9*(3), 198–210. doi:10.1057/palgrave.crr.1550025

Lorz, M., Müller, S., & Volery, T. (2011). Entrepreneurship Education: A Meta- Analysis of Impact Studies and Applied Methodologies. *FGF G Forum 2011*.

Lundvall, B. (1988). Innovation as an interactive process: From user-producer interaction to the national system of innovation. In G. Dosi, C. Freeman, R. Nelson, G. Silverberg, & L. Soete (Eds.), *Technical change and economic theory*. London: Pinter.

Lu, Y. (2012). *An investigation of the relationship between cluster brands and individual brands: A place branding perspective*. Ames, IA: Iowa State University; doi:10.31274/etd-180810-2983

Lyons, A., & Powell, D. (2010). *Airport terminal facility activation techniques*. Available at: http://www.nap.edu/catalog/14394

MacBride, E. (2016, January 31). *Forbes*. Retrieved August 29, 2018 from Lessons From Startup Success In Dubai: To Win As An Entrepreneur, Do This One Thing, Fast: https://www.forbes.com/sites/elizabethmacbride/2016/01/31/dubai-based-adrelated-draws-attention-from-google-and-elsewhere-for-its-innovation/#6e56d58a3140

Maddison, A. (1998). *Chinese economic performance in the long run*. Paris: Development Centre of the Organisation for Economic Co-Operation and Development.

Malek, C. (2018). *Meet the young Arab entrepreneurs paving the way for the region's future*. Retrieved from The National: https://www.thenational.ae/uae/meet-the-young-arab-entrepreneurs-paving-the-way-for-region-s-future-1.693816?videoId=5716439907001

Malerba, F., & Nelson, R. (2011). Learning and catching up in different sectoral systems: Evidence from six industries. *Industrial and Corporate Change*, *20*(6), 1645–1675. doi:10.1093/icc/dtr062

Malik, R. (1997). *Chinese Entrepreneurs in the Economic Development of China*. London: Praeger.

Manna, R., Adebanjob, D., Laosirihongthong, T., & Punnakitikashem, P. (2011). Awareness and impact of business excellence in Asia. Routledge Taylor & Francis.

Marcotte, C. (2013). Measuring entrepreneurship at the country level: A review and research agenda. *Entrepreneurship and Regional Development*, *25*(3-4), 174–194. doi:10.1080/08985626.2012.710264

Marquardt, A. J. (2013). Relationship quality as a resource to build industrial brand equity when products are uncertain and future-based. *Industrial Marketing Management*, *42*(8), 1386–1397. doi:10.1016/j.indmarman.2013.07.017

Marshall, A., Ojiako, U., Wang, V., Lin, F., & Chipulu, M. (2018). Forecasting Unknown-Unknowns by Boosting the Risk Radar within the Risk Intelligent Organisation. *International Journal of Forecasting*.

Marshall, A. (1920). *Principes of Economics* (8th ed.). London: Macmillan.

Martinez, J. A. (2005). Equilibrium entrepreneurship rate, economic development and growth: Evidence from Spanish regions. *Entrepreneurship and Regional Development: An International Journal*, *17*(2), 61–145.

Masrom, M., Rahim, M., Mohamed, S., Chen, G. K., & Yunus, R. (2015). Successful criteria for large infrastructure projects in Malaysia. *Procedia Engineering*, *125*, 143–149. doi:10.1016/j.proeng.2015.11.021

Mauroner, O. (2015). Innovation clusters and public policy—The case of a research-driven cluster in Germany. *American Journal of Industrial and Business Management*, *5*(12), 736-747.

Mauroner, O., & Zorn, J. (2017). Cluster branding – a case study on regional cluster initiatives, cluster management, and cluster brands. *International Journal of Innovative Research and Development*, *7*(4), 289–312. doi:10.1504/IJIRD.2017.086234

McFarland, D. A. G. (2013). *Organizational Analysis*. Stanford, CA: Stanford University.

McLean, S., Protti, D., & Sheikh, A. (2011). Telehealthcare for long term conditions. *BMJ*, *342*(2), d120-d120.

Memba, S. F., Gakure, W. R., & Karanja, K. (2012). Venture capital (VC): Its impact on growth of small and medium enterprises in Kenya. *International Journal of Business and Social Science*, *3*(6), 32–38.

Méndez-Picazo, M., Galindo-Martín, M., & Ribeiro-Soriano, D. (2012). Governance, entrepreneurship and economic growth. *Entrepreneurship and Regional Development*, *24*(9-10), 865–877. doi:10.1080/08985626.2012.742323

Menon, A., & Menon, A. (1997). Enviropreneurial marketing strategy: The emergence of corporate environmentalism as marketing strategy. *Journal of Marketing*, *61*(1), 51–67. doi:10.1177/002224299706100105

Mensi, W., Hammoudeh, S., & Yoon, S. (2015). Structural breaks, dynamic correlations, asymmetric volatility transmission, and hedging strategies for petroleum prices and USD exchange rate. *Energy Economics*, *48*(1), 46–60. doi:10.1016/j.eneco.2014.12.004

Mensi, W., Hammoudeh, S., & Yoon, S.-M. (2014). Structural breaks and long memory in modeling and forecasting the volatility of foreign exchange markets of oil exporters: The importance of scheduled and unscheduled news announcements. *International Review of Economics & Finance*, *30*(1), 101–119. doi:10.1016/j.iref.2013.10.004

Michell, P., King, J., & Reast, J. (2001). Brand values related to industrial products. *Industrial Marketing Management*, *30*(5), 415–425. doi:10.1016/S0019-8501(99)00097-8

Michie, S., Johnston, M., Abraham, C., Lawton, R., Parker, D., & Walker, A. (2005). Making psychological theory useful for implementing evidence based practice: A consensus approach. *Quality & Safety in Health Care*, *14*(1), 26–33. doi:10.1136/qshc.2004.011155 PMID:15692000

Michie, S., van Stralen, M., & West, R. (2011). The behaviour change wheel: A new method for characterising and designing behaviour change interventions. *Implementation Science; IS*, *6*(1), 42. doi:10.1186/1748-5908-6-42 PMID:21513547

Middle East Makes a Play for Fintech Glory. (n.d.). Retrieved from https://amp.ft.com/content/201a0580-e72d-11e8-8a85-04b8afea6ea3

Miller, W. R., & Rollnick, S. (2012). *Motivational interviewing: Helping people change*. Guilford Press.

Ministry of Climate Change. (2019, March 25). *Mission & Vision & Values*. Retrieved from the Ministry of Climate Change: https://www.moccae.gov.ae/en/about-ministry/about-the-ministry/missionvision-and-values.aspx

Minniti, M., & Levesque, M. (2006). *Entrepreneurial types and economic growth*. Paper presented at the international conference on entrepreneurship in emerging regions, Hyderabad, India.

Minniti, M., Bygrave, W. D., & Autio, E. (2005). *Global entrepreneurship monitor: 2005 executive report*. Wellesley, MA: Babson College.

Mintzberg, H., Ahlstrand, B., & Lampel, J. (1998). *Strategy Safari: A Guide Through the Wilds of Strategic Management*. New York: Free Press.

Mitussis, D. (2010). SME innovation in Zhejiang, China: Potential constraints to development of widespread innovation. *Journal of Knowledge-based Innovation in China*, *2*(1), 89–105. doi:10.1108/17561411011032007

MOei.gov.ae. (2019). *Innovation Science Technology & Innovation Policy*. Retrieved from moei.gov.ae: https://www.moei.gov.ae/en/innovation/innovation-science-technology-and-innovation-policy.aspx

Molla, A., & Licker, P. (2005). Perceived e-readiness factors in e-commerce adoption: An empirical investigation in a developing country. *International Journal of Electronic Commerce*, *10*(1), 83–110. doi:10.1080/10864415.2005.11043963

Moreno, A. M., & Casillas, J. C. (2007). High-growth SMEs version non-high-growth SMEs: A discriminant analysis. *Entrepreneurship and Regional Development*, *19*(1), 69–88. doi:10.1080/08985620601002162

Morgan, N. A., Vorhies, D. W., & Mason, C. H. (2009). Market orientation, marketing capabilities, and firm performance. *Strategic Management Journal*, *30*(8), 909–920. doi:10.1002mj.764

Morosan, C. (2016). An empirical examination of US travellers' intentions to use biometric e-gates in airports. *Journal of Air Transport Management*, *55*, 120–128. doi:10.1016/j.jairtraman.2016.05.005

Morris, P. (1983). Managing project interfaces — key points for project success. In D. I. Cleland & W. R. King (Eds.), *Project Management Handbook*. Van Nostrand.

Morris, P. (1997). Managing project interfaces—key points for project success. In D. I. Cleland & W. R. King (Eds.), *Project management handbook* (2nd ed.). Hoboken, NJ: John Wiley & Sons, Inc. doi:10.1002/9780470172353.ch2

Motwani, J., Subramanian, R., & Gopala Krishna, P. (2005). Critical factors for successful ERP implementation: Exploratory findings from four case studies. *Computers in Industry*, *56*(6), 529–544. doi:10.1016/j.compind.2005.02.005

Mowery, D. (1995). The Boundaries of the US Firm in R&D. In N. R. Lamoreaux & D. M. G. Raff (Eds.), *Coordination and Information: Historical Perspectives on the Organization of Enterprise* (pp. 147–172). Chicago: Chicago University Press.

Mumayiz, S. (1989). Development of airport terminal design concepts—A new perspective. *Transportation Planning and Technology*, *13*(4), 303–320. doi:10.1080/03081068908717408

Muro, M., & Katz, B. (2010). The new "cluster moment": How regional innovation clusters can foster the next economy. *Brookings Institution*. Available from: https://www.brookings.edu/research/the-new-cluster-moment-how-regional-innovation-clusters-can-foster-the-next-economy/

Narver, J. C., & Slater, S. F. (1990). The Effect of a Market Orientation on Business Profitability. *Journal of Marketing*, *54*(4), 20–35. doi:10.1177/002224299005400403

National Research Council. (2011). *Growing Innovation Clusters for American Prosperity: Summary of a Symposium*. Washington, DC: The National Academies Press.

Naude, W. (2008). Entrepreneurship in economic development. World Institute for Development Economics Research.

Naughton, B. (2007). *The Chinese economy: Transitions and growth*. Cambridge, MA: The MIT Press.

Nelson, J., Raskind-Hood, C., Galvin, V. G., Essien, J., & Levine, L. (1999). Positioning for partnerships - Assessing public health agency readiness. *American Journal of Preventive Medicine*, *16*(1), 103–117. doi:10.1016/S0749-3797(99)00003-3 PMID:10198687

Nelson, R. (1988). Institutions supporting technical change in the United States. In G. Dosi, C. Freeman, R. Nelson, G. Silverberg, & L. Soete (Eds.), *Technical change and economic theory*. London: Pinter.

Ng, S. C. H., Rungtusanatham, J. M., Zhao, X., & Ivanova, A. (2015). TQM and environmental uncertainty levels: Profits, fit, and firm performance. *International Journal of Production Research*, *53*(14), 4266–4286. doi:10.1080/00207543.2014.994076

Nijkamp, P., & Poot, J. (1998). Spatial perspectives on new theories of economic growth. *The Annals of Regional Science*, *32*(1), 7–38. doi:10.1007001680050061

Nissan, E., Galindo, M. A., & Mendez, M. T. (2011). Relationship between organizations, institutions, entrepreneurship and economic growth process. *The International Entrepreneurship and Management Journal*, *7*(3), 24–311. doi:10.100711365-011-0191-2

Norman, W., & MacDonald, C. (2004). Getting to the bottom of "Triple Bottom Line.". *Business Ethics Quarterly*, *14*(2), 243–262. doi:10.5840/beq200414211

North, D. (1990). *Institutions, Institutional Change and Economic Performance*. Cambridge, UK: Cambridge University Press. doi:10.1017/CBO9780511808678

Nossair, A., Al-Tamimi, A., Al Amri, A., Al-Katheeri, K., Hann, T., & Finigan, T. (2012). Mega projects integrated readiness assurance process. In Abu Dhabi international petroleum conference and exhibition. Abu Dhabi, UAE: Society of Petroleum Engineers. doi:10.2118/159116-MS

O'Connell, J. (2011). The rise of the Arabian Gulf carriers: An insight into the business model of Emirates Airline. *Journal of Air Transport Management*, *17*(6), 339–346. doi:10.1016/j.jairtraman.2011.02.003

O'Connor, E., & Fiol, C. (2006). Creating readiness and involvement. *Physician Executive*, *32*(1), 72–74. PMID:16509406

OECD. (2010). *SMEs, Entrepreneurship, and Innovation*. Paris: OECD.

OECD. (2016). *Financing SMEs and Entrepreneurs 2016- An OECD Scoreboard*. Paris: OECD Publishing.

OECD. (2017g). *Small, Medium, Strong. Trends in SME Performance and Business Conditions*. Paris: OECD Publishing.

Ojiako, U., Maguire, S., & Chipulu, M. (2013). Thematic elements underlying the delivery of services in high-contact public service encounters. *Production Planning and Control*, *24*(6), 532–545. doi:10.1080/09537287.2011.642485

Okasha, A. (2017). *How to be Successful in Dubai: 12 Lessons that I Learnt running a small business in Dubai*. Amazon Kindle Publishing.

Oosterbeek, H., Van Praag, M., & Ijsselstein, A. (2010). The impact of entrepreneurship education on entrepreneurship skills and motivation. *European Economic Review*, *54*(3), 442–454. doi:10.1016/j.euroecorev.2009.08.002

OptoNet. (2018). A powerful network. *OptoNet*. Available from: http://www.optonet-jena.de/english-pages

Orser, B. J., Hogarth-Scott, S., & Riding, A. L. (2000). Performance, firm size, and management problem solving. *Journal of Small Business Management*, *38*(4), 42–58.

Ozawa, T. (2005). *Institutions, industrial upgrading, and economic performance in Japan: the 'flying-geese' paradigm of catch-up growth*. Cheltenham, UK: Edward Elgar. doi:10.4337/9781845425678

Papadopoulos, N., & Heslop, L. (2002). Country equity and country branding: Problems and prospects. *Journal of Brand Management*, *9*(4), 294–314. doi:10.1057/palgrave.bm.2540079

Parasuraman, A. (2000). Technology Readiness Index (TRI) a multiple-item scale to measure readiness to embrace new technologies. *Journal of Service Research*, *2*(4), 307–320. doi:10.1177/109467050024001

PaulKenny. (2019). *Paulkenny.com*. Retrieved from About Paul: https://www.paul-kenny.com/#contact

Perna, L. (2005). The Benefits of Higher Education: Sex, Racial/Ethnic, and Socioeconomic Group Differences. *The Review Of Higher Education*, *29*(1), 23–52. doi:10.1353/rhe.2005.0073

Petch, N. (2018). *Startup success by the numbers – battling the odds*. Retrieved August 29, 2018 from Virtuzone: https://vz.ae/startup-success-by-the-numbers-battling-the-odds/

Petra, C. M. (2013). Document Management for the Implementation and Maintenance of Management Systems Case study - Sherlock Web. Quality - Access to Success, 14(134), 80.

Philippidis, A. (2018). Top 10 U.S. biopharma clusters. *Genetic Engineering and Biotechnology News*. Available from: http://www.genengnews.com/lists/top-10-u-s-biopharma-clusters-5

Pinto, J., & Winch, G. (2015). The unsettling of 'settled science:' The past and future of the management of projects. *International Journal of Project Management, 34*(2), 237–245. doi:10.1016/j.ijproman.2015.07.011

Pistrui, D., Huang, W., Oksoy, D., Jing, Z., & Welsch, H. (2001). Entrepreneurship in China: Characteristics, Attributes, and Family Forces Shaping the Emerging Private Sector. *Family Business Review*, *XIV*, 2, 141–152.

Ponzini, D. (2011). Large scale development projects and star architecture in the absence of democratic politics: The case of Abu Dhabi, UAE. *Cities (London, England)*, *28*(3), 251–259. doi:10.1016/j.cities.2011.02.002

Porter, M. (1990). *The competitive advantage of nations*. New York: Free Press. doi:10.1007/978-1-349-11336-1

Porter, M. E. (2000). Location, competition, and economic development: Local clusters in a global economy. *Economic Development Quarterly*, *14*(1), 15–20. doi:10.1177/089124240001400105

Portney, K. (2015). *Sustainability*. Cambridge, MA: MIT Press.

Poutziouris, P., Wang, Y., & Chan, S. (2002). Chinese entrepreneurship: The development of small family firms in China. *Journal of Small Business and Enterprise Development*, *9*(4), 383–399. doi:10.1108/14626000210450568

Powell, W., & Snellman, K. (2004). The knowledge economy. *Annual Review of Sociology*, *30*(1), 199–220. doi:10.1146/annurev.soc.29.010202.100037

Power Technology. (n.d.). *Mohammed bin Rashid Al Maktoum Solar Park Phase II, Dubai.* Retrieved from https://www.power-technology.com/projects/mohammed-bin-rashid-al-maktoum-solar-park-phase-ii-dubai/

Prochaska, J., & DiClemente, C. C. (1983). Stages and processes of self-change of smoking: Toward an integrative model of change. *Journal of Consulting and Clinical Psychology*, *51*(3), 390–395. doi:10.1037/0022-006X.51.3.390 PMID:6863699

profitableventure.com. (2018). *50 Best Small Business ideas in Germany for 2018*. Retrieved August 28, 2018 from profitableventure.com: https://www.profitableventure.com/business-ideas-in-germany/

Project Management Institute. (2013). *A guide to the project management body of knowledge (PMBOK Guide)* (5th ed.). Project Management Institute.

Pye, L. (2000). Asian values: From dynamos to dominoes? In L. Harrison & S. Huntington (Eds.), *Culture matters how values shape human progress* (pp. 244–255). New York: Basic Books.

Qualsys. (2018). Retrieved from Context of the organization: http://quality.eqms.co.uk/iso-9001-2015-revision-explained-context-of-the-organisation

Rakthin, S., Calantone, R. J., & Wang, J. F. (2016). Managing market intelligence: The comparative role of absorptive capacity and market orientation. *Journal of Business Research*, *69*(12), 5569–5577. doi:10.1016/j.jbusres.2016.03.064

Ramsay, W. (2011). Revisiting the Resource Curse: Natural Disasters, the Price of Oil, and Democracy. *International Organization*, *65*(3), 507–529. doi:10.1017/S002081831100018X

Ravussin, E., & Ryan, D. (2017). Three New Perspectives on the Perfect Storm: What's Behind the Obesity Epidemic? *Obesity (Silver Spring, Md.)*, *26*(1), 9–10. doi:10.1002/oby.22085 PMID:29265770

Razzaque, A., Hamdan, A., Al-Hashimi, M., & Al-Dhaen, E. (2019). Learning readiness when sharing knowledge while e-learning. In *13th International Conference on e-Learning - MCCSIS 2019*. Porto, Portugal: MCCSIS 2019.

Richardson, P. (1999). *Economic change in China, c. 1800-1950*. Cambridge, UK: Cambridge University Press. doi:10.1017/CBO9781139171229

Robson, P. J., & Obeng, B. A. (2008). The barriers to growth in Ghana. *Small Business Economics*, *30*(4), 385–403. doi:10.100711187-007-9046-1

Rodrigues, A., & Williams, T. (1998). System dynamics in project management: Assessing the impacts of client behaviour on project performance. *The Journal of the Operational Research Society*, *49*(1), 1–24. doi:10.1057/palgrave.jors.2600490

Ro, H. (2012). Moderator and mediator effects in hospitality research. *International Journal of Hospitality Management*, *31*(1), 952–961. doi:10.1016/j.ijhm.2011.11.003

Romer, P. M. (1990). Endogenous Technical Change. *Journal of Political Economy*, *98*(1), 71–102. doi:10.1086/261725

Rosser, A. (2007). Escaping the Resource Curse: The Case of Indonesia. *Journal of Contemporary Asia*, *37*(1), 38–58. doi:10.1080/00472330601104557

Rust, R. (1998). Editorial: What Is the Domain of Service Research? *Journal of Service Research*, *1*(November), 107. doi:10.1177/109467059800100201

Sabella, A. R., Farraj, W. A., Burbar, M., & Qaimary, D. (2014). Entrepreneurship and Economic Growth in West Bank, Palestine. *Journal of Developmental Entrepreneurship*, *19*(01), 1450003. doi:10.1142/S1084946714500034

Sachs, D. and Andrew M. (1995). *Natural Resource Abundance and Economic Growth*. Technical Report Development Discussion, Paper no. 517a Harvard Institute for International Development Cambridge.

Salter, A., & Martin, B. (2001). The economic benefits of publicly funded basic research: A critical review. *Research Policy*, *30*(3), 509–532. doi:10.1016/S0048-7333(00)00091-3

Santander. (2019, March 25). *United Arab Emirates: Foreign Investment.* Retrieved from Santander.com: https://en.portal.santandertrade.com/establish-overseas/united-arab-emirates/foreign-investment

Schaper, M. (2002). The Essence of Ecopreneurship. *Greener Management International.*, *38*(38), 26–30. doi:10.9774/GLEAF.3062.2002.su.00004

Schmitz, J. A. Jr. (1989). Imitation, entrepreneurship and long–run growth. *Journal of Political Economy*, *97*(3), 721–739. doi:10.1086/261624

Schultz, T. W. (1975). The value of the ability to deal with disequilibria. *Journal of Economic Literature*, *13*(3), 827–846.

Schumpeter, J. A. (1911). The Theory of Economic Development. Cambridge, MA: Harvard University Press.

Shamuzova, S. (2018). *t's action time for female entrepreneurs in the UAE.* Retrieved from Khaleejtimes.com: https://www.khaleejtimes.com/business/local/its-action-time-for-female-entrepreneurs-in-the-uae

Simpson, M., Padmore, J., & Newman, N. (2012). Towards a new model of success and performance in SMEs. *International Journal of Entrepreneurial Behaviour & Research*, *18*(3), 264–285. doi:10.1108/13552551211227675

Singh, R. K., Garg, S. K., & Deshmukh, S. G. (2009). The competitiveness of SMEs in a globalized economy: Observations from China and India. *Management Research Review*, *33*(1), 54–65. doi:10.1108/01409171011011562

Sirmon, D. G., Arregle, J.-L., Hitt, M. A., & Webb, J. W. (2008). The role of family influence in firms' strategic responses to threat of imitation. *Entrepreneurship Theory and Practice*, *32*(6), 979–998. doi:10.1111/j.1540-6520.2008.00267.x

Sirois, F., Kitner, R., & Hirsch, J. (2014). Supplemental Material for Self-Compassion, Affect, and Health-Promoting Behaviors. *Health Psychology.*

Skerlavaj, M. S., Štemberger, M. I., Škrinjar, R., & Dimovski, V. (2007). Organizational learning culture – the missing link between business process change and organizational performance. *International Journal of Production Economics*, *106*(2), 346–367. doi:10.1016/j.ijpe.2006.07.009

SKGEP. (2019). *Sheikh Khalifa Government Excellence.* Retrieved from https://www.skgep.gov.ae/en

SmallandMediumEnterprises. (2018). *About Us*. Retrieved 2018 from SME.ae.

Smart S. M. E. MENA. (2019). *SME Sector & GCC.* Retrieved from: https://smartsmemena.com/smart-sme-mena-sme-and-gcc/

SME Dubai. (2014). *The state of Small & Medium Enterprises (SMEs) in Dubai – a Report by Dubai SMEs- An agency of the Department of Economic Development.* Retrieved December 1, 2018, from http://www.sme.ae/studiesandresearchdocument/sme_report_english.pdf

Sniehotta, F. F., Scholz, U., & Schwarzer, R. (2005). Bridging the intention–behaviour gap: Planning, self-efficacy, and action control in the adoption and maintenance of physical exercise. *Psychology & Health, 20*(2), 143–160. doi:10.1080/08870440512331317670

Sölvell, Ö., Lindqvist, G., & Ketels, C. (2003). *The cluster initiative greenbook.* Stockholm: Ivory Tower.

Sorli, M., & Stokic, D. (2009). *Innovating in Product/Process Development: Gaining Pace in New Product Development.* Springer Science & Business Media. doi:10.1007/978-1-84882-545-1

stalawfirm. (2018). *Intellectual Property Guide.* Retrieved August 30, 2018 from stalawfirm.com: https://www.stalawfirm.com/public/uploads/downloads/UAE-Intellectual-Property-Guide.pdf

Statistica. (2018). *Crowdfunding.* Retrieved 2018 from Statistica: https://www.statista.com/outlook/335/100/crowdfunding/worldwide

Steinfeld, E. S. (2004). China's shallow integration: Networked production and the new challenges for late internationalisation. *World Development, 32*(11), 1971–1987. doi:10.1016/j.worlddev.2004.04.003

Step Feed. (2018). Retrieved from https://stepfeed.com/here-s-how-the-uae-is-creating-the-next-wave-of-innovators-0348

Sternberg, R., & Wennekers, S. (2005). Determinants and Effects of New Business Creation Using Global Entrepreneurship Monitor Data. *Small Business Economics, 24*(3), 193–203. doi:10.100711187-005-1974-z

Stevens, G. (2013). Toward a process-based approach of conceptualizing change readiness. *The Journal of Applied Behavioral Science, 49*(3), 333–360. doi:10.1177/0021886313475479

Stok, F., De Vet, E., Wardle, J., Chu, M., De Wit, J., & De Ridder, D. (2015). Navigating the obesogenic environment: How psychological sensitivity to the food environment and self-regulatory competence are associated with adolescent unhealthy snacking. *Eating Behaviors, 17*, 19–22. doi:10.1016/j.eatbeh.2014.12.003 PMID:25528719

Stryjecki, C., Alyass, A., & Meyre, D. (2017). Ethnic and population differences in the genetic predisposition to human obesity. *Obesity Reviews, 19*(1), 62–80. doi:10.1111/obr.12604 PMID:29024387

Suarez-Villa, L. (2000). *Invention and the rise of technocapitalism.* New York: Rowan & Littlefield.

SuccessHarbor. (2017). *What Percentage of Businesses Fail – The Real Number*. Retrieved August 28, 2018 from Success Harbor: https://www.successharbor.com/percentage-businesses-fail-09092015/

Sun, S. L. (2009). Internationalization Strategy of MNEs from Emerging Economies: The Case of Huawei. *Multinational Business Review*, *17*(2), 129–156. doi:10.1108/1525383X200900013

Sustainable Development Knowledge Platform. (n.d.). Retrieved from http://sustainabledevelopment.un.org/

Svejvig, P., & Andersen, P. (2015). Rethinking project management: A structured literature review with a critical look at the brave new world. *International Journal of Project Management*, *33*(2), 278–290. doi:10.1016/j.ijproman.2014.06.004

Szabo, S., Osenenko, K., Qatami, L., Korenblat Donato, B., Korol, E., Al Madani, A., ... Levy, A. R. (2015). Quality of Care for Patients with Type 2 Diabetes Mellitus in Dubai: A HEDIS-Like Assessment. *International Journal of Endocrinology*, *2015*, 1–8. doi:10.1155/2015/413276 PMID:26089885

Takebayashi, M. (2012). Managing the multiple airport system by coordinating short/long-haul flights. *Journal of Air Transport Management*, *22*, 16–20. doi:10.1016/j.jairtraman.2012.01.004

Tang, L., & Koveos, P. E. (2004). Venture entrepreneurship, innovation entrepreneurship and economic growth. *Journal of Developmental Entrepreneurship*, *9*(2), 161–171.

Taryam, M., Al Faisal, W., Hussein, H., Suliman, E., Al Janahi, T., Al Salaq, A., & Wasfy, A. (2017). Hypertension among Dubai Population, Prevalence and Patterns, Reflected in Dubai Household Health Survey 2014. *American Journal Of Food Science And Health*, *3*(1), 14–17.

Taylor, S., Kemeny, M., Reed, G., Bower, J., & Gruenewald, T. (2000). Psychological resources, positive illusions, and health. *The American Psychologist*, *55*(1), 99–109. doi:10.1037/0003-066X.55.1.99 PMID:11392870

TenTwenty. (n.d.). *DIFC: The Leading International Financial Hub & Destination for Lifestyle, Arts & Culture*. Retrieved from https://www.difc.ae/

Thawani, S. (2014). *UAE Journey Towards Excellence*. Academic Press.

The National. (2019). *Dubai home to first solar-powered hydrogen facility in Mena*. Retrieved from https://www.thenational.ae/business/energy/dubai-home-to-first-solar-powered-hydrogen-facility-in-mena-1.821303

The national.ae. (2017). *Elon Musk launches Tesla in the UAE*. Retrieved from The national.ae: https://www.thenational.ae/arts-culture/elon-musk-launches-tesla-in-the-uae-1.30459

The Official Portal of the UAE Government. (n.d.) *Crowdfunding in the UAE*. Retrieved from: https://www.government.ae/en/information-and-services/business/crowdfunding

The Official Portal of the UAE Government. (n.d.). *Green Economy for Sustainable Development.* Retrieved from https://government.ae/about-the-uae/economy/green-economy-for-sustainable-development

The Paris Agreement. (n.d.). Retrieved from https://unfccc.int/process-and-meetings/the-paris-agreement/the-paris-agreement

The State Council. (2017). *China remains world's largest manufacturer and major network power the people republic of China.* Retrieved October 23, from http://english.gov.cn/state_council/ministries/2017/02/17/content_281475570357858.htm

The UAE Government. (2019, March 25). *Green Economy for Sustainable Development.* Retrieved from Government.ae

The World Bank. (2019). Retrieved from: https://data.worldbank.org/indicator/ic.reg.durs

Thomas, S. C. (2007). China's Economic development from 1860 to the present: the roles of sovereignty and the global economy. *Forum on Public policy: A Journal of the Oxford Round Table. Academic OneFile.* Retrieved October 23, from https://link.galegroup.com/apps/doc/A244026614/AONE?u=googlescholar&sid=AONE&xid=64fb8a7d

Thomas, J., Al-Qarni, N., & Furber, S. (2015). Conceptualising mental health in the United Arab Emirates: The perspective of traditional healers. *Mental Health, Religion & Culture*, *18*(2), 134–145. doi:10.1080/13674676.2015.1010196

Thomson Reuters. (2015). *State of the Global Islamic Economy.* Dubai, UAE: Thomson Reuters.

Tian, M., Li, D., & Yin, X. (2012). Literature Review about Strategic emerging industries for China. *Interdisciplinary Journal of Contemporary Research in Business*, *4*(7), 42–48.

Times, K. (2017, December 4). *How the UAE is empowering women.* Retrieved August 28, 2018 from Khaleej Times: https://www.khaleejtimes.com/business/local/how-the-uae-is-empowering-women

Times, K. (2017, October 14). *SMEs key to driving UAE's economic growth.* Retrieved August 28, 2018 from Khaleej Times: https://www.khaleejtimes.com/smes-key-to-drive-uaes-economic-growth

Tomiyama, A., Carr, D., Granberg, E., Major, B., Robinson, E., Sutin, A., & Brewis, A. (2018). How and why weight stigma drives the obesity 'epidemic' and harms health. *BMC Medicine*, *16*(1), 123. doi:10.118612916-018-1116-5 PMID:30107800

TradingEconomics. (2019, March 25). *Ease of Doing Business in the United Arab Emirates.* Retrieved from Tradingeconomics.com: https://tradingeconomics.com/united-arab-emirates/ease-of-doing-business

Tribe, M., & Johnson, R. (2008). Effective capital project commissioning. In *Pulp and Paper Industry Technical Conference, 2008. PPIC 2008. Conference Record of 2008 54th Annual* (pp. 106-119). IEEE. 10.1109/PAPCON.2008.4585812

Tylecote, A., & Macdonald, S. (2008). *Information for innovation in Chinese firms: personal relationships versus personal networks.* Paper presented at 1st Asian Management and Entrepreneurship Workshop: New and Old Chinese, Indian and Japanese Firms, European Institute for Advanced Studies in Management (EIASM), Brussels, Belgium.

UAE Government. (2019). *The future.* Retrieved from government.ae: https://www.government.ae/en/about-the-uae/uae-future

UAE MFT. (2012). *Why UAE: Unlimited Opportunity Yearbook 2012.* Ministry of Foreign Trade Publications.

UAE Ministry of Economy. (2018). *Annual Economic Report 2018.* Abu Dhabi: UAE Ministry of Economy.

UAE Ministry of Economy. (2019, March 25). *Economy.* Retrieved from government.ae: https://www.government.ae/en/about-the-uae/economy

UAE Ministry of Finance. (2018). *Intellectual Properties Sector.* Retrieved August 30, 2018 from UAE Ministry of Finance: http://www.economy.gov.ae/english/Ministry/MinistrySectors/Pages/CopyRightSector.aspx

Uchino, B., Bowen, K., de Grey, R., Mikel, J., & Fisher, E. (2018). Social Support and Physical Health: Models, Mechanisms, and Opportunities. In Principles and Concepts of Behavioral Medicine (pp. 341-372). Springer.

Uddin, J., Parvin, S., & Rahman, M. L. (2013). Factors Influencing Importance of Country of Brand and Country of Manufacturing in Consumer Product Evaluation. *International Journal of Business and Management, 8*(4), 65–74. doi:10.5539/ijbm.v8n4p65

UNCTAD. (2019, March 25). *World Investment Report 2018.* Retrieved from UNCTAD.org: https://unctad.org/en/pages/PublicationWebflyer.aspx?publicationid=2130

United Arab Emirates Ministry of Climate Change & Environment. (n.d.). *UAE State of Green Economy Report 2017.* Retrieved from http://un- page.org/files/public/uae_state_of_green_economy_report_2017_0.pdf

United Nations Environment Program. (2011). *Towards a Green Economy: Pathways to Sustainable Development and Poverty Eradication.* Retrieved from http://www.unep.org/greeneconomy

United Nations Statistical Division. (1997). *Glossary of Environment Statistics, Studies in Methods (Series F, No. 67).* New York, NY: United Nations.

Uowdubai. (2013). *Cobone CEO inspires entrepreneurs of the future*. Retrieved from uowdubai.com: https://www.uowdubai.ac.ae/news/cobone-ceo-inspires-entrepreneurs-future

Valentin, E. K. (2001). Swot Analysis from a Resource-Based View. *Journal of Marketing Theory and Practice*, *9*(2), 54–69. doi:10.1080/10696679.2001.11501891

Valliere, D., & Peterson, R. (2009). Entrepreneurship and economic growth: Evidence from emerging and developed countries. *Entrepreneurship and Regional Development*, *21*(5-6), 459–480. doi:10.1080/08985620802332723

Vanguard, C. (2018). *vanguard-method.net*. Retrieved from systems-principles: https://vanguard-method.net/library/systems-principles/demings-seven-deadly-diseases/

Vedung, E. (1998). Policy instruments: Typologies and theories. In M. L. Bemelmans-Videc, R. C. Rist, & E. O. Vedung (Eds.), *Carrots, Sticks and Sermons: Policy Instruments and Their Evaluation*. London, UK: Transaction Publishers.

Ventre, K., Barry, J., Davis, D., Baiamonte, V., Wentworth, A. C., Pietras, M., ... Barley, G. (2014). Using in situ simulation to evaluate operational readiness of a children's hospital-based obstetrics unit. Simulation in Healthcare. *Journal of the Society for Simulation in Healthcare*, *9*(2), 102–111. doi:10.1097/SIH.0000000000000005 PMID:24401917

Vivian, A., & Wohar, M. (2012). Commodity volatility breaks. *Journal of International Financial Markets, Institutions and Money*, *22*(2), 395–422. doi:10.1016/j.intfin.2011.12.003

Von Graevenitz, G., Harhoff, D., & Weber, R. (2010). The effects of entrepreneurship education. *Journal of Economic Behavior & Organization*, *76*(1), 90–112.

Vos, J. P. (2005). Developing strategic self descriptions of SMEs. *Technovation*, *25*(9), 989–999. doi:10.1016/j.technovation.2004.02.014

Wagner, E. T. (2013, September 12). *Five Reasons 8 Out Of 10 Businesses Fail*. Retrieved August 28, 2018 from Forbs: https://www.forbes.com/sites/ericwagner/2013/09/12/five-reasons-8-out-of-10-businesses-fail/#4b1d35ad6978

Walker, E., & Brown, A. (2004). What success factors are important to small business owners? *International Small Business Journal*, *22*(6), 577–594. doi:10.1177/0266242604047411

Wanberg, C. R., & Banas, J. (2000). Predictors and outcomes of openness to changes in a reorganizing workplace. *The Journal of Applied Psychology*, *85*(1), 132–142. doi:10.1037/0021-9010.85.1.132 PMID:10740964

Weiner, B. (2009). A theory of organizational readiness for change. *Implementation Science; IS*, *4*(67). doi:10.1186/1748-5908-4-67 PMID:19840381

Weiner, B., Amick, H., & Lee, S. (2008). Conceptualization and measurement of organizational readiness for change: A review of the literature in health services research and other fields. *Medical Care Research and Review : MCRR*, *65*, 379–436. doi:10.1177/1077558708317802 PMID:18511812

Weiss, D., & Maher, M. W. (2009). Operational hedging against adverse circumstances. *Journal of Operations Management*, *27*(5), 362–373. doi:10.1016/j.jom.2008.10.003

Wennekers, S., Van Stel, A., Thurik, R., & Reynolds, P. (2005). *Nascent Entrepreneurship and the Level of Economic Development*. Discussion Paper no. 2005–14, Growth and Public Policy, Max Planck Institute of Economics.

Wennekers, S., & Thurik, R. (1999). Linking entrepreneurship and economic growth. *Small Business Economics*, *13*(1), 27–55. doi:10.1023/A:1008063200484

Wikipedia. (2019, March 25). *Ease of doing business index*. Retrieved from Wikipedia.org: https://en.wikipedia.org/wiki/Ease_of_doing_business_index#Ranking

Wiklund, J., Davidsson, P., & Delmar, F. (2003). What do they think and feel about growth? An expectancy-value approach to small business managers' attitudes toward growth. *Entrepreneurship Theory and Practice*, *27*(3), 247–270. doi:10.1111/1540-8520.t01-1-00003

Willis, K. (2015). Can Dubai's design district 'hipster village' attract the right type of goatee-wearing individualist? *The Independent*. Available from: https://www.independent.co.uk/arts-entertainment/architecture/can-dubais-design-district-hipster-village-attract-the-right-type-of-goatee-wearing-individualist-10277373.html

Wilson, M., Hejna, W., & Hosking, J. (2004). Activation and operational planning: ensuring a successful transition. *Journal of Healthcare Management / American College of Healthcare Executives*, *49*(6), 358–362.

Winch, G., & Leiringer, R. (2015). Owner project capabilities for infrastructure development: A review and development of the 'strong owner' concept. *International Journal of Project Management*, *34*(2), 271–281. doi:10.1016/j.ijproman.2015.02.002

Wolff, J. A., & Pett, T. L. (2000). Internationalization of small firms: An examination of export competitive patterns, firm size, and export performance. *Journal of Small Business Management*, *38*(2), 34–47.

Wonglimpiyarat, J. (2015). New economics of innovation: Strategies to support high-tech SMEs. *The Journal of High Technology Management Research*, *26*(2), 186–195. doi:10.1016/j.hitech.2015.09.006

Wong, P. K., Ho, Y. P., & Autio, E. (2005). Entrepreneurship, innovation and economic growth: Evidence from GEM data. *Small Business Economics*, *24*(3), 335–350. doi:10.100711187-005-2000-1

Wood, M. (2018, July 27). *The 5 Most Profitable Small Businesses in 2018*. Retrieved August 28, 2018 from Fundera.com: https://www.fundera.com/blog/most-profitable-industries

Woo, W. T. (1997). Chinese economic growth: sources and prospects. In M. Fouquin & F. Lemoine (Eds.), *The Chinese Economy*. London: Economica.

World Bank. (1997). *China 2020: development challenges in the New Century*. Washington, DC: World Bank.

World Commission on Environment and Development. (1987). *Our Common Future (Brundtland Commission)*. Oxford, UK: Oxford University Press.

WorldAtlas. (2019, March 25). *Muslim Population By Country*. Retrieved from WorldAtlas: https://www.worldatlas.com/articles/countries-with-the-largest-muslim-populations.html

WorldData.info. (2019). *Average income around the world*. Retrieved from WorldData.info: https://www.worlddata.info/average-income.php

Wubbeke, J., & Conrad, B. (2015). 'Industrie 4.0': Will German Technology Help China Catch Up with the West? *MERICS China Monitor*. Retrieve December 2, from https://www.merics.org/sites/default/files/2017-09/China_Monitor_23_Industrie40_EN.pdf

Xie, X. M., Zeng, S. X., & Tam, C. M. (2010). Overcoming barriers to innovation in SMEs in China: A perspective based cooperation network. *Innovation, Management. Policy & Practice*, *12*(3), 298–310. doi:10.5172/impp.12.3.298

Xie, X., Zeng, S., Peng, Y., & Tam, C. (2013). What affects the innovation performance of small and medium-sized enterprises in China? Innovation: Management. *Policy & Practice*, *15*(3), 271–286. doi:10.5172/impp.2013.15.3.271

Xiong, M. H., Tor, S. B., Bhatnagar, R., Khoo, L. P., & Venkat, S. (2006). A DSS approach to managing customer enquiry stage. *International Journal of Production Economics*, *103*(1), 332–346. doi:10.1016/j.ijpe.2005.08.008

Yang, J., Liu, H., Gao, S., & Li, Y. (2012). Technological innovation of firms in China: Past, present, and future. *Asia Pacific Journal of Management*, *29*(3), 819–840. doi:10.100710490-010-9243-3

Yang, T. T., & Li, C. R. (2011). Competence Exploration and Exploitation in New Product Development: The Moderating Effects of Environmental Dynamism and Competitiveness. *Management Decision*, *49*(9), 1444–1470. doi:10.1108/00251741111173934

Yan, H.-D. (2012). Entrepreneurship, Competitive Strategies, and Transforming Firms from OEM to OBM in Taiwan. *Journal of Asia-Pacific Business*, *13*(1), 16–36. doi:10.1080/10599231.2012.629877

Yeung, H. (2006). Change and continuity in Southeast Asian Chinese business. *Asia Pacific Journal of Management*, *23*(3), 229–254. doi:10.100710490-006-9007-2

Yongyoon, S., & Kim, M. S. (2012). Effects of SME collaboration on R&D in the servicesector in open innovation, Innovation: Management. *Policy & Practice*, *14*(3), 349–362. doi:10.5172/impp.2012.14.3.349

Zahra, S. A., & George, G. (2002). Absorptive capacity: A review, reconceptualization, and extension. *Academy of Management Review*, *27*(2), 185–203. doi:10.5465/amr.2002.6587995

Zaneldin, E. (2006). Construction claims in United Arab Emirates: Types, causes, and frequency. *International Journal of Project Management*, *24*(5), 453–459. doi:10.1016/j.ijproman.2006.02.006

Zeemering, E. (2009). What Does Sustainability Mean to City Officials? *Urban Affairs Review*, *45*(2), 247–273. doi:10.1177/1078087409337297

Zeng, D. Z. (2012). China's Special Economic Zones and Industrial Clusters: The Engines for Growth. *Journal of International Commerce. Economic Policy*, *3*(3), 1–28.

Zerjav, V., Edkins, A., & Davies, A. (2018). Project capabilities for operational outcomes in inter-organisational settings: The case of London Heathrow Terminal 2. *International Journal of Project Management*, *36*(3), 444–459. doi:10.1016/j.ijproman.2018.01.004

Zhang, X., Ma, X., Wang, Y., Li, X., & Huo, D. (2016). What drives the internationalization of Chinese SMEs? The joint effects of international entrepreneurship characteristics, network ties, and firm ownership. *International Business Review*, *25*(2), 522–534. doi:10.1016/j.ibusrev.2015.09.001

Zhu, Y. M., & Sanderson, J. W. (2009). The key obstacles and countermeasure against development of innovative SMEs in China. *China Soft Science*, *9*, 23–31.

Zhu, Y., Wittmann, X., & Peng, M. W. (2012). Institution-based barriers to innovation in SMEs in China. *Asia Pacific Journal of Management*, *29*(4), 1131–1142. doi:10.100710490-011-9263-7

Related References

To continue our tradition of advancing information science and technology research, we have compiled a list of recommended IGI Global readings. These references will provide additional information and guidance to further enrich your knowledge and assist you with your own research and future publications.

Abtahi, M. S., Behboudi, L., & Hasanabad, H. M. (2017). Factors Affecting Internet Advertising Adoption in Ad Agencies. *International Journal of Innovation in the Digital Economy*, *8*(4), 18–29. doi:10.4018/IJIDE.2017100102

Agrawal, S. (2017). The Impact of Emerging Technologies and Social Media on Different Business(es): Marketing and Management. In O. Rishi & A. Sharma (Eds.), *Maximizing Business Performance and Efficiency Through Intelligent Systems* (pp. 37–49). Hershey, PA: IGI Global. doi:10.4018/978-1-5225-2234-8.ch002

Alnoukari, M., Razouk, R., & Hanano, A. (2016). BSC-SI: A Framework for Integrating Strategic Intelligence in Corporate Strategic Management. *International Journal of Social and Organizational Dynamics in IT*, *5*(2), 1–14. doi:10.4018/IJSODIT.2016070101

Alnoukari, M., Razouk, R., & Hanano, A. (2016). BSC-SI, A Framework for Integrating Strategic Intelligence in Corporate Strategic Management. *International Journal of Strategic Information Technology and Applications*, *7*(1), 32–44. doi:10.4018/IJSITA.2016010103

Altındağ, E. (2016). Current Approaches in Change Management. In A. Goksoy (Ed.), *Organizational Change Management Strategies in Modern Business* (pp. 24–51). Hershey, PA: IGI Global. doi:10.4018/978-1-4666-9533-7.ch002

Alvarez-Dionisi, L. E., Turner, R., & Mittra, M. (2016). Global Project Management Trends. *International Journal of Information Technology Project Management, 7*(3), 54–73. doi:10.4018/IJITPM.2016070104

Anantharaman, R. N., Rajeswari, K. S., Angusamy, A., & Kuppusamy, J. (2017). Role of Self-Efficacy and Collective Efficacy as Moderators of Occupational Stress Among Software Development Professionals. *International Journal of Human Capital and Information Technology Professionals, 8*(2), 45–58. doi:10.4018/IJHCITP.2017040103

Aninze, F., El-Gohary, H., & Hussain, J. (2018). The Role of Microfinance to Empower Women: The Case of Developing Countries. *International Journal of Customer Relationship Marketing and Management, 9*(1), 54–78. doi:10.4018/IJCRMM.2018010104

Arsenijević, O. M., Orčić, D., & Kastratović, E. (2017). Development of an Optimization Tool for Intangibles in SMEs: A Case Study from Serbia with a Pilot Research in the Prestige by Milka Company. In M. Vemić (Ed.), *Optimal Management Strategies in Small and Medium Enterprises* (pp. 320–347). Hershey, PA: IGI Global. doi:10.4018/978-1-5225-1949-2.ch015

Aryanto, V. D., Wismantoro, Y., & Widyatmoko, K. (2018). Implementing Eco-Innovation by Utilizing the Internet to Enhance Firm's Marketing Performance: Study of Green Batik Small and Medium Enterprises in Indonesia. *International Journal of E-Business Research, 14*(1), 21–36. doi:10.4018/IJEBR.2018010102

Atiku, S. O., & Fields, Z. (2017). Multicultural Orientations for 21st Century Global Leadership. In N. Baporikar (Ed.), *Management Education for Global Leadership* (pp. 28–51). Hershey, PA: IGI Global. doi:10.4018/978-1-5225-1013-0.ch002

Atiku, S. O., & Fields, Z. (2018). Organisational Learning Dimensions and Talent Retention Strategies for the Service Industries. In N. Baporikar (Ed.), *Global Practices in Knowledge Management for Societal and Organizational Development* (pp. 358–381). Hershey, PA: IGI Global. doi:10.4018/978-1-5225-3009-1.ch017

Ávila, L., & Teixeira, L. (2018). The Main Concepts Behind the Dematerialization of Business Processes. In M. Khosrow-Pour, D.B.A. (Ed.), Encyclopedia of Information Science and Technology, Fourth Edition (pp. 888-898). Hershey, PA: IGI Global. doi:10.4018/978-1-5225-2255-3.ch076

Bartens, Y., Chunpir, H. I., Schulte, F., & Voß, S. (2017). Business/IT Alignment in Two-Sided Markets: A COBIT 5 Analysis for Media Streaming Business Models. In S. De Haes & W. Van Grembergen (Eds.), *Strategic IT Governance and Alignment in Business Settings* (pp. 82–111). Hershey, PA: IGI Global. doi:10.4018/978-1-5225-0861-8.ch004

Bashayreh, A. M. (2018). Organizational Culture and Organizational Performance. In W. Lee & F. Sabetzadeh (Eds.), *Contemporary Knowledge and Systems Science* (pp. 50–69). Hershey, PA: IGI Global. doi:10.4018/978-1-5225-5655-8.ch003

Bedford, D. A. (2018). Sustainable Knowledge Management Strategies: Aligning Business Capabilities and Knowledge Management Goals. In N. Baporikar (Ed.), *Global Practices in Knowledge Management for Societal and Organizational Development* (pp. 46–73). Hershey, PA: IGI Global. doi:10.4018/978-1-5225-3009-1.ch003

Benmoussa, F., Nakara, W. A., & Jaouen, A. (2016). The Use of Social Media by SMEs in the Tourism Industry. In I. Lee (Ed.), *Encyclopedia of E-Commerce Development, Implementation, and Management* (pp. 2159–2170). Hershey, PA: IGI Global. doi:10.4018/978-1-4666-9787-4.ch155

Berger, R. (2016). Indigenous Management and Bottom of Pyramid Countries: The Role of National Institutions. In U. Aung & P. Ordoñez de Pablos (Eds.), *Managerial Strategies and Practice in the Asian Business Sector* (pp. 107–123). Hershey, PA: IGI Global. doi:10.4018/978-1-4666-9758-4.ch007

Bharwani, S., & Musunuri, D. (2018). Reflection as a Process From Theory to Practice. In M. Khosrow-Pour, D.B.A. (Ed.), Encyclopedia of Information Science and Technology, Fourth Edition (pp. 1529-1539). Hershey, PA: IGI Global. doi:10.4018/978-1-5225-2255-3.ch132

Bhatt, G. D., Wang, Z., & Rodger, J. A. (2017). Information Systems Capabilities and Their Effects on Competitive Advantages: A Study of Chinese Companies. *Information Resources Management Journal, 30*(3), 41–57. doi:10.4018/IRMJ.2017070103

Bhushan, M., & Yadav, A. (2017). Concept of Cloud Computing in ESB. In R. Bhadoria, N. Chaudhari, G. Tomar, & S. Singh (Eds.), *Exploring Enterprise Service Bus in the Service-Oriented Architecture Paradigm* (pp. 116–127). Hershey, PA: IGI Global. doi:10.4018/978-1-5225-2157-0.ch008

Bhushan, S. (2017). System Dynamics Base-Model of Humanitarian Supply Chain (HSCM) in Disaster Prone Eco-Communities of India: A Discussion on Simulation and Scenario Results. *International Journal of System Dynamics Applications, 6*(3), 20–37. doi:10.4018/IJSDA.2017070102

Biswas, A., & De, A. K. (2017). On Development of a Fuzzy Stochastic Programming Model with Its Application to Business Management. In S. Trivedi, S. Dey, A. Kumar, & T. Panda (Eds.), *Handbook of Research on Advanced Data Mining Techniques and Applications for Business Intelligence* (pp. 353–378). Hershey, PA: IGI Global. doi:10.4018/978-1-5225-2031-3.ch021

Bücker, J., & Ernste, K. (2018). Use of Brand Heroes in Strategic Reputation Management: The Case of Bacardi, Adidas, and Daimler. In A. Erdemir (Ed.), *Reputation Management Techniques in Public Relations* (pp. 126–150). Hershey, PA: IGI Global. doi:10.4018/978-1-5225-3619-2.ch007

Bureš, V. (2018). Industry 4.0 From the Systems Engineering Perspective: Alternative Holistic Framework Development. In R. Brunet-Thornton & F. Martinez (Eds.), *Analyzing the Impacts of Industry 4.0 in Modern Business Environments* (pp. 199–223). Hershey, PA: IGI Global. doi:10.4018/978-1-5225-3468-6.ch011

Buzady, Z. (2017). Resolving the Magic Cube of Effective Case Teaching: Benchmarking Case Teaching Practices in Emerging Markets – Insights from the Central European University Business School, Hungary. In D. Latusek (Ed.), *Case Studies as a Teaching Tool in Management Education* (pp. 79–103). Hershey, PA: IGI Global. doi:10.4018/978-1-5225-0770-3.ch005

Campatelli, G., Richter, A., & Stocker, A. (2016). Participative Knowledge Management to Empower Manufacturing Workers. *International Journal of Knowledge Management, 12*(4), 37–50. doi:10.4018/IJKM.2016100103

Căpusneanu, S., & Topor, D. I. (2018). Business Ethics and Cost Management in SMEs: Theories of Business Ethics and Cost Management Ethos. In I. Oncioiu (Ed.), *Ethics and Decision-Making for Sustainable Business Practices* (pp. 109–127). Hershey, PA: IGI Global. doi:10.4018/978-1-5225-3773-1.ch007

Carneiro, A. (2016). Maturity in Health Organization Information Systems: Metrics and Privacy Perspectives. *International Journal of Privacy and Health Information Management*, *4*(2), 1–18. doi:10.4018/IJPHIM.2016070101

Chan, R. L., Mo, P. L., & Moon, K. K. (2018). Strategic and Tactical Measures in Managing Enterprise Risks: A Study of the Textile and Apparel Industry. In K. Strang, M. Korstanje, & N. Vajjhala (Eds.), *Research, Practices, and Innovations in Global Risk and Contingency Management* (pp. 1–19). Hershey, PA: IGI Global. doi:10.4018/978-1-5225-4754-9.ch001

Chandan, H. C. (2016). Motivations and Challenges of Female Entrepreneurship in Developed and Developing Economies. In N. Baporikar (Ed.), *Handbook of Research on Entrepreneurship in the Contemporary Knowledge-Based Global Economy* (pp. 260–286). Hershey, PA: IGI Global. doi:10.4018/978-1-4666-8798-1.ch012

Charlier, S. D., Burke-Smalley, L. A., & Fisher, S. L. (2018). Undergraduate Programs in the U.S: A Contextual and Content-Based Analysis. In J. Mendy (Ed.), *Teaching Human Resources and Organizational Behavior at the College Level* (pp. 26–57). Hershey, PA: IGI Global. doi:10.4018/978-1-5225-2820-3.ch002

Chaudhuri, S. (2016). Application of Web-Based Geographical Information System (GIS) in E-Business. In U. Panwar, R. Kumar, & N. Ray (Eds.), *Handbook of Research on Promotional Strategies and Consumer Influence in the Service Sector* (pp. 389–405). Hershey, PA: IGI Global. doi:10.4018/978-1-5225-0143-5.ch023

Choudhuri, P. S. (2016). An Empirical Study on the Quality of Services Offered by the Private Life Insurers in Burdwan. In U. Panwar, R. Kumar, & N. Ray (Eds.), *Handbook of Research on Promotional Strategies and Consumer Influence in the Service Sector* (pp. 31–55). Hershey, PA: IGI Global. doi:10.4018/978-1-5225-0143-5.ch002

Dahlberg, T., Kivijärvi, H., & Saarinen, T. (2017). IT Investment Consistency and Other Factors Influencing the Success of IT Performance. In S. De Haes & W. Van Grembergen (Eds.), *Strategic IT Governance and Alignment in Business Settings* (pp. 176–208). Hershey, PA: IGI Global. doi:10.4018/978-1-5225-0861-8.ch007

Damnjanović, A. M. (2017). Knowledge Management Optimization through IT and E-Business Utilization: A Qualitative Study on Serbian SMEs. In M. Vemić (Ed.), *Optimal Management Strategies in Small and Medium Enterprises* (pp. 249–267). Hershey, PA: IGI Global. doi:10.4018/978-1-5225-1949-2.ch012

Daneshpour, H. (2017). Integrating Sustainable Development into Project Portfolio Management through Application of Open Innovation. In M. Vemić (Ed.), *Optimal Management Strategies in Small and Medium Enterprises* (pp. 370–387). Hershey, PA: IGI Global. doi:10.4018/978-1-5225-1949-2.ch017

Daniel, A. D., & Reis de Castro, V. (2018). Entrepreneurship Education: How to Measure the Impact on Nascent Entrepreneurs. In A. Carrizo Moreira, J. Guilherme Leitão Dantas, & F. Manuel Valente (Eds.), *Nascent Entrepreneurship and Successful New Venture Creation* (pp. 85–110). Hershey, PA: IGI Global. doi:10.4018/978-1-5225-2936-1.ch004

David, F., van der Sijde, P., & van den Besselaar, P. (2016). Enterpreneurial Incentives, Obstacles, and Management in University-Business Co-Operation: The Case of Indonesia. In J. Saiz-Álvarez (Ed.), *Handbook of Research on Social Entrepreneurship and Solidarity Economics* (pp. 499–518). Hershey, PA: IGI Global. doi:10.4018/978-1-5225-0097-1.ch024

David, R., Swami, B. N., & Tangirala, S. (2018). Ethics Impact on Knowledge Management in Organizational Development: A Case Study. In N. Baporikar (Ed.), *Global Practices in Knowledge Management for Societal and Organizational Development* (pp. 19–45). Hershey, PA: IGI Global. doi:10.4018/978-1-5225-3009-1.ch002

Delias, P., & Lakiotaki, K. (2018). Discovering Process Horizontal Boundaries to Facilitate Process Comprehension. *International Journal of Operations Research and Information Systems*, *9*(2), 1–31. doi:10.4018/IJORIS.2018040101

Denholm, J., & Lee-Davies, L. (2018). Success Factors for Games in Business and Project Management. In *Enhancing Education and Training Initiatives Through Serious Games* (pp. 34–68). Hershey, PA: IGI Global. doi:10.4018/978-1-5225-3689-5.ch002

Deshpande, M. (2017). Best Practices in Management Institutions for Global Leadership: Policy Aspects. In N. Baporikar (Ed.), *Management Education for Global Leadership* (pp. 1–27). Hershey, PA: IGI Global. doi:10.4018/978-1-5225-1013-0.ch001

Deshpande, M. (2018). Policy Perspectives for SMEs Knowledge Management. In N. Baporikar (Ed.), *Knowledge Integration Strategies for Entrepreneurship and Sustainability* (pp. 23–46). Hershey, PA: IGI Global. doi:10.4018/978-1-5225-5115-7.ch002

Dezdar, S. (2017). ERP Implementation Projects in Asian Countries: A Comparative Study on Iran and China. *International Journal of Information Technology Project Management, 8*(3), 52–68. doi:10.4018/IJITPM.2017070104

Domingos, D., Martinho, R., & Varajão, J. (2016). Controlled Flexibility in Healthcare Processes: A BPMN-Extension Approach. In M. Cruz-Cunha, I. Miranda, R. Martinho, & R. Rijo (Eds.), *Encyclopedia of E-Health and Telemedicine* (pp. 521–535). Hershey, PA: IGI Global. doi:10.4018/978-1-4666-9978-6.ch040

Domingos, D., Respício, A., & Martinho, R. (2017). Reliability of IoT-Aware BPMN Healthcare Processes. In C. Reis & M. Maximiano (Eds.), *Internet of Things and Advanced Application in Healthcare* (pp. 214–248). Hershey, PA: IGI Global. doi:10.4018/978-1-5225-1820-4.ch008

Dosumu, O., Hussain, J., & El-Gohary, H. (2017). An Exploratory Study of the Impact of Government Policies on the Development of Small and Medium Enterprises in Developing Countries: The Case of Nigeria. *International Journal of Customer Relationship Marketing and Management, 8*(4), 51–62. doi:10.4018/IJCRMM.2017100104

Durst, S., Bruns, G., & Edvardsson, I. R. (2017). Retaining Knowledge in Smaller Building and Construction Firms. *International Journal of Knowledge and Systems Science, 8*(3), 1–12. doi:10.4018/IJKSS.2017070101

Edvardsson, I. R., & Durst, S. (2017). Outsourcing, Knowledge, and Learning: A Critical Review. *International Journal of Knowledge-Based Organizations, 7*(2), 13–26. doi:10.4018/IJKBO.2017040102

Edwards, J. S. (2018). Integrating Knowledge Management and Business Processes. In M. Khosrow-Pour, D.B.A. (Ed.), Encyclopedia of Information Science and Technology, Fourth Edition (pp. 5046-5055). Hershey, PA: IGI Global. doi:10.4018/978-1-5225-2255-3.ch437

Ejiogu, A. O. (2018). Economics of Farm Management. In *Agricultural Finance and Opportunities for Investment and Expansion* (pp. 56–72). Hershey, PA: IGI Global. doi:10.4018/978-1-5225-3059-6.ch003

Ekanem, I., & Abiade, G. E. (2018). Factors Influencing the Use of E-Commerce by Small Enterprises in Nigeria. *International Journal of ICT Research in Africa and the Middle East, 7*(1), 37–53. doi:10.4018/IJICTRAME.2018010103

Ekanem, I., & Alrossais, L. A. (2017). Succession Challenges Facing Family Businesses in Saudi Arabia. In P. Zgheib (Ed.), *Entrepreneurship and Business Innovation in the Middle East* (pp. 122–146). Hershey, PA: IGI Global. doi:10.4018/978-1-5225-2066-5.ch007

El Faquih, L., & Fredj, M. (2017). Ontology-Based Framework for Quality in Configurable Process Models. *Journal of Electronic Commerce in Organizations, 15*(2), 48–60. doi:10.4018/JECO.2017040104

El-Gohary, H., & El-Gohary, Z. (2016). An Attempt to Explore Electronic Marketing Adoption and Implementation Aspects in Developing Countries: The Case of Egypt. *International Journal of Customer Relationship Marketing and Management, 7*(4), 1–26. doi:10.4018/IJCRMM.2016100101

Entico, G. J. (2016). Knowledge Management and the Medical Health Librarians: A Perception Study. In J. Yap, M. Perez, M. Ayson, & G. Entico (Eds.), *Special Library Administration, Standardization and Technological Integration* (pp. 52–77). Hershey, PA: IGI Global. doi:10.4018/978-1-4666-9542-9.ch003

Faisal, M. N., & Talib, F. (2017). Building Ambidextrous Supply Chains in SMEs: How to Tackle the Barriers? *International Journal of Information Systems and Supply Chain Management, 10*(4), 80–100. doi:10.4018/IJISSCM.2017100105

Fernandes, T. M., Gomes, J., & Romão, M. (2017). Investments in E-Government: A Benefit Management Case Study. *International Journal of Electronic Government Research, 13*(3), 1–17. doi:10.4018/IJEGR.2017070101

Fouda, F. A. (2016). A Suggested Curriculum in Career Education to Develop Business Secondary Schools Students' Career Knowledge Management Domains and Professional Thinking. *International Journal of Technology Diffusion, 7*(2), 42–62. doi:10.4018/IJTD.2016040103

Gallardo-Vázquez, D., & Pajuelo-Moreno, M. L. (2016). How Spanish Universities are Promoting Entrepreneurship through Your Own Lines of Teaching and Research? In L. Carvalho (Ed.), *Handbook of Research on Entrepreneurial Success and its Impact on Regional Development* (pp. 431–454). Hershey, PA: IGI Global. doi:10.4018/978-1-4666-9567-2.ch019

Gao, S. S., Oreal, S., & Zhang, J. (2018). Contemporary Financial Risk Management Perceptions and Practices of Small-Sized Chinese Businesses. In I. Management Association (Ed.), Global Business Expansion: Concepts, Methodologies, Tools, and Applications (pp. 917-931). Hershey, PA: IGI Global. doi:10.4018/978-1-5225-5481-3.ch041

Garg, R., & Berning, S. C. (2017). Indigenous Chinese Management Philosophies: Key Concepts and Relevance for Modern Chinese Firms. In B. Christiansen & G. Koc (Eds.), *Transcontinental Strategies for Industrial Development and Economic Growth* (pp. 43–57). Hershey, PA: IGI Global. doi:10.4018/978-1-5225-2160-0.ch003

Gencer, Y. G. (2017). Supply Chain Management in Retailing Business. In U. Akkucuk (Ed.), *Ethics and Sustainability in Global Supply Chain Management* (pp. 197–210). Hershey, PA: IGI Global. doi:10.4018/978-1-5225-2036-8.ch011

Giacosa, E. (2016). Innovation in Luxury Fashion Businesses as a Means for the Regional Development. In L. Carvalho (Ed.), *Handbook of Research on Entrepreneurial Success and its Impact on Regional Development* (pp. 206–222). Hershey, PA: IGI Global. doi:10.4018/978-1-4666-9567-2.ch010

Giacosa, E. (2018). The Increasing of the Regional Development Thanks to the Luxury Business Innovation. In L. Carvalho (Ed.), *Handbook of Research on Entrepreneurial Ecosystems and Social Dynamics in a Globalized World* (pp. 260–273). Hershey, PA: IGI Global. doi:10.4018/978-1-5225-3525-6.ch011

Gianni, M., & Gotzamani, K. (2016). Integrated Management Systems and Information Management Systems: Common Threads. In P. Papajorgji, F. Pinet, A. Guimarães, & J. Papathanasiou (Eds.), *Automated Enterprise Systems for Maximizing Business Performance* (pp. 195–214). Hershey, PA: IGI Global. doi:10.4018/978-1-4666-8841-4.ch011

Gianni, M., Gotzamani, K., & Linden, I. (2016). How a BI-wise Responsible Integrated Management System May Support Food Traceability. *International Journal of Decision Support System Technology*, *8*(2), 1–17. doi:10.4018/IJDSST.2016040101

Glykas, M., & George, J. (2017). Quality and Process Management Systems in the UAE Maritime Industry. *International Journal of Productivity Management and Assessment Technologies*, *5*(1), 20–39. doi:10.4018/IJPMAT.2017010102

Glykas, M., Valiris, G., Kokkinaki, A., & Koutsoukou, Z. (2018). Banking Business Process Management Implementation. *International Journal of Productivity Management and Assessment Technologies*, *6*(1), 50–69. doi:10.4018/IJPMAT.2018010104

Gomes, J., & Romão, M. (2017). The Balanced Scorecard: Keeping Updated and Aligned with Today's Business Trends. *International Journal of Productivity Management and Assessment Technologies*, *5*(2), 1–15. doi:10.4018/IJPMAT.2017070101

Gomes, J., & Romão, M. (2017). Aligning Information Systems and Technology with Benefit Management and Balanced Scorecard. In S. De Haes & W. Van Grembergen (Eds.), *Strategic IT Governance and Alignment in Business Settings* (pp. 112–131). Hershey, PA: IGI Global. doi:10.4018/978-1-5225-0861-8.ch005

Grefen, P., & Turetken, O. (2017). Advanced Business Process Management in Networked E-Business Scenarios. *International Journal of E-Business Research*, *13*(4), 70–104. doi:10.4018/IJEBR.2017100105

Haider, A., & Saetang, S. (2017). Strategic IT Alignment in Service Sector. In S. Rozenes & Y. Cohen (Eds.), *Handbook of Research on Strategic Alliances and Value Co-Creation in the Service Industry* (pp. 231–258). Hershey, PA: IGI Global. doi:10.4018/978-1-5225-2084-9.ch012

Haider, A., & Tang, S. S. (2016). Maximising Value Through IT and Business Alignment: A Case of IT Governance Institutionalisation at a Thai Bank. *International Journal of Technology Diffusion*, *7*(3), 33–58. doi:10.4018/IJTD.2016070104

Hajilari, A. B., Ghadaksaz, M., & Fasghandis, G. S. (2017). Assessing Organizational Readiness for Implementing ERP System Using Fuzzy Expert System Approach. *International Journal of Enterprise Information Systems*, *13*(1), 67–85. doi:10.4018/IJEIS.2017010105

Haldorai, A., Ramu, A., & Murugan, S. (2018). Social Aware Cognitive Radio Networks: Effectiveness of Social Networks as a Strategic Tool for Organizational Business Management. In H. Bansal, G. Shrivastava, G. Nguyen, & L. Stanciu (Eds.), *Social Network Analytics for Contemporary Business Organizations* (pp. 188–202). Hershey, PA: IGI Global. doi:10.4018/978-1-5225-5097-6.ch010

Hall, O. P. Jr. (2017). Social Media Driven Management Education. *International Journal of Knowledge-Based Organizations*, *7*(2), 43–59. doi:10.4018/IJKBO.2017040104

Hanifah, H., Halim, H. A., Ahmad, N. H., & Vafaei-Zadeh, A. (2017). Innovation Culture as a Mediator Between Specific Human Capital and Innovation Performance Among Bumiputera SMEs in Malaysia. In N. Ahmad, T. Ramayah, H. Halim, & S. Rahman (Eds.), *Handbook of Research on Small and Medium Enterprises in Developing Countries* (pp. 261–279). Hershey, PA: IGI Global. doi:10.4018/978-1-5225-2165-5.ch012

Hartlieb, S., & Silvius, G. (2017). Handling Uncertainty in Project Management and Business Development: Similarities and Differences. In Y. Raydugin (Ed.), *Handbook of Research on Leveraging Risk and Uncertainties for Effective Project Management* (pp. 337–362). Hershey, PA: IGI Global. doi:10.4018/978-1-5225-1790-0.ch016

Hass, K. B. (2017). Living on the Edge: Managing Project Complexity. In Y. Raydugin (Ed.), *Handbook of Research on Leveraging Risk and Uncertainties for Effective Project Management* (pp. 177–201). Hershey, PA: IGI Global. doi:10.4018/978-1-5225-1790-0.ch009

Hassan, A., & Privitera, D. S. (2016). Google AdSense as a Mobile Technology in Education. In J. Holland (Ed.), *Wearable Technology and Mobile Innovations for Next-Generation Education* (pp. 200–223). Hershey, PA: IGI Global. doi:10.4018/978-1-5225-0069-8.ch011

Hassan, A., & Rahimi, R. (2016). Consuming "Innovation" in Tourism: Augmented Reality as an Innovation Tool in Digital Tourism Marketing. In N. Pappas & I. Bregoli (Eds.), *Global Dynamics in Travel, Tourism, and Hospitality* (pp. 130–147). Hershey, PA: IGI Global. doi:10.4018/978-1-5225-0201-2.ch008

Hawking, P., & Carmine Sellitto, C. (2017). Developing an Effective Strategy for Organizational Business Intelligence. In M. Tavana (Ed.), *Enterprise Information Systems and the Digitalization of Business Functions* (pp. 222–237). Hershey, PA: IGI Global. doi:10.4018/978-1-5225-2382-6.ch010

Hawking, P., & Sellitto, C. (2017). A Fast-Moving Consumer Goods Company and Business Intelligence Strategy Development. *International Journal of Enterprise Information Systems, 13*(2), 22–33. doi:10.4018/IJEIS.2017040102

Hawking, P., & Sellitto, C. (2017). Business Intelligence Strategy: Two Case Studies. *International Journal of Business Intelligence Research, 8*(2), 17–30. doi:10.4018/IJBIR.2017070102

Haynes, J. D., Arockiasamy, S., Al Rashdi, M., & Al Rashdi, S. (2016). Business and E Business Strategies for Coopetition and Thematic Management as a Sustained Basis for Ethics and Social Responsibility in Emerging Markets. In M. Al-Shammari & H. Masri (Eds.), *Ethical and Social Perspectives on Global Business Interaction in Emerging Markets* (pp. 25–39). Hershey, PA: IGI Global. doi:10.4018/978-1-4666-9864-2.ch002

Hee, W. J., Jalleh, G., Lai, H., & Lin, C. (2017). E-Commerce and IT Projects: Evaluation and Management Issues in Australian and Taiwanese Hospitals. *International Journal of Public Health Management and Ethics, 2*(1), 69–90. doi:10.4018/IJPHME.2017010104

Hernandez, A. A. (2018). Exploring the Factors to Green IT Adoption of SMEs in the Philippines. *Journal of Cases on Information Technology, 20*(2), 49–66. doi:10.4018/JCIT.2018040104

Hernandez, A. A., & Ona, S. E. (2016). Green IT Adoption: Lessons from the Philippines Business Process Outsourcing Industry. *International Journal of Social Ecology and Sustainable Development*, *7*(1), 1–34. doi:10.4018/IJSESD.2016010101

Hollman, A., Bickford, S., & Hollman, T. (2017). Cyber InSecurity: A Post-Mortem Attempt to Assess Cyber Problems from IT and Business Management Perspectives. *Journal of Cases on Information Technology*, *19*(3), 42–70. doi:10.4018/JCIT.2017070104

Igbinakhase, I. (2017). Responsible and Sustainable Management Practices in Developing and Developed Business Environments. In Z. Fields (Ed.), *Collective Creativity for Responsible and Sustainable Business Practice* (pp. 180–207). Hershey, PA: IGI Global. doi:10.4018/978-1-5225-1823-5.ch010

Ilahi, L., Ghannouchi, S. A., & Martinho, R. (2016). A Business Process Management Approach to Home Healthcare Processes: On the Gap between Intention and Reality. In M. Cruz-Cunha, I. Miranda, R. Martinho, & R. Rijo (Eds.), *Encyclopedia of E-Health and Telemedicine* (pp. 439–457). Hershey, PA: IGI Global. doi:10.4018/978-1-4666-9978-6.ch035

Iwata, J. J., & Hoskins, R. G. (2017). Managing Indigenous Knowledge in Tanzania: A Business Perspective. In P. Jain & N. Mnjama (Eds.), *Managing Knowledge Resources and Records in Modern Organizations* (pp. 198–214). Hershey, PA: IGI Global. doi:10.4018/978-1-5225-1965-2.ch012

Jabeen, F., Ahmad, S. Z., & Alkaabi, S. (2016). The Internationalization Decision-Making of United Arab Emirates Family Businesses. In N. Zakaria, A. Abdul-Talib, & N. Osman (Eds.), *Handbook of Research on Impacts of International Business and Political Affairs on the Global Economy* (pp. 1–22). Hershey, PA: IGI Global. doi:10.4018/978-1-4666-9806-2.ch001

Jain, P. (2017). Ethical and Legal Issues in Knowledge Management Life-Cycle in Business. In P. Jain & N. Mnjama (Eds.), *Managing Knowledge Resources and Records in Modern Organizations* (pp. 82–101). Hershey, PA: IGI Global. doi:10.4018/978-1-5225-1965-2.ch006

Jamali, D., Abdallah, H., & Matar, F. (2016). Opportunities and Challenges for CSR Mainstreaming in Business Schools. *International Journal of Technology and Educational Marketing*, *6*(2), 1–29. doi:10.4018/IJTEM.2016070101

James, S., & Hauli, E. (2017). Holistic Management Education at Tanzanian Rural Development Planning Institute. In N. Baporikar (Ed.), *Management Education for Global Leadership* (pp. 112–136). Hershey, PA: IGI Global. doi:10.4018/978-1-5225-1013-0.ch006

Janošková, M., Csikósová, A., & Čulková, K. (2018). Measurement of Company Performance as Part of Its Strategic Management. In R. Leon (Ed.), *Managerial Strategies for Business Sustainability During Turbulent Times* (pp. 309–335). Hershey, PA: IGI Global. doi:10.4018/978-1-5225-2716-9.ch017

Jean-Vasile, A., & Alecu, A. (2017). Theoretical and Practical Approaches in Understanding the Influences of Cost-Productivity-Profit Trinomial in Contemporary Enterprises. In A. Jean Vasile & D. Nicolò (Eds.), *Sustainable Entrepreneurship and Investments in the Green Economy* (pp. 28–62). Hershey, PA: IGI Global. doi:10.4018/978-1-5225-2075-7.ch002

Jha, D. G. (2016). Preparing for Information Technology Driven Changes. In S. Tiwari & L. Nafees (Eds.), *Innovative Management Education Pedagogies for Preparing Next-Generation Leaders* (pp. 258–274). Hershey, PA: IGI Global. doi:10.4018/978-1-4666-9691-4.ch015

Joia, L. A., & Correia, J. C. (2018). CIO Competencies From the IT Professional Perspective: Insights From Brazil. *Journal of Global Information Management, 26*(2), 74–103. doi:10.4018/JGIM.2018040104

Juma, A., & Mzera, N. (2017). Knowledge Management and Records Management and Competitive Advantage in Business. In P. Jain & N. Mnjama (Eds.), *Managing Knowledge Resources and Records in Modern Organizations* (pp. 15–28). Hershey, PA: IGI Global. doi:10.4018/978-1-5225-1965-2.ch002

K., I., & A, V. (2018). Monitoring and Auditing in the Cloud. In K. Munir (Ed.), *Cloud Computing Technologies for Green Enterprises* (pp. 318-350). Hershey, PA: IGI Global. doi:10.4018/978-1-5225-3038-1.ch013

Kabra, G., Ghosh, V., & Ramesh, A. (2018). Enterprise Integrated Business Process Management and Business Intelligence Framework for Business Process Sustainability. In A. Paul, D. Bhattacharyya, & S. Anand (Eds.), *Green Initiatives for Business Sustainability and Value Creation* (pp. 228–238). Hershey, PA: IGI Global. doi:10.4018/978-1-5225-2662-9.ch010

Kaoud, M. (2017). Investigation of Customer Knowledge Management: A Case Study Research. *International Journal of Service Science, Management, Engineering, and Technology, 8*(2), 12–22. doi:10.4018/IJSSMET.2017040102

Kara, M. E., & Fırat, S. Ü. (2016). Sustainability, Risk, and Business Intelligence in Supply Chains. In M. Erdoğdu, T. Arun, & I. Ahmad (Eds.), *Handbook of Research on Green Economic Development Initiatives and Strategies* (pp. 501–538). Hershey, PA: IGI Global. doi:10.4018/978-1-5225-0440-5.ch022

Katuu, S. (2018). A Comparative Assessment of Enterprise Content Management Maturity Models. In N. Gwangwava & M. Mutingi (Eds.), *E-Manufacturing and E-Service Strategies in Contemporary Organizations* (pp. 93–118). Hershey, PA: IGI Global. doi:10.4018/978-1-5225-3628-4.ch005

Khan, M. A. (2016). MNEs Management Strategies in Developing Countries: Establishing the Context. In M. Khan (Ed.), *Multinational Enterprise Management Strategies in Developing Countries* (pp. 1–33). Hershey, PA: IGI Global. doi:10.4018/978-1-5225-0276-0.ch001

Khan, M. A. (2016). Operational Approaches in Organizational Structure: A Case for MNEs in Developing Countries. In M. Khan (Ed.), *Multinational Enterprise Management Strategies in Developing Countries* (pp. 129–151). Hershey, PA: IGI Global. doi:10.4018/978-1-5225-0276-0.ch007

Kinnunen, S., Ylä-Kujala, A., Marttonen-Arola, S., Kärri, T., & Baglee, D. (2018). Internet of Things in Asset Management: Insights from Industrial Professionals and Academia. *International Journal of Service Science, Management, Engineering, and Technology*, *9*(2), 104–119. doi:10.4018/IJSSMET.2018040105

Klein, A. Z., Sabino de Freitas, A., Machado, L., Freitas, J. C. Jr, Graziola, P. G. Jr, & Schlemmer, E. (2017). Virtual Worlds Applications for Management Education. In L. Tomei (Ed.), *Exploring the New Era of Technology-Infused Education* (pp. 279–299). Hershey, PA: IGI Global. doi:10.4018/978-1-5225-1709-2.ch017

Kożuch, B., & Jabłoński, A. (2017). Adopting the Concept of Business Models in Public Management. In M. Lewandowski & B. Kożuch (Eds.), *Public Sector Entrepreneurship and the Integration of Innovative Business Models* (pp. 10–46). Hershey, PA: IGI Global. doi:10.4018/978-1-5225-2215-7.ch002

Kumar, J., Adhikary, A., & Jha, A. (2017). Small Active Investors' Perceptions and Preferences Towards Tax Saving Mutual Fund Schemes in Eastern India: An Empirical Note. *International Journal of Asian Business and Information Management*, *8*(2), 35–45. doi:10.4018/IJABIM.2017040103

Lassoued, Y., Bouzguenda, L., & Mahmoud, T. (2016). Context-Aware Business Process Versions Management. *International Journal of e-Collaboration*, *12*(3), 7–33. doi:10.4018/IJeC.2016070102

Lavassani, K. M., & Movahedi, B. (2017). Applications Driven Information Systems: Beyond Networks toward Business Ecosystems. *International Journal of Innovation in the Digital Economy*, *8*(1), 61–75. doi:10.4018/IJIDE.2017010104

Lazzareschi, V. H., & Brito, M. S. (2017). Strategic Information Management: Proposal of Business Project Model. In G. Jamil, A. Soares, & C. Pessoa (Eds.), *Handbook of Research on Information Management for Effective Logistics and Supply Chains* (pp. 59–88). Hershey, PA: IGI Global. doi:10.4018/978-1-5225-0973-8.ch004

Lederer, M., Kurz, M., & Lazarov, P. (2017). Usage and Suitability of Methods for Strategic Business Process Initiatives: A Multi Case Study Research. *International Journal of Productivity Management and Assessment Technologies*, *5*(1), 40–51. doi:10.4018/IJPMAT.2017010103

Lee, I. (2017). A Social Enterprise Business Model and a Case Study of Pacific Community Ventures (PCV). In V. Potocan, M. Ünğan, & Z. Nedelko (Eds.), *Handbook of Research on Managerial Solutions in Non-Profit Organizations* (pp. 182–204). Hershey, PA: IGI Global. doi:10.4018/978-1-5225-0731-4.ch009

Lee, L. J., & Leu, J. (2016). Exploring the Effectiveness of IT Application and Value Method in the Innovation Performance of Enterprise. *International Journal of Enterprise Information Systems*, *12*(2), 47–65. doi:10.4018/IJEIS.2016040104

Lee, Y. (2016). Alignment Effect of Entrepreneurial Orientation and Marketing Orientation on Firm Performance. *International Journal of Customer Relationship Marketing and Management*, *7*(4), 58–69. doi:10.4018/IJCRMM.2016100104

Leon, L. A., Seal, K. C., Przasnyski, Z. H., & Wiedenman, I. (2017). Skills and Competencies Required for Jobs in Business Analytics: A Content Analysis of Job Advertisements Using Text Mining. *International Journal of Business Intelligence Research, 8*(1), 1–25. doi:10.4018/IJBIR.2017010101

Leu, J., Lee, L. J., & Krischke, A. (2016). Value Engineering-Based Method for Implementing the ISO14001 System in the Green Supply Chains. *International Journal of Strategic Decision Sciences, 7*(4), 1–20. doi:10.4018/IJSDS.2016100101

Levy, C. L., & Elias, N. I. (2017). SOHO Users' Perceptions of Reliability and Continuity of Cloud-Based Services. In M. Moore (Ed.), *Cybersecurity Breaches and Issues Surrounding Online Threat Protection* (pp. 248–287). Hershey, PA: IGI Global. doi:10.4018/978-1-5225-1941-6.ch011

Levy, M. (2018). Change Management Serving Knowledge Management and Organizational Development: Reflections and Review. In N. Baporikar (Ed.), *Global Practices in Knowledge Management for Societal and Organizational Development* (pp. 256–270). Hershey, PA: IGI Global. doi:10.4018/978-1-5225-3009-1.ch012

Lewandowski, M. (2017). Public Organizations and Business Model Innovation: The Role of Public Service Design. In M. Lewandowski & B. Kożuch (Eds.), *Public Sector Entrepreneurship and the Integration of Innovative Business Models* (pp. 47–72). Hershey, PA: IGI Global. doi:10.4018/978-1-5225-2215-7.ch003

Lhannaoui, H., Kabbaj, M. I., & Bakkoury, Z. (2017). A Survey of Risk-Aware Business Process Modelling. *International Journal of Risk and Contingency Management, 6*(3), 14–26. doi:10.4018/IJRCM.2017070102

Li, J., Sun, W., Jiang, W., Yang, H., & Zhang, L. (2017). How the Nature of Exogenous Shocks and Crises Impact Company Performance?: The Effects of Industry Characteristics. *International Journal of Risk and Contingency Management, 6*(4), 40–55. doi:10.4018/IJRCM.2017100103

Lu, C., & Liu, S. (2016). Cultural Tourism O2O Business Model Innovation-A Case Study of CTrip. *Journal of Electronic Commerce in Organizations, 14*(2), 16–31. doi:10.4018/JECO.2016040102

Machen, B., Hosseini, M. R., Wood, A., & Bakhshi, J. (2016). An Investigation into using SAP-PS as a Multidimensional Project Control System (MPCS). *International Journal of Enterprise Information Systems, 12*(2), 66–81. doi:10.4018/IJEIS.2016040105

Malega, P. (2017). Small and Medium Enterprises in the Slovak Republic: Status and Competitiveness of SMEs in the Global Markets and Possibilities of Optimization. In M. Vemić (Ed.), *Optimal Management Strategies in Small and Medium Enterprises* (pp. 102–124). Hershey, PA: IGI Global. doi:10.4018/978-1-5225-1949-2.ch006

Malewska, K. M. (2017). Intuition in Decision-Making on the Example of a Non-Profit Organization. In V. Potocan, M. Ünğan, & Z. Nedelko (Eds.), *Handbook of Research on Managerial Solutions in Non-Profit Organizations* (pp. 378–399). Hershey, PA: IGI Global. doi:10.4018/978-1-5225-0731-4.ch018

Maroofi, F. (2017). Entrepreneurial Orientation and Organizational Learning Ability Analysis for Innovation and Firm Performance. In N. Baporikar (Ed.), *Innovation and Shifting Perspectives in Management Education* (pp. 144–165). Hershey, PA: IGI Global. doi:10.4018/978-1-5225-1019-2.ch007

Martins, P. V., & Zacarias, M. (2017). A Web-based Tool for Business Process Improvement. *International Journal of Web Portals, 9*(2), 68–84. doi:10.4018/IJWP.2017070104

Matthies, B., & Coners, A. (2017). Exploring the Conceptual Nature of e-Business Projects. *Journal of Electronic Commerce in Organizations, 15*(3), 33–63. doi:10.4018/JECO.2017070103

McKee, J. (2018). Architecture as a Tool to Solve Business Planning Problems. In M. Khosrow-Pour, D.B.A. (Ed.), Encyclopedia of Information Science and Technology, Fourth Edition (pp. 573-586). Hershey, PA: IGI Global. doi:10.4018/978-1-5225-2255-3.ch050

McMurray, A. J., Cross, J., & Caponecchia, C. (2018). The Risk Management Profession in Australia: Business Continuity Plan Practices. In N. Bajgoric (Ed.), *Always-On Enterprise Information Systems for Modern Organizations* (pp. 112–129). Hershey, PA: IGI Global. doi:10.4018/978-1-5225-3704-5.ch006

Meddah, I. H., & Belkadi, K. (2018). Mining Patterns Using Business Process Management. In R. Hamou (Ed.), *Handbook of Research on Biomimicry in Information Retrieval and Knowledge Management* (pp. 78–89). Hershey, PA: IGI Global. doi:10.4018/978-1-5225-3004-6.ch005

Mendes, L. (2017). TQM and Knowledge Management: An Integrated Approach Towards Tacit Knowledge Management. In D. Jaziri-Bouagina & G. Jamil (Eds.), *Handbook of Research on Tacit Knowledge Management for Organizational Success* (pp. 236–263). Hershey, PA: IGI Global. doi:10.4018/978-1-5225-2394-9.ch009

Mnjama, N. M. (2017). Preservation of Recorded Information in Public and Private Sector Organizations. In P. Jain & N. Mnjama (Eds.), *Managing Knowledge Resources and Records in Modern Organizations* (pp. 149–167). Hershey, PA: IGI Global. doi:10.4018/978-1-5225-1965-2.ch009

Mokoqama, M., & Fields, Z. (2017). Principles of Responsible Management Education (PRME): Call for Responsible Management Education. In Z. Fields (Ed.), *Collective Creativity for Responsible and Sustainable Business Practice* (pp. 229–241). Hershey, PA: IGI Global. doi:10.4018/978-1-5225-1823-5.ch012

Muniapan, B. (2017). Philosophy and Management: The Relevance of Vedanta in Management. In P. Ordóñez de Pablos (Ed.), *Managerial Strategies and Solutions for Business Success in Asia* (pp. 124–139). Hershey, PA: IGI Global. doi:10.4018/978-1-5225-1886-0.ch007

Muniapan, B., Gregory, M. L., & Ling, L. A. (2016). Marketing Education in Sarawak: Looking at It from the Employers' Viewpoint. In B. Smith & A. Porath (Eds.), *Global Perspectives on Contemporary Marketing Education* (pp. 112–130). Hershey, PA: IGI Global. doi:10.4018/978-1-4666-9784-3.ch008

Murad, S. E., & Dowaji, S. (2017). Using Value-Based Approach for Managing Cloud-Based Services. In A. Turuk, B. Sahoo, & S. Addya (Eds.), *Resource Management and Efficiency in Cloud Computing Environments* (pp. 33–60). Hershey, PA: IGI Global. doi:10.4018/978-1-5225-1721-4.ch002

Mutahar, A. M., Daud, N. M., Thurasamy, R., Isaac, O., & Abdulsalam, R. (2018). The Mediating of Perceived Usefulness and Perceived Ease of Use: The Case of Mobile Banking in Yemen. *International Journal of Technology Diffusion*, *9*(2), 21–40. doi:10.4018/IJTD.2018040102

Naidoo, V. (2017). E-Learning and Management Education at African Universities. In N. Baporikar (Ed.), *Management Education for Global Leadership* (pp. 181–201). Hershey, PA: IGI Global. doi:10.4018/978-1-5225-1013-0.ch009

Naidoo, V., & Igbinakhase, I. (2018). Opportunities and Challenges of Knowledge Retention in SMEs. In N. Baporikar (Ed.), *Knowledge Integration Strategies for Entrepreneurship and Sustainability* (pp. 70–94). Hershey, PA: IGI Global. doi:10.4018/978-1-5225-5115-7.ch004

Nayak, S., & Prabhu, N. (2017). Paradigm Shift in Management Education: Need for a Cross Functional Perspective. In N. Baporikar (Ed.), *Management Education for Global Leadership* (pp. 241–255). Hershey, PA: IGI Global. doi:10.4018/978-1-5225-1013-0.ch012

Ndede-Amadi, A. A. (2016). Student Interest in the IS Specialization as Predictor of the Success Potential of New Information Systems Programmes within the Schools of Business in Kenyan Public Universities. *International Journal of Information Systems and Social Change*, *7*(2), 63–79. doi:10.4018/IJISSC.2016040104

Nedelko, Z., & Potocan, V. (2016). Management Practices for Processes Optimization: Case of Slovenia. In G. Alor-Hernández, C. Sánchez-Ramírez, & J. García-Alcaraz (Eds.), *Handbook of Research on Managerial Strategies for Achieving Optimal Performance in Industrial Processes* (pp. 545–561). Hershey, PA: IGI Global. doi:10.4018/978-1-5225-0130-5.ch025

Nedelko, Z., & Potocan, V. (2017). Management Solutions in Non-Profit Organizations: Case of Slovenia. In V. Potocan, M. Üngan, & Z. Nedelko (Eds.), *Handbook of Research on Managerial Solutions in Non-Profit Organizations* (pp. 1–22). Hershey, PA: IGI Global. doi:10.4018/978-1-5225-0731-4.ch001

Nedelko, Z., & Potocan, V. (2017). Priority of Management Tools Utilization among Managers: International Comparison. In V. Wang (Ed.), *Encyclopedia of Strategic Leadership and Management* (pp. 1083–1094). Hershey, PA: IGI Global. doi:10.4018/978-1-5225-1049-9.ch075

Nedelko, Z., Raudeliūnienė, J., & Črešnar, R. (2018). Knowledge Dynamics in Supply Chain Management. In N. Baporikar (Ed.), *Knowledge Integration Strategies for Entrepreneurship and Sustainability* (pp. 150–166). Hershey, PA: IGI Global. doi:10.4018/978-1-5225-5115-7.ch008

Nguyen, H. T., & Hipsher, S. A. (2018). Innovation and Creativity Used by Private Sector Firms in a Resources-Constrained Environment. In S. Hipsher (Ed.), *Examining the Private Sector's Role in Wealth Creation and Poverty Reduction* (pp. 219–238). Hershey, PA: IGI Global. doi:10.4018/978-1-5225-3117-3.ch010

Nycz, M., & Pólkowski, Z. (2016). Business Intelligence as a Modern IT Supporting Management of Local Government Units in Poland. *International Journal of Knowledge and Systems Science*, *7*(4), 1–18. doi:10.4018/IJKSS.2016100101

Obaji, N. O., Senin, A. A., & Olugu, M. U. (2016). Supportive Government Policy as a Mechanism for Business Incubation Performance in Nigeria. *International Journal of Information Systems and Social Change*, *7*(4), 52–66. doi:10.4018/IJISSC.2016100103

Obicci, P. A. (2017). Risk Sharing in a Partnership. In *Risk Management Strategies in Public-Private Partnerships* (pp. 115–152). Hershey, PA: IGI Global. doi:10.4018/978-1-5225-2503-5.ch004

Obidallah, W. J., & Raahemi, B. (2017). Managing Changes in Service Oriented Virtual Organizations: A Structural and Procedural Framework to Facilitate the Process of Change. *Journal of Electronic Commerce in Organizations*, *15*(1), 59–83. doi:10.4018/JECO.2017010104

Ojasalo, J., & Ojasalo, K. (2016). Service Logic Business Model Canvas for Lean Development of SMEs and Start-Ups. In N. Baporikar (Ed.), *Handbook of Research on Entrepreneurship in the Contemporary Knowledge-Based Global Economy* (pp. 217–243). Hershey, PA: IGI Global. doi:10.4018/978-1-4666-8798-1.ch010

Ojo, O. (2017). Impact of Innovation on the Entrepreneurial Success in Selected Business Enterprises in South-West Nigeria. *International Journal of Innovation in the Digital Economy*, *8*(2), 29–38. doi:10.4018/IJIDE.2017040103

Okdinawati, L., Simatupang, T. M., & Sunitiyoso, Y. (2017). Multi-Agent Reinforcement Learning for Value Co-Creation of Collaborative Transportation Management (CTM). *International Journal of Information Systems and Supply Chain Management*, *10*(3), 84–95. doi:10.4018/IJISSCM.2017070105

Ortner, E., Mevius, M., Wiedmann, P., & Kurz, F. (2016). Design of Interactional Decision Support Applications for E-Participation in Smart Cities. *International Journal of Electronic Government Research, 12*(2), 18–38. doi:10.4018/IJEGR.2016040102

Pal, K. (2018). Building High Quality Big Data-Based Applications in Supply Chains. In A. Kumar & S. Saurav (Eds.), *Supply Chain Management Strategies and Risk Assessment in Retail Environments* (pp. 1–24). Hershey, PA: IGI Global. doi:10.4018/978-1-5225-3056-5.ch001

Palos-Sanchez, P. R., & Correia, M. B. (2018). Perspectives of the Adoption of Cloud Computing in the Tourism Sector. In J. Rodrigues, C. Ramos, P. Cardoso, & C. Henriques (Eds.), *Handbook of Research on Technological Developments for Cultural Heritage and eTourism Applications* (pp. 377–400). Hershey, PA: IGI Global. doi:10.4018/978-1-5225-2927-9.ch018

Parry, V. K., & Lind, M. L. (2016). Alignment of Business Strategy and Information Technology Considering Information Technology Governance, Project Portfolio Control, and Risk Management. *International Journal of Information Technology Project Management, 7*(4), 21–37. doi:10.4018/IJITPM.2016100102

Pashkova, N., Trujillo-Barrera, A., Apostolakis, G., Van Dijk, G., Drakos, P. D., & Baourakis, G. (2016). Business Management Models of Microfinance Institutions (MFIs) in Africa: A Study into Their Enabling Environments. *International Journal of Food and Beverage Manufacturing and Business Models, 1*(2), 63–82. doi:10.4018/IJFBMBM.2016070105

Patiño, B. E. (2017). New Generation Management by Convergence and Individual Identity: A Systemic and Human-Oriented Approach. In N. Baporikar (Ed.), *Innovation and Shifting Perspectives in Management Education* (pp. 119–143). Hershey, PA: IGI Global. doi:10.4018/978-1-5225-1019-2.ch006

Pawliczek, A., & Rössler, M. (2017). Knowledge of Management Tools and Systems in SMEs: Knowledge Transfer in Management. In A. Bencsik (Ed.), *Knowledge Management Initiatives and Strategies in Small and Medium Enterprises* (pp. 180–203). Hershey, PA: IGI Global. doi:10.4018/978-1-5225-1642-2.ch009

Pejic-Bach, M., Omazic, M. A., Aleksic, A., & Zoroja, J. (2018). Knowledge-Based Decision Making: A Multi-Case Analysis. In R. Leon (Ed.), *Managerial Strategies for Business Sustainability During Turbulent Times* (pp. 160–184). Hershey, PA: IGI Global. doi:10.4018/978-1-5225-2716-9.ch009

Perano, M., Hysa, X., & Calabrese, M. (2018). Strategic Planning, Cultural Context, and Business Continuity Management: Business Cases in the City of Shkoder. In A. Presenza & L. Sheehan (Eds.), *Geopolitics and Strategic Management in the Global Economy* (pp. 57–77). Hershey, PA: IGI Global. doi:10.4018/978-1-5225-2673-5.ch004

Pereira, R., Mira da Silva, M., & Lapão, L. V. (2017). IT Governance Maturity Patterns in Portuguese Healthcare. In S. De Haes & W. Van Grembergen (Eds.), *Strategic IT Governance and Alignment in Business Settings* (pp. 24–52). Hershey, PA: IGI Global. doi:10.4018/978-1-5225-0861-8.ch002

Perez-Uribe, R., & Ocampo-Guzman, D. (2016). Conflict within Colombian Family Owned SMEs: An Explosive Blend between Feelings and Business. In J. Saiz-Álvarez (Ed.), *Handbook of Research on Social Entrepreneurship and Solidarity Economics* (pp. 329–354). Hershey, PA: IGI Global. doi:10.4018/978-1-5225-0097-1.ch017

Pérez-Uribe, R. I., Torres, D. A., Jurado, S. P., & Prada, D. M. (2018). Cloud Tools for the Development of Project Management in SMEs. In R. Perez-Uribe, C. Salcedo-Perez, & D. Ocampo-Guzman (Eds.), *Handbook of Research on Intrapreneurship and Organizational Sustainability in SMEs* (pp. 95–120). Hershey, PA: IGI Global. doi:10.4018/978-1-5225-3543-0.ch005

Petrisor, I., & Cozmiuc, D. (2017). Global Supply Chain Management Organization at Siemens in the Advent of Industry 4.0. In L. Saglietto & C. Cezanne (Eds.), *Global Intermediation and Logistics Service Providers* (pp. 123–142). Hershey, PA: IGI Global. doi:10.4018/978-1-5225-2133-4.ch007

Pierce, J. M., Velliaris, D. M., & Edwards, J. (2017). A Living Case Study: A Journey Not a Destination. In N. Silton (Ed.), *Exploring the Benefits of Creativity in Education, Media, and the Arts* (pp. 158–178). Hershey, PA: IGI Global. doi:10.4018/978-1-5225-0504-4.ch008

Radosavljevic, M., & Andjelkovic, A. (2017). Multi-Criteria Decision Making Approach for Choosing Business Process for the Improvement: Upgrading of the Six Sigma Methodology. In J. Stanković, P. Delias, S. Marinković, & S. Rochhia (Eds.), *Tools and Techniques for Economic Decision Analysis* (pp. 225–247). Hershey, PA: IGI Global. doi:10.4018/978-1-5225-0959-2.ch011

Radovic, V. M. (2017). Corporate Sustainability and Responsibility and Disaster Risk Reduction: A Serbian Overview. In M. Camilleri (Ed.), *CSR 2.0 and the New Era of Corporate Citizenship* (pp. 147–164). Hershey, PA: IGI Global. doi:10.4018/978-1-5225-1842-6.ch008

Raghunath, K. M., Devi, S. L., & Patro, C. S. (2018). Impact of Risk Assessment Models on Risk Factors: A Holistic Outlook. In K. Strang, M. Korstanje, & N. Vajjhala (Eds.), *Research, Practices, and Innovations in Global Risk and Contingency Management* (pp. 134–153). Hershey, PA: IGI Global. doi:10.4018/978-1-5225-4754-9.ch008

Raman, A., & Goyal, D. P. (2017). Extending IMPLEMENT Framework for Enterprise Information Systems Implementation to Information System Innovation. In M. Tavana (Ed.), *Enterprise Information Systems and the Digitalization of Business Functions* (pp. 137–177). Hershey, PA: IGI Global. doi:10.4018/978-1-5225-2382-6.ch007

Rao, Y., & Zhang, Y. (2017). The Construction and Development of Academic Library Digital Special Subject Databases. In L. Ruan, Q. Zhu, & Y. Ye (Eds.), *Academic Library Development and Administration in China* (pp. 163–183). Hershey, PA: IGI Global. doi:10.4018/978-1-5225-0550-1.ch010

Ravasan, A. Z., Mohammadi, M. M., & Hamidi, H. (2018). An Investigation Into the Critical Success Factors of Implementing Information Technology Service Management Frameworks. In K. Jakobs (Ed.), *Corporate and Global Standardization Initiatives in Contemporary Society* (pp. 200–218). Hershey, PA: IGI Global. doi:10.4018/978-1-5225-5320-5.ch009

Renna, P., Izzo, C., & Romaniello, T. (2016). The Business Process Management Systems to Support Continuous Improvements. In W. Nuninger & J. Châtelet (Eds.), *Handbook of Research on Quality Assurance and Value Management in Higher Education* (pp. 237–256). Hershey, PA: IGI Global. doi:10.4018/978-1-5225-0024-7.ch009

Rezaie, S., Mirabedini, S. J., & Abtahi, A. (2018). Designing a Model for Implementation of Business Intelligence in the Banking Industry. *International Journal of Enterprise Information Systems*, *14*(1), 77–103. doi:10.4018/IJEIS.2018010105

Riccò, R. (2016). Diversity Management: Bringing Equality, Equity, and Inclusion in the Workplace. In J. Prescott (Ed.), *Handbook of Research on Race, Gender, and the Fight for Equality* (pp. 335–359). Hershey, PA: IGI Global. doi:10.4018/978-1-5225-0047-6.ch015

Romano, L., Grimaldi, R., & Colasuonno, F. S. (2017). Demand Management as a Success Factor in Project Portfolio Management. In L. Romano (Ed.), *Project Portfolio Management Strategies for Effective Organizational Operations* (pp. 202–219). Hershey, PA: IGI Global. doi:10.4018/978-1-5225-2151-8.ch008

Rostek, K. B. (2016). Risk Management: Role and Importance in Business Organization. In D. Jakóbczak (Ed.), *Analyzing Risk through Probabilistic Modeling in Operations Research* (pp. 149–178). Hershey, PA: IGI Global. doi:10.4018/978-1-4666-9458-3.ch007

Rouhani, S., & Savoji, S. R. (2016). A Success Assessment Model for BI Tools Implementation: An Empirical Study of Banking Industry. *International Journal of Business Intelligence Research*, *7*(1), 25–44. doi:10.4018/IJBIR.2016010103

Ruan, Z. (2016). A Corpus-Based Functional Analysis of Complex Nominal Groups in Written Business Discourse: The Case of "Business". *International Journal of Computer-Assisted Language Learning and Teaching*, *6*(2), 74–90. doi:10.4018/IJCALLT.2016040105

Ruhi, U. (2018). Towards an Interdisciplinary Socio-Technical Definition of Virtual Communities. In M. Khosrow-Pour, D.B.A. (Ed.), Encyclopedia of Information Science and Technology, Fourth Edition (pp. 4278-4295). Hershey, PA: IGI Global. doi:10.4018/978-1-5225-2255-3.ch371

Ryan, J., Doster, B., Daily, S., & Lewis, C. (2016). A Case Study Perspective for Balanced Perioperative Workflow Achievement through Data-Driven Process Improvement. *International Journal of Healthcare Information Systems and Informatics*, *11*(3), 19–41. doi:10.4018/IJHISI.2016070102

Safari, M. R., & Jiang, Q. (2018). The Theory and Practice of IT Governance Maturity and Strategies Alignment: Evidence From Banking Industry. *Journal of Global Information Management*, *26*(2), 127–146. doi:10.4018/JGIM.2018040106

Sahoo, J., Pati, B., & Mohanty, B. (2017). Knowledge Management as an Academic Discipline: An Assessment. In B. Gunjal (Ed.), *Managing Knowledge and Scholarly Assets in Academic Libraries* (pp. 99–126). Hershey, PA: IGI Global. doi:10.4018/978-1-5225-1741-2.ch005

Saini, D. (2017). Relevance of Teaching Values and Ethics in Management Education. In N. Baporikar (Ed.), *Management Education for Global Leadership* (pp. 90–111). Hershey, PA: IGI Global. doi:10.4018/978-1-5225-1013-0.ch005

Sambhanthan, A. (2017). Assessing and Benchmarking Sustainability in Organisations: An Integrated Conceptual Model. *International Journal of Systems and Service-Oriented Engineering*, *7*(4), 22–43. doi:10.4018/IJSSOE.2017100102

Sambhanthan, A., & Potdar, V. (2017). A Study of the Parameters Impacting Sustainability in Information Technology Organizations. *International Journal of Knowledge-Based Organizations*, *7*(3), 27–39. doi:10.4018/IJKBO.2017070103

Sánchez-Fernández, M. D., & Manríquez, M. R. (2018). The Entrepreneurial Spirit Based on Social Values: The Digital Generation. In P. Isaias & L. Carvalho (Eds.), *User Innovation and the Entrepreneurship Phenomenon in the Digital Economy* (pp. 173–193). Hershey, PA: IGI Global. doi:10.4018/978-1-5225-2826-5.ch009

Sanchez-Ruiz, L., & Blanco, B. (2017). Process Management for SMEs: Barriers, Enablers, and Benefits. In M. Vemić (Ed.), *Optimal Management Strategies in Small and Medium Enterprises* (pp. 293–319). Hershey, PA: IGI Global. doi:10.4018/978-1-5225-1949-2.ch014

Sanz, L. F., Gómez-Pérez, J., & Castillo-Martinez, A. (2018). Analysis of the European ICT Competence Frameworks. In V. Ahuja & S. Rathore (Eds.), *Multidisciplinary Perspectives on Human Capital and Information Technology Professionals* (pp. 225–245). Hershey, PA: IGI Global. doi:10.4018/978-1-5225-5297-0.ch012

Sarvepalli, A., & Godin, J. (2017). Business Process Management in the Classroom. *Journal of Cases on Information Technology*, *19*(2), 17–28. doi:10.4018/JCIT.2017040102

Satpathy, B., & Muniapan, B. (2016). Ancient Wisdom for Transformational Leadership and Its Insights from the Bhagavad-Gita. In U. Aung & P. Ordoñez de Pablos (Eds.), *Managerial Strategies and Practice in the Asian Business Sector* (pp. 1–10). Hershey, PA: IGI Global. doi:10.4018/978-1-4666-9758-4.ch001

Saygili, E. E., Ozturkoglu, Y., & Kocakulah, M. C. (2017). End Users' Perceptions of Critical Success Factors in ERP Applications. *International Journal of Enterprise Information Systems*, *13*(4), 58–75. doi:10.4018/IJEIS.2017100104

Saygili, E. E., & Saygili, A. T. (2017). Contemporary Issues in Enterprise Information Systems: A Critical Review of CSFs in ERP Implementations. In M. Tavana (Ed.), *Enterprise Information Systems and the Digitalization of Business Functions* (pp. 120–136). Hershey, PA: IGI Global. doi:10.4018/978-1-5225-2382-6.ch006

Seidenstricker, S., & Antonino, A. (2018). Business Model Innovation-Oriented Technology Management for Emergent Technologies. In M. Khosrow-Pour, D.B.A. (Ed.), Encyclopedia of Information Science and Technology, Fourth Edition (pp. 4560-4569). Hershey, PA: IGI Global. doi:10.4018/978-1-5225-2255-3.ch396

Senaratne, S., & Gunarathne, A. D. (2017). Excellence Perspective for Management Education from a Global Accountants' Hub in Asia. In N. Baporikar (Ed.), *Management Education for Global Leadership* (pp. 158–180). Hershey, PA: IGI Global. doi:10.4018/978-1-5225-1013-0.ch008

Sensuse, D. I., & Cahyaningsih, E. (2018). Knowledge Management Models: A Summative Review. *International Journal of Information Systems in the Service Sector, 10*(1), 71–100. doi:10.4018/IJISSS.2018010105

Sensuse, D. I., Wibowo, W. C., & Cahyaningsih, E. (2016). Indonesian Government Knowledge Management Model: A Theoretical Model. *Information Resources Management Journal, 29*(1), 91–108. doi:10.4018/irmj.2016010106

Seth, M., Goyal, D., & Kiran, R. (2017). Diminution of Impediments in Implementation of Supply Chain Management Information System for Enhancing its Effectiveness in Indian Automobile Industry. *Journal of Global Information Management, 25*(3), 1–20. doi:10.4018/JGIM.2017070101

Seyal, A. H., & Rahman, M. N. (2017). Investigating Impact of Inter-Organizational Factors in Measuring ERP Systems Success: Bruneian Perspectives. In M. Tavana (Ed.), *Enterprise Information Systems and the Digitalization of Business Functions* (pp. 178–204). Hershey, PA: IGI Global. doi:10.4018/978-1-5225-2382-6.ch008

Shaikh, A. A., & Karjaluoto, H. (2016). On Some Misconceptions Concerning Digital Banking and Alternative Delivery Channels. *International Journal of E-Business Research, 12*(3), 1–16. doi:10.4018/IJEBR.2016070101

Shams, S. M. (2016). Stakeholder Relationship Management in Online Business and Competitive Value Propositions: Evidence from the Sports Industry. *International Journal of Online Marketing, 6*(2), 1–17. doi:10.4018/IJOM.2016040101

Shamsuzzoha, A. (2016). Management of Risk and Resilience within Collaborative Business Network. In R. Addo-Tenkorang, J. Kantola, P. Helo, & A. Shamsuzzoha (Eds.), *Supply Chain Strategies and the Engineer-to-Order Approach* (pp. 143–159). Hershey, PA: IGI Global. doi:10.4018/978-1-5225-0021-6.ch008

Shaqrah, A. A. (2018). Analyzing Business Intelligence Systems Based on 7s Model of McKinsey. *International Journal of Business Intelligence Research, 9*(1), 53–63. doi:10.4018/IJBIR.2018010104

Sharma, A. J. (2017). Enhancing Sustainability through Experiential Learning in Management Education. In N. Baporikar (Ed.), *Management Education for Global Leadership* (pp. 256–274). Hershey, PA: IGI Global. doi:10.4018/978-1-5225-1013-0.ch013

Shetty, K. P. (2017). Responsible Global Leadership: Ethical Challenges in Management Education. In N. Baporikar (Ed.), *Innovation and Shifting Perspectives in Management Education* (pp. 194–223). Hershey, PA: IGI Global. doi:10.4018/978-1-5225-1019-2.ch009

Sinthupundaja, J., & Kohda, Y. (2017). Effects of Corporate Social Responsibility and Creating Shared Value on Sustainability. *International Journal of Sustainable Entrepreneurship and Corporate Social Responsibility*, *2*(1), 27–38. doi:10.4018/IJSECSR.2017010103

Škarica, I., & Hrgović, A. V. (2018). Implementation of Total Quality Management Principles in Public Health Institutes in the Republic of Croatia. *International Journal of Productivity Management and Assessment Technologies*, *6*(1), 1–16. doi:10.4018/IJPMAT.2018010101

Smuts, H., Kotzé, P., Van der Merwe, A., & Loock, M. (2017). Framework for Managing Shared Knowledge in an Information Systems Outsourcing Context. *International Journal of Knowledge Management*, *13*(4), 1–30. doi:10.4018/IJKM.2017100101

Soares, E. R., & Zaidan, F. H. (2016). Information Architecture and Business Modeling in Modern Organizations of Information Technology: Professional Career Plan in Organizations IT. In G. Jamil, J. Poças Rascão, F. Ribeiro, & A. Malheiro da Silva (Eds.), *Handbook of Research on Information Architecture and Management in Modern Organizations* (pp. 439–457). Hershey, PA: IGI Global. doi:10.4018/978-1-4666-8637-3.ch020

Sousa, M. J., Cruz, R., Dias, I., & Caracol, C. (2017). Information Management Systems in the Supply Chain. In G. Jamil, A. Soares, & C. Pessoa (Eds.), *Handbook of Research on Information Management for Effective Logistics and Supply Chains* (pp. 469–485). Hershey, PA: IGI Global. doi:10.4018/978-1-5225-0973-8.ch025

Spremic, M., Turulja, L., & Bajgoric, N. (2018). Two Approaches in Assessing Business Continuity Management Attitudes in the Organizational Context. In N. Bajgoric (Ed.), *Always-On Enterprise Information Systems for Modern Organizations* (pp. 159–183). Hershey, PA: IGI Global. doi:10.4018/978-1-5225-3704-5.ch008

Steenkamp, A. L. (2018). Some Insights in Computer Science and Information Technology. In *Examining the Changing Role of Supervision in Doctoral Research Projects: Emerging Research and Opportunities* (pp. 113–133). Hershey, PA: IGI Global. doi:10.4018/978-1-5225-2610-0.ch005

Studdard, N., Dawson, M., Burton, S. L., Jackson, N., Leonard, B., Quisenberry, W., & Rahim, E. (2016). Nurturing Social Entrepreneurship and Building Social Entrepreneurial Self-Efficacy: Focusing on Primary and Secondary Schooling to Develop Future Social Entrepreneurs. In Z. Fields (Ed.), *Incorporating Business Models and Strategies into Social Entrepreneurship* (pp. 154–175). Hershey, PA: IGI Global. doi:10.4018/978-1-4666-8748-6.ch010

Sun, Z. (2016). A Framework for Developing Management Intelligent Systems. *International Journal of Systems and Service-Oriented Engineering*, *6*(1), 37–53. doi:10.4018/IJSSOE.2016010103

Swami, B., & Mphele, G. T. (2016). Problems Preventing Growth of Small Entrepreneurs: A Case Study of a Few Small Entrepreneurs in Botswana Sub-Urban Areas. In N. Baporikar (Ed.), *Handbook of Research on Entrepreneurship in the Contemporary Knowledge-Based Global Economy* (pp. 479–508). Hershey, PA: IGI Global. doi:10.4018/978-1-4666-8798-1.ch020

Tabach, A., & Croteau, A. (2017). Configurations of Information Technology Governance Practices and Business Unit Performance. *International Journal of IT/Business Alignment and Governance*, *8*(2), 1–27. doi:10.4018/IJITBAG.2017070101

Talaue, G. M., & Iqbal, T. (2017). Assessment of e-Business Mode of Selected Private Universities in the Philippines and Pakistan. *International Journal of Online Marketing*, *7*(4), 63–77. doi:10.4018/IJOM.2017100105

Tam, G. C. (2017). Project Manager Sustainability Competence. In *Managerial Strategies and Green Solutions for Project Sustainability* (pp. 178–207). Hershey, PA: IGI Global. doi:10.4018/978-1-5225-2371-0.ch008

Tambo, T. (2018). Fashion Retail Innovation: About Context, Antecedents, and Outcome in Technological Change Projects. In I. Management Association (Ed.), Fashion and Textiles: Breakthroughs in Research and Practice (pp. 233-260). Hershey, PA: IGI Global. doi:10.4018/978-1-5225-3432-7.ch010

Tambo, T., & Mikkelsen, O. E. (2016). Fashion Supply Chain Optimization: Linking Make-to-Order Purchasing and B2B E-Commerce. In S. Joshi & R. Joshi (Eds.), *Designing and Implementing Global Supply Chain Management* (pp. 1–21). Hershey, PA: IGI Global. doi:10.4018/978-1-4666-9720-1.ch001

Tandon, K. (2016). Innovative Andragogy: The Paradigm Shift to Heutagogy. In S. Tiwari & L. Nafees (Eds.), *Innovative Management Education Pedagogies for Preparing Next-Generation Leaders* (pp. 238–257). Hershey, PA: IGI Global. doi:10.4018/978-1-4666-9691-4.ch014

Tantau, A. D., & Frăţilă, L. C. (2018). Information and Management System for Renewable Energy Business. In *Entrepreneurship and Business Development in the Renewable Energy Sector* (pp. 200–244). Hershey, PA: IGI Global. doi:10.4018/978-1-5225-3625-3.ch006

Teixeira, N., Pardal, P. N., & Rafael, B. G. (2018). Internationalization, Financial Performance, and Organizational Challenges: A Success Case in Portugal. In L. Carvalho (Ed.), *Handbook of Research on Entrepreneurial Ecosystems and Social Dynamics in a Globalized World* (pp. 379–423). Hershey, PA: IGI Global. doi:10.4018/978-1-5225-3525-6.ch017

Trad, A., & Kalpić, D. (2016). The E-Business Transformation Framework for E-Commerce Architecture-Modeling Projects. In I. Lee (Ed.), *Encyclopedia of E-Commerce Development, Implementation, and Management* (pp. 733–753). Hershey, PA: IGI Global. doi:10.4018/978-1-4666-9787-4.ch052

Trad, A., & Kalpić, D. (2016). The E-Business Transformation Framework for E-Commerce Control and Monitoring Pattern. In I. Lee (Ed.), *Encyclopedia of E-Commerce Development, Implementation, and Management* (pp. 754–777). Hershey, PA: IGI Global. doi:10.4018/978-1-4666-9787-4.ch053

Trad, A., & Kalpić, D. (2018). The Business Transformation Framework, Agile Project and Change Management. In M. Khosrow-Pour, D.B.A. (Ed.), Encyclopedia of Information Science and Technology, Fourth Edition (pp. 620-635). Hershey, PA: IGI Global. doi:10.4018/978-1-5225-2255-3.ch054

Trad, A., & Kalpić, D. (2018). The Business Transformation and Enterprise Architecture Framework: The Financial Engineering E-Risk Management and E-Law Integration. In B. Sergi, F. Fidanoski, M. Ziolo, & V. Naumovski (Eds.), *Regaining Global Stability After the Financial Crisis* (pp. 46–65). Hershey, PA: IGI Global. doi:10.4018/978-1-5225-4026-7.ch003

Turulja, L., & Bajgoric, N. (2018). Business Continuity and Information Systems: A Systematic Literature Review. In N. Bajgoric (Ed.), *Always-On Enterprise Information Systems for Modern Organizations* (pp. 60–87). Hershey, PA: IGI Global. doi:10.4018/978-1-5225-3704-5.ch004

van Wessel, R. M., de Vries, H. J., & Ribbers, P. M. (2016). Business Benefits through Company IT Standardization. In K. Jakobs (Ed.), *Effective Standardization Management in Corporate Settings* (pp. 34–53). Hershey, PA: IGI Global. doi:10.4018/978-1-4666-9737-9.ch003

Vargas-Hernández, J. G. (2017). Professional Integrity in Business Management Education. In N. Baporikar (Ed.), *Management Education for Global Leadership* (pp. 70–89). Hershey, PA: IGI Global. doi:10.4018/978-1-5225-1013-0.ch004

Vasista, T. G., & AlAbdullatif, A. M. (2017). Role of Electronic Customer Relationship Management in Demand Chain Management: A Predictive Analytic Approach. *International Journal of Information Systems and Supply Chain Management, 10*(1), 53–67. doi:10.4018/IJISSCM.2017010104

Vergidis, K. (2016). Rediscovering Business Processes: Definitions, Patterns, and Modelling Approaches. In P. Papajorgji, F. Pinet, A. Guimarães, & J. Papathanasiou (Eds.), *Automated Enterprise Systems for Maximizing Business Performance* (pp. 97–122). Hershey, PA: IGI Global. doi:10.4018/978-1-4666-8841-4.ch007

Vieru, D., & Bourdeau, S. (2017). Survival in the Digital Era: A Digital Competence-Based Multi-Case Study in the Canadian SME Clothing Industry. *International Journal of Social and Organizational Dynamics in IT*, *6*(1), 17–34. doi:10.4018/IJSODIT.2017010102

Vijayan, G., & Kamarulzaman, N. H. (2017). An Introduction to Sustainable Supply Chain Management and Business Implications. In M. Khan, M. Hussain, & M. Ajmal (Eds.), *Green Supply Chain Management for Sustainable Business Practice* (pp. 27–50). Hershey, PA: IGI Global. doi:10.4018/978-1-5225-0635-5.ch002

Vlachvei, A., & Notta, O. (2017). Firm Competitiveness: Theories, Evidence, and Measurement. In A. Vlachvei, O. Notta, K. Karantininis, & N. Tsounis (Eds.), *Factors Affecting Firm Competitiveness and Performance in the Modern Business World* (pp. 1–42). Hershey, PA: IGI Global. doi:10.4018/978-1-5225-0843-4.ch001

von Rosing, M., Fullington, N., & Walker, J. (2016). Using the Business Ontology and Enterprise Standards to Transform Three Leading Organizations. *International Journal of Conceptual Structures and Smart Applications*, *4*(1), 71–99. doi:10.4018/IJCSSA.2016010104

von Rosing, M., & von Scheel, H. (2016). Using the Business Ontology to Develop Enterprise Standards. *International Journal of Conceptual Structures and Smart Applications*, *4*(1), 48–70. doi:10.4018/IJCSSA.2016010103

Walczak, S. (2016). Artificial Neural Networks and other AI Applications for Business Management Decision Support. *International Journal of Sociotechnology and Knowledge Development*, *8*(4), 1–20. doi:10.4018/IJSKD.2016100101

Wamba, S. F., Akter, S., Kang, H., Bhattacharya, M., & Upal, M. (2016). The Primer of Social Media Analytics. *Journal of Organizational and End User Computing*, *28*(2), 1–12. doi:10.4018/JOEUC.2016040101

Wang, C., Schofield, M., Li, X., & Ou, X. (2017). Do Chinese Students in Public and Private Higher Education Institutes Perform at Different Level in One of the Leadership Skills: Critical Thinking?: An Exploratory Comparison. In V. Wang (Ed.), *Encyclopedia of Strategic Leadership and Management* (pp. 160–181). Hershey, PA: IGI Global. doi:10.4018/978-1-5225-1049-9.ch013

Wang, F., Raisinghani, M. S., Mora, M., & Wang, X. (2016). Strategic E-Business Management through a Balanced Scored Card Approach. In I. Lee (Ed.), *Encyclopedia of E-Commerce Development, Implementation, and Management* (pp. 361–386). Hershey, PA: IGI Global. doi:10.4018/978-1-4666-9787-4.ch027

Wang, J. (2017). Multi-Agent based Production Management Decision System Modelling for the Textile Enterprise. *Journal of Global Information Management*, *25*(4), 1–15. doi:10.4018/JGIM.2017100101

Wiedemann, A., & Gewald, H. (2017). Examining Cross-Domain Alignment: The Correlation of Business Strategy, IT Management, and IT Business Value. *International Journal of IT/Business Alignment and Governance, 8*(1), 17–31. doi:10.4018/IJITBAG.2017010102

Wolf, R., & Thiel, M. (2018). Advancing Global Business Ethics in China: Reducing Poverty Through Human and Social Welfare. In S. Hipsher (Ed.), *Examining the Private Sector's Role in Wealth Creation and Poverty Reduction* (pp. 67–84). Hershey, PA: IGI Global. doi:10.4018/978-1-5225-3117-3.ch004

Wu, J., Ding, F., Xu, M., Mo, Z., & Jin, A. (2016). Investigating the Determinants of Decision-Making on Adoption of Public Cloud Computing in E-government. *Journal of Global Information Management, 24*(3), 71–89. doi:10.4018/JGIM.2016070104

Xu, L., & de Vrieze, P. (2016). Building Situational Applications for Virtual Enterprises. In I. Lee (Ed.), *Encyclopedia of E-Commerce Development, Implementation, and Management* (pp. 715–724). Hershey, PA: IGI Global. doi:10.4018/978-1-4666-9787-4.ch050

Yablonsky, S. (2018). Innovation Platforms: Data and Analytics Platforms. In *Multi-Sided Platforms (MSPs) and Sharing Strategies in the Digital Economy: Emerging Research and Opportunities* (pp. 72–95). Hershey, PA: IGI Global. doi:10.4018/978-1-5225-5457-8.ch003

Yusoff, A., Ahmad, N. H., & Halim, H. A. (2017). Agropreneurship among Gen Y in Malaysia: The Role of Academic Institutions. In N. Ahmad, T. Ramayah, H. Halim, & S. Rahman (Eds.), *Handbook of Research on Small and Medium Enterprises in Developing Countries* (pp. 23–47). Hershey, PA: IGI Global. doi:10.4018/978-1-5225-2165-5.ch002

Zanin, F., Comuzzi, E., & Costantini, A. (2018). The Effect of Business Strategy and Stock Market Listing on the Use of Risk Assessment Tools. In *Management Control Systems in Complex Settings: Emerging Research and Opportunities* (pp. 145–168). Hershey, PA: IGI Global. doi:10.4018/978-1-5225-3987-2.ch007

Zgheib, P. W. (2017). Corporate Innovation and Intrapreneurship in the Middle East. In P. Zgheib (Ed.), *Entrepreneurship and Business Innovation in the Middle East* (pp. 37–56). Hershey, PA: IGI Global. doi:10.4018/978-1-5225-2066-5.ch003

About the Contributors

Heather Webb is an Assistant Professor of Business at Higher Colleges of Technology, Dubai Men's College where she teaches strategy, entrepreneurship, marketing and other international business courses. She received her PhD in Management from The University of Edinburgh, her MSc in International Business and Emerging Markets (IBEM) from The University of Edinburgh, and her BA in History from the University of Washington. Her research focuses on aspects of strategy, innovation, sustainability and entrepreneurship. Past research has focused on strategies to successfully operate in institutional voids, mobile payment systems and sustainable innovation. She has presented her work at the Academy of Management (AOM) and at the Academy of International Business (AIB). Heather is from Seattle, WA and has lived in Edinburgh, Scotland, and currently resides in Dubai, UAE.

***

Muneer M. S. Al Mubarak (PhD, University of Leeds; MBA, Durham University) is an Associate Professor of Management and Marketing, and Acting Vice President for Admin and Finance at Ahlia University. His main research interests are Relationship Marketing, Competitive Advantage, Entrepreneurship, Corporate Governance, SCR, CRM, SMEs and International Business.

Allam Hamdan is a Full Professor, Dean of College of Business and Finance, Ahlia University. He has many papers published in regional and international journals that discussed several accounting, financial and economic issues concerning the Arab world. In addition, he has interests in educational related issues in the Arab world universities like educational governance, investment in education and its relation with economic growth. Awarded the First Prize of Al-Owais Creative Award, UAE, 2019 and 2017;

the Second Prize of Rashid bin Humaid Award for Culture and Science, UAE, 2016; the Third Prize of Arab Prize for the Social Sciences and Humanities, Qatar, 2015, and the First Prize of "Durrat Watan", UAE, 2013. Member of National Qualifications Framework NQF – Validation Panel, and appeal committee, General Directorate of NQF, Kingdom of Bahrain. Member of Steering Committee in International Arab Conference of Quality Assurance of Higher Education.

Reem Khamis is a PhD Scholar in Brunel University London, UK. She was awarded an MBA degree in Finance from Ahlia University, Bahrain in 2013. Her major research area is in corporate governance, board of directors and ownership structure.

Fenfang Lin is a lecturer in Marketing at the University of Southampton. She holds a PhD in Marketing from the University of Edinburgh with a number of years working experience in different industries. Her research interests lie in B2B SMEs branding, strategic marketing, and marketing capability development.

Shubo Liu has a PhD in Management from Edinburgh University; Assistant Professor at Business School, Central University of Finance and Economics, Beijing, China. Research interests include Sustainability, Business Ethics, International Business.

Alasdair Marshall After gaining his PhD from Glasgow University in Scotland, Dr Marshall worked for five years in risk research at Caledonian Business School in Glasgow before spending the last ten years lecturing in risk management at Southampton University. Dr Marshall publishes widely in business journals, where he applies risk-related theory to a broad range of business contexts such as project management, supply chain management, performance management, competition and innovation.

Okasha Nada is an aspiring clinical health psychologist with an active interest in policy change and intervention design on a national level as well as providing one-to-one psychotherapy. I am qualified to Stage 1 in Health Psychology from King's College, London. I am currently working as an Assistant Psychologist for children and adolescents with East London Foundation Trust, working towards my qualification with the British Psychological Society as a Chartered Health Psychologist.

Udechukwu (Udi) Ojiako is Professor of Engineering Management & Law at the University of Sharjah, United Arab Emirates. He is also Visiting Professor in Management at the Risk Institute, University of Hull and Visiting Professor in Business at UNIZIK Business School, Nnamdi Azikiwe University, Nigeria. He has held prior academic positions in the UK, South Africa and now the United Arab Emirates. Udi holds a PhD in Project Management (2005) obtained from the University of Northumbria, a second PhD (in Business) obtained from University of Hull (2015) and an LLB in Laws obtained from the University of London (2017). His articles have been accepted and published in journals such as International Journal of Project Management, Project Management Journal and Production Planning & Control.

Ahmad Okasha has over than 18 years of health care experience. He brings leadership and extensive expertise in the fields of healthcare management. Dr. Okasha has set up multiple healthcare businesses in Dubai. He also held various leadership positions at major multinational companies. For instance, Dr. Okasha was a Business Director for Zynx Health, a company specializing in evidence based medicine and before that, he was a healthcare business advisor at Oracle, before that, he was a General Manager for MISYS Healthcare ME. In addition, Dr. Okasha was a Director at Belhoul Life care overseeing two hospitals, and prior to that he developed IBM Healthcare business in the region for 4 years. Dr. Okasha is currently teaching health sciences at the Canadian University Dubai. Dr. Okasha has recently published a book on running a healthcare business in Dubai titled 12 Lessons that I learnt running a small business in Dubai". Dr. Okasha earned his Ph.D in Health Management from Medical College of Virginia in the USA.

Anjum Razzaque, Ph.D., is an American and British educated Assistant Professor and Chairperson of MIS department at the College of Business & Finance at Ahlia University in Bahrain. Dr Anjum is teaching Management of Information Systems courses. He attained his Ph.D. from Brunel University's Business School, London, UK. His doctoral dissertation was "Assessing physicians' Virtual Community on Knowledge shared Decision Making". Furthermore, Dr. Anjum attained his M.Sc. in Computer Science from New York Institute of Technology, New York, USA and B.Sc. in Computerized Design and Graphics from Vaughn College of Aeronautics and Technology, New York, USA.

Konstantinos Tsanis is currently leading the innovation part of the first digital bank of Africa, Alat, created by WEMA Bank, as its Chief Innovation Officer. He is a seasoned financial technology and digitalization executive, with 12+ years hands on experience across different continents and industries [Energy (Oil, Gas and Utilities), Consulting, High Tech, Academic, Military and Financial], having worked on roles with much different skill requirements, having a 360° view for both start ups and large corporates. In his past roles he focused on the growth of the corporate incubator within Thomson Reuters, with a particular focus in Start Ups and SMEs across MENA, led the strategy and sales department of Bayzat, the most successfull FinTech in the Middle East, helped the business development of Bloomberg LP across the Middle East and Africa, advised multiple Fortune 500 companies with Kaiser Associates, worked as a strategic advisor on improving the performance of EDF Energy (now called UK Power Networks), while simultaneously having retained his academic engagement by delivering multiple lectures and conducting academic research at the same time. Active in the community, contributing intellectual capital, through both academic and applied research publications, and as a member/founder of industry and professional associations.

Index

www.ingramcontent.com/pod-product-compliance
Lightning Source LLC
LaVergne TN
LVHW080603300926
849162LV00005B/1031